SPORT IN CONTEMPORARY SOCIETY

SPORT IN CONTEMPORARY SOCIETY

An Anthology

Ninth Edition

Edited by
D. Stanley Eitzen

Paradigm Publishers
Boulder • London

Published in the United States by Paradigm Publishers, 2845 Wilderness Place, Boulder, CO 80301 USA.

Paradigm Publishers is the trade name of Birkenkamp & Company, LLC,
Dean Birkenkamp, President and Publisher.

Library of Congress Cataloging-in-Publication Data

Sport in contemporary society : an anthology / edited by D. Stanley Eitzen.—9th ed.
p. cm.
Includes bibliographical references.
ISBN 978-1-61205-032-4 (pbk. : alk. paper)
1. Sports—Social aspects. 2. Sports—Social aspects—United States. I. Eitzen, D. Stanley.
GV706.5.S733 2011
306.4'83—dc23

2011018697

Printed and bound in the United States of America on acid-free paper that meets the standards of the American National Standard for Permanence of Paper for Printed Library Materials.

Designed and Typeset by Straight Creek Bookmakers.

16 15 14 13 12 1 2 3 4 5

Contents

List of Figures, Tables, and Boxes xi
Preface xiii

Part One
SPORT AS A MICROCOSM OF SOCIETY **1**

1 Sports—An Offer We Can't Refuse 3
Dave Zirin
2 American Sport in the New Millennium 8
D. Stanley Eitzen
3 The Great Recession and Sport 13
D. Stanley Eitzen
For Further Study 21

Part Two
SPORT AND SOCIALIZATION: ORGANIZED SPORTS AND YOUTH **23**

4 Play Group versus Organized Competitive Team: A Comparison 25
Jay J. Coakley
5 Anyone Up for Stickball? In a PlayStation World, Maybe Not 34
Timothy Williams and Cassi Feldman
6 Boyhood, Organized Sports, and the Construction of Masculinities 38
Michael A. Messner
For Further Study 55

Part Three
SPORT AND SOCIALIZATION: THE MASS MEDIA **57**

7 The Televised Sports Manhood Formula 59
Michael A. Messner, Michele Dunbar, and Darnell Hunt
8 Gender in Televised Sports 73
Michael A. Messner and Cheryl Cooky
For Further Study 77

Part Four
SPORT AND SOCIALIZATION: SYMBOLS **79**

9 American Flags as Big as Fields 81
John Branch
10 "Redskins" Is No Honor, It's an Insult 84
Bill Plaschke
11 The De-Athleticization of Women: The Naming and Gender Marking of Collegiate Sport Teams 87
D. Stanley Eitzen and Maxine Baca Zinn
For Further Study 97

Part Five
PROBLEMS OF EXCESS: OVERZEALOUS ATHLETES, PARENTS, AND COACHES **99**

12 Female Gymnasts and Ice Skaters: The Dark Side 101
Joan Ryan
13 Bench the Parents 108
Buzz Bissinger
14 Harm to Children in Youth Sports 112
Mark Hyman
15 Missed Opportunities: Boston's Student-Athletes Face a Sports Program in Distress 116
Bob Hohler
For Further Study 122

Part Six
PROBLEMS OF EXCESS: SPORT AND DEVIANCE **123**

16 Ethical Dilemmas in American Sport: The Dark Side of Competition 125
D. Stanley Eitzen
17 Crime and Athletes: New Racial Stereotypes 135
Richard E. Lapchick
For Further Study 146

Part Seven
PROBLEMS OF EXCESS: PERFORMANCE-ENHANCING DRUGS IN SPORTS **147**

18 Creating the Frankenstein Athlete: The Drug Culture in Sports 149
Fran Zimniuch

19 Finding the Golden Genes 155
Patrick Barry
20 Outraged over the Steroids Outrage 162
Robert Lipsyte
For Further Study 165

Part Eight
PROBLEMS OF EXCESS: BIG-TIME COLLEGE SPORT 167

21 College Sports 101: A Primer on Money, Athletics, and Higher Education in the 21st Century 169
The Knight Commission on Intercollegiate Athletics
22 Admissions Exemptions Benefit Athletes 191
Alan Scher Zagier
23 Is Sports in Your Mission Statement? 194
Charles T. Clotfelter
24 The Big-Time College Sports Plantation and the Slaves Who Drive It 197
D. Stanley Eitzen
For Further Study 208

Part Nine
PROBLEMS OF EXCESS: SPORT AND MONEY 209

25 Does Football Cost Too Much? 211
Sally Jenkins
26 When Domes Attack 214
Dave Zirin
27 Corporate Titans Competing for Olympic Gold: How Ad Wars Have Hijacked the Games 228
Geoff Dembicki
For Further Study 235

Part Ten
STRUCTURED INEQUALITY: SPORT AND RACE/ETHNICITY 237

28 Sporting Dreams Die on the "Rez" 239
Kevin Simpson
29 Say It Ain't So, Big Leagues: The Downside for Latin American Players 246
Dave Zirin
30 The 2010 Racial and Gender Report Card: National Football League 250
Richard Lapchick with Jamile M. Kitnurse and Austin Moss II

31 Racism, Ethnic Discrimination, and Exclusion of Migrants and Minorities in Sport: A Comparative Overview of the Situation in the European Union 256
European Union Agency for Fundamental Rights
For Further Study 260

Part Eleven
STRUCTURED INEQUALITY: SPORT AND GENDER **263**

32 Are We There Yet? Thirty-Seven Years Later, Title IX Hasn't Fixed It All 265
R. Vivian Acosta and Linda Jean Carpenter
33 Her Life Depends On It II: Sport, Physical Activity, and the Health and Well-Being of American Girls and Women 270
Women's Sports Foundation
34 The Meaning of Success: The Athletic Experience and the Development of Male Identity 276
Michael A. Messner
For Further Study 291

Part Twelve
STRUCTURED INEQUALITY: SPORT AND SEXUALITY **293**

35 Changing the Game: Homophobia, Sexism, and Lesbians in Sport 295
Pat Griffin
36 Gay Athletes' Dilemma 312
Anthony Cotton
37 On the Team: Equal Opportunity for Transgender Student Athletes 317
Pat Griffin and Helen J. Carroll
For Further Study 327

Part Thirteen
EXPANDING THE HORIZONS: SPORT AND GLOBALIZATION **329**

38 Growing the Game: The Globalization of Major League Baseball 331
Alan M. Klein
39 Nike's Crimes 338
David Macaray

40 New Media and Global Sports 340
George H. Sage
For Further Study 348

About the Editor *349*

List of Figures, Tables, and Boxes

Figure 4-1	A Formal Organization Continuum for Groups in Competitive Physical Activities	26
Table 4-1	Comparison of Two Groups	26
Table 7-1	Race and Sex of Announcers	61
Table 7-2	Sex Composition of 722 Commercials	62
Table 7-3	Instances of Women Being Depicted as Sexy Props or Prizes for Men	63
Table 7-4	Racial Composition of 722 Commercials	64
Table 7-5	Statements Lauding Aggression or Criticizing Lack of Aggression	64
Table 7-6	Humorous or Sarcastic Discussion of Fights or Near-Fights	65
Table 7-7	Comments on the Heroic Nature of Playing Hurt	66
Table 7-8	Martial Metaphors and Language of War and Weaponry	67
Table 7-9	Depictions of Guts in Face of Danger, Speed, Hits, Crashes	68
Table 11-1	Naming Practices That De-Athleticize Women's Teams	93
Table 11-2	Prevalence of Sexist Team Names by Type of School	93
Table 11-3	Prevalence of Sexist Team Names by Region	94
Table 11-4	Naming Practices That De-Athleticize Women's Teams by Region	94
Table 30-1	NFL Offense	254
Table 30-2	NFL Defense	255
Table 30-3	NFL Special Teams	255
Table 40-1	Top Seven World Internet Users	341
Table 40-2	Top Five U.S. Sports Websites in November 2008	342
Box 40-1	Twitter and Global Social Networking in Sports	344
Box 40-2	Facebook and Global Sports Applications	345

Preface

Most North Americans are at least somewhat interested in sport, and many are downright fanatical about it. They attend games, read the sports pages and sport magazines, participate in fantasy leagues, and talk endlessly about the subject. But even those fans who astound us with their knowledge of the most obscure facts about sport do not necessarily *understand* sport.

Do sport buffs know how sport is linked to other institutions of society? Do they understand the role of sport in socializing youngsters in both positive and negative ways? Do they know that the assumption that sport builds character is open to serious debate? Do they know that racism continues in sport? What about the ways in which sport perpetuates gender-role stereotypes in society? How do owners, coaches, and other sport authorities exercise power to maintain control over athletes? These are some of the issues this book examines.

There are two fundamental reasons for the ignorance of most North Americans about the role of sport in society. First, they have had to rely mainly on sportswriters and sportscasters for their information, and these journalists have typically been little more than describers and cheerleaders. Until recent years journalists have rarely examined sport critically. Instead they have perpetuated myths: "Football helped a whole generation of sons of coal miners escape the mines" or "Sport is an island free of prejudice and racism."

The second reason for our sports illiteracy is that sport has been ignored, for the most part, by North American academics. Only in the past generation or so have North American social scientists and physical educators begun to investigate seriously the social aspects of sport. Previously, as with sports journalism, academic research on sport has tended to be biased in support of existing myths. In particular, the early research by physical educators was aimed at proving that sports participation builds character. In this limited perspective, phenomena common to sport such as cheating, excessive violence, coaching tyranny, and the consequences of failure were, for the most part, simply ignored.

Today, however, not only academics but also a new breed of sports journalists are making insightful analyses of the role of sport in society. They examine the positive *and* negative consequences of sport for people, communities, schools, and nations. They demystify and demythologize sport. Most significantly, they document the reciprocal impact of sport on the various institutions of society: religion, education, politics, and economics. There is no danger that sport will suffer from such examination. Critical reflection leads, sometimes, to positive changes. Moreover, the scholarly scrutiny of sport reveals a subject far more complex and far more interesting than what we see on the fields and arenas and what we read in the sports pages.

This book is a collection of the writings representing this new era of critical appraisal. It includes contributions from both journalists and academics. The overriding criterion for inclusion of a particular article was whether it critically examined the role of sport in society. The praise of sport is not omitted, but such praise, as with condemnation, must be backed by fact, not mythology or dogma. (Occasionally a dogmatic piece has been included to challenge the critical faculties of the reader.) The selection of each article was also guided by such questions as: Is it interesting? Is it informative? Is it thought provoking? Does it communicate without the use of unnecessary jargon and sophisticated methodologies?

In short, the selections presented here not only afford the reader an understanding of sport that transcends the still prevalent stereotypes and myths; they also yield fascinating and important insights into the nature of society. Thus, this book has several groups of potential readers. First, it is intended to be the primary or supplementary text for courses in the sociology of sport, sport and society, and foundations of physical education. Second, the book can be used as a supplemental text for sociology courses such as the introduction to sociology, American society, and social institutions. A third audience for this book is general readers who wish to deepen their understanding and appreciation of sport.

The ninth edition of *Sport in Contemporary Society* has undergone extensive revision, with half of the forty selections new to this edition. In keeping with my plan from previous editions, gender- and race-related articles are found throughout the collection, not just "ghettoized" into their appropriate sections. The result is an anthology of lively and timely chapters that will sharpen the reader's analysis and understanding both of sport *and* society.

I am indebted to the authors of the chapters in this volume. My thanks to them for their scholarship and, most significant, for their insights that help us unravel the mysteries of this intriguing and important part of social life.

D. Stanley Eitzen

SPORT IN CONTEMPORARY SOCIETY

PART ONE

Sport as a Microcosm of Society

The early part of the twenty-first century was a disheartening time in sports. Greed seemed to go unchecked. New stadiums were built at taxpayer expense *and the price of tickets went up.* Elite athletes were given astronomical salaries. Professional team owners threatened to move to different cities if they did not receive more subsidies. Parents were spending up to $100,000 annually to have their children groomed for the world of big-time sport. Scandals were commonplace in big-time college sport. Player and fan violence seemed rampant inside and outside the arenas. "Against this tawdry backdrop we've again been forced to face up to the sad truth that sport isn't a sanctuary. It reflects, often all too clearly, society. And, yes, today greed and violence are a big part of society."[1]

My thesis is that sport is a microcosm of society. If we know how sport is organized, the type of games played, the way winners and losers are treated, the type and amount of compensation given the participants, and the way rules are enforced, then we surely also know a great deal about the larger society in which it exists. Conversely, if we know the values of a society, the type of economy, the way minority groups are treated, and the political structure, then we would also have important clues about how sport in that society is likely organized.

The United States, for example, is a capitalistic society. It is not surprising, then, that in the corporate sport that dominates, American athletes are treated as property. In the professional ranks they are bought and sold. At the college level players once enrolled are unable to switch teams without waiting for a year. Even in youth sports, players are drafted and become the "property" of a given team.

Capitalism is also evident as team owners "carpetbag," i.e., move teams to more lucrative markets. At the same time these owners insist that the cities subsidize the construction of new stadiums, thereby making their franchises more profitable. The players, too, appear to have more loyalty to money than to their teams or fans.

Americans are highly competitive. This is easily seen at work, at school, in dating, and in sport. Persons are evaluated not on their intrinsic worth but on the criterion of achievement. As George H. Sage has written, "Sports have consented to measure the results of sports efforts in terms of performance and product—the terms which prevail in the factory and department store."[2]

Athletes are expected to deny self and sacrifice for the needs of the sponsoring organization. This requires, foremost, an acquiescence to authority. The coach is the ultimate authority and the players must obey. This is the way bureaucracies operate, and American society is highly bureaucratic whether it be in government, school, church, or business. As Paul Hoch has stated, "In football, like business ... every pattern of movement on the field is increasingly being brought under control of a group of nonplaying managerial technocrats who sit up in the stands ... with their headphones and dictate offenses, defense, special plays, substitutions, and so forth to the players below."[3]

Thus, American sport, like American society, is authoritarian, bureaucratic, and product-oriented. Winning is everything. Athletes use drugs to enhance their performances artificially in order to succeed. Coaches teach their athletes to bend the rules (to feign a foul, to hold without getting caught) in order to win. Even at America's most prestigious universities, coaches offer illegal inducements to athletes to attend their schools. And, as long as they win, the administrators at these offending schools usually look the other way. After all, the object is to win, and this mentality permeates sport as it does politics and the business world.

These are but some of the ways in which sport mirrors society. In this section we shall examine this relationship further through three selections. The first is from the introduction to sportswriter Dave Zirin's book *What's My Name, Fool? Sports and Resistance in the United States.* Zirin is a critical journalist with a keen eye for the inconsistencies, myths, and inequities in sport.

The second selection is by D. Stanley Eitzen. This piece examines several paradoxes of U.S. sport at the beginning of the millennium: (1) Although seemingly a trivial pursuit, sport is important; (2) sport has the capacity to build character as well as encourage bad character; (3) while the nature of sport is competition where ability tells, the reality is that race restricts; and (4) schools emphasize sports because of the personal and social benefits for participants, yet these same schools have generally resisted efforts by girls and women for participation and resources equal to those of boys and men.

The third selection was written expressly for this edition. It looks at the consequences of the Great Recession and the resulting New Economy on sport.

NOTES

1. E. M. Switch, "Giving His All," *Sports Illustrated* (December 19, 1994): 88.
2. George H. Sage, "Sports, Culture, and Society," paper presented at the Basic Science of Sport Medicine Conference, Philadelphia (July 14–16, 1974), pp. 10–11.
3. Paul Hoch, *Rip Off the Big Game* (Garden City, NY: Doubleday Anchor, 1972), p. 9.

1

Sports—An Offer We Can't Refuse

Dave Zirin

In *The Godfather, Part II,* dying mob boss Hymen Roth wheezes the obscene truth to young Don Michael Corleone. "Michael," he whispers, "we're bigger than U.S. Steel." This scene updated for today would have Yankees kingpin George Steinbrenner booming at pubescent Dallas Mavericks owner Mark Cuban, "Screw U.S. Steel. We're bigger than the damn mafia."

Just like Hymen Roth, "Big Stein" would be telling no lies. Professional sports are now the tenth largest industry in the United States, generating $220 billion in revenue every year. And just like Mr. Roth's rackets, it's a business that can stink to high heaven.

ROTTEN ROOTS

If, in 1900, a forward thinking person had predicted that sports would some day stand as one of the great pillars of American industry, that person would have been proclaimed mad and then subjected to some combination of leeching and lobotomy. Before the 1880s, everything from the World Series to a daily sports page was just a gleam in Uncle Sam's eye. The Victorian idea that sports undermined character and promoted a slothful work ethic dominated most people's perceptions of organized

Source: Dave Zirin, *What's My Name, Fool? Sports and Resistance in the United States* (Chicago: Haymarket Books, 2005): 17–22.

play. (The Victorians clearly considered child labor and building a better chastity belt more noble pursuits.) Their attitude, however, is easy to understand when you consider class. Competitive sports were a working-class pastime that reflected the brutality of early industrial life. Popular sports of the day included bare-knuckled boxing, "stick-battling," cock fighting, and animal baiting, which involved setting starved dogs against a bull or bear.

But at the end of the nineteenth century, an upstart generation of wealthy industrialists forged a new idea about these innocuous games. Industrialist J. P. Morgan and former President Teddy Roosevelt argued that organized athletics could be the means for instilling the character and values deemed necessary to make America a global power in the century to come. Sports could breed a sense of hard work, self-discipline, and the win-at-all-cost ethic of competition. Roosevelt once said, presumably while swinging a big stick,

> Virile, masterful qualities alone can maintain and defend this very civilization. There is no better way [to develop this] than by encouraging the sports which develop such qualities as courage, resolution, and endurance. No people has ever yet done great and lasting work if its physical type was infirm and weak.

Teddy and his ilk backed their words with bucks. Business scions funded organizations like the YMCA to teach sports and specifically to exclude "undesirable" ethnic groups, women, and Blacks.

As the popularity of sports rose among working people, factory owners began to see the benefit of starting plant teams as a form of labor management. This synthesis bore team factory names that remain today like the Green Bay Packers and the Milwaukee Brewers. The Chicago Bears, who used to be rooted in Decatur, Illinois, were known as the Decatur Staleys, named after the A. E. Staley Company. Their first coach, George "Papa Bear" Halas, was a Staley manager. Organized athletics became less a place to toughen up Teddy Roosevelt's gentlemen of leisure than a narrow window of opportunity for immigrants, white urban youth, and people right off the farm to claw their way out of poverty. Players who captured the country's imagination included a Baltimore orphan named "Babe" Ruth, Native American Olympic star Jim Thorpe, and the first renowned female athlete, a daughter of immigrants named Mildred "Babe" Didrikson. As another first-generation American, Joe DiMaggio, once said, "A ball player's got to be kept hungry to become a big-leaguer. That's why no boy from a rich family ever made the big leagues."

As the United States urbanized, it was evident that people would pay to see sports played at their highest level. The 1920s and 1950s, two decades with very similar economic landscapes, saw this take root. Both were periods of expansion and urbanization. Both eras saw revolutions in technology—radio in the 1920s and then TV in the 1950s—that could deliver sports into people's homes. But, most critically, both were times after brutal world wars that saw a population in the United States looking for relief, escape, and leisure.

SPORTS AND LEE GREENWOOD

In addition to becoming a profitable form of mass entertainment, pro sports were used by the political and financial elite as a way to package their values and ideas. This is why sports in this country reflect a distinctly U.S. project, rooted in aspirations for greatness as well as conquest and oppression. That's why the United States is so singular in its sports presentation. We are unique in playing the national anthem before every game (and, since 9/11, playing "God Bless America" during baseball's seventh inning stretch—even for all-American teams like the Toronto Blue Jays). We are unique in employing scantily clad women to tell us when to "cheer." We are unique in calling the winners of our domestic leagues "world champions." We are unique in the very sports we imbibe most heartily—especially football. (And don't tout NFL Europe as counter-evidence. There are more U.S. study-abroad students at those games than at your typical Amsterdam hash bar.) In many cities, the average Sunday NFL game contains more patriotic overkill than a USO show in Kuwait. First there's a military drum line to midfield. Then a standing sing-along to "I'm Proud to Be an American (Where at Least I Know I'm Free)" by Lee Greenwood. And then comes the "Star-Spangled Banner." You are certainly "free" to not stand, as long as you know that the person behind you will feel "free" to pour beer on your head. Save me, Lee Greenwood!

WHY SPORTS MATTERS

Many throughout the U.S. are repelled by pro sports today for a laundry list of reasons. People who otherwise enjoy competitive play performed at its highest levels don't want to be party to the cutthroat competition at its core. Many are also put off by the insane salaries of the games' top players, others by the backroom dealings that produce publicly funded stadiums at taxpayer expense. Then there is the abuse of steroids and other performance enhancing drugs, which some feel have taken long-hallowed baseball records and reduced them to rubbish. When you pile on the way racism and sexism can be used to sell sports, it can all seem about as appealing as a Sunday in the park with George Steinbrenner.

The way that the games have been shaped by profit and patriotism has quite understandably led many people to conclude that sports are little more than a brutal reflection of the savage inequalities that stream through our world. As esteemed left-wing critic Noam Chomsky noted in *Manufacturing Consent,*

> Sports keeps people from worrying about things that matter to their lives that they might have some idea of doing something about. And in fact it's striking to see the intelligence that's used by ordinary people in sports [as opposed to political and social issues]. I mean, you listen to radio stations where people call in—they have the most exotic information and understanding about all kinds of arcane issues. And the press undoubtedly does a lot with this.... Sports is a major factor

> in controlling people. Workers have minds; they have to be involved in something and it's important to make sure they're involved in things that have absolutely no significance. So professional sports is perfect. It instills total passivity.

Chomsky quite correctly highlights how people use sports as a balm to protect themselves from the harsh realities of the world. He is also right that the intelligence and analysis many of us invest in sports far outstrips our dissecting of the broader world. It is truly amazing how we can be moved to fits of fury by a missed call or a blown play, but remain too under-confident to raise our voices in anger when we are laid off, lose our healthcare, or suffer the slings and arrows of everyday life in the United States. The weakness in Chomsky's argument, however, is that it disregards how the very passion we invest in sports can transform it from a kind of mindless escape into a site of resistance. It can become an arena where the ideas of our society are not only presented but also challenged. Just as sports can reflect the dominant ideas of our society, they can also reflect struggle. The story of the women's movement is incomplete without mention of Billie Jean King's match against Bobby Riggs. The struggle for gay rights has to include a chapter on Martina Navratilova. When we think about the Black freedom struggle, we picture Jackie Robinson and Muhammad Ali in addition to Martin Luther King Jr. and Malcolm X. And, of course, when remembering the movement for Black Power, we can't help but visualize one of the most stirring sights of our sports century: Tommie Smith and John Carlos's black-gloved medal-stand salute at the 1968 Olympics.

Chomsky's view also reflects a lack of understanding of why sports are, at their core, so appealing. Amid the politics and pain that engulf and sometimes threaten to smother big-time sports, there is also artistry that can take your breath away. To see Michael Vick zigzag his way through an entire defense, or Mia Hamm crush a soccer ball past a goalie's outstretched hands, or LeBron James use the eyes in the back of his head to spot a teammate cutting to the basket can be a glorious sight at the end of a tough day. It is a bolt of beauty in an otherwise very gray world. As a good friend said to me long ago, "Magic Johnson will always be my Miles Davis."

Lester "Red" Rodney, the editor of the *Daily Worker* sports section from 1934 to 1958 and a groundbreaking fighter in the battle to smash baseball's color line, puts it perfectly:

> Of course there is exploitation but there is fun and beauty too. I mean, what's more beautiful than a 6-4-3 double play perfectly executed where the shortstop fields a ground ball and flips it toward second base in one motion, the second baseman takes the throw in stride, pivots, avoids the base runner, and fires it to first on time. That's not a put-on. That's not fake. That's beyond all the social analysis of the game. The idea of people coming together and amazing the rest of us.

Sports as a whole do not represent black and white, good or bad, red state or blue state issues. Sports are neither to be defended nor vilified. Instead we need to look at sports for what they are, so we can take apart the disgusting, the beautiful, the ridiculous, and even the radical.

This book aims to recall moments of resistance past and rescue the underreported shows of struggle and humanity by athletes of the present, so we can appreciate the beauty of sports independent of the muck and fight for a future where skill, art, glory, and the joy of play belong to all of us.

2

American Sport in the New Millennium

D. Stanley Eitzen

I want to examine sport by focusing on several paradoxes that are central to sport as it has come to be.

Paradox: While seemingly a trivial pursuit, sport is important. On the one hand, sport is entertainment, a fantasy, a diversion from the realities of work, relationships, and survival. But if sport is just a game, why do we take it so seriously? Among the many reasons, let's consider four: First, sport mirrors the human experience. The introductory essay in *The Nation,* which was devoted to sport, said this:

> Sport elaborates in its rituals what it means to be human: the play, the risk, the trials, the collective impulse to games, the thrill of physicality, the necessity of strategy; defeat, victory, defeat again, pain, transcendence and, most of all, the certainty that nothing is certain—that everything can change and be changed.

Second, sport mirrors society in other profound ways as well. Sociologists, in particular, find the study of sport fascinating because we find there the basic elements and expressions of bureaucratization, commercialization, racism, sexism, homophobia, greed, exploitation of the powerless, alienation, and the ethnocentrism found in the larger society. Of special interest, too, is how sport has been transformed from an activity for individuals involved in sport for its own sake, to a money-driven, corporate entity where sport is work rather than play, and where loyalty to players,

Source: D. Stanley Eitzen, "American Sport at Century's End," *Vital Speeches of the Day* 65 (January 1, 1999): 189–191. Revised in 2008.

coaches, and owners is a quaint notion that is now rarely held. Also, now athletes are cogs in a machine where decisions by coaches and bureaucracies are less and less player-centered. I am especially concerned with the decisions made by big business bureaucracies (universities, leagues, cartels such as the NCAA, corporations, and sports conglomerates such as Rupert Murdoch's empire, which just in the U.S. includes ownership of the Fox network, FX, 22 local cable channels, the *New York Post,* 20 percent of L.A.'s Staples center, and the partial rights to broadcast NFL games for eight years and major league baseball for five years). Another powerful sports conglomerate is the Walt Disney Corporation, which owns ABC-TV, ESPN, and like Murdoch, partial rights for NFL games and major league baseball games. Time Warner is another sports empire, including ownership of *Sports Illustrated, Time Magazine,* CNN, HBO, TNT, TBS, and Warner Brothers. Obviously, sport is not a trivial pursuit by these media giants.

A third reason why sports are so compelling is that they combine spectacle with drama. Sports, especially football, involve pageantry, bands forming a liberty bell or unfurling a flag as big as the football field, and militaristic displays with the drama of a situation where the outcome is not perfectly predictable. Moreover, we see excellence, human beings transcending the commonplace to perform heroic deeds. There is also clarity—we know, unlike in many other human endeavors, exactly who won, by how much, and how they did it.

Finally, there is the human desire to identify with something larger than oneself. For athletes, it is to be part of a team, working and sacrificing together to achieve a common goal. For fans, by identifying with a team or a sports hero, they bond with others who share their allegiance; they belong and they have an identity. This bond of allegiance is becoming more and more difficult as players through free agency move from team to team, as coaches are hired and fired, and because many times when coaches are successful they break their contracts to go to a more lucrative situation, leaving their players, assistants, and fans in their wake. The owners of many professional teams blackmail their cities for more lucrative subsidies by threatening to move, which they sometimes do, leaving diehard fans without teams.

Paradox: Sport has the capacity to build character as well as encourage bad character. On the one hand, sports participation encourages hard work, perseverance, self-discipline, sacrifice, following the rules, obeying authority, and working with teammates to achieve a common goal. Sport promotes fair play. There are countless examples where competitors show respect for one another, where sportsmanship rules.

But for all of the honor and integrity found in sport there is also much about sport that disregards the ideals of fair play. Good sportsmanship may be a product of sport, but so is bad sportsmanship. Let me cite a few examples: (1) trash-talking and taunting opponents; (2) dirty play (an article in *Sports Illustrated* documented dirty play in the NFL, citing the ten worst offenders, saying that "there's a nasty breed of players who follow one cardinal rule: Anything goes, and that means biting, kicking, spearing, spitting, and leg-whipping"); (3) coaches who teach their players how to hold and not get caught; (4) faking being fouled so that a referee who is out of position will call an undeserved foul on the opponent; (5) trying to hurt an opponent; (6) coaches rewarding players for hurting an opponent; (7) throwing a spitter or corking a bat; (8) using illegal drugs to enhance performance; (9) crushing an opponent (a Laramie, Wyoming, girls junior high basketball team won a game a few years ago by a score of 81–1, using a full-court press the entire game); (10) fans yelling racial slurs; (11) coaches who, like Pat Riley of the Miami Heat, demand that their players not show respect for their opponents (Riley fines his players $1,500 if they help an opposing player get off the floor); (12) coaches who are sexist and homophobic, calling their male players "pussies" or "fags" if they are not aggressive enough; (13) a male locker room culture that tends to promote homophobia, sexism, and aggressive behaviors; and (14) coaches who recruit illegally, who alter transcripts and bribe teachers to keep players eligible, and who exploit players with no regard for their health or their education.

What lesson is being taught and caught when a coach openly asks a player to cheat? Consider this example. A few years ago, the Pretty Prairie Kansas High School had twin boys on its team. One of the twins was injured but suited up for a game where his brother was in foul trouble at half time. The coach had the twins change jerseys so that the foul-plagued twin would be in the second half with no fouls charged to the player's number he was now wearing....

My point is that we live in a morally distorted sports world—a world where winning often supersedes all other considerations, where moral values have become confused with the bottom line. In this in-your-face, whip-your-butt climate, winning at any price often becomes the prevailing code of conduct. And when it does, I assert, sport does build character, but it is bad character. When we make the value of winning so important that it trumps morality, then we and sport are diminished.

Paradox: While the nature of sport is competition where ability tells, the reality is that race restricts. Just as in other social realms, we find in sport that the ascribed status of race gives advantage to some and disadvantage to others. Let's look at racism in sport, focusing on African Americans since they are the dominant racial minority in American sport.

At first glance, its seems impossible that Blacks are victims of discrimination in sport since some of them make huge fortunes from their athletic prowess, such as LaBron James who signed a seven-year deal with Nike for $90 million before he graduated from high school, and Tiger Woods who makes about $120 million annually. Moreover, it is argued that Blacks in sport are not victims of discrimination because, while only constituting 12 percent of the general population, they comprise 67 percent of the players in professional football, 77 percent of professional basketball players, and 8 percent of the players in major league baseball (and where Latinos constitute another 24 percent). Also about 60 percent of the football and basketball players in big-time college programs are African Americans.

Despite these empirical facts that seem to contradict racism in sport, it is prevalent in several forms. Let me cite some examples. First, Blacks are rarely found in those sports that require the facilities, coaching, and competition usually provided only in private—and typically racially segregated—clubs; sports such as swimming, golf, skiing, and tennis. Black athletes also are rarely found where it takes extraordinary up-front money, usually from corporate sponsors, to participate such as in automobile racing.

But even in the team sports where African Americans dominate numerically, there is evidence of discrimination. Sociologists have long noted that Blacks tend to be relegated to those team positions where the physical attributes of strength, size, speed, aggressiveness, and "instinct" are important but that they are underrepresented at those playing positions that require thinking and leadership and are the most crucial for outcome control. This phenomenon, known as stacking, continues today, at both the college and professional levels in football and baseball. Using professional football as the example, African Americans are underrepresented on offense and if on offense they tend to be at wide receiver and running back—the whitest positions are center, offensive guard, quarterback, punter, placekicker, and placekick holder. Blacks are overrepresented at all positions on defense, except middle linebacker. The existence of stacking reinforces negative stereotypes about racial minorities, as Whites appear, by the positions they play, to be superior to Blacks in cognitive ability and leadership qualities but behind them in physical prowess.

African Americans are also underrepresented in nonplaying leadership positions. At the professional level team ownership is an exclusively all-White club. In the league offices of the NCAA, major league baseball, the NBA, and the NFL, the employees are disproportionately White. The same is true, of course, for head coaches in big-time college and professional sports.

African Americans are also underrepresented in ancillary sports positions such as sports information director, ticket manager, trainer, equipment manager, scout, accountant, sportswriting, and sports broadcasting, especially play-by-play announcing. . . .

Paradox: Schools emphasize sports because of the personal and social benefits for participants, yet these same schools have generally resisted efforts by girls and women for participation and resources equal to that of boys and men. Research shows many benefits from sports for girls and women. When female athletes are compared to their nonathlete peers, they are found to have higher self-esteem and better body image. For high school girls, athletes are less likely than nonathletes to use illicit drugs; they are more likely to be virgins; if sexually active they are more likely to begin intercourse at a later age; and they are much less likely to get pregnant. These advantages are in addition to the standard benefits of learning to work with teammates for a common goal, striving for excellence, and the lessons of what it takes to win and how to cope with defeat. Yet, historically, women have been denied these benefits. And, even today, the powerful male establishment in sport continues to drag its collective feet on gender equity.

Title IX, passed in 1972, mandated gender equity in school sports programs. While this affected schools at all levels, I'll focus on the college level because this is where women have met the most resistance. Since 1972 women's intercollegiate programs have made tremendous strides, with participation quadrupling from 30,000 women in 1971 to 160,000 in 2004. Athletic scholarships for women were virtually unknown in 1972; now women athletes receive 45 percent of college athletic scholarship dollars. These increases in a generation represent the good news concerning gender equity in collegiate sport. The bad news, however, is quite significant. The Women's Sports Foundation has noted the following disparities by gender in big-time (Division I-A) programs:

1. Even though female students comprise 57 percent of college student populations, female athletes receive only 43 percent of participation opportunities compared to their male counterparts.
2. Women's teams receive only 38 percent of college sport operating dollars and 33 percent of college athletic team recruitment spending.
3. Women coach 43 percent of women's teams and only 2 percent of men's teams, and hold only 8 percent of athletic director positions.
4. Head coaches of women's teams receive on average $932,700 less than head coaches of men's teams.

Clearly, as these data show, gender equity is not part of big-time college sports programs. In my view, universities must address the question: Is it appropriate for a college or university to deny women the same opportunities that it provides men? Shouldn't our daughters have the same possibilities as our sons in all aspects of higher education? Women are slightly more than half of the undergraduates in U.S. higher education. They receive half of all the master's degrees. Should they be second-class in any aspect of the university's activities? The present unequal state of affairs in sport is not inevitable. Choices have been made in the past that have given men advantage in university sports. They continue to do so, to the detriment of not only women's sports but so to the so-called minor sports for men.

These are a few paradoxes concerning contemporary sport in the United States. There are more but I'll let my colleagues and the other contributors speak directly or indirectly to them. Let me conclude my remarks with this statement and a plea. We celebrate sport for many good reasons. It excites and it inspires. We savor the great moments of sport when an athlete does the seemingly impossible or when the truly gifted athlete makes the impossible routine. We exult when a team or an athlete overcomes great odds to succeed. We are touched by genuine camaraderie among teammates and between competitors. We are uplifted by the biographies of athletes who have used sport to get an education that they would have been denied because of economic circumstance or who have used sport to overcome delinquency and drugs. But for all of our love and fascination with sport and our extensive knowledge of it, do we truly understand it? Can we separate the hype from the reality and the myths from the facts? Do we accept the way sport is organized without questioning? Unfortunately for many fans and participants alike there is a superficial, uncritical, and taken-for-granted attitude concerning sport. Sportswriter Rick Reilly of *Sports Illustrated* has written that "sport deserves a more critical examination. We need to ask more probing questions about sport." That has always been my goal; it continues to be my goal; and I hope that it is yours as well.

3

The Great Recession and Sport

D. Stanley Eitzen

"In the past, I've felt baseball was recession-proof but this is different. I've never seen anything like [this] economy and its impact on Major League Baseball."
—Bud Selig, Commissioner of Major League Baseball

THE GREAT RECESSION

Several powerful forces converged in 2007, creating a "perfect storm" of economic devastation. The "housing bubble" burst when subprime borrowers (people with questionable credit ratings) defaulted on their mortgages. That sent housing prices tumbling, unleashing a domino effect on mortgage-backed securities. Banks, insurance companies, and brokerages, basically unregulated by the government, that had borrowed money to increase their leverage had to raise capital quickly. Some of these firms had to sell their assets at bargain rates. Others failed. The stock market dropped precipitously. Credit dried up. Business slowed, causing companies to lay off workers by the tens of thousands. Consumers reduced their buying. The result was the worst economic downturn in the United States since the Great Depression of the 1930s (Eitzen, Baca Zinn, and Smith, 2012). Consider these negative facts from the "Great Recession":

Source: D. Stanley Eitzen, "The Great Recession and Sport," written expressly for the ninth edition of *Sport in Contemporary Society.*

- The stock market lost 35 percent, resulting in the loss of retirement savings for millions.
- Eight million jobs were lost, with the official unemployment rate doubling from 5 percent to 10 percent.
- Housing wealth declined by $6 trillion.
- The average net worth of households was 20 percent lower in 2010 than it was in 2006.
- The income of one-fifth of Americans was down by 25 percent.
- Two million homes a year were lost to foreclosures and bank repossessions.
- The official poverty rate rose from 13.2 percent in 2008 to 14.3 percent in 2009—an increase of 4 million impoverished people.
- The number of people without health insurance rose by 4.4 million from 2008 to 2009.

These statistics have important implications for societal stability, the decline of the middle class, government policy, and a deepening public discontent and mistrust of societal institutions.

CONSEQUENCES OF THE GREAT RECESSION FOR SPORT

The unique qualities of sports would seem to make them exempt from the troubles that plague the larger economy. Watching games and identifying with a team offer an escape for fans (Eitzen, 2009, pp. 8–11). Sport is fascinating because it transcends everyday routine experiences with excitement, heroics, spectacle, drama, excellence, unpredictability, and clarity (we know who won and who lost and why). As Scott Simon of National Public Radio puts it: "You can tell yourself: It's just sports, nothing real; it has nothing to do with your life, no resonance in the real world of living, dying, and struggling. And you'd be right. Then, something happens. MJ leaps! Mac swings! Flutie scores! And inside, where your body cannot kid you, something takes over and it feels real" (2000). Finally, there is the human desire to identify with something greater than oneself. For athletes, this is being part of a team, working and sacrificing together to achieve a common goal. For fans, identifying with a team or a sports hero bonds them with others who share their allegiance; they belong and they have an identity. Sports analyst Frank Deford says this: "In today's world, where we are so fragmented, an arena is one place left where we come together to share" (1999). The question: Will sport's powerful attractions immunize it from the negative pulls of the Great Recession? To answer this question we examine attendance, alternative options to attending, and corporate sponsorships.

Attendance

Attendance at sports events has declined since the beginning of the Great Recession in late 2007. Let's begin with the National Football League, the most popular professional sport in the United States. Despite its popularity, ticket sales and average game attendance for the NFL through 2009 fell for three consecutive seasons and is expected to drop another 1 percent to 2 percent, and season ticket sales are expected to fall by 5 percent in 2010 (McCarthy, 2010). The cost of attending a game has become too great for many in difficult economic times; the average cost to take a family of four to an NFL game was $420 in 2010 (Leahy, 2010). "The NFL, long thought to be recession proof is feeling the squeeze. In the best of times, football is a blue-collar game at white-collar prices. But this year attendance has dropped, in no small part because ticket prices remain prohibitive even amidst the crisis" (Zirin, 2009b).

Alternatives to Attendance

The decline in attendance at NFL games, however, does not indicate a loss of fan interest in the sport. To the contrary, the popularity of Fantasy Football continues to increase. So, too, is watching NFL games on television. In 2010, viewing games increased 13 percent from the 2009 season, making that season the most watched in NFL history (Leahy, 2011). In difficult economic times, watching a game at home on a big-screen, high-definition television is an attractive alternative to attending high-priced games in person. The downside to this for the television fan is that when NFL games are not sold out 48 hours before game time, the game will not be shown locally on television. With attendance down, the number of television blackouts increased considerably during the 2009 and 2010 seasons.

The NFL's premier event—the Super Bowl—is an extravaganza of commercial excess, but the Great Recession even curbed this hugely popular event. Sports columnist Dave Zirin (2009a) dubbed the 2009 Super Bowl "America's first Recession Super Bowl." He noted that the city of Tampa, which hosted the Super Bowl, took in $30 million less than expected, that some pre-game corporate-sponsored parties were cancelled, and that game tickets were being sold in the shadow market for below retail. Television ratings, on the other hand, set records with the 2010 Super Bowl watched by 106.5 million in the United States, up 8 percent from 2009 (Gregory-Bristol, 2010b).

Here are two additional indicators of hard times for professional football: (1) In 2009 the NFL commissioner's office cut over 10 percent of its staff (150 out of 1,100); and (2) the Arena Football League, in existence for twenty-two years, folded in 2009.

Ticket sales in major league baseball declined for three consecutive years beginning in 2007. The most celebrated team—the New York Yankees—defied this trend with attendance surpassing three million in each year of the Great Recession. The majority of teams, however, suffered a different fate. Indicative of declining fan attendance, 16 of the 30 franchises in MLB froze or cut season ticket prices in 2009. The Milwaukee Brewers executive vice president of business operations said, "In sports, the news is all good, but on the financial pages, the news keeps getting worse. We have to do everything to make the product affordable" (quoted in Antonen and Lacques, 2008). Unlike the case for professional football, television ratings for baseball were flat.

Similarly, attendance in men's professional basketball was down during the Great Recession. In 2008–2009 NBA attendance declined by 2.4 percent from the previous season and was down another 2.9 percent in 2009–2010 with three teams having double-digit declines (*Sports Business Daily,* 2010).

While fan attendance slipped, television viewing of NBA games increased 11 percent.

Attendance for women's professional basketball (the Women's National Basketball Association) in 2009 was down 3.7 percent from the previous year. In 2008 the WNBA folded its Houston team because of finances.

For professional hockey, attendance in 2009–2010 was down 2.2 percent from the previous season. But while attendance declined in 17 of 24 U.S. markets, television ratings for NHL hockey were up in 17 of 24 markets (*Sports Business Daily,* reported in Zona, 2010).

Attendance at stock car races (NASCAR) in 2009 was down 10 percent from the previous year, with television viewing down a whopping 25 percent in 2009 (Gregory-Bristol, 2010a). Further evidence of economic difficulties in NASCAR: the organization suspended stock car testing at NASCAR-sanctioned tracks in 2008 and many racing teams either laid off employees or merged with other racing teams (Macur and Caldwell, 2008).

Big-time college sports (Division I football and men's basketball) also experienced a drop in attendance coinciding with the Great Recession. In football, attendance declined 3 percent from 2008–2009, and another 2.2 percent from 2009–2010 (Burton, 2010). For basketball, every one of the 12 top-drawing conferences saw attendance fall in 2009 (Weiberg, 2009). It is important to point out, however, that the glamorous and successful teams in big-time college football and basketball, just as the Yankees in baseball and the Los Angeles Lakers in basketball, did not fall off in attendance during the Great Recession.

Big-time college women's basketball defied the downward trend with similar attendance records from year-to-year, despite the difficult economy. This could be a function of lower ticket prices for women's basketball games. The most successful women's programs—Connecticut and Tennessee—sustained rising attendance.

Corporate Sponsorships

Companies sponsor sports through buying the naming rights to stadiums and arenas, purchasing the rights to a successful athlete for advertising, and contracting the rights to identify exclusively with a team. These sponsorships are believed to increase awareness of the company's product and to enhance an image that distinguishes the product/company from its competitors. These sponsorships are expensive, and in difficult times, corporations have reduced or eliminated their support of athletes and teams. In 2009 spending on sports sponsorships shrank by $100 million, most notably the sponsorship of golf tournaments and race car advertising. (Fitch, Ozanian, and Badenhausen, 2010). Other examples of diminished sponsorship include the following: Bank of America dropped its 16-year-old sponsorship of the U.S.

Olympic team. Corporate sponsorship of cycling declined by $12 million (partially the consequence of drug cheating). Pepsi split with soccer star David Beckham, a ten-year relationship worth $4 million a year. Microsoft declined to renew a two-year $1 million deal with LeBron James. In 2009 Frontier Airlines ended its sponsorship of the Denver Nuggets, Colorado Avalanche, the Crush, and the Colorado Mammoth. Also, in 2009 the Professional Golf Association Tour lost one tournament due to not having enough sponsors. The Ladies Professional Golf Association Tour scheduled three fewer tournaments in 2009 than in the previous year.

A Case Study in Declining Corporate Sponsorship: General Motors

General Motors was hit hard by the recession. Consumer demand was low. Debt exceeded income. And bankruptcy was a real possibility until the federal government came to its rescue with a bailout. Faced with these and other enormous economic difficulties, the company decided that spending on sport was not prudent. As a result G.M. made the following decisions:

- Cadillac withdrew its sponsorship of the Masters golf tournament and the Buick Open.
- G.M. ended its relationships with two NASCAR racetracks.
- In 2009 General Motors did not purchase television commercials for the 2009 Super Bowl broadcast. G.M. had spent $77.1 million on Super Bowl advertising in the fifteen years prior to 2009.
- G.M. did not purchase stadium advertising inside the Detroit Tigers park in 2009.
- Buick ended an $8 million annual deal with Tiger Woods.

THE NEW ECONOMY AND THE SPORTS BUSINESS

Most economists believe that the effects of the Great Recession, just as happened after the Great Depression, will be relatively long lasting. Technically, the recession, which began in December 2007, ended in June 2009 when general business activity in the United States reached a low point and the recovery began. Unfortunately, reality trumped the technical definition of a recession's end. Consumer demand and bank lending remained weak. Unemployment rates remained high and real estate values stayed low. Foreclosures and bankruptcies were in the millions. While some economic indicators slowly become more positive, the Great Recession has shifted U.S. society to a New Economy (Wingfield, 2010; Reich, 2010). Compared to the time prior to the "bubble bursting" in 2007, the middle and lower classes in 2010 had less discretionary income; consumers were more thrifty; investors were more cautious, saving more and investing less; federal, state, and local governments were deeply in debt and unwilling or unable to fund new projects; and businesses seemed more interested in replacing labor with technology and in offshoring and outsourcing their activities rather than hiring. Thus, the aftermath of the Great Recession is a bridge to a New Economy—an economy characterized by personal and public debt, stagnant wages, high unemployment, and weak consumer demand. These factors feed on each other, resulting in continuing economic woes.

The New Economy has consequences for the sports business. As we have seen, the ravages of the Great Recession affected professional sports leagues and big-time college sport by declines in ticket sales and corporate sponsorship of athletes, teams, and sporting events. Are these temporary phenomena or will they be long lasting?

In a new era of thrift brought about by the Great Recession, ticket sales are down because prices are too high for the limited incomes of many fans, resulting in continued downward levels of attendance. But the Great Recession has had an additional effect. Just as it has fostered resentment and anger in the electorate (e.g., the Tea Party), the Great Recession has fostered a growing resentment and anger by fans aimed at professional team owners who they feel do not care about them. In Dave Zirin's words: "Because of publicly funded stadium construction, luxury box licenses, sweetheart cable deals, globalized merchandizing plans, and other 'revenue streams,' the need for owners to cater to a local working- and middle-class fan base has shrunk dramatically" (2010b). Adding to the alienation of many are owners who show no loyalty to fans by threatening to move their franchises in order to secure greater subsidies for new stadiums.

Sports at institutions of higher learning are also meeting increased resistance from fans, students, and faculty who, fueled by economic hard times, question the excessive costs of big-time programs. Several situations stoke the smoldering embers. For fans, the cost of tickets at big-time programs is expensive. Moreover, athletic departments often charge fans a seat license—that is, a sports mortgage that guarantees the holder the right to purchase tickets for that seat. For students, the high cost of athletic programs is subsidized by them through their fees (whether they attend events or not) and indirectly when money budgeted for educational purposes is funneled by administrators to the athletic department. In 2008, for instance, some $826 million in student fees and university subsidies propped up athletic programs in big-time programs (Gillum, Upton, and Berkowitz, 2010). This upsets the faculty who see huge athletic budgets and coaching salaries while academic hiring and salary raises are frozen. At the University of California–Berkeley, for example, the athletic department in 2009 had a $430 million building program underway at the same time that tuition was raised 32 percent and departments across campus were asked to make significant budget reductions. Moreover, the athletic department was subsidized by student fees and administrative financial help totaling $12.1 million in 2009–2010, up from $7.4 million in 2007–2008 (Berkowitz, 2010). At the University of Texas, during a time of belt-tightening across campus in 2010, the Board of Regents upped the total compensation of the football coach, Mack Brown, from $3 million to $5 million a year. As a professor at Texas said: "College sports is widely viewed as an out-of-control train on a collision course with academia" (quoted in Zirin, 2010a).

The future of Corporate Sport (professional and big-time college) is and will continue to be shaped by the Great Recession. Questions exist in this New Economy:

Will cash-strapped fans continue to purchase expensive tickets, parking, concessions, and travel or will attendance continue to drop? Will corporations continue to subsidize corporate sport when their profits are thin and the future uncertain? Will citizens (fans and non-fans) vote to raise their taxes to subsidize the building of stadiums and arenas for wealthy team owners? Will college students and their parents, faced with rising tuition, accept costly fees to support bloated athletic departments? So, too, will those in academia acquiesce to the current situation where the sport "dog" wags the education "tail" or will administrators and academics retake their universities and reclaim the primacy of education? In effect, have we entered a new era in which the sports establishment is tamed by the new economic realities and in which many are questioning and resisting the sports establishment?

REFERENCES

Antonen, Mel, and Gabe Lacques. 2008. "MLB Clubs Cutting Ticket Prices," *USA Today* (December 4).

Berkowitz, Steve. 2010. "Cal's Cuts Reveal Budget Pressures," *USA Today* (September 29).

Burton, Larry. 2010. "NCAA Football Attendance Figures Down," *Bleacher Report* (May 30).

Deford, Frank. 1999. "Why We Love Sports," *CNN/Sports Illustrated* (December 29).

Eitzen, D. Stanley. 2009. *Fair and Foul: Beyond the Myths and Paradoxes of Sport,* 4th ed. Lanham, MD: Rowman and Littlefield.

Eitzen, D. Stanley, Maxine Baca Zinn, and Kelly Eitzen Smith. 2012. *Social Problems,* 12th ed. Boston: Allyn and Bacon.

Fitch, Stephane, Mike Ozanian, and Kurt Badenhausen. 2010. "When Big Money Doesn't Play Ball," *Sports Illustrated* (January 18).

Gillum, Jack, Jodi Upton, and Steve Berkowitz. 2010. "College Athletics Soaking Up Subsidies, Fees," *USA Today* (January 14).

Gregory-Bristol, Sean. 2010a. "NASCAR Needs Another Gear," *Time* (April 26).

Gregory-Bristol, Sean. 2010b. "Why Sports Ratings Are Surging on TV," *Time* (August 14).

Leahy, Sean. 2010. "NFL Ticket Prices Rise Again in 2010, Up 30% Since 2005," *USA Today* (September 22).

Leahy, Sean. 2011 "2011 NFL Season Was Most-Watched in History," *USA Today* (January 13).

Macur, Juliet, and Dave Caldwell. 2008. "Poor Economy Starting to Shape Sports Landscape," *New York Times* (November 15).

McCarthy, Michael. 2010. "League Expects Drop in Ticket Sales Again," *USA Today* (September 2).

Reich, Robert B. 2010. *Aftershock: The Next Economy and America's Future.* New York: Alfred A. Knopf.

Reuters. 2010. "NFL Television Ratings Expected to Skyrocket" (July 27).

Simon, Scott. 2000. *Home and Away.* New York: Hyperion.

Sports Business Daily. 2010. "NBA Regular Season Attendance Down 2% from '08-09 Campaign" (April 15).

Wieberg, Steve. 2009. "Economy Hits Hardwood: Attendance Down at NCAA Games," *USA Today* (March 13).

Wingfield, Brian. 2010. "The End of the Great Recession? Hardly," *Forbes* (September 20).

Zirin, Dave. 2009a. "Recession Bowl," *Progressive Populist* (March 1).

Zirin, Dave. 2009b. "The Coming Labor War in the NFL," *Edge of Sports* (November 2).
Zirin, Dave. 2010a. "Faculty Protest Coach's Raise," *Progressive Populist* (February 1).
Zirin, Dave. 2010b. *Bad Sports: How Owners Are Ruining the Games We Love.* New York: Scribner.
Zona, Derek. 2010. "2009–2010 NHL Attendance & Television Ratings," *fromtherink.com* (April 20).

* FOR FURTHER STUDY *

Coakley, Jay. 2007. *Sport in Society: Issues and Controversies.* 9th ed. New York: McGraw-Hill.

Coakley, Jay, and Eric Dunning, eds. 2000. *Handbook of Sport Studies.* London: Sage.

Crapeau, Dick. 1991–2001. Special Issue of *Aethlon: The Journal of Sport Literature* 20 (Fall).

Eitzen, D. Stanley. 2009. *Fair and Foul: Beyond the Myths and Paradoxes of Sport.* 4th ed. Lanham, MD: Rowman and Littlefield.

Eitzen, D. Stanley, and George H. Sage. 2009. *Sociology of North American Sport.* 8th ed. Boulder, CO: Paradigm.

Foer, Franklin. 2005. *How Soccer Explains the World.* New York: Harper Perennial.

Gerdy, John R. 2002. *Sports: The All-American Addiction.* Jackson: University of Mississippi Press.

Giulianotti, Richard. 2002. "Supporters, Followers, Fans, and *Flaneurs.*" *Journal of Sport and Social Issues* 26 (February): 25–46.

Lever, Janet. 1983. *Soccer Madness.* Chicago: University of Chicago Press.

Loy, John W., and Jay Coakley. 2007. "Sport." Pp. 4643–4653 in *Blackwell Encyclopedia of Sport.* Vol. 9.

Nixon, Howard L. II. 2008. *Sport in a Changing World.* Boulder, CO: Paradigm.

Paolantonio, Sal. 2008. *How Football Explains America.* Chicago: Triumph.

Prettyman, Sandra Spickard, and Brian Lampman (eds.). 2011. *Learning Culture Through Sports: Perspectives on Society and Organized Sports,* 2nd ed. Lanham, MD: Rowman and Littlefield.

Sage, George H. 1998. *Power and Ideology in American Sport: A Critical Perspective.* 2nd ed. Champaign, IL: Human Kinetics.

Zirin, Dave. 2008. *A People's History of Sports in the United States: 250 Years of Politics, Protest, People, and Play.* New York: New Press.

PART TWO

Sport and Socialization: Organized Sports and Youth

The involvement of young people in adult-supervised sport is characteristic of contemporary American society. Today, millions of boys and girls are involved in organized baseball, football, hockey, basketball, and soccer leagues. Others are involved in swimming, skating, golf, tennis, and gymnastics at a highly competitive level. School-sponsored sports begin about the seventh grade and are highly organized, win-oriented activities.

Why do so many parents in so many communities strongly support organized sports programs for youth? Primarily because most people believe that sports participation has positive benefits for those involved. The following quotation from *Time* summarizes this assumption.

> Sport has always been one of the primary means of civilizing the human animal, of inculcating the character traits a society desires. Wellington in his famous aphorism insisted that the Battle of Waterloo had been won on the playing fields of Eton. The lessons learned on the playing field are among the most basic: the setting of goals and joining with others to achieve them; an understanding of and respect for rules; the persistence to hone ability into skill, prowess into perfection. In games, children learn that success is possible and that failure can be overcome. Championships may be won; when lost, wait until next year. In practicing such skills as fielding a grounder and hitting a tennis ball, young athletes develop work patterns and attitudes that carry over into college, the marketplace and all of life.[1]

However, parents often ignore the negative side of sports participation, a position that is summarized by Charles Banham:

> It [the conventional argument that sport builds character] is not sound because it assumes that everyone will benefit from sport in the complacently prescribed manner. A minority do so benefit. A few have the temperament that responds healthily to all the demands. These are the only ones able to develop an attractively active character. Sport can put fresh air in the mind, if it's the right mind; it can give muscle to the personality, if it's the right personality. But for the rest, it encourages selfishness, envy, conceit, hostility, and bad temper. Far from ventilating the mind, it stifles it. Good sportsmanship may be a product of sport, but so is bad sportsmanship.[2]

The problem is that sports produce positive and negative outcomes. This dualistic quality of sport is summarized by Terry Orlick: "For every positive psychological or social outcome in sports, there are possible negative outcomes. For example, sports can offer a child group membership or group exclusion, acceptance or rejection, positive feedback or negative feedback, a sense of accomplishment or a sense of failure, evidence of self-worth or a lack of evidence of self-worth. Likewise, sports can develop cooperation and a concern for others, but they can also develop intense rivalry and a complete lack of concern for others."[3]

The first selection in this part, by sociologist Jay J. Coakley, describes the organized youth sports of today and compares them with the spontaneous games more characteristic of youth in previous generations.

The second selection expresses a concern over the change in children's play as they are now more engaged in solitary computer games. This change stifles creativity, physical activity, and social engagement.

The final selection, by sociologist Michael Messner, reports his research on the meanings that males attribute to their boyhood participation in organized sport. Messner concludes: "Organized sports is a 'gendered institution'—an institution constructed by gender relations. As such, its structure and values . . . reflect dominant conceptions of masculinity and femininity."

NOTES

1. "Comes the Revolution: Joining the Game at Last, Women Are Transforming American Athletics," *Time* (June 26, 1978): 55.
2. Charles Banham, "Man at Play," *Contemporary Review* 207 (August 1965): 62.
3. T. D. Orlick, "The Sports Environment: A Capacity to Enhance—A Capacity to Destroy," paper presented at the Canadian Symposium of Psycho-Motor Learning and Sports Psychology (1974), 2.

4

Play Group versus Organized Competitive Team

A Comparison

Jay J. Coakley

One way to begin to grasp the nature and extent of the impact of participation in sport is to try to understand the sport group as a context for the behavior and the relationships of youngsters. In a 1968 symposium on the sociology of sport, Gunther Luschen from the University of Illinois delivered a paper entitled "Small Group Research and the Group in Sport." While discussing the variety of different group contexts in which sport activities occur, he contrasted the spontaneously formed casual play group with the organized competitive team. He was primarily interested in the social organization and the amount of structural differentiation existing in sport groups in general, but some of his ideas give us a basis for comparing the characteristics of the spontaneous play group and the organized competitive Little League team in terms of their implications for youngsters. In general, any group engaging in competitive physical activity can be described in terms of the extent and complexity of its formal organization. Simply put, we can employ a continuum along which such groups could be located depending on how formally organized they are. Figure 4-1 illustrates this idea.

The spontaneous play group is an example of a context for competitive physical activities in which formal organization is absent. Its polar opposite is the sponsored

---

Source: "Play Group versus Organized Competitive Team: A Comparison" by Jay J. Coakley. From *Sport in Society: Issues and Controversies* by Jay J. Coakley.

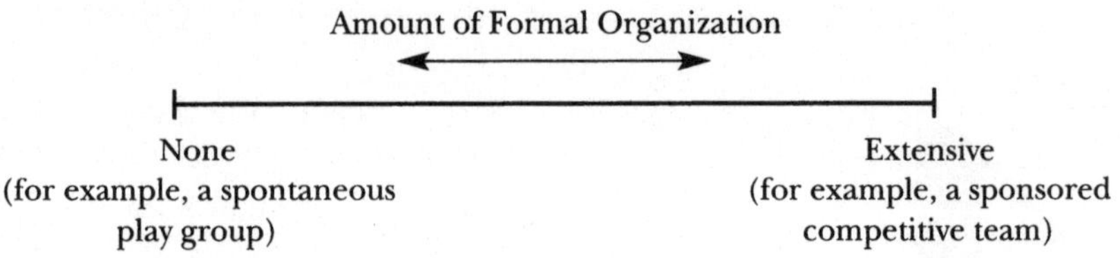

Figure 4-1 A Formal Organization Continuum for Groups in Competitive Physical Activities

Table 4-1 Comparison of Two Groups

The Spontaneous Play Group: No Formal Organization	*The Sponsored Competitive Team: High Formal Organization*
Action is an outgrowth of the interpersonal relationships and of the decision-making processes of participating members.	Action is an outgrowth of a predesignated system of role relationships and of the role-learning abilities of group members.
Rewards are primarily intrinsic and are a function of the experience and the extent of the interpersonal skills of the group members.	Rewards are primarily extrinsic and are a function of the combined technical skills of group members.
Meanings attached to actions and situations are emergent and are subject to changes over time.	Meanings are predominantly predefined and are relatively static from one situation to the next.
Group integration is based on the process of exchange between group members.	Group integration is based on an awareness of and conformity to a formalized set of norms.
Norms governing action are emergent, and interpretation is variable.	Norms are highly formalized and specific, with variability resulting from official judgments.
Social control is internally generated among members and is dependent on commitment.	Social control is administered by an external agent and is dependent on obedience.
Sanctions are informal and are directly related to the maintenance of action in the situation	Sanctions are formal and are related to the preservation of values as well as order.
Individual freedom is high, with variability a function of the group's status structure.	Individual freedom is limited to the flexibility tolerated within role expectations.
Group is generally characterized by structural instability.	Group is generally characterized by structural stability.

competitive team in an organized league. It follows that the amount of formal organization has implications for the actions of group members, for their relationships with one another, and for the nature of their experiences. Table 4-1 outlines the characteristics of the two groups that would most closely approximate the polar extremes on the continuum.

Before going any further, I should point out that the two descriptions in Table 4-1 represent "ideal type" groups. In other words, the respective sets of characteristics represent hypothetical concepts that emphasize each group's most identifiable and important elements. Ideal types are necessarily extreme or exaggerated examples of the phenomenon under investigation and as such are to be used for purposes of comparison rather than as depictions of reality. Our concern here is to look at an actual group in which youngsters participate and to compare the actual group with the ideal types in order to make an assessment of what the real group might be like as a context for experience. Of course, the real group will not be an exact replica of either of the ideal types, but will more or less resemble one or the other.

GETTING THE GAME STARTED

The characteristics of each group suggest that the differences between the spontaneous play group and the organized competitive team would be quite apparent as soon as initial contact between the participants occurs. In the spontaneous play group, we might expect that the majority of time would be spent on dealing with organizational problems, such as establishing goals, defining means to those goals, and developing expectations of both a general and a specific nature for each of the participants. Being a member of a *completely* spontaneous play group would probably be similar to being involved in the initial organizational meeting of a group of unacquainted college freshmen who are supposed to come up with a class project. Both would involve a combination of some fun, a good deal of confusion, much talking, and little action. For the context of the organized competitive team, we might imagine a supervisor (coach) blowing a whistle that brings a group of preselected youngsters of similar ages and abilities running to fall into a routine formation to await an already known command. This would resemble a "brave new world" of sport where there would be some action, a good deal of listening to instructions, much routinization, and little fun. Fortunately, most group contexts for youngsters' sport participation fall somewhere between these two extremes. The trick is, of course, to find which points on the continuum would have a maximization of both fun and action along with the other characteristics seen as most beneficial to the young participants' development.

From my observations of youngsters in backyards, gyms, parks, and playgrounds, I have concluded that, for the most part, they are quite efficient in organizing their sport activities. The primary organizational details are often partially worked out by physical setting, available equipment, and time of the year, all of which influence the choice of activity and the form the activity will take. To the extent that the participants know one another and have played with each other before, there will be a minimum amount of time devoted to formation of norms—rules from previous games can be used. But despite the ability of most youngsters to get a competitive physical activity going, there seems to be a tendency for adults to become impatient with some of the "childish" disagreements of the young participants. Adults often become impatient because they do not understand the youngsters' "distortions" of the games—games the adults know are supposed to be played another way. Adults who want to teach youngsters to play the game the *right way* and to help young players avoid disagreements and discussions in order to build up more action time seem to be everywhere. These adults see a very clear need for organization, that is, establishing regular practice times, scheduling contests, and giving positive rewards and encouragement to those whose performances are seen as deserving. Although their motives may be commendable, these adults usually fail to consider all of the differences between the informally organized group and the formally organized team.

Most importantly, the game in the park is in the control of the youngsters themselves, whereas the organized competitive team is supervised and controlled by adults. In the play group, getting the game under way depends on the group members being able to communicate well enough to make organizational decisions and to evoke enough cooperation so that a sufficient amount of the group's behavior is conducive to the achievement of the goals of the game, however they have been defined. In this situation, interpersonal skills are crucial, and youngsters will probably be quick to realize that playing the game depends on being able to develop and maintain positive relationships or, at least, learning to cope with interpersonal problems in a way that will permit cooperative action. This constitutes a valuable set of experiences that become less available to participants as the amount of the group's formal organization increases. It is a rare adult coach who allows youngsters to make many decisions on how the game should be organized and played. In fact, most decisions have been made for the coach; the availability of the practice field has been decided, the roles defined, the rules made, the sanctions outlined, the team colors picked, the games scheduled, etc. Occasionally the players are allowed to vote on their team name, but that happens only if the team is new and does not already have one. In all, *the emphasis in the organized setting is on the development of sport skills, not on the development of interpersonal skills.*

PLAY OF THE GAME

Differences between the two groups do not disappear once the game begins. For the spontaneous play group, the game experience is likely to be defined as an end in itself, whereas for the organized team, the game is a means to an end. In the play group, the game is unlikely to have implications beyond the setting in which it occurs, and the participants are primarily concerned with managing the situation so that action can be preserved for as long as possible. To this end, it is quite common for the participating youngsters to develop sets of norms accompanied by rather complex sets of qualifications and to establish handicaps for certain participants. These tactics serve to compensate for skill differences and to ensure that the game proceeds with scores close enough so that excitement and satisfaction can be maximized for as many of the players as possible. For example, if one of the pitchers in an informal baseball game were bigger or stronger than the rest of the youngsters, he/she would be required to pitch the ball with "an arch on it" to minimize the ball's speed and to allow all the batters a chance to hit it. Exceptionally good batters might be required to bat left-handed (if they were right-handed) to minimize the chances of hitting a home run every time they came to bat. A youngster having a hard time hitting the ball might be given more than three strikes, and the pitcher might make a special effort to "put the ball over the plate" so that the batter would have a good chance of hitting the ball rather than striking out. Since a strikeout is a relatively unexciting event in a game where the primary goal is the involvement of all players, one of the most frequently made comments directed to the pitcher by his/her teammates in the field is "C'mon, let 'em hit it!"

Similar examples of norm qualifications and handicap systems can be found in other sport groups characterized by a low degree of formal organization. Sometimes these little adaptations can be very clever, and, of course, some participants have to be warned if they seem to be taking unfair advantage of them. This may occur in cases where a young player tends to call time-outs whenever the opposition has his team at a disadvantage or when someone begins to overuse an interference or a "do-over" call to nullify a mistake or a failure to make a play. Although the system of qualifications and handicaps may serve to allow the participants to have another chance when they make mistakes and to avoid the embarrassment associated with a relative lack of skills, the major function of such systems seems to be to equalize not only the players, but also the teams competing against one another. Through such techniques, scores will remain close enough that neither team will give up and destroy the game by quitting. In a sense, the players make an attempt to control the competition so that the fun of all will be safeguarded. Adults do the same thing when given the chance. None of us enjoys being overwhelmed by an opponent or overcoming an opponent so weak that we never had to make an effort.

For the formally organized competitive team, however, the play of the game may be considerably different. The goal of victory or the promotion of the team's place in the league standings replaces the goal of maximizing individual participant satisfaction. The meanings and rewards attached to the game are largely a function of how the experience is related to a desired outcome—either victory or "a good show." Players may even be told that a good personal performance is almost always nullified by a team defeat and that to feel satisfied with yourself without a team victory is selfish (as they say in the locker room, "There is no 'u' in team" or "Defeat is worse than death because you have to live with defeat").

Since victories are a consequence of the combined skills of the team members, such skills are to be practiced and improved and then utilized in ways that maximize the chances for team success. Granting the other team a handicap is quite rare unless any chance for victory is out of their grasp. If this is the case, the weaker players may be substituted in the lineup of the stronger team *unless,* of course, a one-sided score will serve the purpose of increasing the team's prestige or intimidating future opponents.

Also, if one player's skill level far exceeds that of the other participants, that player will often be used where he can be most effective. In the Little League game, it is frequently the bigger youngster with the strongest arm who is made the pitcher. This may help to ensure a team's chances for victory, but it also serves to nearly eliminate the rest of the team's chances for making fielding plays and for being involved in the defensive play of the game. In a 6-inning game, the fact that a large number of the 18 total outs for the opponents come as strikeouts means that a number of fielders may never have a chance to even touch the ball while they are out in the field. A similar thing happens in football. The youth-league team often puts its biggest and strongest players in the backfield rather than in the line. The game then consists of giving those youngsters the ball on nearly every play. For the smaller players on the defensive team, the primary task may be getting out of the way of the runner to avoid being stepped on. Thus on the organized team, intimidation may become a part of playing strategy. Unfortunately, intimidation increases apprehension and inhibits some of the action in the game as well as the involvement of some of the players. Generally, it seems that on the organized team the tendency to employ the skills of the players to win games takes precedence over devising handicaps to ensure fun and widespread participation.

One way to become aware of some of the differences between the informal play group and the formally organized competitive team is to ask the participants in each group the scores of their games. In the formally organized setting, the scores are often one-sided with members of the winning team even boasting about how they won their last football game 77 to 6, their last baseball games 23 to 1, or their last soccer game 14 to 0. Such scores lead me to question the amount of fun had by the players. In the case of the losers it would be rare to find players who would be able to maintain an interest in a game when they are so completely beaten. If the winners say they enjoyed themselves, the lesson they may be learning through such an experience should be seriously questioned. It may be that the major lesson is if your opponents happen to be weak, take advantage of that weakness so totally that they will never be able to make a comeback. Such experiences, instead of instilling positive relationships and a sincere interest in sport activities, are apt to encourage distorted assessments of self-worth and to turn youngsters off to activities that, in modified forms, could provide them with years of enjoyment.

In addition to the differences in how the game is organized and how the action is initiated, there are also differences in how action for the two groups is maintained. In the informally organized group, the members are held together through the operation of some elementary processes of exchange that, in a sense, serve as the basis for the participants obtaining what they think they deserve out of the experience (Polgar, 1976). When the range of abilities is great, the older, bigger, more talented participants have to compromise some of their abilities so that the younger, smaller, and less talented will have a chance to gain the rewards necessary to continue playing. The play of the game depends on maintaining a necessary level of commitment among all participants. This commitment then serves as a basis for social control during the action. Although there are some exceptions, those in the groups with the highest combined skill and social prestige levels act as leaders and serve as models of normal behavior. For these individuals to deviate from the norms in any consistent manner would most likely earn them the reputation of being cheaters or bad sports.

In fact, consistent deviation from the group norms by any of the participants is likely to be defined by the others as disruptive, and the violator will be reminded of his/her infraction through some type of warning or through a threat of future exclusion from group activities. When sanctions are employed in the informal play group, they usually serve an instrumental function—they bring behavior in line so that the game can continue. Sanctions are usually not intended to reinforce status distinctions, to preserve an established social structure, or to safeguard values and principles. Interestingly, self-enforcement of norms in the play group is usually quite effective. Deviation is not totally eliminated, but it is kept within the limits necessary to preserve action in the game. The emphasis is not so much on keeping norms sacred, but on making sure that the norms serve to maintain the goal of action. In fact, norms may change or be reinterpreted for specific individuals or in specific situations so that the level of action in the play activities can be maximized. The importance of maintaining a certain level of action is demonstrated by the informal sanctions directed at a participant who might always be insisting on too rigid an enforcement of norms. This is the person who continually cries "foul" or who always spots a penalty. To be persistent in such a hard-nosed approach to norm enforcement will probably earn the player the nonendearing reputation of being a baby, a crier, or a complainer.

In the informally organized play group, the most disruptive kind of deviant is the one who does not care about the game. It is interesting that the group will usually tolerate any number of different performance styles, forms, and individual innovations as long as they do not destroy action. Batting left-handed when one is right-handed is okay if the batter is at least likely to hit the ball, thus keeping the action going. Throwing behind-the-back passes and trying a crazy shot in basketball or running an unplanned pass pattern in football are all considered part of the game in the play group *if action is not destroyed.* Joking around will frequently be tolerated and sometimes even encouraged *if action can continue.* But if such behavior moves beyond the level of seriousness required to maintain satisfying action for all the participants, commitment decreases, and the group is likely to dissolve. In line with this, usually those participants with the highest amount of skill are allowed the greatest amount of freedom to play "as the spirit moves them." Although such behavior may seem to indicate a lack of seriousness to the outsider, the skill of the player is developed enough to avoid a "disruptive" amount of mistakes. At the same time, such freedom gives high-ability participants a means through which their interest level can be maintained. Similar free-wheeling behavior by a low-ability participant would be viewed with disfavor, since the behavior would frequently bring the action level below what would be defined as acceptable by the rest of the group.

In contrast to the play group, the maintenance of action on the formally organized team depends on an initial commitment to playing as a part of the team. This commitment then serves as a basis for learning and conforming to a preestablished set of norms.[1] The norms apply equally to everyone, and control is administered through the coach-supervisor. Regardless of how priorities are set with respect to goals, goal achievement rests primarily on obedience to the coach's directives rather than on the generation of personal interests based on mutually satisfying social exchange processes. Within the structure of the organized competitive team, deviation from the norms is defined as serious not only when it disrupts action, but also when it could have been disruptive or when it somehow challenges the organized structure through which action occurs. Thus sanctions take on a value-supportive function as well as an instrumental function. This is demonstrated by the coaches who constantly worry about their own authority, that is, whether they command the respect of their players.

In the interest of developing technical skills, the norms for the formally organized competitive team restrict not only the range of a player's action, but also the form of such actions. Unique batting, throwing, running, shooting, or kicking styles must be abandoned in the face of what the coach considers to be correct form. Joking around on the part of any team member is usually not tolerated regardless of the player's abilities, and the demonstration of skills is usually limited to the fundamentals of the game.

If commitment cannot be maintained under these circumstances, players are often not allowed to quit. They may be told by the coach that "We all have to take our bumps to be part of the team" or "Quitters never win and winners never quit." Parents may also point out that "Once you join a team, it is your duty to stick it out for the whole season" or "We paid our money for you to play the whole season; don't waste what we've given you." With this kind of feedback, even a total absence of personal commitment to the sport activity may not lead to withdrawal from participation. What keeps youngsters going is a commitment to personal honor and integrity or obedience to a few significant people in their lives.

WHEN THE GAME IS OVER: MEANING AND CONSEQUENCES

The implications of the game after completion are different for the members of the informal play group than they are for the members of the formally organized competitive team. For the latter, the game goes on record as a win or a loss. If the score was close, both winners and losers may initially qualify the outcome in terms of that closeness.[2] But, as other games are played, all losses and wins are grouped respectively regardless of the closeness of scores. In the informal play group, the score of a game may be discussed while walking home; however, it is usually forgotten quickly and considered insignificant in light of the actions of individual players. Any feelings of elation that accompany victory or of let-down that accompany defeat are short-lived in the play group—you always begin again on the next day, in the next game, or with the next activity. For the organized competitive team, such feelings are less transitory and are often renewed at some future date when there is a chance to avenge a previous loss or to show that a past victory was not just a fluke. Related to this is the fact that the organized team is usually geared to winning, with the coaches and players always reminding themselves, in the Norman Vincent Peale tradition, that "we can win . . . if we only play like we can." This may lead to defining victories as the expected outcomes of games and losses as those outcomes that occur when you do not perform as you are able. When this happens, the elation and satisfaction associated with winning can be buried by the determination to win the next one, the next one, and so on. Losses, however, are not so quickly put away. They tend to follow you as a reminder of past failures to accomplish what you could have if you had executed your collective skills properly. The element of fun in such a setting is of only minor importance and may be eliminated by the seriousness and determination associated with the activity.

The final difference between the two groups is related to the stability of each. The informal play group is characteristically unstable, whereas the opposite is true of the organized team. If minimal levels of commitment cannot be maintained among some members of the play group, the group may simply dissolve. Dissolution may also result from outside forces. For example, since parents are not involved in the organization of the play group, they may not go out of their way to plan for their youngster's participation by delaying or arranging family activities around the time of the group's existence. When a parent calls a youngster home, the entire group may be in serious jeopardy. Other problems that contribute to instability are being told that you cannot play in the street, that someone's yard is off limits, that park space is inaccessible, or that necessary equipment is broken or unavailable. These problems usually do not exist for the organized team. Consent by parents almost guarantees the presence of a player at a scheduled practice or game, space and equipment are reserved in advance, and substitute players are available when something happens to a regular team member. Because the team is built around a structure of roles rather than a series of interacting persons, players can be replaced without serious disruption, and the action can continue.

NOTES

1. In some cases, "commitment" may not be totally voluntary on the part of the player. Parents may sign up a son or daughter without the youngster's full consent or may, along with peers, subtly coerce the youngster to play.

2. Such qualifications are, of course, used for different effects. Winners use them to show that their challengers were able or that victory came under pressure. Losers use them to show how close they came to victory.

5

Anyone Up for Stickball?

In a PlayStation World, Maybe Not

Timothy Williams and Cassi Feldman

On a few dirty squares of sidewalk in Crown Heights, Brooklyn, is a chalk drawing as mysterious to the uninitiated as hieroglyphics. Someone had, with great care, marked off a series of squares and given each a numerical value, although there did not seem to be any obvious pattern.

The drawing is a skelly board, for a game once so popular on the streets of New York that on some blocks adults had to walk in the street to avoid interrupting any of several games under way.

In a time before video games, trans fat or car alarms, in a city that seemed like a smaller version of present-day New York, screaming children ruled the streets. There was the whack of stickball on the asphalt, the singsong rhymes of double dutch jump-rope on the sidewalk, the smack of curb ball in the gutter, the pained yelps arising out of a game called "booty's up," and the frantic counting of hide-and-seek in unexpected corners.

With joyous abandon, kids roller-skated, played ring-a-levio and steal the bacon, used sticks to roll discarded tires down the street, built go-carts and forts out of debris and wrenched open fire hydrants, drenching whoever dared go past.

Today, such loosely organized street play, outside of skateboarding and basketball, is on its last gasp in the city, a vestige of a simpler age for which a fast-paced world has little time.

Source: Timothy Williams and Cassi Feldman, "Anyone Up for Stickball? In a PlayStation World, Maybe Not," *New York Times*, July 1, 2007, 25–26.

"Parents drive children at a very young age to get them on the right track for success, so every waking moment is programmed, which doesn't leave lots of time for play," said Steven Zeitlin, executive director of City Lore, a nonprofit group on the Lower East Side of Manhattan that studies the nation's cultural heritage. "A lot is being lost as these old forms of play die out."

From the 1920s (and perhaps earlier) to the 1980s, the block in front of an apartment building in many neighborhoods was not just a child's backyard, but an extension of the living room and the classroom—a place where children learned to play by the rules, the simpler the better.

If, like Stephen Swid, a kid was lucky enough to live a few blocks from Yankee Stadium in the 1950s, players like Mickey Mantle or Tony Kubek might stop by to take a turn at stickball. Sometimes, it got even better.

Mr. Swid, 66, former chief executive officer of Knoll International Holdings and Spin magazine, said he remembered a day when Mantle hit a ball over a six-story building on Sheridan Avenue. Another day, a rival stickball team showed up wearing uniforms—an unusual touch for a working-class neighborhood. Later, Mr. Swid learned the black and gold uniforms had been designed by one of the team's adolescent players, Ralph Lifshitz, now known as Ralph Lauren.

The fun stopped, or moved inside, depending upon whom you ask, thanks to (pick two or three): television; two-income families; air-conditioning; digital technology; organized sports, crime; smaller families and roomier apartments; too much homework and other responsibilities; diverse, less cohesive neighborhoods; and perhaps most significantly, steady traffic, even on side streets.

Additionally, parents have not passed the games on to children, and newer immigrants have chosen to play soccer, cricket and badminton—sports not necessarily conducive to being played on the street.

While the games have largely faded away from city streets—and any sort of play beyond basketball, bicycle riding, handball or skateboarding has become unusual—some of the old games have held on, albeit with updated rules.

Brandon Santos, an 11-year-old with a crew cut who lives in the East Village, said his favorite is "off-the-ledge baseball," which years ago would have been called curb ball. A player throws a rubber ball against the curb, sending it airborne over the street. If a member of the opposing team falls to catch it, the thrower gets to run the bases, although in Brandon's version there is no running. Instead, the bases are accumulated in one's head.

"It's imaginary," he explained. "We don't run. We're kind of lazy." He and his friend Taylon Wilson, also 11, are part of a group of neighborhood kids that ebbs and swells as friends pass by on their way home, or appear from around a corner. The two, who had been playing handball, rattled off their favorite street games: fishies, fishies, cross my ocean; off-the-ledge baseball; booty's up; manhunt; taps.

Just off Avenue C, Brandon showed where he and friends had spray-painted a skelly board on the concrete—a task that in years past had been done with chalk.

They play their share of video games as well, said Taylon, who speaks in excited bursts, but the boys sometimes prefer to play on the street.

"It's kind of more fun," he said. "You get to make it like your own. You get to design your game and make the rules."

And besides, Taylon said about video games: "After a while, they kind of make your eyes water up. You start to drool." He pretended to drool. "You get bored of them."

As the boys came and went, Raynard Rembert, a 46-year-old security guard who grew up in the nearby Jacob Riis Houses, walked over after overhearing snippets of the conversation. His nickname, he said, is Radar.

One of Mr. Rembert's favorite childhood games was "Johnny-on-the-pony." The game, which had been among the most popular street games, involves two teams. One crouches into a single-file line, each person holding the waist of the person ahead of them. There are variations, but generally, members of they second team try one by one to hop atop the "pony" and to stay on for a certain amount of time before they are shaken off. Other versions involve jumping onto the pony, trying to make everyone fall to the ground.

Mr. Rembert said he had also played booty's up, though he and his friends called it "bunky's up" because they were not allowed to use the word "booty." That game involved throwing a hard rubber Spaldeen ball at someone's backside from close range. Few people seem to remember the precise rules, and doubt there were many anyhow.

The old games, Mr. Rembert said fondly, are "physical and they're challenging. They take coordination and balance and focus."

Perhaps allowing the sepia-tinged haze of his memories to forget the many welts raised by a round of booty's up and the noses bloodied during Johnny-on-the-pony, Mr. Rembert added, "It's good to pass down sports where the kids are competing but aren't trying to hurt each other."

For several years, a diverse collection of people have sought to revive street play in the city, not only with an eye on their own nostalgic views of childhood, but also with the belief that such games contribute to social cohesion and to healthier children.

"It was expected that you would go out after school, roam the neighborhood and play these games, and then come home for dinner," said Nick Green, a 53-year-old social worker who lives in South Jamaica, Queens, and operates a Web site, Streetplay.com, that celebrates the old games. "We didn't realize it at the time, but that was probably the golden age for children."

Last summer, Anthony Gigante, 48, of Brooklyn, organized a league to play what may be the most resilient of the traditional games—stickball—although its slow demise has been lamented for years.

The game is still played by a few adult leagues in the city, including the Major Stick-Ball League, which plays on schoolyard playgrounds, but Mr. Gigante wanted to teach the game to children after he learned that many could not afford the cost of participating in youth baseball leagues.

He got permission from the city to close Bay 22nd Street near Bath Avenue in Bensonhurst on Sunday mornings from 9 to noon. Every week, about 40 children, ages 5 to 11, showed up.

"We played ball every Sunday," he said. "We played stickball, box ball, Johnny-on-the-pony. You don't see kids playing on the street anymore because there's so many cars. It's a different culture."

The old games were rarely complicated, although their rules and names would often vary from block to block.

Skelly, for instance, is also known as skully, skilsies, skelsies, bottle caps and dead box. The game calls for players to use pieces, typically bottle caps, to navigate a board drawn on the pavement. The object is for a player to navigate through the board's 13 squares and back again. That player then has the right to roam the board, harassing other players, including "blasting" a rival's piece off the board.

Last year in Boerum Hill, Brooklyn, 58-year-old Delores Hadden Smith organized a street festival at the Gowanus Houses and had adults teach children games with candy-coated names that sounded like the made-up concoctions they were.

There was red devil; box ball; bluebird, bluebird through my window; hot peas and butter; a variation of ring-a-levio called cocolevio; steal the bacon; look who's here punch-a-nella; knockout; and duck duck goose.

"The older people said, 'No, that's not going to work, these children are too bad,'" Ms. Hadden Smith, a public school teacher, said triumphantly. "In the end, we had more than 300 people register, and we went all day without a single curse word."

Actually, Ms. Hadden Smith didn't last until the end of the day. She went to bed about 11 p.m. The games continued past midnight.

"We laughed and we hollered and we cried," she said. "We had the time of our lives."

It didn't matter that none of the children had known how to play the games, including performing simple tasks like turning a jump-rope, she said.

"Who's going to teach them?" she asked. "You don't see a lot of people jumping rope, do you?"

This summer, Ms. Hadden Smith expects an even larger turnout.

"The children were children like when we were children," she said. "They weren't little fidgety adults or little thugs or thugettes. Every single weekend since then, I can't go out to the corner store without them coming up to me saying, 'I'm ready! I'm ready! When are we going to do that again?'"

6

Boyhood, Organized Sports, and the Construction of Masculinities

Michael A. Messner

The rapid expansion of feminist scholarship in the past two decades has led to fundamental reconceptualizations of the historical and contemporary meanings of organized sport. In the nineteenth and twentieth centuries, modernization and women's continued movement into public life created widespread "fears of social feminization," especially among middle-class men (Hantover 1978; Kimmel 1987). One result of these fears was the creation of organized sport as a homosocial sphere in which competition and (often violent) physicality was valued, while "the feminine" was devalued. As a result, organized sport has served to bolster a sagging ideology of male superiority, and has helped to reconstitute masculine hegemony (Bryson 1987; Hall 1988; Messner 1988; Theberge 1981).

The feminist critique has spawned a number of studies of the ways that women's sport has been marginalized and trivialized in the past (Greendorfer 1977; Oglesby 1978; Twin 1978), in addition to illuminating the continued existence of structural and ideological barriers to gender equality within sport (Birrell 1987). Only recently, however, have scholars begun to use feminist insights to examine men's experiences in sport (Kidd 1987; Messner 1987; Sabo 1985). This article explores the relationship between the construction of masculine identity and boyhood participation in organized sports.

Source: Michael A. Messner, *Journal of Contemporary Ethnography*, 18, no. 4 (January 1990): 416–444,

I view gender identity not as a "thing" that people "have," but rather as a *process of construction* that develops, comes into crisis, and changes as a person interacts with the social world. Through this perspective, it becomes possible to speak of "gendering" identities rather than "masculinity" or "femininity" as relatively fixed identities or statuses.

There is an agency in this construction; people are not passively shaped by their social environment. As recent feminist analyses of the construction of feminine gender identity have pointed out, girls and women are implicated in the construction of their own identities and personalities, both in terms of the ways that they participate in their own subordination and the ways that they resist subordination (Benjamin 1988; Haug 1987). Yet this self-construction is not a fully conscious process. There are also deeply woven, unconscious motivations, fears, and anxieties at work here. So, too, in the construction of masculinity. Levinson (1978) has argued that masculine identity is neither fully "formed" by the social context, nor is it "caused" by some internal dynamic put into place during infancy. Instead, it is shaped and constructed through the interaction between the internal and the social. The internal gendering identity may set developmental "tasks," may create thresholds of anxiety and ambivalence, yet it is only through a concrete examination of people's interactions with others within social institutions that we can begin to understand both the similarities and differences in the construction of gender identities.

In this study I explore and interpret the meanings that males themselves attribute to their boyhood participation in organized sport. In what ways do males construct masculine identities within the institution of organized sports? In what ways do class and racial differences mediate this relationship and perhaps lead to the construction of different meanings, and perhaps different masculinities? And what are some of the problems and contradictions within these constructions of masculinity?

DESCRIPTION OF RESEARCH

Between 1983 and 1985, I conducted interviews with 30 male former athletes. Most of the men I interviewed had played the (U.S.) "major sports"—football, basketball, baseball, track. At the time of the interview, each had been retired from playing organized sports for at least five years. Their ages ranged from 21 to 48, with the median, 33; 14 were black, 14 were white, and two were Hispanic; 15 of the 16 black and Hispanic men had come from poor or working-class families, while the majority (9 of 14) of the white men had come from middle-class or professional families. All had at some time in their lives based their identities largely on their roles as athletes and could therefore be said to have had "athletic careers." Twelve had played organized sports through high school, 11 through college, and seven had been professional athletes. Though the sample was not randomly selected, an effort was made to see that the sample had a range of difference in terms of race and social class backgrounds, and that there was some variety in terms of age, types of sports played, and levels of success in athletic careers. Without exception, each man contacted agreed to be interviewed.

The tape-recorded interviews were semistructured and took from one and one-half to six hours, with most taking about three hours. I asked each man to talk about four broad eras in his life: (1) his earliest experiences with sports in boyhood, (2) his athletic career, (3) retirement or disengagement from the athletic career, and (4) life after the athletic career. In each era, I focused the interview on the meanings of "success and failure," and on the boy's/man's relationships with family, with other males, with women, and with his own body.

In collecting what amounted to life histories of these men, my overarching purpose was to use feminist theories of masculine gender identity to explore how masculinity develops and changes as boys and men interact within the socially constructed world of organized sports. In addition to using the data to move toward some generalizations about the relationship between "masculinity and sport," I was also concerned with sorting out some of the variations among boys, based on class and racial inequalities, that led them to relate differently to athletic careers. I divided my sample into two comparison groups. The first group was made up of 10 men from higher-status backgrounds, primarily white, middle-class, and professional families. The second group was made up of 20 men from lower-status backgrounds, primarily minority, poor, and working-class families.

BOYHOOD AND THE PROMISE OF SPORTS

Zane Grey once said, "All boys love baseball. If they don't they're not real boys" (as cited in Kimmel 1990). This is, of course, an ideological statement; in fact, some boys do *not* love baseball, or any other sports, for that matter. There are millions of males who at an early age are rejected by, become alienated from, or lose interest in organized sports. Yet all boys are, to a greater or lesser extent, judged according to their ability, or lack of ability, in competitive sports (Eitzen, 1975; Sabo, 1985). In this study I focus on those males who did become athletes—males who eventually poured thousands of hours into the development of specific physical skills. It is in boyhood that we can discover the roots of their commitment to athletic careers.

How did organized sports come to play such a central role in these boy's lives? When asked to recall how and why they initially got into playing sports, many of the men interviewed for this study seemed a bit puzzled: after all, playing sports was "just the thing to do." A 42-year-old black man who had played college basketball put it this way:

> It was just what you did. It's kind of like, you went to school, you played athletics, and if you didn't, there was something wrong with you. It was just like brushing your teeth: it's just what you did. It's part of your existence.

Spending one's time playing sports with other boys seemed as natural as the cycle of the seasons: baseball in the spring and summer, football in the fall, basketball in the winter—and then it was time to get out the old baseball glove and begin again. As a black 35-year-old former professional football star said:

> I'd say when I wasn't in school, 95 percent of the time was spent in the park playing. It was the only thing to do. It just came as natural.

And a black, 34-year-old professional basketball player explained his early experiences in sports:

> My principal and teacher said, "Now if you work at this you might be pretty damned good." So it was more or less a community thing—everybody in the community said, "Boy, if you work hard and keep your nose clean, you gonna be good." Cause it was natural instinct.

"It was natural instinct." "I was a natural." Several athletes used words such as these to explain their early attraction to sports. But certainly there is nothing "natural" about throwing a ball through a hoop, hitting a ball with a bat, or jumping over hurdles. A boy, for instance, may have amazingly dexterous inborn hand–eye coordination, but this does not predispose him to a career of hitting baseballs any more than it predisposes him to a life as a brain surgeon. When one listens closely to what these men said about their early experiences in sports, it becomes clear that their adoption of the self-definition of "natural athlete" was the result of what Connell (1990) has called "a collective practice" that constructs masculinities. The boyhood development of masculine identity and status—truly problematic in a society that offers no official rite of passage into adulthood—results from a process of interaction with people and social institutions. Thus, in discussing early motivations in sports, men commonly talk of the importance of relationships with family members, peers, and the broader community.

FAMILY INFLUENCES

Though most of the men in this study spoke of their mothers with love, respect, even reverence, their descriptions of their earliest experiences in sports are stories of an exclusively male world. The existence of older brothers or uncles who served as teachers and athletic role models—as well as sources of competition for attention and status within the family—was very common. An older brother, uncle, or even close friend of the family who was a successful athlete appears to have acted as a sort of standard of achievement against whom to measure oneself. A 34-year-old black man who had been a three-sport star in high school said:

> My uncles—my Uncle Harold went to the Detroit Tigers, played pro ball—all of 'em, everybody played sports, so I wanted to be better than anybody else. I knew

> that everybody in this town knew them—their names were something. I wanted my name to be just like theirs.

Similarly, a black 41-year-old former professional football player recalled:

> I was the younger of three brothers and everybody played sports, so consequently I was more or less forced into it. 'Cause one brother was always better than the next brother and then I came along and had to show them that I was just as good as them. My oldest brother was an all-city ballplayer, then my other brother comes along he's all-city and all-state, and then I have to come along.

For some, attempting to emulate or surpass the athletic accomplishments of older male family members created pressures that were difficult to deal with. A 33-year-old white man explained that he was a good athlete during boyhood, but the constant awareness that his two older brothers had been better made it difficult for him to feel good about himself, or to have fun in sports:

> I had this sort of reputation that I followed from the playgrounds through grade school, and through high school. I followed these guys who were all-conference and all-state.

Most of these men, however, saw their relationships with their athletic older brothers and uncles in a positive light; it was within these relationships that they gained experience and developed motivations that gave them a competitive "edge" within their same-aged peer group. As a 33-year-old black man describes his earliest athletic experiences:

> My brothers were role models. I wanted to prove—especially to my brothers—that I had heart, you know, that I was a man.

When asked, "What did it mean to you to be 'a man' at that age?" he replied:

> Well, it meant that I didn't want to be a so-called scaredy-cat. You want to hit a guy even though he's bigger than you to show that, you know, you've got this macho image. I remember that at that young an age, that feeling was exciting to me. And that carried over, and as I got older, I got better and I began to look around me and see, well hey! I'm competitive with these guys, even though I'm younger, you know? And then of course all the compliments come—and I began to notice a change, even in my parents—especially in my father—he was proud of that, and that was very important to me. He was extremely important … he showed me more affection, now that I think of it.

As this man's words suggest, if men talk of their older brothers and uncles mostly as role models, teachers, and "names" to emulate, their talk of their relationships with their fathers is more deeply layered and complex. Athletic skills and competition for status may often be learned from older brothers, but it is in boys' relationships with fathers that we find many of the keys to the emotional salience of sports in the development of masculine identity.

RELATIONSHIPS WITH FATHERS

The fact that boys' introductions to organized sports are often made by fathers who might otherwise be absent or emotionally distant adds a powerful emotional charge to these early experiences (Osherson 1986). Although playing organized sports eventually came to feel "natural" for all of the men interviewed in this study, many needed to be "exposed" to sports, or even gently "pushed" by their fathers to become involved in activities like Little League baseball. A white, 33-year-old man explained:

> I still remember it like it was yesterday—Dad and I driving up in his truck, and I had my glove and my hat and all that—and I said, "Dad, I don't want to do it." He says, "What?" I says, "I don't want to do it." I was nervous. That I might fail. And he says, "Don't be silly. Lookit: There's Joey and Petey and all your friends out there." And so Dad says, "You're gonna do it, come on." And in my memory he's never said that about anything else; he just knew I needed a little kick in the pants and I'd do it. And once you're out there and you see all the other kids making errors and stuff, and you know you're better than those guys, you know: Maybe I *do* belong here. As it turned out, Little League was a good experience.

Some who were similarly "pushed" by their fathers were not so successful as the aforementioned man had been in Little League baseball, and thus the experience was not altogether a joyous affair. One 34-year-old white man, for instance, said he "inherited" his interest in sports from his father, who started playing catch with him at the age of four. Once he got into Little League, he felt pressured by his father, one of the coaches, who expected him to be the star of the team:

> I'd go 0-for-four sometimes, strike out three times in a Little League game, and I'd dread the ride home. I'd come home and he'd say, "Go in the bathroom and swing the bat in the mirror for an hour," to get my swing level ... It didn't help much, though, I'd go out and strike out three or four times again the next game too [laughs ironically].

When asked if he had been concerned with having his father's approval, he responded:

> Failure in his eyes? Yeah, I always thought that he wanted me to get some kind of [athletic] scholarship. I guess I was afraid of him when I was a kid. He didn't

> hit that much, but he had a rage about him—he'd rage, and that voice would just rattle you.

Similarly, a 24-year-old black man described his awe of his father's physical power and presence, and his sense of inadequacy in attempting to emulate him:

> My father had a voice that sounded like rolling thunder. Whether it was intentional on his part or not, I don't know, but my father gave me a sense, an image of him being the most powerful being on earth, and that no matter what I ever did I would never come close to him.... There were definite feelings of physical inadequacy that I couldn't work around.

It is interesting to note how these feelings of physical inadequacy relative to the father lived on as part of this young man's permanent internalized image. He eventually became a "feared" high school football player and broke school records in weight-lifting, yet,

> As I grew older, my mother and friends told me that I had actually grown to be a larger man than my father. Even though in time I required larger clothes than he, which should have been a very concrete indication, neither my brother nor I could ever bring ourselves to say that I was bigger. We simply couldn't conceive of it.

Using sports activities as a means of identifying with and "living up to" the power and status of one's father was not always such a painful and difficult task for the men I interviewed. Most did not describe fathers who "pushed" them to become sports stars. The relationship between their athletic strivings and their identification with their fathers was more subtle. A 48-year-old black man, for instance, explained that he was not pushed into sports by his father, but was aware from an early age of the community status his father had gained through sports. He saw his own athletic accomplishments as a way to connect with and emulate his father:

> I wanted to play baseball because my father had been quite a good baseball player in the Negro leagues before baseball was integrated, and so he was kind of a model for me. I remember, quite young, going to a baseball game he was in—this was before the war and all—I remember being in the stands with my mother and seeing him on first base, and being aware of the crowd ... I was aware of people's confidence in him as a serious baseball player. I don't think my father ever said anything to me like "play sports" ... [But] I knew he would like it if I did well. His admiration was important ... he mattered.

Similarly, a 24-year-old white man described his father as a somewhat distant "role model" whose approval mattered:

> My father was more of an example ... he definitely was very much in touch with and still had very fond memories of being an athlete and talked about it, bragged about it.... But he really didn't do that much to teach me skills, and he didn't always go to every game I played like some parents. But he approved and that was important, you know. That was important to get his approval. I always knew that playing sports was important to him, so I knew implicitly that it was good and there was definitely a value on it.

First experiences in sports might often come through relationships with brothers or older male relatives, and the early emotional salience of sports was often directly related to a boy's relationship with his father. The sense of commitment that these young boys eventually made to the development of athletic careers is best explained as a process of development of masculine gender identity and status in relation to same-sex peers.

MASCULINE IDENTITY AND EARLY COMMITMENT TO SPORTS

When many of the men in this study said that during childhood they played sports because "it's just what everybody did," they of course meant that it was just what *boys* did. They were introduced to organized sports by older brothers and fathers, and once involved, found themselves playing within an exclusively male world. Though the separate (and unequal) gendered worlds of boys and girls came to appear as "natural," they were in fact socially constructed. Thorne's observations of children's activities in schools indicated that rather than "naturally" constituting "separate gendered cultures," there is considerable interaction between boys and girls in classrooms and on playgrounds. When adults set up legitimate contact between boys and girls, Thorne observed, this usually results in "relaxed interactions." But when activities in the classroom or on the playground are presented to children as sex-segregated activities and gender is marked by teachers and other adults ("boys line up here, girls over there"), "gender boundaries are heightened, and mixed-sex interaction becomes an explicit arena of risk" (Thorne 1986; 70). Thus sex-segregated activities such as organized sports as structured by adults, provide the context in which gendered identities and separate "gendered cultures" develop and come to appear natural. For the boys in this study, it became "natural" to equate masculinity with competition, physical strength, and skills. Girls simply did not (could not, it was believed) participate in these activities.

Yet it is not simply the separation of children, by adults, into separate activities that explains why many boys came to feel such a strong connection with sports activities, while so few girls did. As I listened to men recall their earliest experiences in organized sports, I heard them talk of insecurity, loneliness, and especially a need to connect with other people as a primary motivation in their early sports strivings. As a 42-year-old white man stated, "The most important thing was just being out there with the rest of the guys—being friends." Another 32-year-old interviewee was born in Mexico and moved to the United States at a fairly young age. He never knew his father, and his mother died when he was only nine years old. Suddenly he felt rootless, and threw himself into sports. His initial motivations, however, do not appear to be based on a need to compete and win:

> Actually, what I think sports did for me is it brought me into kind of an instant family. By being on a Little League team, or even just playing with all kinds of different kids in the neighborhood, it brought what I really wanted, which was some kind of closeness. It was just being there, and being friends.

Clearly, what these boys needed and craved was that which was most problematic for them: connection and unity with other people. But why do these young males find *organized sports* such an attractive context in which to establish "a kind of closeness" with others? Comparative observations of young boys' and girls' game-playing behaviors yield important insights into this question. Piaget (1965) and Lever (1976) both observed that girls tend to have more "pragmatic" and "flexible" orientations to the rules of games; they are more prone to make exceptions and innovations in the middle of a game in order to make the game more "fair." Boys, on the other hand, tend to have a more firm, even inflexible orientation to the rules of a game; to them, the rules are what protects any fairness. This difference, according to Gilligan (1982), is based on the fact that early developmental experiences have yielded deeply rooted differences between males' and females' developmental tasks, needs, and moral reasoning. Girls, who tend to define themselves primarily through connection with others, experience highly competitive situations (whether in organized sports or in other hierarchical institutions) as threats to relationships, and thus to their identities. For boys, the development of gender identity involves the construction of positional identities, where a sense of self is solidified through separation from others (Chodorow 1978). Yet feminist psychoanalytic theory has tended to oversimplify the internal lives of men (Lichterman 1986). Males do appear to develop positional identities, yet despite their fears of intimacy, they also retain a human need for closeness and unity with others. This ambivalence toward intimate relationships is a major thread running through masculine development throughout the life course. Here we can conceptualize what Craib (1987) calls the "elective affinity" between personality and social structure: For the boy who both seeks and fears attachment with others, the rule-bound structure of organized sports can promise to be a safe place in which to seek nonintimate attachment with others within a context that maintains clear boundaries, distance, and separation.

COMPETITIVE STRUCTURES AND CONDITIONAL SELF-WORTH

Young boys may initially find that sports gives them the opportunity to experience "some kind of closeness" with others, but the structure of sports and athletic careers often undermines the possibility of boys learning to transcend their fears of intimacy, thus becoming able to develop truly close and intimate relationships with others (Kidd 1990; Messner 1987). The sports world is extremely hierarchical, and an incredible amount of importance is placed on winning, on "being number one." For instance, a few years ago I observed a basketball camp put on for boys by a professional basketball coach and his staff. The youngest boys, about eight years old (who could barely reach the basket with their shots) played a brief scrimmage. Afterwards, the coaches lined them up in a row in front of the older boys who were sitting in the grandstands. One by one, the coach would stand behind each boy, put his hand on the boy's head (much in the manner of a priestly benediction), and the older boys in the stands would applaud and cheer, louder or softer, depending on how well or poorly the young boy was judged to have performed. The two or three boys who were clearly the exceptional players looked confident that they would receive the praise they were due. Most of the boys, though, had expressions ranging from puzzlement to thinly disguised terror on their faces as they awaited the judgments of the older boys.

This kind of experience teaches boys that it is not "just being out there with the guys—being friends," that ensures the kind of attention and connection that they crave; it is being *better* than the other guys—*beating* them—that is the key to acceptance. Most of the boys in this study did have some early successes in sports, and thus their ambivalent need for connection with others was met, at least for a time. But the institution of sport tends to encourage the development of what Schafer (1975) has called "conditional self-worth" in boys. As boys become aware that acceptance by others is contingent upon being good—a "winner"—narrow definitions of success, based upon performance and winning become increasingly important to them. A 33-year-old black man said that by the time he was in his early teens:

> It was expected of me to do well in all my contests—I mean by my coaches, my peers, and my family. So I in turn expected to do well, and if I didn't do well, then I'd be very disappointed.

The man from Mexico, discussed above, who said that he had sought "some kind of closeness" in his early sports experiences began to notice in his early teens that if he played well, was a *winner,* he would get attention from others:

> It got to the point where I started realizing, noticing that people were always there for me, backing me all the time—sports got to be really fun because I always had some people there backing me. Finally my oldest brother started going to all my games, even though I had never really seen who he was [laughs]—after the game, you know, we never really saw each other, but he was at all my baseball games, and it seemed like we shared a kind of closeness there, but only in those situations. Off the field, when I wasn't in uniform, he was never around.

By high school, he said, he felt "up against the wall." Sports hadn't delivered what he had hoped it would, but he thought if he just tried harder, won one more championship trophy, he would get the attention he truly craved. Despite his efforts, this attention was not forthcoming. And, sadly, the pressures he had put on himself to excel in sports had taken most of the fun out of playing.

For many of the men in this study, throughout boyhood and into adolescence, this conscious striving for successful achievement became the primary means through which they sought connection with other people (Messner 1987). But it is important to recognize that young males' internalized ambivalences about intimacy do not fully determine the contours and directions of their lives. Masculinity continues to develop through interaction with the social world—and because boys from different backgrounds are interacting with substantially different familial, educational, and other institutions, these differences will lead them to make different choices and define situations in different ways. Next, I examine the differences in the ways that boys from higher- and lower-status families and communities related to organized sports.

STATUS DIFFERENCES AND COMMITMENTS TO SPORTS

In discussing early attractions to sports, the experiences of boys from higher- and lower-status backgrounds are quite similar. Both groups indicate the importance of fathers and older brothers in introducing them to sports. Both groups speak of the joys of receiving attention and acceptance among family and peers for early successes in sports. Note the similarities, for instance, in the following descriptions of boyhood athletic experiences of two men. First, a man born in a white, middle-class family:

> I loved playing sports so much from a very early age because of early exposure. A lot of the sports came easy at an early age, and because they did, and because you were successful at something, I think that you're inclined to strive for that gratification. It's like, if you're good, you like it, because it's instant gratification. I'm doing something that I'm good at and I'm gonna keep doing it.

Second, a black man from a poor family:

> Fortunately I had some athletic ability, and, quite naturally, once you start doing good in whatever it is—I don't care if it's jacks—you show off what you do. That's your ability, that's your blessing, so you show it off as much as you can.

For boys from both groups, early exposure to sports, the discovery that they had some "ability," shortly followed by some sort of family, peer, and community recognition, all eventually led to the commitment of hundreds and thousands of hours of playing, practicing, and dreaming of future stardom. Despite these similarities, there are also some identifiable differences that begin to explain the tendency of males from lower-status backgrounds to develop higher levels of commitment to sports careers. The most clear-cut difference was that while men from higher-status backgrounds are likely to describe their earliest athletic experiences and motivations almost exclusively in terms of immediate family, men from lower-status backgrounds more commonly describe the importance of a broader community context. For instance, a 46-year-old man who grew up in a "poor working class" black family in a small town in Arkansas explained:

> In that community, at the age of third or fourth grade, if you're a male, they expect you to show some kind of inclination, some kind of skill in football or basketball. It was an expected thing, you know? My mom and my dad, they didn't push at all. It was the general environment.

A 48-year-old man describes sports activities as a survival strategy in his poor black community:

> Sports protected me from having to compete in gang stuff, or having to be good with my fists. If you were an athlete and got into the fist world, that was your business, and that was okay—but you didn't have to if you didn't want to. People would generally defer to you, give you your space away from trouble.

A 35-year-old man who grew up in "a poor black ghetto" described his boyhood relationship to sports similarly:

> Where I came from, either you were one of two things: you were in sports or you were out on the streets being a drug addict, or breaking into places. The guys who were in sports, we had it a little easier, because we were accepted by both groups.... So it worked out to my advantage, cause I didn't get into a lot of trouble—some trouble, but not a lot.

The fact that boys in lower-status communities faced these kinds of realities gave salience to their developing athletic identities. In contrast, sports were important to boys from higher-status backgrounds, yet the middle-class environment seemed more secure, less threatening, and offered far more options. By the time most of these boys got into junior high or high school, many had made conscious decisions to shift their attentions away from athletic careers to educational and (nonathletic) career goals. A 32-year-old white college athletic director told me that he had seen his chance to pursue a pro baseball career as "pissing in the wind," and instead, focused on education. Similarly, a 33-year-old white dentist who was a three-sport star in high school, decided not to play sports in college, so he could focus on getting into dental school. As he put it,

> I think I kind of downgraded the stardom thing. I thought it was small potatoes. And sure, that's nice in high school and all that, but on a broad scale, I didn't think it amounted to all that much.

This statement offers an important key to understanding the construction of masculine identity within a middle-class context. The status that this boy got through sports had been *very* important to him, yet he could see that "on a broad scale," this sort of status was "small potatoes." This sort of early recognition is more than a result of the oft-noted middle-class tendency to raise "future-oriented" children (Rubin 1976; Sennett and Cobb 1973). Perhaps more important, it is that the *kinds* of future orientations developed by boys from higher-status backgrounds are consistent with the middle-class context. These men's descriptions of their boyhoods reveal that they grew up immersed in a wide range of institutional frameworks, of which organized sports was just one. And—importantly—they could see that the status of adult males around them was clearly linked to their positions within various professions, public institutions, and bureaucratic organizations. It was clear that access to this sort of institutional status came through educational achievement, not athletic prowess. A 32-year-old black man who grew up in a professional-class family recalled that he had idolized Wilt Chamberlain and dreamed of being a pro basketball player, yet his father discouraged his athletic strivings:

> He knew I liked the game. I *loved* the game. But basketball was not recommended; my dad would say, "That's a stereotyped image for black youth.... When your basketball is gone and finished, what are you gonna do? One day, you might get injured. What are you gonna look forward to?" He stressed education.

Similarly, a 32-year-old man who was raised in a white, middle-class family, had found in sports a key means of gaining acceptance and connection in his peer group. Yet he was simultaneously developing an image of himself as a "smart student," and becoming aware of a wide range of nonsports life options:

> My mother was constantly telling me how smart I was, how good I was, what a nice person I was, and giving me all sorts of positive strokes, and those positive strokes became a self-motivating kind of thing. I had this image of myself as smart, and I lived up to that image.

It is not that parents of boys in lower-status families did not also encourage their boys to work hard in school. Several reported that their parents "stressed books first, sports second." It's just that the broader social context—education, economy, and community—was more likely to *narrow* lower-status boys' perceptions of real-life options, while boys from higher-status backgrounds faced an expanding world of options. For instance, with a different socioeconomic background, one 35-year-old black man might have become a great musician instead of a star professional football running back. But he did not. When he was a child, he said, he was most interested in music:

> I wanted to be a drummer. But we couldn't afford drums. My dad couldn't go out and buy me a drum set or a guitar even—it was just one of those things; he was just trying to make ends meet.

But he *could* afford, as could so many in his socioeconomic condition, to spend countless hours at the local park, where he was told by the park supervisor

> that I was a natural—not only in gymnastics or baseball—whatever I did, I was a natural. He told me I shouldn't waste this talent, and so I immediately started watching the big guys then.

In retrospect, this man had potential to be a musician or any number of things, but his environment limited his options to sports, and he made the best of it. Even within sports, he, like most boys in the ghetto, was limited:

> We didn't have any tennis courts in the ghetto—we used to have a lot of tennis balls, but no racquets. I wonder today how good I might be in tennis if I had gotten a racquet in my hands at an early age.

It is within this limited structure of opportunity that many lower-status young boys found sports to be *the* place, rather than *a* place, within which to construct masculine identity, status, the relationships. A 36-year-old white man explained that his father left the family when he was very young and his mother faced a very difficult struggle to make ends meet. As his words suggest, the more limited a boy's options, and the more insecure his family situation, the more likely he is to make an early commitment to an athletic career:

> I used to ride my bicycle to Little League practice—if I'd waited for someone to pick me up and take me to the ball park I'd have never played. I'd get to the ball park and all the other kids would have their dad bring them to practice or games. But I'd park my bike to the side and when it was over I'd get on it and go home. Sports was the way for me to move everything to the side—family problems, just all the embarrassments—and think about one thing, and that was sports ... In the third grade, when the teacher went around the classroom and asked everybody, "What do you want to be when you grow up?," I said, "I want to be a major league baseball player," and everybody laughed their heads off.

This man eventually did enjoy a major league baseball career. Most boys from lower-status backgrounds who make similar early commitments to athletic careers are not so successful. As stated earlier, the career structure of organized sports is highly competitive and hierarchical. In fact, the chances of attaining professional status in sports are approximately 4:100,000 for a white man, 2:100,000 for a black man, and 3:1 million for a Hispanic man in the United States (Leonard and Reyman 1988). Nevertheless, the immediate rewards (fun, status, attention), along with the constricted (nonsports) structure of opportunity, attract disproportionately large numbers of boys from lower-status backgrounds to athletic careers as their major means of constructing a masculine identity. These are the boys who later, as young men, had to struggle with "conditional self-worth," and, more often than not, occupational dead ends.

Boys from higher-status backgrounds, on the other hand, bolstered their boyhood, adolescent, and early adult status through their athletic accomplishments. Their wider range of experiences and life chances led to an early shift away from sports careers as the major basis of identity (Messner 1989).

CONCLUSION

The conception of the masculinity–sports relationship developed here begins to illustrate the idea of an "elective affinity" between social structure and personality. Organized sports is a "gendered institution"—an institution constructed by gender relations. As such, its structure and values (rules, formal organization, sex composition, etc.), reflect dominant conceptions of masculinity and femininity. Organized sports is also a "gendering institution"—an institution that helps to construct the current gender order. Part of this construction of gender is accomplished through the "masculinizing" of male bodies and minds.

Yet boys do not come to their first experiences in organized sports as "blank slates," but arrive with already "gendering" identities due to early developmental experiences and previous socialization. I have suggested here that an important thread running through the development of masculine identity is males' ambivalence toward intimate unity with others. Those boys who experience early athletic successes find in the structure of organized sport an affinity with this masculine ambivalence toward intimacy: The rule-bound, competitive, hierarchical world of sport offers boys an attractive means of establishing an emotionally distant (and thus "safe") connection with others. Yet as boys begin to define themselves as "athletes," they learn that in order to be accepted (to have connection) through sports, they must be winners. And in order to be winners, they must construct relationships with others (and with themselves) that are consistent with the competitive and hierarchical values and structure of the sports world. As a result, they often develop a "conditional self-worth" that leads them to construct more instrumental relationships with themselves and others. This ultimately exacerbates their difficulties in constructing intimate relationships with others. In effect, the interaction between the young male's preexisting internalized ambivalence toward intimacy with the competitive hierarchical institution of sport has resulted in the construction of a masculine personality that is characterized by instrumental rationality, goal orientation, and difficulties with intimate connection and expression (Messner 1987).

This theoretical line of inquiry invites us not simply to examine how social institutions "socialize" boys, but also to explore the ways that boys' already-gendering identities interact with social institutions (which, like organized sport, are themselves the product of gender relations). This study has also suggested that it is not some singular "masculinity" that is being constructed through athletic careers. It may be correct, from a psychoanalytic perspective, to suggest that all males bring ambivalences toward intimacy to their interactions with the world, but "the world" is a very different place for males from different racial and socioeconomic backgrounds. Because males have substantially different interactions with the world, based on class, race, and other differences and inequalities, we might expect the construction of masculinity to take on different meanings for boys and men from differing backgrounds (Messner 1989). Indeed, this study has suggested that boys from higher-status backgrounds face a much broader range of options than do their lower-status counterparts. As a result, athletic careers take on different meanings for these boys. Lower-status boys are likely to see athletic careers as *the* institutional context for the construction of their masculine status and identities, while higher-status males make an early shift away from athletic careers toward other institutions (usually education and nonsports careers). A key line of inquiry for future studies might begin by exploring this irony of sports careers: Despite the fact that "the athlete" is currently an example of an exemplary form of masculinity in public ideology, the vast majority of boys who become most committed to athletic careers are never well-rewarded for their efforts. The fact that class and racial dynamics lead boys from higher-status backgrounds, unlike their lower-status counterparts, to move into nonsports careers illustrates how the construction of different kinds of masculinities is a key component of the overall construction of the gender order.

REFERENCES

Birrell, S. 1987. "The Woman Athlete's College Experience: Knowns and Unknowns." *Journal of Sport and Social Issues* 11: 82–96.

Benjamin, J. 1988. *The Bonds of Love: Psychoanalysis, Feminism, and the Problem of Domination.* New York: Pantheon.

Bryson, L. 1987. "Sport and the Maintenance of Masculine Hegemony." *Women's Studies International Forum* 10: 349–360.

Chodorow, N. 1978. *The Reproduction of Mothering.* Berkeley: University of California Press.

Connell, R. W. 1987. *Gender and Power.* Stanford, CA: Stanford University Press.

Connell, R. W. (1990) "An Iron Man: The Body and Some Contradictions of Hegemonic Masculinity." In M. A. Messner and D. F. Sabo, eds., *Sport, Men and the Gender Order: Critical Feminist Perspectives.* Champaign, IL: Human Kinetics.

Craib, I. 1987. "Masculinity and Male Dominance." *Sociological Review* 38: 721–743.

Eitzen, D. S. 1975. "Athletics in the Status System of Male Adolescents: A Replication of Coleman's *The Adolescent Society.*" *Adolescence* 10: 268–276.

Gilligan, C. 1982. *In a Different Voice: Psychological Theory and Women's Development.* Cambridge, MA: Harvard University Press.

Greendorfer, S. L. 1977. "The Role of Socializing Agents in Female Sport Involvement." *Research Quarterly* 48: 304–310.

Hall, M. A. 1988. "The Discourse on Gender and Sport: From Femininity to Feminism." *Sociology of Sport Journal* 5: 330–340.

Hantover, J. 1978. "The Boy Scouts and the Validation of Masculinity." *Journal of Social Issues* 34: 184–195.

Haug, F. 1987. *Female Sexualization.* London: Verso.

Kidd, B. 1987. "Sports and Masculinity." Pp. 250–265 in M. Kaufman, ed., *Beyond Patriarchy: Essays by Men on Pleasure, Power, and Change.* Toronto: Oxford University Press.

———. 1990. "The Men's Cultural Centre: Sports and the Dynamic of Women's Oppression/Men's Repression." In M. A. Messner and D. F. Sabo, eds., *Sport, Men and the Gender Order: Critical Feminist Perspectives.* Champaign, IL: Human Kinetics.

Kimmel, M. S. 1987. "Men's Responses to Feminism at the Turn of the Century." *Gender and Society* 1: 261–283.

———. 1990. "Baseball and the Reconstitution of American Masculinity: 1880–1920." In M. A. Messner and D. F. Sabo, eds., *Sport, Men and the Gender Order: Critical Feminist Perspectives.* Champaign, IL: Human Kinetics.

Leonard, W. M. II, and J. M. Reyman. 1988. "The Odds of Attaining Professional Athlete Status: Refining the Computations." *Sociology of Sport Journal* 5: 162–169.

Lever, J. 1976. "Sex Differences in the Games Children Play." *Social Problems* 23: 478–487.

Levinson, D. J. et al. 1978. *The Seasons of a Man's Life.* New York: Ballantine.

Lichterman, P. 1986. "Chodorow's Psychoanalytic Sociology: A Project Half-Completed." *California Sociologist* 9: 147–166.

Messner, M. 1987. "The Meaning of Success: The Athletic Experience and the Development of Male Identity." Pp. 193–210 in H. Brod, ed., *The Making of Masculinities: The New Men's Studies.* Boston: Allen and Unwin.

———. 1988. "Sports and Male Domination: The Female Athlete as Contested Ideological Terrain." *Sociology of Sport Journal* 5: 197–211.

———. 1989. "Masculinities and Athletic Careers." *Gender and Society* 3: 71–88.

Oglesby, C. A., ed. 1978. *Women and Sport: From Myth to Reality.* Philadelphia: Lea and Febiger.

Osherson, S. 1986. *Finding Our Fathers: How a Man's Life Is Shaped by His Relationship with His Father.* New York: Fawcett Columbine.

Piaget, J. H. 1965. *The Moral Judgment of the Child.* New York: Free Press.

Rubin, L. B. 1976. *Worlds of Pain: Life in the Working Class Family.* New York: Basic Books.

Sabo, D. 1985. "Sport, Patriarchy, and Male Identity: New Questions about Men and Sport." *Arena Review* 9: 2.

Schafer, W. E. 1975. "Sport and Male Sex Role Socialization." *Sport Sociology Bulletin* 4: 47–54.

Sennett, R., and J. Cobb. 1973. *The Hidden Injuries of Class.* New York: Random House.

Theberge, N. 1981. "A Critique of Critiques: Radical and Feminist Writings on Sport." *Social Forces* 60: 2.

Thome, B. 1986. "Girls and Boys Together ... but Mostly Apart: Gender Arrangements in Elementary Schools." Pp. 167–184 in W. W. Hartup and Z. Rubin, eds., *Relationships and Development.* Hillsdale, NJ: Lawrence Erlbaum.

Twin, S. L., ed. 1978. *Out of the Bleachers: Writings on Women and Sport.* Old Westbury, NY: Feminist Press.

* FOR FURTHER STUDY *

Bissenger, H. G. 1990. *Friday Night Lights: A Town, A Team, and a Dream.* New York: Perseus.

Cavanaugh, Ed. 2003. "Basketball Lifts Cairo's Gloom." *Chicago Tribune,* March 14, 1, 28.

Coakley, Jay. 2007. *Sports in Society: Issues and Controversies,* 9th ed. New York: McGraw-Hill.

Curry, Timothy Jon. 2001. Reply to "A Conversation (Re)Analysis of Fraternal Bonding in the Locker Room." *Sociology of Sport Journal* 18 (3): 339–344.

Curtis, James, William McTeer, and Philip White. 2003. "Do High School Athletes Earn More Pay? Youth Sports Participation and Earnings as an Adult." *Sociology of Sport Journal* 20 (1): 60–76.

Eitle, Tamela McNulty, and David J. Eitle. 2002. "Just Don't Do It: High School Sports Participation and Young Female Adult Sexual Behavior." *Sociology of Sport Journal* 19 (4): 403–418.

Eitzen, D. Stanley. 2009. *Fair and Foul: Beyond the Myths and Paradoxes of Sport.* 4th ed. Lanham, MD: Rowman and Littlefield.

Eitzen, D. Stanley, and George H. Sage, 2009. *Sociology of North American Sport.* 8th ed. Boulder, CO: Paradigm.

Ferguson, Andrew. 1999. "Inside the Crazy Culture of Kids Sports." *Time* (July 12): 52–60.

Foley, Douglas E. 1990. *Learning Capitalist Culture: Deep in the Heart of Tejas.* Philadelphia: University of Pennsylvania Press.

Frey, Darcy. 1991. *The Last Shot: City Streets, Basketball Dreams.* Boston: Houghton Mifflin.

Gatz, Margaret, Michael A. Messner, and Sandra J. Ball-Rokeach, eds. 2002. *Paradoxes of Youth and Sport.* Albany: State University of New York Press.

Goldsmith, Pat Antonio. 2003. "Race Relations and Racial Patterns in School Sports Participation." *Sociology of Sport Journal* 20 (2): 147–171.

Hyman, Mark. 2001. "Reading, Writing—and Winning." *Business Week* (April 2): 58–60.

Jimerson, Jason B. 2001. "A Conversation (Re)Analysis of Fraternal Bonding in the Locker Room." *Sociology of Sport Journal* 18 (3): 317–338.

Latimer, Clay. 2003. "Pulling Strings: For Better or Worse, Parents' Role in Prep Sports Evolving into More Agent than Cheerleader." *Rocky Mountain News,* March 8, 1B, 11B-13B.

May, Reuben A. Buford. 2001. "The Sticky Situation of Sportsmanship: Contexts and Contradictions in Sportsmanship among High School Boys Basketball Players." *Journal of Sport and Social Issues* 25 (November): 372–389.

Messner, Michael A. 2009. *It's All for the Kids: Gender, Families, and Youth Sports.* Berkeley: University of California Press.

Nixon, Howard L. II. 2008. *Sport in a Changing World.* Boulder, CO: Paradigm.

Rees, C. Roger, and Andrew W. Miracle. 2001. "Education and Sport." Pp. 277–290 in Jay Coakley and Eric Dunning eds., *Handbook of Sports Studies.* London: Sage.

Ryan, Joan. 1995. *Little Girls in Pretty Boxes: The Making and Breaking of Elite Gymnasts and Figure Skaters.* New York: Warner.

Telander, Rick. 1976. *Heaven Is a Playground.* New York: Simon and Schuster.

Watts, Jay. 2002. "Perspectives on Sport Specialization." *JOPERD* 73 (October): 33–37, 50.

Wolff, Alexander. 2002. "The High School Athlete." *Sports Illustrated,* three-part series (November 18, 25, and December 2).

PART THREE

Sport and Socialization: The Mass Media

The mass media have a tremendous impact on sports. First, the popularity of sport is due in large measure to the enormous attention it receives from the mass media. Second, television has infused huge sums of money into sport, affecting franchise moves and salaries. Third, television (and the money it offers) has changed the way sports are played (for example, the scheduling of games, the interruption of the flow of games for commercial breaks, the shift from match play to medal play in tournament golf, and rule changes such as liberalizing offensive holding in football to increase scoring and, therefore, viewer interest). Fourth, television has affected college sports by making recruiting more national than regional and by focusing the nation's attention (and heaping television's money) on the games by a relatively few schools. Thus, television has exacerbated the gap between the "haves" and the "have nots." Moreover, since television money goes to the successful, it has heightened the pressure to win, and for some, the necessity to cheat in order to win.

Another consequence of the media—the effect on perceptions—is the focus of this section. The media direct attention toward certain acts and away from others. While the media appear to simply report what is happening, or what has just happened, during a sporting event, they actually provide a constructed view by what they choose to cover, their focus, and the narrative themes they pursue.[1] As Alan and John Clarke have said:

> It selects *between* sports for those which make "good television," and it selects *within* a particular event, it highlights particular aspects for the viewers. This selective highlighting is not "natural" or inevitable—it is based on certain criteria, certain media assumptions about what is "good television." But the media do not only select, they also provide us with definitions of what has been selected. They interpret events for us, provide us with frameworks of meaning in which to make sense of

the event. To put it simply, television does not merely consist of pictures, but also involves a commentary on the pictures—a commentary which explains to us what we are seeing.... These selections are socially constructed—they involve decisions about what to reveal to the viewers. The presentation of sport through the media involves an active process of re-presentation: what we see is not the event, but the event transformed into something else—a media event.[2]

The first selection in this section, by Michael A. Messner, Michele Dunbar, and Darnell Hunt, explores themes in televised sports that combine to construct a masculinity formula consistent with the entrenched interests of the sports/media/commercial complex.

The second selection tracks the progress or lack thereof in the coverage of women's sport on television. The startling conclusion of sociologists Messner and Cooky is that viewers are actually receiving less time devoted to women's sports than they were twenty years ago.

NOTES

1. D. Stanley Eitzen and George H. Sage, *Sociology of North American Sport,* 8th ed. (Boulder, CO: Paradigm Publishers, 2008), chap. 9.
2. Alan Clarke and John Clarke, "Highlights and Action Replays—Ideology, Sport, and the Media," in *Sport, Culture, and Ideology,* Jennifer Hargreaves, ed. (Boston: Routledge and Kegan Paul, 1982), pp. 69, 71.

7

The Televised Sports Manhood Formula

Michael A. Messner, Michele Dunbar, and Darnell Hunt

A recent national survey found 8- to 17-year-old children to be avid consumers of sports media, with television most often named as the preferred medium (Amateur Athletic Foundation of Los Angeles, 1999). Although girls watch sports in great numbers, boys are markedly more likely to report that they are regular consumers of televised sports. The most popular televised sports with boys, in order, are pro football, men's pro basketball, pro baseball, pro wrestling, men's college basketball, college football, and Extreme sports.[1] Although counted separately in the Amateur Athletic Foundation (AAF) study, televised sports highlights shows also were revealed to be tremendously popular with boys.

What are boys seeing and hearing when they watch these programs? What kinds of values concerning gender, race, aggression, violence, and consumerism are boys exposed to when they watch their favorite televised sports programs, with their accompanying commercials? This chapter, based on a textual analysis, presents the argument that televised sports, and their accompanying commercials, consistently present boys with a narrow portrait of masculinity, which we call the Televised Sports Manhood Formula.

SAMPLE AND METHOD

We analyzed a range of televised sports that were identified by the AAF study as those programs most often watched by boys. Most of the programs in our sample aired

Source: Michael A. Messner, Michele Dunbar, and Darnell Hunt, "The Televised Sports Manhood Formula," *Journal of Sport and Social Issues* 24 (November 2000): 380–394.

during a single week, May 23–29, 1999, with one exception. Because pro football is not in season in May, we acquired tapes of two randomly chosen National Football League (NFL) *Monday Night Football* games from the previous season to include in our sample. We analyzed televised coverage, including commercials and pregame, halftime, and postgame shows (when appropriate), for the following programs:

1. two broadcasts of *SportsCenter* on ESPN (2 hours of programming);
2. two broadcasts of Extreme sports, one on ESPN and one on Fox Sports West (approximately 90 minutes of programming);
3. two broadcasts of professional wrestling, including *Monday Night Nitro* on TNT and *WWF Superstars* on USA (approximately 2 hours of programming);
4. two broadcasts of National Basketball Association (NBA) play-off games, one on TNT and the other on NBC (approximately 7 hours of programming);
5. two broadcasts of NFL *Monday Night Football* on ABC (approximately 7 hours of programming); and
6. one broadcast of Major League Baseball (MLB) on TBS (approximately 3 hours of programming).

We conducted a textual analysis of the sports programming and the commercials. In all, we examined about 23 hours of sports programming, nearly one quarter of which was time taken up by commercials. We examined a total of 722 commercials, which spanned a large range of products and services. We collected both quantitative and qualitative data. Although we began with some sensitizing concepts that we knew we wanted to explore (e.g., themes of violence, images of gender and race, etc.), rather than starting with preset categories we used an inductive method that allowed the dominant themes to emerge from our reading of the tapes.

Each taped show was given a first reading by one of the investigators, who then constructed a preliminary analysis of the data. The tape was then given a second reading by another of the investigators. This second independent reading was then used to modify and sharpen the first reading. Data analysis proceeded along the lines of the categories that emerged in the data collection. The analyses of each separate sport were then put into play with each other and common themes and patterns were identified. In one case, the dramatic pseudosport of professional wrestling, we determined that much of the programming was different enough that it made little sense to directly compare it with the other sports shows; therefore, we only included data on wrestling in our comparisons when it seemed to make sense to do so.

DOMINANT THEMES IN TELEVISED SPORTS

Our analysis revealed that sports programming presents boys with narrow and stereotypical messages about race, gender, and violence. We identified 10 distinct themes that, together, make up the Televised Sports Manhood Formula.

Table 7-1 Race and Sex of Announcers

White Men	White Women	Black Men	Black Women
24	3	3	1

White Males Are the Voices of Authority

Although one of the two *SportsCenter* segments in the sample did feature a White woman coanchor, the play-by-play and ongoing color commentary in NFL, wrestling, NBA, Extreme sports, and MLB broadcasts were conducted exclusively by White, male play-by play commentators (see Table 7-1).

With the exception of *SportsCenter,* women and Blacks never appeared as the main voices of authority in the booth conducting play-by-play or ongoing color commentary. The NFL broadcasts occasionally cut to field-level color commentary by a White woman, but her commentary was very brief (about 3½ minutes of the nearly 3 hours of actual game and pregame commentary). Similarly, one of the NBA broadcasts used a Black man for occasional on-court analysis and a Black man for pregame and halftime analysis, whereas the other NBA game used a White woman as host in the pregame show and a Black woman for occasional on-court analysis. Although viewers commonly see Black male athletes—especially on televised NBA games—they rarely hear or see Black men or women as voices of authority in the broadcast booth (Sabo and Jansen, 1994). In fact, the only Black commentators that appeared on the NBA shows that we examined were former star basketball players (Cheryl Miller, Doc Rivers, and Isaiah Thomas). A Black male briefly appeared to welcome the audience to open one of the Extreme sports shows but he did not do any play-by-play; in fact, he was used only to open the show with a stylish, street, hip-hop style for what turned out to be an almost totally White show.

Sports Is a Man's World

Images or discussion of women athletes is almost entirely absent in the sports programs that boys watch most. *SportsCenter*'s mere 2.9 percent of news time devoted to women's sports is slightly lower than the 5 percent to 6 percent of women's sports coverage commonly found in other sports news studies (Duncan and Messner, 1998). In addition, *SportsCenter*'s rare discussion of a women's sport seemed to follow men's in newsworthiness (e.g., a report on a Professional Golfers' Association [PGA] tournament was followed by a more brief report on a Ladies Professional Golf Association [LPGA] tournament). The baseball, basketball, wrestling, and football programs we watched were men's contests so they could not perhaps have been expected to cover or mention women athletes. However, Extreme sports are commonly viewed as "alternative" or "emerging" sports in which women are challenging masculine hegemony (Wheaton and Tomlinson, 1998). Despite this, the Extreme sports shows we watched devoted only a single 50-second interview segment to a woman athlete.

Table 7-2 Sex Composition of 722 Commercials

Men Only	Women Only	Women and Men	No People
279 (38.6%)	28 (3.9%)	324 (44.9%)	91 (12.6%)

This segment constituted about 1 percent of the total Extreme sports programming and, significantly, did not show this woman athlete in action. Perhaps this limited coverage of women athletes on the Extreme sports shows we examined is evidence of what Rinehart (1998) calls a "pecking order" in alternative sports, which develops when new sports are appropriated and commodified by the media.

Men Are Foregrounded in Commercials

The idea that sports is a man's world is reinforced by the gender composition and imagery in commercials. Women almost never appear in commercials unless they are in the company of men, as Table 7-2 shows.

That 38.6 percent of all commercials portray only men actually understates the extent to which men dominate these commercials for two reasons. First, nearly every one of the 91 commercials that portrayed no visual portrayals of people included a male voice-over. When we include this number, we see that more than 50 percent of commercials provide men-only images and/or voiceovers, whereas only 3.9 percent portray only women. Moreover, when we combine men-only and women and men categories, we see that men are visible in 83.5 percent of all commercials and men are present (when we add in the commercials with male voice-overs) in 96.1 percent of all commercials. Second, in the commercials that portray both women and men, women are often (although not exclusively) portrayed in stereotypical, and often very minor, background roles.

Women Are Sexy Props or Prizes for Men's Successful Sport Performances or Consumption Choices

Although women were mostly absent from sports commentary, when they did appear it was most often in stereotypical roles as sexy, masculinity-validating props, often cheering the men on. For instance, "X-sports" on Fox Sports West used a bikini-clad blonde woman as a hostess to welcome viewers back after each commercial break as the camera moved provocatively over her body Although she mentioned the show's sponsors, she did not narrate the actual sporting event. The wrestling shows generously used scantily clad women (e.g., in pink miniskirts or tight Spandex and high heels) who overtly displayed the dominant cultural signs of heterosexy attractiveness[2] to escort the male wrestlers to the ring, often with announcers discussing the women's provocative physical appearance. Women also appeared in the wrestling shows as sexually provocative dancers (e.g., the "Gorgeous Nitro Girls" on TNT).

In commercials, women are numerically more evident, and generally depicted in more varied roles, than in the sports programming. Still, women are underrepresented

Table 7-3 Instances of Women Being Depicted as Sexy Props or Prizes for Men

	SportsCenter	Extreme	Wrestling	NBA	MLB	NFL
Commercials	5	5	3	10	4	6
Sport programs	0	5	13	3	0	4
Total	5	10	16	13	4	10

Note: NBA = National Basketball Association, MLB = Major League Baseball, and NFL = National Football League.

and rarely appear in commercials unless they are in the company of men. Moreover, as Table 7-3 illustrates, the commercials' common depiction of women as sexual objects and as "prizes" for men's successful consumption choices articulates with the sports programs' presentation of women primarily as sexualized, supportive props for men's athletic performances. For instance, a commercial for Keystone Light Beer that ran on *SportsCenter* depicted two White men at a baseball game. When one of the men appeared on the stadium big screen and made an ugly face after drinking an apparently bitter beer, women appeared to be grossed out by him. But then he drank a Keystone Light and reappeared on the big screen looking good with two young, conventionally beautiful (fashion-model-like) women adoring him. He says, "I hope my wife's not watching!" as the two women flirt with the camera.

As Table 7-3 shows, in 23 hours of sports programming, viewers were exposed to 58 incidents of women being portrayed as sexy props and/or sexual prizes for men's successful athletic performances or correct consumption choices. Put another way, a televised sports viewer is exposed to this message, either in commercials or in the sports program itself, on an average of twice an hour. The significance of this narrow image of women as heterosexualized commodities should be considered especially in light of the overall absence of a wider range of images of women, especially as athletes (Duncan and Messner, 1998; Kane and Lenskyj, 1998).

Whites Are Foregounded in Commercials

The racial composition of the commercials is, if anything, more narrow and limited than the gender composition. As Table 7-4 shows, Black, Latino, or Asian American people almost never appear in commercials unless the commercial also has White people in it (the multiracial category in the table).

To say that 52.2 percent of the commercials portrayed only Whites actually understates the extent to which images of White people dominated the commercials for two reasons. First, if we subtract the 91 commercials that showed no actual people, then we see that the proportion of commercials that actually showed people was 59.7 percent White only. Second, when we examine the quality of the portrayals of Blacks, Latinos, and Asian Americans in the multiracial commercials, we see that people of color are far more often than not relegated to minor roles, literally in the background of scenes that feature Whites, and/or they are relegated to stereotypical or negative roles.

Table 7-4 Racial Composition of 722 Commercials

White Only	Black Only	Latino/a Only	Asian Only	Multiracial	Undeter-mined	No People
377 (52.2%)	28 (3.9%)	3 (0.4%)	2 (0.3%)	203 (28.1%)	18 (2.5%)	91 (12.6%)

For instance, a Wendy's commercial that appeared on several of the sports programs in our sample showed White customers enjoying a sandwich with the White owner while a barely perceptible Black male walked by in the background.

Aggressive Players Get the Prize; Nice Guys Finish Last

As Table 7-5 illustrates, viewers are continually immersed in images and commentary about the positive rewards that come to the most aggressive competitors and of the negative consequences of playing "soft" and lacking aggression.

Commentators consistently lauded athletes who most successfully employed physical and aggressive play and toughness. For instance, after having his toughness called into question, NBA player Brian Grant was awarded redemption by *SportsCenter* because he showed that he is "not afraid to take it to Karl Malone." *SportsCenter* also informed viewers that "the aggressor usually gets the calls [from the officials] and the Spurs were the ones getting them." In pro wrestling commentary, this is a constant theme (and was therefore not included in our tallies for Table 7-5 because the theme permeated the commentary, overtly and covertly). The World Wrestling Federation (WWF) announcers praised the "raw power" of wrestler "Shamrock" and approvingly dubbed "Hardcore Holly" as "the world's most dangerous man." NBA commentators suggested that it is okay to be a good guy off the court but one must be tough and aggressive on the court: Brian Grant and Jeff Hornacek are "true gentlemen of the NBA … as long as you don't have to play against them. You know they're great off the court; on the court, every single guy out there *should* be a killer."

When players were not doing well, they were often described as "hesitant" and lacking aggression, emotion, and desire (e.g., for a loose ball or rebound). For instance, commentators lamented that "the Jazz aren't going to the hoop, they're being pushed and shoved around," that Utah was responding to the Blazers' aggression "passively, in a reactive mode," and that "Utah's got to get Karl Malone toughened up." *SportsCenter* echoed this theme, opening one show with a depiction of Horace

Table 7-5 Statements Lauding Aggression or Criticizing Lack of Aggression

SportsCenter	Extreme	NBA	MLB	NFL
3	4	40	4	15

Note: NBA = National Basketball Association, MLB = Major League Baseball, and NFL = National Football League.

Grant elbowing Karl Malone and asking of Malone, "Is he feeble?" Similarly, NFL broadcasters waxed on about the virtues of aggression and domination. Big "hits"; ball carriers who got "buried," "stuffed," or "walloped" by the defense; and players who get "cleaned out" or "wiped out" by a blocker were often shown on replays, with announcers enthusiastically describing the plays. By contrast, they clearly declared that it is a very bad thing to be passive and to let yourself get pushed around and dominated at the line of scrimmage. Announcers also approvingly noted that going after an opposing player's injured body part is just smart strategy: In one NFL game, the Miami strategy to blitz the opposing quarterback was lauded as "brilliant"—"When you know your opposing quarterback is a bit nicked and something is wrong, Boomer, you got to come after him."

Previous research has pointed to this heroic framing of the male body-as-weapon as a key element in sports' role in the social construction of narrow conceptions of masculinity (Messner, 1992; Trujillo, 1995).

This injunction for boys and men to be aggressive, not passive, is reinforced in commercials, where a common formula is to play on the insecurities of young males (e.g., that they are not strong enough, tough enough, smart enough, rich enough, attractive enough, decisive enough, etc.) and then attempt to convince them to avoid, overcome, or mask their fears, embarrassments, and apparent shortcomings by buying a particular product. These commercials often portray men as potential or actual geeks, nerds, or passive schmucks who can overcome their geekiness (or avoid being a geek like the guy in the commercial) by becoming decisive and purchasing a particular product.

Boys Will Be (Violent) Boys

Announcers often took a humorous "boys will be boys" attitude in discussing fights or near-fights during contests, and they also commonly used a recent fight, altercation, or disagreement between two players as a "teaser" to build audience excitement (see Table 7-6).

Fights, near-fights, threats of fights, or other violent actions were overemphasized in sports coverage and often verbally framed in sarcastic language that suggested that this kind of action, although reprehensible, is to be expected. For instance, as *SportsCenter* showed NBA centers Robinson and O'Neill exchanging forearm shoves, the commentators said, simply, "much love." Similarly, in an NFL game, a brief scuffle between players is met with a sarcastic comment by the broadcaster that the players

Table 7-6 Humorous or Sarcastic Discussion of Fights or Near-Fights

SportsCenter	Extreme	NBA	MLB	NFL
10	1	2	2	7

Note: NBA = National Basketball Association, MLB = Major League Baseball, and NFL = National Football League.

are simply "making their acquaintance." This is, of course, a constant theme in pro wrestling (which, again, we found impossible and less than meaningful to count because this theme permeates the show). We found it noteworthy that the supposedly spontaneous fights outside the wrestling ring (what we call unofficial fights) were given more coverage time and focus than the supposedly official fights inside the ring. We speculate that wrestling producers know that viewers already watch fights inside the ring with some skepticism as to their authenticity so they stage the unofficial fights outside the ring to bring a feeling of spontaneity and authenticity to the show and to build excitement and a sense of anticipation for the fight that will later occur inside the ring.

Give Up Your Body for the Team

Athletes who are "playing with pain," "giving up their body for the team," or engaging in obviously highly dangerous plays or maneuvers were consistently framed as heroes; conversely, those who removed themselves from games due to injuries had questions raised about their character, their manhood (see Table 7-7).

This theme cut across all sports programming. For instance, *SportsCenter* asked, "Could the dominator be soft?" when a National Hockey League (NHL) star goalie decided to sit out a game due to a groin injury. Heroically taking risks while already hurt was a constant theme in Extreme sports commentary. For instance, one bike competitor was lauded for "overcoming his fear" and competing "with a busted up ankle" and another was applauded when he "popped his collarbone out in the street finals in Louisville but he's back on his bike here in Richmond, just 2 weeks later!" Athletes appear especially heroic when they go against doctors' wishes not to compete. For instance, an X Games interviewer adoringly told a competitor, "Doctors said don't ride but you went ahead and did it anyway and escaped serious injury" Similarly, NBA player Isaiah Rider was lauded for having "heart" for "playing with that knee injury." Injury discussions in NFL games often include speculation about whether the player will be able to return to this or future games. A focus on a star player in a pregame or halftime show, such as the feature on 49ers' Garrison Hearst, often contain commentary about heroic overcoming of serious injuries (in this case, a knee blowout, reconstructive surgery, and rehabilitation). As one game began, commentators noted that 37-year-old "Steve Young has remained a rock ... not bad for a guy who a lotta people figured was, what, one big hit from ending his career." It's especially impressive when an injured player is able and willing to continue to play with aggressiveness and reckless abandon: "Kurt Scrafford at right guard-bad neck

Table 7-7 Comments on the Heroic Nature of Playing Hurt

SportsCenter	Extreme	NBA	MLB	NFL
9	12	6	4	15

Note: NBA = National Basketball Association, MLB = Major League Baseball, and NFL = National Football League.

and all—is just out there wiping out guys." And announcers love the team leader who plays hurt:

> Drew Bledsoe gamely tried to play in loss to Rams yesterday; really admirable to try to play with that pin that was surgically implanted in his finger during the week; I don't know how a Q.B. could do that. You know, he broke his finger the time we had him on Monday night and he led his team to two come-from-behind victories, really gutted it out and I think he took that team on his shoulders and showed he could play and really elevated himself in my eyes, he really did.

Sports Is War

Commentators consistently (an average of nearly five times during each hour of sports commentary) used martial metaphors and language Of war and weaponry to describe sports action (e.g., battle, kill, ammunition, weapons, professional sniper, depth charges, taking aim, fighting, shot in his arsenal, reloading, detonate, squeezes the trigger, attack mode, firing blanks, blast, explosion, blitz, point of attack, a lance through the heart, etc.) (see Table 7-8).

Some shows went beyond commentators' use of war terminology and actually framed the contests as wars. For instance, one of the wrestling shows offered a continual flow of images and commentary that reminded the viewers that "RAW is WAR!" Similarly, both NFL *Monday Night Football* broadcasts were introduced with explosive graphics and an opening song that included lyrics "Like a rocket burning through time and space, the NFL's best will rock this place ... the battle lines are drawn." This sort of use of sport/war metaphors has been a common practice in televised sports commentary for many years, serving to fuse (and confuse) the distinctions between values of nationalism with team identity and athletic aggression with military destruction (Jansen and Sabo, 1994). In the shows examined for this study, war themes also were reinforced in many commercials, including commercials for movies, other sports programs, and in the occasional commercial for the U.S. military.

Show Some Guts!

Commentators continually depicted and replayed exciting incidents of athletes engaging in reckless acts of speed, showing guts in the face of danger, big hits, and violent crashes (see Table 7-9).

Table 7-8 Martial Metaphors and Language of War and Weaponry

SportsCenter	Extreme	Wrestling	NBA	MLB	NFL
9	3	15	27	6	23

Note: NBA = National Basketball Association, MLB = Major League Baseball, and NFL = National Football League.

Table 7-9 Depictions of Guts in Face of Danger, Speed, Hits, Crashes

SportsCenter	Extreme	NBA	MLB	NFL
4	21	5	2	8

Note: NBA = National Basketball Association, MLB = Major League Baseball, and NFL = National Football League.

This theme was evident across all of the sports programs but was especially predominant in Extreme sports that continually depicted crashing vehicles or bikers in an exciting manner. For instance, when one race ended with a crash, it was showed again in slow-motion replay, with commentators approvingly dubbing it "unbelievable" and "original." Extreme sports commentators; commonly raised excitement levels by saying "he's on fire" or "he's going huge!" when a competitor was obviously taking greater risks. An athlete's ability to deal with the fear of a possible crash, in fact, is the mark of an "outstanding run": "Watch out, Richmond," an X-games announcer shouted to the crowd, "He's gonna wreck this place!" A winning competitor laughingly said, "I do what I can to smash into [my opponents] as much as I can." Another competitor said, "If I crash, no big deal; I'm just gonna go for it." NFL commentators introduced the games with images of reckless collisions and during the game a "fearless" player was likely to be applauded: "There's no chance that Barry Sanders won't take when he's running the football." In another game, the announcer noted that receiver "Tony Simmons plays big. And for those of you not in the NFL, playing big means you're not afraid to go across the middle and catch the ball and make a play out of it after you catch the ball." Men showing guts in the face of speed and danger was also a major theme in 40 of the commercials that we analyzed.

THE TELEVISED SPORTS MANHOOD FORMULA

Tens of millions of U.S. boys watch televised sports programs with their accompanying commercial advertisements. This study sheds light on what these boys are seeing when they watch their favorite sports programs. What values and ideas about gender, race, aggression, and violence are being promoted? Although there are certainly differences across different kinds of sports, as well as across different commercials, when we looked at all of the programming together, we identified 10 recurrent themes, which we have outlined above. Taken together, these themes codify a consistent and (mostly) coherent message about what it means to be a man. We call this message the Televised Sports Manhood Formula:

> What is a Real Man? A Real Man is strong, tough, aggressive, and above all, a winner in what is still a Man's World. To be a winner he has to do what needs to be done. He must be willing to compromise his own long term health by showing guts in the face of danger, by fighting other men when necessary, and by "play-

ing hurt" when he's injured. He must avoid being soft; he must be the aggressor, both on the "battle fields" of sports and in his consumption choices. Whether he is playing sports or making choices about which snack food or auto products to purchase, his aggressiveness will net him the ultimate prize: the adoring attention of conventionally beautiful women. He will know if and when he has arrived as a Real Man when the Voices of Authority—White Males—*say* he is a Real Man. But even when he has finally managed to win the big one, has the good car and the right beer, and is surrounded by beautiful women, he will be reminded by these very same Voices of Authority just how fragile this Real Manhood really is: After all, he has to come out and prove himself all over again tomorrow. You're only as good as your last game (or your last purchase).

The major elements of the Televised Sports Manhood Formula are evident, in varying degrees, in the football, basketball, baseball, Extreme sports, and *SportsCenter* programs and in their accompanying commercials. But it is in the dramatic spectacle of professional wrestling that the Televised Sports Manhood Formula is most clearly codified and presented to audiences as an almost seamless package. Boys and young men are drawn to televised professional wrestling in great numbers. Consistently each week, from four to six pro wrestling shows rank among the top 10 rated shows on cable television. Professional wrestling is not a real sport in the way that baseball, basketball, football, or even Extreme sports are. In fact, it is a highly stylized and choreographed "sport as theatre" form of entertainment. Its producers have condensed—and then amplified—all of the themes that make up the Televised Sports Manhood Formula. For instance, where violence represents a thread in the football or basketball commentary, violence makes up the entire fabric of the theatrical narrative of televised pro wrestling. In short, professional wrestling presents viewers with a steady stream of images and commentary that represents a constant fusion of all of the themes that make up the Televised Sports Manhood Formula: This is a choreographed sport where all men (except losers) are Real Men, where women are present as sexy support objects for the men's violent, monumental "wars" against each other. Winners bravely display muscular strength, speed, power, and guts. Bodily harm is (supposedly) intentionally inflicted on opponents. The most ruthlessly aggressive men win, whereas the passive or weaker men lose, often shamefully. Heroically wrestling while injured, rehabilitating oneself from former injuries, and inflicting pain and injury on one's opponent are constant and central themes in the narrative.

GENDER AND THE SPORTS/MEDIA/ COMMERCIAL COMPLEX

In 1984, media scholar Sut Jhally pointed to the commercial and ideological symbiosis between the institutions of sport and the mass media and called it the sports/media complex. Our examination of the ways that the Televised Sports Manhood Formula reflects and promotes hegemonic ideologies concerning race, gender, sexuality, aggression, violence, and consumerism suggests adding a third dimension to Jhally's analysis: the huge network of multi-billion-dollar automobile, snack food, alcohol, entertainment, and other corporate entities that sponsor sports events and broadcasts. In fact, examining the ways that the Televised Sports Manhood Formula cuts across sports programming and its accompanying commercials may provide important clues as to the ways that ideologies of hegemonic masculinity are both promoted by—and in turn serve to support and stabilize—this collection of interrelated institutions that make up the sports/media/commercial complex. The Televised Sports Manhood Formula is a master discourse that is produced at the nexus of the institutions of sport, mass media, and corporations who produce and hope to sell products and services to boys and men. As such, the Televised Sports Manhood Formula appears well suited to discipline boys' bodies, minds, and consumption choices within an ideological field that is conducive to the reproduction of the entrenched interests that profit from the sports/media/commercial complex. The perpetuation of the entrenched commercial interests of the sports/media/commercial complex appears to be predicated on boys accepting—indeed glorifying and celebrating—a set of bodily and relational practices that resist and oppose a view of women as fully human and place boys' and men's long-term health prospects in jeopardy.

At a historical moment when hegemonic masculinity has been destabilized by socioeconomic change, and by women's and gay liberation movements, the Televised Sports Manhood Formula provides a remarkably stable and concrete view of masculinity as grounded in bravery, risk taking, violence, bodily strength, and heterosexuality. And this view of masculinity is given coherence against views of women as sexual support objects or as invisible and thus irrelevant to men's public struggles for glory. Yet, perhaps to be successful in selling products, the commercials sometimes provide a less than seamless view of masculinity. The insecurities of masculinity in crisis are often tweaked in the commercials, as we see weak men, dumb men, and indecisive men being eclipsed by strong, smart, and decisive men and sometimes being humiliated by smarter and more decisive women. In short, this commercialized version of hegemonic masculinity is constructed partly in relation to images of men who don't measure up.

This analysis gives us hints at an answer to the commonly asked question of why so many boys and men continue to take seemingly irrational risks, submit to pain and injury, and risk long-term debility or even death by playing hurt. A critical examination of the Televised Sports Manhood Formula tells us why: The costs of masculinity (especially pain and injury), according to this formula, appear to be well worth the price; the boys and men who are willing to pay the price always seem to get the glory, the championships, the best consumer products, and the beautiful women. Those who don't—or can't—pay the price are humiliated or ignored by women and left in the dust by other men. In short, the Televised Sports Manhood Formula is a pedagogy through which boys are taught that paying the price, be it one's bodily health or one's money, gives one access to the privileges that have been historically linked to hegemonic masculinity—money, power, glory, and women. And the barrage of images of femininity as model-like beauty displayed for and in the service of successful men suggests that heterosexuality is a major lynchpin of the Televised Sports

Manhood Formula, and on a larger scale serves as one of the major linking factors in the conservative gender regime of the sports/media/commercial complex.

On the other hand, we must be cautious in coming to definitive conclusions as to how the promotion of the values embedded in the Televised Sports Manhood Formula might fit into the worlds of young men. It is not possible, based merely on our textual analysis of sports programs, to explicate precisely what kind of impact these shows, and the Televised Sports Manhood Formula, have on their young male audiences. That sort of question is best approached through direct research with audiences. Most such research finds that audiences interpret, use, and draw meanings from media variously, based on factors such as social class, race/ethnicity, and gender (Hunt, 1999; Whannel, 1998). Research with various subgroups of boys that explores their interpretations of the sports programs that they watch would enhance and broaden this study.

Moreover, it is important to go beyond the preferred reading presented here that emphasizes the persistent themes in televised sports that appear to reinforce the hegemony of current race, gender, and commercial relations (Sabo and Jansen, 1992). In addition to these continuities, there are some identifiable discontinuities within and between the various sports programs and within and among the accompanying commercials. For instance, commercials are far more varied in the ways they present gender imagery than are sports programs themselves. Although the dominant tendency in commercials is either to erase women or to present them as stereotypical support or sex objects, a significant minority of commercials present themes that set up boys and men as insecure and/or obnoxious schmucks and women as secure, knowledgeable, and authoritative. Audience research with boys who watch sports would shed fascinating light on how they decode and interpret these more complex, mixed, and paradoxical gender images against the dominant, hegemonic image of the Televised Sports Manhood Formula.

NOTES

1. There are some differences, and some similarities, in what boys and girls prefer to watch. The top seven televised sports reported by girls are, in order, gymnastics, men's pro basketball, pro football, pro baseball, swimming/diving, men's college basketball, and women's pro or college basketball.

2. Although images of feminine beauty shift, change, and are contested throughout history, female beauty is presented in sports programming and commercials in narrow ways. Attractive women look like fashion models (Banet-Weiser, 1999): They are tall, thin, young, usually (although not always) White, with signs of heterosexual femininity encoded and overtly displayed through hair, makeup, sexually provocative facial and bodily gestures, large (often partially exposed) breasts, long (often exposed) legs, and so forth.

REFERENCES

Amateur Athletic Foundation of Los Angeles. 1999. *Children and Sports Media.* Los Angeles: Author.

Banet-Weiser, S. 1999. *The Most Beautiful Girl in the World: Beauty Pageants and National Identity.* Berkeley: University of California Press.

Duncan, M. C., and Messner, M. A. 1998. "The Media Image of Sport and Gender." Pp. 170–195 in L. A. Wenner, ed., *MediaSport.* New York: Routledge.

Hunt, D. 1999. *O.J. Simpson: Facts and Fictions,* New York: Cambridge University Press.

Jansen, S. C., and Sabo, D. 1994. The "Sport/War Metaphor: Hegemonic Masculinity, the Persian Gulf War, and the New World Order." *Sociology of Sport Journal* 11: 1–17.

Jhally, S. 1984. "The Spectacle of Accumulation: Material and Cultural Factors in the Evolution of the Sports/Media Complex." *Insurgent Sociologist* 12, no. 3: 41–52.

Kane, M. J., and Lenskyj, H. J. 1998. "Media Treatment of Female Athletes: Issues of Gender and Sexualities." Pp. 186–201 in L. A. Wenner, ed., *MediaSport.* New York: Routledge.

Messner, M. A. 1992. *Power at Play: Sports and the Problem of Masculinity.* Boston: Beacon.

Rinehart, R. 1998. "Inside of the Outside: Pecking Orders within Alternative Sport at ESPN's 1995 'The eXtreme Games.'" *Journal of Sport and Social Issues* 22: 398–415.

Sabo, D., and Jansen, S. C. 1992. "Images of Men in Sport Media: The Social Reproduction of Masculinity." Pp. 169–184 in S. Craig, ed., *Men, Masculinity, and the Media.* Newbury Park, CA: Sage.

———. 1994. "Seen but Not Heard: Images of Black Men in Sports Media." Pp. 150–160 in M. A. Messner and D. F. Sabo, eds., *Sex, Violence, and Power in Sports: Rethinking Masculinity.* Freedom, CA: Crossing Press.

Trujillo, N. 1995. "Machines, Missiles, and Men: Images of the Male Body on ABC's *Monday Night Football.*" *Sociology of Sport Journal* 12: 403–423.

Whannel, G. 1998. "Reading the Sports Media Audience." Pp. 221–232 in L. A. Wenner, ed., *MediaSport.* New York: Routledge.

Wheaton, B., and Tomlinson, A. 1998. "The Changing Gender Order in Sport? The Case of Windsurfing Subcultures." *Journal of Sport and Social Issues* 22: 252–274.

8

Gender in Televised Sports

Michael A. Messner and Cheryl Cooky

I. INTRODUCTION

By Diana Nyad

For two decades, the GENDER IN TELEVISED SPORTS report has tracked the progress—as well as the lack of progress—in the coverage of women's sports on television news and highlights shows. One of the positive outcomes derived from past editions of this valuable study has been a notable improvement in the often-derogatory ways that sports commentators used to routinely speak of women athletes. The good news in this report is that there is far less insulting and overtly sexist treatment of women athletes than there was twenty or even ten years ago. The bad news, in these times of women's empowerment and success in most spheres of our society, is that the overall coverage of women's sports has declined to a level of outrageously small numbers.

As a former world-class athlete, and through my thirty years working in sports television and radio, I have certainly come to know the uphill challenges we women face in the male bastion of sports. I am also fully aware of the market forces at work in shaping the everyday programming decisions in televised sports. But in reading this most current edition of GENDER IN TELEVISED SPORTS, I confess to being shocked to learn that since 1989 very little has changed in the world of televised sports news. As a matter of fact, for women athletes, and fans of women's sports,

---

Source: Michael A. Messner and Cheryl Cooky, "Gender in Televisted Sports: News and Highlights Shows, 1989–2009." Los Angeles: Center for Feminist Research, University of Southern California (June 2010), excerpts. Reprinted with permission of the University of Southern California Center for Feminist Research.

things have devolved, rather than having evolved. It is frankly unfathomable, and unacceptable, that viewers are actually receiving *less* coverage of women's sports than they were twenty years ago . . . and that the sports news is still being delivered almost exclusively by men.

There is no doubt that there has been a gender revolution in American sports in recent decades. Millions of girls play sports every day. Tens of thousands of women compete in college and professional athletics. Women's athletic skill levels have risen astronomically over the past twenty years in sports from basketball to volleyball, from swimming to soccer. It is time for television news and highlights shows to keep pace with this revolution. I can only hope that, five years from now, when this study is conducted again, it will find a substantial number of women among the ranks of sports news and highlights commentators, and that they, along with men commentators, will have joined the Twenty-first Century by reporting fairly and equitably on women's sports. The coverage today misrepresents both the participation and the interest in women's sports across our population at large.

II. SUMMARY OF FINDINGS

Coverage of Women's Sports: Lower Than Ever

- Women's sports were underreported in the six weeks of early evening and late night television sports news on the three network affiliates sampled in the study. Men's sports received 96.3% of the airtime, women's sports 1.6%, and gender neutral topics 2.1%. This is a precipitous decline in the coverage of women's sports since 2004, when 6.3% of the airtime was devoted to women's sports, and the lowest proportion ever recorded in this study.
- ESPN's nationally televised program *SportsCenter* devoted only 1.4% of its airtime to coverage of women's sports, a decline in their coverage of women's sports compared with 1999 (2.2%) and 2004 (2.1%).
- ESPN and two of the network affiliates (KNBC and KCBS), continually ran a scrolling ticker text bar at the bottom of the screen, reporting scores and other sports news. The proportion of "ticker time" devoted to women's sports on KNBC and KCBS was 4.6%, more than triple the thin airtime they devoted to women's sports in their main broadcasts. *SportsCenter* devoted 2.7% of its ticker time to women's sports, down from 8.5% in 2004.

Men's "Big Three" Sports: In or Out of Season, Always the Central Focus

- 100% of the *SportsCenter* programs and 100% of the sports news shows in the sample led with a men's sports story. Lead stories tend to be among the longest stories in the broadcast, containing the highest production values.
- 72% of all airtime (main and ticker coverage) focused on men's basketball, football,

and baseball. Other men's sports, especially most individual sports, were pushed to the margins along with the few women's sports that received any coverage.

- Reporters continually devoted airtime to men's sports that were out of season—pro and college football in March and July, pro baseball in November, or pro basketball in July—while failing to report on women's sports that were currently in season.

Women's and Men's Pro and College Basketball: Separate and Unequal

- The WNBA received a tiny fraction of the coverage that was devoted to the NBA, both when in-season, and when out-of-season.
- College basketball in March is a sport being played both by women's and men's teams during the same time frame. The three network affiliate news shows devoted zero time, and *SportsCenter* gave token attention to women's college basketball, while lavishing huge amounts of airtime to men's college basketball.
- News and highlights shows' scant coverage of pro or college women's basketball was usually relegated to the margins, appearing more often on the scrolling ticker at the bottom of the screen rather than in the program's main coverage.

Views of Women: Less Sexual Objectification; Sparing Servings of Respect

- Past studies observed that women athletes (and women spectators) were frequently portrayed in demeaning ways—as sexual objects, or as the brunt of commentators' sarcastic humor in stories on marginal pseudo-sports. There was far less of this sort of sexist humor about women in 2009, though this may in part reflect that women in any form were increasingly absent from the broadcasts.
- A large chunk of ESPN's *SportsCenter*'s meager coverage of women's sports was devoted to a short March series, "Celebrating Women's History Month: Her Triumph, Her Story." These features had high technical quality, and were delivered in a respectful tone, but were cordoned off from regular *SportsCenter* highlights, and presented as something separate and different.
- A handful of women's sports stories made their way into news and highlights shows when the story line was focused on a rule-breaking incident like a fight, or on some other controversy in women's sport.
- On the rare occasions when women were featured in sports news and highlights shows, they were usually presented in stereotypical ways: as wives or girlfriends of famous male athletes or as mothers.

Sports Commentators: Racially Diverse, Sex-Segregated

- Past studies revealed that news and highlights commentators were racially diverse, but most were men. This dual pattern of racial diversity and sex segregation continued in 2009. The three network affiliates included no women sports announcers, while women announcers appeared in a small number of *SportsCenter* broadcasts. Unlike general TV news anchor or weather positions, the TV sports news and highlights position is still defined almost exclusively as a male occupation.

* FOR FURTHER STUDY *

Bishop, Ronald. 2003. "Missing in Action: Feature Coverage of Women's Sports in *Sports Illustrated.*" *Journal of Sport and Social Issues* 27 (May): 184–194.

Brookes, R. 2002. *Representing Sport.* London: Arnold.

Coakley, Jay. 2007. *Sports in Society: Issues and Controversies.* New York: McGraw-Hill.

Crawford, Garry. 2004. *Consuming Sport: Fans, Sport, and Culture.* New York: Routledge.

Denham, Bryan E., Andrew C. Billings, and Kelby K. Halone. 2002. "Differential Accounts of Race in Broadcast Commentary of the 2000 NCAA Men's and Women's Final Four Basketball Tournaments." *Sociology of Sport Journal* 19 (3): 315–332.

Duncan, Margaret Carlisle, and Michael A. Messner. 2005. *Gender in Televised Sports: News and Highlights Shows, 1989–2004.* Los Angeles: Amateur Athletic Foundation.

Eitzen, D. Stanley, and George H. Sage. 2009. *Sociology of North American Sport.* 8th ed. Boulder, CO: Paradigm.

Juffer, Jane. 2002. "Who's the Man? Sammy Sosa, Latinos, and Televisual Redefinitions of the 'American' Pastime." *Journal of Sport and Social Issues* 26 (November): 381–402.

Malcolm, Dominic. 2007. "Sports Industry." Pp. 4713–4717 in *Blackwell Encyclopedia of Sport.* Vol. 9.

Messner, Michael A., Margaret Carlisle Duncan, and Cheryl Cooky. 2003. "Silence, Sports Bras, and Wrestling Porn." *Journal of Sport and Social Issues* 27 (February): 38–51.

Messner, Michael A., Margaret Carlisle Duncan, and Kerry Jensen. "Separating the Men from the Girls: The Gendered Language of Televised Sports." *Gender and Society* 7 (1992): 121–137.

Nixon, Howard L. II. 2008. *Sport in a Changing World.* Boulder, CO: Paradigm.

Owusu, Jeanette, and Aretha Faye Marbley. 2008. "Institutional Racism within the Print Media," *Journal for the Study of Sports and Athletes in Education* 2 (Spring): 29–49.

Raney, Arthur A., and Jennings Bryant, eds. 2006. *Handbook of Sports and Media.* Mahwah, NJ: Lawrence Erlbaum.

Stempel, Carl. 2006. "Televised Sports, Masculinist Moral Capital, and Support for the U.S. Invasion of Iraq." *Journal of Sport and Social Issues* 30 (February): 79–106.

Wannel, G. 2000. "Sports and the Media." Pp. 291–308 in Jay Coakley and Eric Dunning, eds., *Handbook of Sport Studies.* London: Sage.

PART FOUR

Sport and Socialization: Symbols

A symbol is anything that carries a particular meaning recognized by members of a culture. A wink, a raised finger (which one is important), a green light, a double stripe on the highway, and a handshake are all symbols with meaning for people in the United States. Part of the socialization process for children or other newcomers to a culture is the learning of symbols. While some symbols are relatively unimportant, others—such as the Constitution, the U.S. flag, or a cross—have great importance to certain segments of the population. Some of the symbols found in sport are very important.

The three selections in this section consider three symbols. The first, by journalist John Branch, examines the trend toward the use of huge U.S. flags at athletic events. The second, by journalist Bill Plaschke, highlights another battle over symbols. Here the issue is the use of a derogatory Native American name—Redskins.

The third selection, by sociologists D. Stanley Eitzen and Maxine Baca Zinn, looks at sexist naming of women's athletic teams. They found in a study of all four-year colleges and universities in the United States that over half had sexist names, logos, or mascots. This use of demeaning symbols for women's teams has several negative functions for women: through their use women are trivialized, made invisible, and de-athleticized.

9

American Flags as Big as Fields

John Branch

On the field before the All-Star Game, Major League Baseball plans to assemble the largest gathering of Hall of Fame players in baseball history. And as fans salute their heroes, the former players will join the crowd in saluting the American flag—one that is roughly 75 feet by 150 feet, as long as a 15-story building is tall, spread horizontally over the Yankee Stadium turf.

That is a relatively small flag by big-event standards in American sports these days. But it will signal the latest can't-miss blend of sports and patriotism, a combination increasingly presenting itself through gigantic American flags, unfurled by dozens or hundreds of people in an attempt to elicit a sense of awe and nationalism in the surrounding crowd.

Once the gaudy lure of attention-seeking car dealerships or other roadside attractions, big flags have found a comfortable home inside the ballparks, arenas and raceways of American sporting events.

"It is an American phenomenon, no doubt about it," said Frank Supovitz, the N.F.L.'s senior vice president for events, who oversees such spectacles as the Super Bowl and has helped stage events around the world.

A small industry has formed to supply the flags, usually at a cost of a few thousand dollars an appearance. Some colleges and bowl games, tired of renting them frequently, have bought their own field-sized flags.

"People are getting more on the bandwagon," said Doug Green, who has long rented giant flags to teams and leagues, and recently supplied one for the Indianapolis 500. "Nascar's doing it more and more, the N.F.L. is doing it more and more."

The trend began nearly 25 years ago, spiked after 9/11 and now seems simply part of the cultural backdrop in American sports. Where there is a big game, there is a big flag, often the size of the playing field itself.

Far too big for a pole, the flags raise something else—the question of whether a bigger flag is a more patriotic one, or just a bigger one.

"For big, spectacular events, big just happens because it paints a more vibrant picture," said Tim Brosnan, the executive vice president for business at Major League Baseball. "I don't think bigger is necessarily better, but it is a celebration."

These can be touchy times for interpreting the use of the flag as a symbol of patriotism. A tiny flag on a lapel, or the absence of one, fueled debate in the presidential campaign. And the Olympics will provide plenty of chances for medal-winning Americans, handed flags as celebratory props, to create a stir with their reaction. Some past Olympians were accused of disrespecting the flag by wrapping themselves in it or wearing it like a cape.

But there is little debate over the use of field-size or court-size flags during the national anthem or other sporting rituals. They have received the tacit approval of the military, which often supplies the people to present the flags, and are routinely greeted with wide-eyed cheers.

"People go ape when they see it," said Jim Alexander, a retired Coast Guard commander who runs Superflag, the company that basically invented the industry and once held the world record for the largest flag, which temporarily hung on the Hoover Dam. It was 255 by 505 feet and has been surpassed by a flag in Israel that measures 2,165 by 330 feet. "It's a feeling. It's a feeling that takes over a whole stadium. If anyone in the stands opened their mouth and objected, there would be hell to pay."

The eccentric founder of Superflag, Thomas Demski, known as Ski, commissioned a 95-by-160-foot American flag—about half the size of a football field—that made its debut in 1984 at Super Bowl XVIII.

Mr. Green soon designed a big flag of his own, made to come apart in 14 pieces for easy transport. Now, as the vice president of Sky's the Limit Productions, he has two football-field-sized flags. The other unfastens into four pieces, packed into separate trunks that, when filled, weigh 400 pounds each. Each of the 50 stars on those flags is about 5 feet across, according to Pete Van de Putte, the president of the Dixie Flag Manufacturing in San Antonio, which has made four football-field-sized flags.

At games, flags are typically unfurled quickly by volunteers, sometimes hundreds of them, creating an effect like a slow-motion firework or a fast-motion blooming of a flower. Once the flag is fully displayed, often at a particular point in the national anthem, the holders sometimes shake their arms, creating ripples to conjure a flag in a breeze.

Mr. Green says that the only complaint he hears is that the flags sometimes touch the ground. Sheer size makes it nearly impossible to avoid. Plastic is often placed on the ground when the flags are packed and unpacked. Superflag recommends having 265 volunteers to hold the football-field-sized flag—most to hold the edges, but about 100 of them to be stationed beneath the flag to help keep it aloft.

Mike Buss, an assistant director at the American Legion's national headquarters in Indianapolis, and the organization's flag guru, said that the belief that a flag that touched the ground was somehow soiled and must be destroyed "is an old wives' tale."

"All we ask is, no matter the size, that the flag is treated with dignity and respect," Mr. Buss said.

Event planners say they sense that there are limits, but do not think they have yet been exceeded. Still, every team is different. Mr. Green has supplied flags to the Yankees for opening days, playoff games and other occasions for about 10 years.

"The Yankees like one of the smallest flags I own—about the size of a basketball court, 45 by 90," Mr. Green said.

That means, for the All-Star Game on July 15, a decision was made by baseball: We need a bigger flag than usual at Yankee Stadium. But not the biggest.

"The smell test is, is it exploitative?" said Mr. Brosnan, the Major League Baseball vice president.

Mr. Buss, from the American Legion, says he has yet to see flags go too far—or too big. "Huge flags?" he said. "That's great."

10

"Redskins" Is No Honor, It's an Insult

Bill Plaschke

On a Saturday night in New York, the sports world vilifies Serena Williams for raining threats upon a line judge.

Yet a day later across the river, the same sports world celebrates a team whose nickname is considered a threat to an entire ethnic group.

Redskins.

A pro football season begins with two noted players banished to the sidelines for "conduct detrimental to the integrity of, and confidence in, the National Football League."

Yet that same league supports a team whose entire identity is forged through a symbol of detrimental conduct known as racism.

Redskins.

It remains one of the great mysteries in sports, a 77 year old crime that remains largely ignored and purposely unsolved.

How does a team from the nation's capital, supported by a fan base of some of the nation's greatest thinkers, maintain a nickname that is the Native American equivalent to the N-word?

Redskins?

"It is the worst thing in the English language you can be called if you are a native person," said Suzan Shown Harjo, a Native American writer and public policy advocate who is the lead plaintiff in one of the most compelling lawsuits in sports history.

Source: Bill Plaschke, "'Redskins' Is No Honor, It's an Insult." *Los Angeles Times* (September 18, 2009). http://www.latimes.com/Sports/la-sp-plaschke18-2009sep18,0,631231.

Seventeen years after challenging the Washington Redskins trademark, Harjo and six others have renewed their fight, petitioning the Supreme Court to examine a lower-court ruling that denied their challenge on a technicality.

It was announced Monday that Harjo's group will appeal the decision that their challenge was made too late and falls outside the statute of limitations.

The Redskins, named in 1933, were registered as a trademark during a vastly different racial climate in 1967.

Harjo's group challenges that, now and then, the trademark violates the Lanham Act, which bars trademarks that "disparage" people living or dead.

She's on time. Of the several high-profile Native American nicknames still alive in sports, nothing is more clearly disparaging than this one.

While the Braves, Indians, Chiefs, and Blackhawks all describe a group of people, the Redskin is the clear slur of an individual.

Look it up. It is listed as "offensive" in most dictionaries, and as the name given an Indian hunter's bounty in several historical publications.

"It is basically characterizing a person by their skin," Harjo said. "How wrong is that?"

The NFL and the Redskins counter with an argument found on Page 326 of the team's media guide, citing that the word "Redskin" actually refers to the red paint used on the skin of Indian warriors.

A league spokesman said they stand by the Redskins in this battle and, in fact, the NFL has paid much of the Redskins' legal fees.

Amazing, isn't it, how the sports world demands civility and good conduct only as long as it doesn't get in the way of tradition? When it comes to Native American mascots, insensitivity dies especially hard.

Chief Illiniwek has been banned from the University of Illinois, yet fans still stand up during halftime of football games and chant his name during the traditional time for his appearance.

Some fans at otherwise educated Dartmouth and Stanford, even though they have long since banned their Indian mascots, still show up at games with painted faces on their shirts.

"People lose their sense of discernment when it comes to sports," Harjo said. "With this particular issue, people just lose their minds."

Particularly in pro sports, and particularly in Washington, where one man's insult has become another man's birthright, and rationalizations run rampant.

It's stunning how many people there will insist that the word "Redskins" pays tribute to Native Americans ... even though none of those people are Native American.

"They say, 'You're being honored' ... we say, 'We're being offended,'" explained Harjo. "They say honored. We say offended. Then they just tell us to shut up."

Unlike the Seminoles of Florida State, there is no tribe that supports "Redskin." Unlike with some other mascots such as Warriors, there are no Native American groups that are even lukewarm about it.

"All national Indian groups support us," said Harjo, who is president of the Morning Star Institute, a Washington-based native cultural organization.

There is, in fact, precedent for changing the Redskins mascot, as it has already been deleted from major college sports with little impact.

Miami of Ohio has become the RedHawks, and it didn't seem to bother quarterback Ben Roethlisberger.

The University of Utah has become the Utes, who weren't any less tough when they nearly stole a national football championship last year.

The name can be changed. The name should be changed. There is not a bigger certifiable slur in sports. There is nothing even close.

And don't even try to compare this to the Fighting Irish, OK?

If you saw a Native American on the street, would you call that person a redskin?

"It's like putting Aunt Jemima on a helmet," Harjo said.

There has long been an argument that young Native Americans don't mind being used as sports symbols, but Harjo isn't buying that as a factor.

"Lots of people are saying, 'Just let us have our gambling and we'll stay out of the way,'" she said. "That doesn't make it right."

Some say Redskins owner Daniel Snyder will never make it right because it will cost too much money in merchandising. But imagine the riches he would reap with new apparel.

Some say NFL Commissioner Roger Goodell would never dare mess with one of the league's cornerstone franchises. But what better way to cement his growing legacy as a curator of equality and fairness?

Of course, it is a formidable task, fighting both men.

"We aren't just fighting Coke, we're fighting Pepsi backed by Coke," Harjo said.

And, indeed, it is a fight they lose every day.

"We are the invisible population," she said of the approximately 4 million Native Americans. "So racism against our population is also invisible."

Then again, there is this:

The original lawsuit was filed in 1992, after the Redskins' Super Bowl victory over the Buffalo Bills. At the time, the Redskins had appeared in four Super Bowls in the previous 10 years.

In the 17 years since, they have appeared in exactly zero Super Bowls.

Hail to the what, exactly?

11

The De-Athleticization of Women

The Naming and Gender Marking of Collegiate Sport Teams

D. Stanley Eitzen and Maxine Baca Zinn

Sport is an institution with enormous symbolic significance that contributes to and perpetuates male dominance in society (Hall, 1984, 1985). This occurs through processes that exclude women completely, or if they do manage to participate, processes that effectively minimize their achievements. Bryson (1987) has argued that sport reproduces patriarchal relations through four minimalizing processes: definition, direct control, ignoring, and trivialization. This chapter examines several of these processes but focuses especially on how the trivialization of women occurs through the sexist naming practices of athletic teams.

THE PROBLEM

American colleges and universities typically have adopted nicknames, songs, colors, emblems, and mascots as identifying and unifying symbols. This practice of using symbols to achieve solidarity and community is a common group practice, as

Source: Reprinted by permission from *Sociology of Sport Journal,* 1989, 6(4): 362–370. © Human Kinetics, Inc.

Durkheim showed in his analysis of primitive religions (Durkheim, 1947). Durkheim noted that people in a locality believed they were related to some totem, which was usually an animal but was occasionally a natural object as well. All members of a common group were identified by their shared symbol, which they displayed by the emblem of their totem. This identification with an animal, bird, or other object is common in institutions of higher learning where students, former students, faculty members, and others who identify with the local academic community display similar colors, wave banners, wear special clothing and jewelry, and chant or sing together. These behaviors usually center around athletic contests. Janet Lever (1983, p. 12) connects these activities with totemism: "Team worship, like animal worship, makes all participants intensely aware of their own group membership. By accepting that a particular team represents them symbolically, people enjoy ritual kinship based on a common bond. Their emblem, be it an insignia or a lapel pin or a scarf with team colors, distinguishes fellow fans from both strangers and enemies."

A school nickname is much more than a tag or a label. It conveys, symbolically as Durkheim posits, the characteristics and attributes that define the institution. In an important way, the school's symbols represent the institution's self-concept. Schools may have names that signify the school's ethnic heritage (e.g., the Bethany College Swedes), state history (University of Oklahoma Sooners), mission (U.S. Military Academy at West Point Cadets), religion (Oklahoma Baptist College Prophets), or founder (Whittier College Poets). Most schools, though, use symbols of aggression and ferocity (e.g., birds such as hawks, animals such as bulldogs, human categories such as pirates, and even the otherworldly such as devils) (see Fuller and Manning, 1987).

While school names tend to evoke strong emotions of solidarity among followers, there is also a potential dark side. The names chosen by some schools are demeaning or derogatory to some groups. In the past two decades or so, Native American activists have raised serious objections to the use of Indians as school names or mascots because their use typically distorts Native American traditions and reinforces negative stereotypes about them by depicting them as savages, scalpers, and the like. A few colleges (e.g., Stanford and Dartmouth) have taken these objections seriously and deleted Indian names and mascots. Most schools using some form of reference to Indians, however, have chosen to continue that practice despite the objections of Native Americans. In fact, Indian or some derivative is a popular name for athletic teams. Of the 1,251 four-year schools reported by Franks (1982), some 21 used Indian, 13 were Warriors, 7 were Chiefs, 6 were Redmen, 5 were Braves, 2 were Redskins, and individual schools were Nanooks, Chippewas, Hurons, Seminoles, Choctaws, Mohawks, Sioux, Utes, Aztecs, Savages, Tribe, and Raiders. Ironically though, Native Americans is the only racial/ethnic category used by schools where they are not a significant part of the student body or heritage of the school. Yet the members of schools and their constituencies insist on retaining their Native American names because these are part of their collective identities. This allegiance to their school symbol is more important, apparently, than an insensitivity to the negative consequences evoked from the appropriation and depiction of Native Americans.

The purpose of this chapter is to explore another area of potential concern by an oppressed group—women—over the names given their teams. The naming of women's teams raises parallel questions to the issues raised by Native Americans. Are the names given to university and college women's sport teams fair to women in general and women athletes in particular, or do they belittle them, diminish them, and reinforce negative images of women and their secondary status?

THEORETICAL BACKGROUND: LANGUAGE AND GENDER

Gender differentiation in language has been extensively documented and analyzed. An expanding body of literature reveals that language reflects and helps maintain the secondary status of women by defining them and their place (Henley, 1987, p. 3). This is because "every language reflects the prejudices of the society in which it evolved" (Miller and Swift, 1980, p. 3). Language places women and men within a system of differentiation and stratification. Language suggests how women and men are to be evaluated. Language embodies negative and positive value stances and valuations related to how certain groups within society are apprised (Van Den Bergh, 1987, p. 132). Language in general is filled with biases about women and men. Specific linguistic conventions are sexist when they isolate or stereotype some aspect of an individual's nature or the nature of a group of individuals based on their sex.

Many studies have pointed to the varied ways in which language acts in the defining, deprecation, and exclusion of women in areas of the social structure (Thorne, Kramarae, and Henley, 1985, p, 3). Our intent is to add to the literature by showing how the linguistic marking systems adopted by many college and university teams promote male supremacy and female subordination.

Names are symbols of identity as well as being essential for the construction of reality. Objects, events, and feelings must be named in order to make sense of the world. But naming is not a neutral process. Naming is an application of principles already in use, an extension of existing rules (Spender, 1980, p. 163). Patriarchy has shaped words, names, and labels for women and men, their personality traits, expressions of emotion, behaviors, and occupations. Names are badges of femininity and masculinity, hence of inferiority and superiority. Richardson (1981, p. 46) has summarized the subconscious rules governing the name preference in middle-class America:

> Male names tend to be short, hard-hitting, and explosive (e.g., Bret, Lance, Mark, Craig, Bruce, etc.). Even when the given name is multisyllabic (e.g., Benjamin, Joshua, William, Thomas), the nickname tends to imply hardness and energy (e.g., Ben, Josh, Bill, Tom, etc.). Female names, on the other hand, are longer, more melodic, and softer (e.g., Deborah, Caroline, Jessica, Christina) and easily succumb to the diminutive "ie" ending form (e.g., Debbie, Carrie, Jessie, Christie). And although feminization of male names (e.g., Fredricka, Roberta, Alexandra) is not uncommon, the inverse rarely occurs.

While naming is an important manifestation of gender differentiation, little research exists on naming conventions other than those associated with gender and given names. Only one study (Fuller and Manning, 1987) examines the naming practices of college sport teams, but it focuses narrowly on the sexism emanating from the violence commonly attributed to these symbols. Because of their emphasis Fuller and Manning considered only three sexist naming practices. The study presented here builds on the insights of Fuller and Manning by looking at eight sexist naming categories. The goal is to show that the naming traditions of sports teams can unwittingly promote the ideology of male superiority and sexual difference.

Our argument is that the names of many women's and men's athletic teams reinforce a basic element of social structure—that of gender division. Team names reflect this division as well as the asymmetry that is associated with it. Even after women's advances in sport since the implementation of Title IX, widespread naming practices continue to mark female athletes as unusual, aberrant, or invisible.

DATA AND METHODS

The data source on the names and mascots of sports teams at 4-year colleges and universities was Franks (1982). This book provides the required information plus a history of how the names were selected for 1,251 schools. Since our research focused on comparing the names for men's and women's teams, those schools limited to one sex were not considered. Also, schools now defunct were omitted from the present analysis. This was determined by eliminating those schools not listed in the latest edition of *American Universities and Colleges* (American Council of Education, 1987). Thus the number of schools in the present study was 1,185.

The decision on whether a school had sexist names for its teams was based on whether the team names violated the rules of gender neutrality. A review of the literature on language and gender revealed a number of gender-linked practices that diminish and trivialize women (Henley, 1987; Lakoff, 1975; Miller and Swift, 1980; Schulz, 1975; Spender, 1980).

1. Physical markers: One common naming practice emphasizes the physical appearance of women ("belle"). As Miller and Swift (1980, p. 87) argue, this practice is sexist because the "emphasis on the physical characteristics of women is offensive in contexts where men are described in terms of achievement."
2. Girl or gal: The use of "girl" or "gal" stresses the presumed immaturity and irresponsibility of women. "Just as *boy* can be blatantly offensive to minority men, so *girl* can have comparable patronizing and demeaning implications for women" (Miller and Swift, 1980, p. 71).
3. Feminine suffixes: This is a popular form of gender differentiation found in the names of athletic, social, and women's groups. The practice not only marks women but it denotes a feminine derivative by establishing a "female

negative trivial category" (Miller and Swift, 1977, p. 58). The devaluation is accomplished by tagging words with feminine suffixes such as "ette" or "esse."

4. Lady: This label has several meanings that demean women athletes. Often "lady" is used to indicate women in roles thought to be unusual, if not unfortunate (Baron, 1986, p. 114). Lady is used to "evoke a standard of propriety, correct behavior, and elegance" (Miller and Swift, 1977, p. 72), characteristics decidedly unathletic. Similarly, lady carries overtones recalling the age of chivalry. "This makes the term seem polite at first, but we must also remember that these implications are perilous: they suggest that a 'lady' is helpless, and cannot do things for herself" (Lakoff, 1975, p. 25).
5. Male as a false generic: This practice assumes that the masculine in language, word, or name choice is the norm while the feminine is ignored altogether. Miller and Swift (1980, p. 9) define this procedure as, "Terms used of a class or group that are not applicable to all members." The use of "mankind" to encompass both sexes has its parallel among athletic teams where both men's and women's teams are the Rams, Stags, or Steers. Dale Spender (1980, p. 3) has called this treatment of the masculine as the norm as "one of the most pervasive and pernicious rules that has been encoded."
6. Male name with a female modifier: This practice applies the feminine to a name that usually denotes a male. This gives females lower status because it indicates inferior quality (Baron, 1986, p. 112). Examples among sports teams are the Lady Friars, Lady Rams, and Lady Gamecocks. Using such oxymorons "reflects role conflict and contributes to the lack of acceptance of women's sport" (Fuller and Manning, 1987, p. 64).
7. Double gender marking: This occurs when the name for the women's team is a diminutive of the men's team name and adding "belle" or "lady" or other feminine modifier. For example, the men's teams at Mississippi College are known as the Choctaws, while the women's teams are designated as the Lady Chocs. At the University of Kentucky the men's teams are the Wildcats and the women's teams are the Lady Kats. By compounding the feminine, the practice intensifies women's secondary status. Double gender marking occurs "perhaps to underline the inappropriateness or rarity of the feminine noun or to emphasize its negativity" (Baron, 1986, p. 115).
8. Male-female-paired polarity: Women's and men's teams can be assigned names that represent a female/male opposition. When this occurs, the names for the men's teams always are positive in that they embody competitive and other traits associated with sport while the names for women's teams are lighthearted or cute. The essence of sports is competition in which physical skills largely determine outcomes. Successful athletes are believed to embody such traits as courage, bravura, boldness, self-confidence, and aggression. When the names given men's teams imply these traits but the names for women's teams suggest that women are playful and cuddly, then women are trivialized and de-athleticized. Some egregious examples of this practice are:

Fighting Scots/Scotties, Blue Hawks/Blue Chicks, Bears/Teddy Bears, and Wildcats/Wildkittens.

Although these eight categories make meaningful distinctions, they are not mutually exclusive. The problem arises with teams using the term lady. They might be coded under "lady" (Lady Threshers), or "male name with a female modifier" (Lady Rams), or "double gender marking" (Lady Kats). Since team names of all three types could be subsumed under the "lady" category, we opted to separate those with lady that could be included in another category. In other words, the category "lady" includes only those teams that could not be placed in either of the other two categories.

FINDINGS

The extent and type of symbolic derogation of women's teams were examined in several ways. We found, first, that of the 1,185 four-year schools in the sample, 451 (38.1 percent) had sexist names for their athletic teams. Examining only team logos (903 schools, or 76 percent of the sample, provided these data), 45.1 percent were sexist. For those schools with complete information on both names and logos, 493 of the 903 (54.6 percent) were sexist on one or both. We found that many schools have contradictory symbols, perhaps having a gender-neutral name for both male and female teams (Bears, Tigers) but then having a logo for both teams that was clearly having stereotypical and therefore unathletic characteristics. The important finding here is that when team names and logos are considered, more than half of the colleges and universities trivialize women's teams and women athletes.

The data on names were analyzed by the mode of discrimination, using the naming practices elaborated in the previous section (see Table 11-1). This analysis reveals, first, that over half the cases (55.0 percent) fall into the category of using a male name as a false generic. This usage contributes to the invisibility of women's teams. The next popular type of sexism in naming is the use of "lady" (25.3 percent) in Table 11-1, but actually 30.8 percent since some of the teams using lady are classified in what we considered more meaningful categories (see second footnote under Table 11-1). This popular usage clearly de-athleticizes women by implying their fragility, elegance, and propriety. This is also the consequence of the use of the feminine suffix (6.4 percent). Another 5.8 percent of the schools with sexist naming patterns use the male/female paired polarity where male teams have names with clear referents to stereotypically masculine traits while the names for women's teams denote presumed feminine traits that are clearly unathletic. The other important category was the use of a male name with a female modifier (4.7 percent). This naming practice clearly implies that men are more important than women; men are represented by nouns whereas women are represented by adjectives. Few schools use the other linguistic categories (physical markers, girl or gal, and double gender marking).

The next question addressed was whether the institutions that diminished women through team naming were clustered among certain types of schools or in

Table 11-1 Naming Practices That De-Athleticize Women's Teams

Naming Practices	*N*	%	*Examples*
Physical markers	2	0.4	Belles, Rambelles
Girl or Gal[a]	1	0.2	Green Gals
Feminine suffix	29	6.4	Tigerettes, Duchesses
Lady[b]	114	25.3	Lady Jets, Lady Eagles
Male as false generic	248	55.0	Cowboys, Hokies, Tomcats
Male name with female modifier	21	4.7	Lady Rams, Lady Centaurs, Lady Dons
Double gender marking	10	2.2	Choctaws/Lady Chocs, Jaguars/Lady Jags
Male-/Female-paired polarity	26	5.8	Panthers/Pink Panthers, Bears/Teddy Bears
Totals	451	100.0	

[a]Several female teams were designated as Cowgirls but they were not included if the male teams were Cowboys. We assumed this difference to be nonsexist.

[b]Actually 139 of the 451 schools (30.8%) used Lady, but we placed 25 of them in other, more meaningful categories.

a particular geographical region. We thought perhaps that religious schools might be more likely to employ traditional notions about women than public schools or private secular schools (see Table 11-2). The data show that while religious colleges and universities are slightly more likely to have sexist naming practices than public or independent schools, the differences were not statistically significant.

We also controlled for region of the country, assuming that southern schools might be less likely than schools in other regions of the United States to be progressive about gender matters (see Table 11-3). The data show that the differences between schools in the South and the non-South are indeed statistically different, with Southern schools more likely to use sexist names for their athletic teams. Table 11-4 analyzes these data by type of discrimination. Three interesting and statistically significant

Table 11-2 Prevalence of Sexist Team Names by Type of School

	PUBLIC[a]		INDEPENDENT		RELIGIOUS	
Naming Practice	*N*	%	*N*	%	*N*	%
Nonsexist	289	64.7	135	63.4	310	59.0
Sexist	158	35.3	78	36.6	215	41.0
Totals	447	100.0	213	100.0	525	100.0

$\chi^2 = 3.45$, $df = 2$, not significant.

[a]The determination of public, independent, or religious was provided in the description of each school in American Council of Education *(1987).*

Table 11-3 Prevalence of Sexist Team Names by Region

	NON-SOUTH		SOUTH[a]	
Naming Practice	*N*	%	*N*	%
Nonsexist	500	65.4	264	34.6
Sexist	264	34.6	187	44.4
Totals	764	100.0	451	100.0

$\chi^2 = 10.79$, corrected for continuity $df = 1, p < .001$.

[a]Included in the South are schools from Missouri, Arkansas, Virginia, West Virginia, Mississippi, Maryland, Texas, Oklahoma, Louisiana, Alabama, Georgia, Kentucky, Tennessee, North Carolina, South Carolina, Florida, and the District of Columbia.

Table 11-4 Naming Practices That De-Athleticize Women's Teams by Region

	NON-SOUTH		SOUTH		*Level of*
Naming Practices	*N*	%	*N*	%	*Significance*
Physical markers	0	0.0	2	100.0	n.s.
Girl or Gal	0	0.0	1	100.0	n.s.
Feminine suffix	10	34.4	19	65.6	p < .025
Lady	47	41.2	67	58.8	p < .001
Male as false generic	173	70.0	75	30.0	p < .001
Male name with female modifier	14	66.7	7	33.3	n.s.
Double gender marking	5	50.0	5	50.0	n.s.
Male-/Female-paired polarity	15	58.0	11	42.0	n.s.
Totals	264	58.5	187	41.0	

differences are found. Southern schools are much more likely than non-Southern schools to incorporate feminine suffixes and use lady in their naming of female teams. Both of these naming practices emphasize traditional notions of femininity. The other difference in this table is in the opposite direction—non-Southern schools are more likely to use male names as a false generic than are Southern schools. This naming practice ignores women's teams. Southern schools on the other hand, with their disproportionate use of feminine suffixes and lady, call attention to their women's teams but emphasize their femininity rather than their athleticism.

DISCUSSION

This research has shown that approximately three-eighths of American colleges and universities employ sexist names and over half have sexist names and/or logos for their athletic teams. This means that the identity symbols for athletic teams contribute to the maintenance of male dominance within college athletics. As Polk (1974) has noted in an article on the sources of male power, since men have shaped society's institutions they tend to fit the value structure of such institutions. Nowhere is this more apparent than in sport. Since the traditional masculine gender role matches most athletic qualities better than the traditional feminine gender role, the images and symbols are male. Women do not fit in this scheme. They are "others" even when they do participate. Their team names and logos tend to perpetuate and strengthen the image of female inferiority by making them either invisible or trivial or consistently nonathletic.

Institutional sexism is deeply entrenched in college sports. The mere changing of sexist names and logos to nonsexist ones will not alter this structural inequality, but it is nevertheless important. As institutional barriers to women's participation in athletics are removed, negative linguistic and symbolic imagery must be replaced with names and images that reflect the new visions of women and men in their expanding and changing roles.

In the past decade the right of women to rename or relabel themselves and their experiences has become a tool of empowerment. For feminists, changing labels to reflect the collective redefinition of what it means to be female has been one way to gain power. As Van Den Bergh (1987) explains, renaming can create changes for the powerless group as well as promoting change in social organization. Renaming gives women a sense of control of their own identity and raises consciousness within their group and that of those in power. Because language is intimately intertwined with the distribution of power in society, the principle of renaming can be an important way of changing reality.

Since language has a large impact on people's values and their conceptions of women's and men's rightful place in the social order, the pervasive acceptance of gender marking in the names of collegiate athletic teams is not a trivial matter. Athletes, whether women or men, need names that convey their self-confidence, their strength, their worth, and their power.

REFERENCES

American Council of Education. 1987. *American Universities and Colleges,* 14th ed. New York: de Gruyter.

Baron, D. 1986. *Grammar and Gender.* New Haven, CT: Yale University Press.

Bryson, L. 1987. "Sport and the Maintenance of Masculine Hegemony." *Women's Studies International Forum* 10: 349–360.

Durkheim, E. 1947. *The Elementary Forms of Religious Life,* trans. J. W. Sivain. New York: Free Press.

Franks, R. 1982. *What's in a Nickname? Exploring the Jungle of College Athletic Mascots.* Amarillo, TX: Ray Franks.

Fuller, J. R., and E. A. Manning. 1987. "Violence and Sexism in College Mascots and Symbols: A Typology." *Free Inquiry in Creative Sociology* 15: 61–64.

Hall, M. A. 1984. "Feminist Prospects for the Sociology of Sport." *Arena Review* 8: 1–9.

———. 1985. "Knowledge and Gender: Epistemological Questions in the Social Analysis of Sport." *Sociology of Sport Journal,* 25–42.

Henley, N. M. 1987. "This New Species That Seeks a New Language: On Sexism in Language and Language Change." Pp. 3–27 in J. Penfield, ed., *Women and Language in Transition.* Albany: State University of New York Press.

Lakoff, R. 1975. *Language and Woman's Place.* New York: Harper and Row.

Lever, J. 1983. *Soccer Madness.* Chicago: University of Chicago Press.

Miller, C., and Swift, K. 1977. *Words and Women: New Language in New Times.* Garden City, NY: Doubleday/Anchor.

Miller, C., and Swift, K. 1980. *The Handbook of Nonsexist Writing.* New York: Lippincott and Crowell.

Polk, B. B. 1974. "Male Power and the Women's Movement." *Journal of Applied Behavioral Sciences* 10, no. 3: 415–431.

Richardson, L. W. 1981. *The Dynamics of Sex and Gender,* 2nd ed. Boston: Houghton Mifflin.

Schulz, M. 1975. "The Semantic Derogation of Women." Pp. 64–75 in B. Thorne and N. Henley, eds., *Language and Sex: Difference and Dominance.* Rowley, MA: Newbury House.

Spender, D. 1980. *Man-Made Language.* London: Routledge and Kegan Paul.

Thorne, B., C. Kramarae, and N. Henley. 1985. "Language, Gender, and Society: Opening a Second Decade of Research." Pp. 7–24 in B. Thorne and N. Henley, eds., *Language, Gender, and Society.* Rowley, MA: Newbury House.

Van Den Bergh, N. 1987. "Renaming: Vehicle for Empowerment." Pp. 130–136 in J. Penfield, ed., *Women and Language and Transition.* Albany: State University of New York Press.

❋ FOR FURTHER STUDY ❋

Charmaz, Kathy. 2006. "The Power of Names." *Journal of Contemporary Ethnography* 35: 396–399.

Churchill, Ward. 1993. "Crimes against Humanity." *Z Magazine* 6: 43–47.

Davis-Delano, Laurel. 2007. "Eliminating Native American Mascots: Ingredients for Success." *Journal of Sport and Social Issues* 31 (4): 340–373.

Eitzen, D. Stanley. 2009. *Fair and Foul: Beyond the Myths and Paradoxes of Sport.* 4th ed. Lanham, MD: Rowman and Littlefield.

King, C. Richard. 2004. "Reclaiming Indianness: Critical Perspectives on Native American Mascots." *Journal of Sport and Social Issues* 28 (February): entire issue.

King, C. Richard, and C. F. Springwood, eds. 2001. *Team Spirits: The Native American Mascots Controversy.* Lincoln: University of Nebraska Press/Bison Books.

King, C. Richard, Ellen J. Staurowsky, Lawrence Baca, Laurel R. Davis, and Cornel Pewewardy. 2002. "Of Polls and Race Prejudice: *Sports Illustrated*'s Errant 'Indian Wars.'" *Journal of Sport and Social Issues* 26 (November): 381–402.

Pelak, Cynthia Fabrizio. 2008. "The Relationship between Sexist Naming Practices and Athletic Opportunities at Colleges and Universities in the Southern United States." *Sociology of Education* 81 (April): 189–210.

Staurowsky, Ellen J. 2000. "The Cleveland 'Indians': A Case Study in American Indian Cultural Dispossession." *Sociology of Sport Journal* 17 (4): 307–330.

Van Den Bergh, Nan. 1987. "Renaming: Vehicle for Empowerment." Pp. 130–136 in Joyce Penfield, ed., *Women and Language in Transition.* Albany: State University of New York Press.

PART FIVE

Problems of Excess: Overzealous Athletes, Parents, and Coaches

This section examines some forms of deviance in sport. One manifestation of this—positive deviance—is by the athletes. We usually think of deviance as the rejection of commonly accepted norms and expectations for behavior. Positive deviance, however, results from the overacceptance of and overconformity to norms and expectations.[1] Athletes may pursue goals in sports with such zeal that it undermines family relationships and work responsibilities. Athletes may harm themselves as they use drugs to become bigger, faster, and stronger. They may starve themselves to meet weight requirements. They may injure themselves by overtraining.

The first selection, by journalist Joan Ryan, shows how positive deviance by the athletes combined with incredibly demanding coaches and ambitious parents results, sometimes, in damaged bodies and psyches of young female elite gymnasts and ice skaters.

The second presentation in this section is authored by journalist Buzz Bissinger, famous for his book on Texas high school football, *Friday Night Lights.* In this piece, Bissinger focuses on the role of parents in the high pressure—winning is everything—world of organized youth baseball.

The third selection, by journalist Mark Hyman, provides examples of how children can be harmed physically and emotionally by the demands of youth and school sports.

Finally, journalist Bob Hohler examines how students are harmed by inadequate funding for school sports supplied by a school district, in this case the city of Boston.

NOTE

1. Jay J. Coakley, *Sport in Society: Issues and Controversies,* 6th ed. (New York: McGraw-Hill, 1998), chap. 6.

12

Female Gymnasts and Ice Skaters

The Dark Side

Joan Ryan

Unlike women's tennis, a sport in which teenage girls rise to the highest echelon year after year in highly televised championships, gymnastics and figure skating flutter across our screens as ephemerally as butterflies. We know about tennis burnout, about Tracy Austin, Andrea Jaeger, Mary Pierce, and, more recently, about Jennifer Capriati, who turned pro with $5 million in endorsement contracts at age thirteen and ended up four years later in a Florida motel room, blank-eyed and disheveled, sharing drugs with runaways. But we hear precious little about the young female gymnasts and figure skaters who perform magnificent feats of physical strength and agility, and even less about their casualties. How do the extraordinary demands of their training shape these young girls? What price do their bodies and psyches pay?

I set out to answer some of these questions during three months of research for an article that ran in the *San Francisco Examiner,* but when I finished I couldn't close my notebook. I took a year's leave to continue my research, focusing this time on the girls who never made it, not just on the champions.

What I found was a story about legal, even celebrated, child abuse. In the dark troughs along the road to the Olympics lay the bodies of the girls who stumbled on the way, broken by the work, pressure, and humiliation. I found a girl whose father left the family when she quit gymnastics at age thirteen, who scraped her arms and legs with razors to dull her emotional pain, and who needed a two-hour pass from a psychiatric hospital to attend her high school graduation. Girls who broke their necks and backs. One who so desperately sought the perfect, weightless gymnastics body that she starved herself to death. Others-many-who became so obsessive about controlling their weight that they lost control of themselves instead, falling into the potentially fatal cycle of bingeing on food, then purging by vomiting or taking laxatives. One who was sexually abused by her coach and one who was sodomized for four years by the father of a teammate. I found a girl who felt such shame at not making the Olympic team that she slit her wrists. A skater who underwent plastic surgery when a judge said her nose was distracting. A father who handed custody of his daughter over to her coach so she could keep skating. A coach who fed his gymnasts so little that federation officials had to smuggle food into their hotel rooms. A mother who hid her child's chicken pox with makeup so she could compete. Coaches who motivated their athletes by calling them imbeciles, idiots, pigs, cows.

I am not suggesting that gymnastics and figure skating in and of themselves are destructive. On the contrary, both sports are potentially wonderful and enriching, providing an arena of competition in which the average child can develop a sense of mastery, self-esteem, and healthy athleticism. But this chapter isn't about recreational sports or the average child. It's about the elite child athlete and the American obsession with winning that has produced a training environment wherein results are bought at any cost, no matter how devastating. It's about how our cultural fixation on beauty and weight and youth has shaped both sports and driven the athletes into a sphere beyond the quest for physical performance.

The well-known story of Tonya Harding and Nancy Kerrigan did not happen in a vacuum; it symbolizes perfectly the stakes now involved in elite competition—itself a reflection of our national character. We created Tonya and Nancy not only by our hunger for winning but by our criterion for winning, an exaggeration of the code that applies to ambitious young women everywhere: Talent counts, but so do beauty, class, weight, clothes, and politics. The anachronistic lack of ambivalence about femininity in both sports is part of their attraction, hearkening back to a simpler time when girls were girls, when women were girls for that matter: coquettish, malleable, eager to please. In figure skating especially, we want our athletes thin, graceful, deferential, and cover-girl pretty. We want eyeliner, lipstick, and hair ribbons. Makeup artists are fixtures backstage at figure-skating competitions, primping and polishing. In figure skating, costumes can actually affect a score. They are so important that skaters spend $1500 and up on one dress—more than they spend on their skates. Nancy Kerrigan's dresses by designer Vera Wang cost upward of $5000 each.

Indeed, the costumes fueled the national fairy tale of Tonya and Nancy. Nancy wore virginal white. She was the perfect heroine, a good girl with perfect white teeth, a 24-inch waist, and a smile that suggested both pluck and vulnerability. She remained safely within skating's pristine circle of grace and femininity. Tonya, on the other hand, crossed all the lines. She wore bordello red-and-gold. She was the perfect villainess, a bad girl with truck stop manners, a racy past, and chunky thighs. When she became convinced Nancy's grace would always win out over her own explosive strength, Tonya crossed the final line, helping to eliminate Nancy from competition. The media frenzy tapped into our own inner wranglings about the good-girl/bad-girl paradox, about how women should behave, about how they should look and what they should say. The story touched a cultural nerve about women crossing societal boundaries—of power, achievement, violence, taste, appearance—and being ensnared by them. In the end, both skaters were trapped, Tonya by her ambition and Nancy by the good-girl image she created for the ice—an image she couldn't live up to. The public turned on Nancy when foolish comments and graceless interviews made it clear she wasn't Snow White after all.

Both sports embody the contradiction of modern womanhood. Society has allowed women to aspire higher, but to do so a woman must often reject that which makes her female, including motherhood. Similarly, gymnastics and figure skating remove the limits of a girl's body, teaching it to soar beyond what seems possible. Yet they also imprison it, binding it like the tiny Victorian waist or the Chinese woman's foot. The girls aren't allowed passage into adulthood. To survive in the sports, they beat back puberty, desperate to stay small and thin, refusing to let their bodies grow up. In this way the sports pervert the very femininity they hold so dear. The physical skills have become so demanding that only a body shaped like a missile—in other words, a body shaped like a boy's—can excel. Breasts and hips slow the spins, lower the leaps, and disrupt the clean, lean body lines that judges reward. "Women's gymnastics" and "ladies' figure skating" are misnomers today. Once the athletes become women, their elite careers wither.

In the meantime, their childhoods are gone. But they trade more than their childhoods for a shot at glory. They risk serious physical and psychological problems that can linger long after the public has turned its attention to the next phenom in pigtails. The intensive training and pressure heaped on by coaches, parents, and federation officials—the very people who should be protecting the children—often result in eating disorders, weakened bones, stunted growth, debilitating injuries, and damaged psyches. In the last six years two U.S. Olympic hopefuls have died as a result of their participation in elite gymnastics.

Because they excel at such a young age, girls in these sports are unlike other elite athletes. They are world champions before they can drive. They are the Michael Jordans and Joe Montanas of their sports before they learn algebra. Unlike male athletes their age, who are playing quarterback in high school or running track for the local club, these girls are competing on a worldwide stage. If an elite gymnast or figure skater fails, she fails globally. She sees her mistake replayed in slow motion on TV and captured in bold headlines in the newspaper. Adult reporters crowd around, asking what she has to say to a country that had hung its hopes on her thin shoulders. Tiffany Chin was seventeen when she entered the 1985 U.S. Figure Skating Championships as the favorite. She was asked at the time how she would feel if she didn't win. She paused, as if trying not to consider the possibility. "Devastated," she said quietly. "I don't know. I'd probably die."

Chin recalled recently that when she did win, "I didn't feel happiness. I felt relief. Which was disappointing." Three months before the 1988 Olympics, Chin retired when her legs began to break down. Some, however, say she left because she could no longer tolerate the pressure and unrelenting drive of her stern mother. "I feel I'm lucky to have gotten through it," she said of skating. "I don't think many people are that lucky. There's a tremendous strain on people who don't make it. The money, the sacrifices, the time. I know people emotionally damaged by it. I've seen nervous breakdowns, psychological imbalances."

An elite gymnast or figure skater knows she takes more than her own ambitions into a competition. Her parents have invested tens of thousands of dollars in her training, sometimes hundreds of thousands. Her coach's reputation rides on her performance. And she knows she might have only one shot. By the next Olympics she might be too old. By the next year she might be too old. Girls in these sports are under pressure not only to win but to win quickly. They're running against a clock that eventually marks the lives of all women, warning them they'd better hurry up and get married and have children before it's too late. These girls hear the clock early. They're racing against puberty.

Boys, on the other hand, welcome the changes that puberty brings. They reach their athletic peak after puberty when their bodies grow and their muscles strengthen. In recent years Michael Chang and Boris Becker won the French Open and Wimbledon tennis titles, respectively, before age eighteen, but in virtually every male sport the top athletes are men, not boys. Male gymnastics and figure-skating champions are usually in their early to mid-twenties; female champions are usually fourteen to seventeen years old in gymnastics and sixteen to early twenties in figure skating.

In staving off puberty to maintain the "ideal" body shape, girls risk their health in ways their male counterparts never do. They starve themselves, for one, often in response to their coaches' belittling insults about their bodies. Starving shuts down the menstrual cycle—the starving body knows it cannot support a fetus—and thus blocks the onset of puberty. It's a dangerous strategy to save a career. If a girl isn't menstruating, she isn't producing estrogen. Without estrogen, her bones weaken. She risks stunting her growth. She risks premature osteoporosis. She risks fractures in all bones, including her vertebrae, and she risks curvature of the spine. In several studies over the last decade, young female athletes who didn't menstruate were found to have the bone densities of postmenopausal women in their fifties, sixties, and seventies. Most elite gymnasts don't begin to menstruate until they retire. Kathy Johnson, a medalist in the 1984 Olympics, didn't begin until she quit the sport at age twenty-five.

Our national obsession with weight, our glorification of thinness, has gone completely unchecked in gymnastics and figure skating. The cultural forces that have produced extravagantly bony fashion models have taken their toll on gymnasts and skaters already insecure about their bodies. Not surprisingly, eating disorders are common in both sports, and in gymnastics they're rampant. Studies of female college gymnasts show that most practice some kind of disordered eating. In a 1994 University of Utah study of elite gymnasts—those training for the Olympics—59 percent admitted to some form of disordered eating. And in interviewing elites for this book, I found only a handful who had not tried starving, throwing up, or taking laxatives or diuretics to control their weight. Several left the sport because of eating disorders. One died. Eating disorders among male athletes, as in the general male population, are virtually unknown.

"Everyone goes through it, but nobody talks about it, because they're embarrassed," gymnast Kristie Phillips told me. "But I don't put the fault on us. It's the pressures that are put on us to be so skinny. It's mental cruelty. It's not fair that all these pressures are put on us at such a young age and we don't realize it until we get older and we suffer from it."

Phillips took laxatives, thyroid pills, and diuretics to lose weight. She had been the hottest gymnast in the mid-1980s, the heir apparent to 1984 Olympic superstar Mary Lou Retton. But she not only didn't win a medal at the 1988 Summer Games, she didn't even make the U.S. team. She left the sport feeling like a failure. She gained weight, then became bulimic, caught in a cycle of bingeing and vomiting. Distraught, she took scissors to her wrists in a botched attempt to kill herself. "I weighed ninety-eight pounds and I was being called [by her coach] an overstuffed Christmas turkey," Phillips said in our interview. "I was told I was never going to make it in life because I was going to be fat. I mean, in *life.* Things I'll never forget."

Much of the direct blame for the young athletes' problems falls on the coaches and parents. Obviously, no parent wakes up in the morning and plots how to ruin his or her child's life. But the money, the fame, and the promise of great achievement can turn a parent's head. Ambition gets perverted. The boundaries of parents and coaches bloat and mutate, with the parent becoming the ruthless coach and coach becoming the controlling parent. One father put gymnastics equipment in his living room and for every mistake his daughter made at the gym she had to repeat the skill hundreds of times at home. He moved the girl to three gyms around the country, pushing her in the sport she came to loathe. He said he did it because he wanted the best for her.

Coaches push because they are paid to produce great gymnasts. They are relentless about weight because physically round gymnasts and skaters don't win. Coaches are intolerant of injuries because in the race against puberty, time off is death. Their job is not to turn out happy, well-adjusted young women; it is to turn out champions. If they scream, belittle, or ignore, if they prod an injured girl to forget her pain, if they push her to drop out of school, they are only doing what the parents have paid them to do. So sorting out the blame when a girl falls apart is a messy proposition; everyone claims he was just doing his job.

The sports' national governing bodies, for their part, are mostly impotent. They try to do well by the athletes, but they, too, often lose their way in a tangle of ambition and politics. They're like small-town governments: personal, despotic, paternalistic, and absolutely without teeth. The federations do not have the power that the commissioners' offices in professional baseball, football, and basketball do. They cannot revoke a coach's or an athlete's membership for anything less than criminal activity. (Tonya Harding was charged and sentenced by the courts before the United States Figure Skating Association expelled her.) They cannot fine or suspend a coach whose athletes regularly leave the sport on stretchers.

There simply is no safety net protecting these children. Not the parents, the coaches, or the federations.

Child labor laws prohibit a thirteen-year-old from punching a cash register for forty hours a week, but that same child can labor for forty hours or more inside a gym or an ice skating rink without drawing the slightest glance from the government. The U.S. government requires the licensing of plumbers. It demands that even the tiniest coffee shop adhere to a fastidious health code. It scrutinizes the advertising claims on packages of low-fat snack food. But it never asks a coach, who holds the lives of his young pupils in his hands, to pass a minimum safety and skills test. Coaches in this country need no license to train children, even in a high-injury sport like elite gymnastics. The government that forbids a child from buying a pack of cigarettes because of health concerns never checks on the child athlete who trains until her hands bleed or her knees buckle, who stops eating to achieve the perfect body, who takes eight Advils a day and offers herself up for another shot of cortisone to dull the pain, who drinks a bottle of Ex-Lax because her coach is going to weigh her in the morning. The government never takes a look inside the gym or the rink to make sure these children are not being exploited or abused or worked too hard. Even college athletes—virtually all of whom are adults—are restricted by the NCAA to just twenty hours per week of formal training. But no laws, no agencies, put limits on the number of hours a child can train or the methods a coach can use.

Some argue that extraordinary children should be allowed to follow extraordinary paths to realize their potential. They argue that a child's wants are no less important than an adult's and thus she should not be denied her dreams just because she is still a child. If pursuing her dream means training eight hours a day in a gym, withstanding abusive language, and tolerating great pain, and if the child wants to do it and the parents believe it will build character, why not let her? Who are we to tell a child what she can and cannot do with her life?

In fact, we tell children all the time what they can and cannot do with their lives. Restricting children from certain activities is hardly a revolutionary concept. Laws prohibit children from driving before sixteen and drinking before twenty-one. They prohibit children from dropping out of school before fifteen and working full-time before sixteen. In our society we put great value on protecting our children from physical harm and exploitation, and sometimes that means protecting them from their own poor judgment and their parents' poor judgment. No one questions the wisdom of the government in forbidding a child to work full-time, so why is it all right for her to train full-time with no rules to ensure her well-being? Child labor laws should address all labor, even that which is technically nonpaid, though top gymnasts and figure skaters *do* labor for money.

In recent years the federations have begun to pay their top athletes a stipend based on their competition results. The girls can earn bonuses by representing the United States in certain designated events. Skaters who compete in the World Figure Skating Championships and the Olympic Games, for example, receive $15,000. They earn lesser amounts for international competitions such as Skate America. They also earn money from corporate sponsors and exhibitions. The money might not cover much more than their training expenses, which can run $75,000 for a top skater and $20,000 to $30,000 per year for a top gymnast, but it's money—money that is paid specifically for the work the athletes do in the gym and the skating rink.

The real payoff for their hard work, however, waits at the end of the road. That's what the parents and athletes hope anyway. When Mary Lou Retton made millions on Madison Avenue after winning the gold medal at the 1984 Olympics, she changed gymnastics forever. "Kids have agents now before they even make it into their teens," Retton says. Now the dream is no longer just about medals but about Wheaties boxes and appearance fees, about paying off mom and dad's home equity loans, and trading in the Toyota for a Mercedes. It doesn't seem to matter that only six girls every four years reach the Olympics and that winning the gold once they get there is the longest of long shots. Even world champion Shannon Miller didn't win the all-around Olympic gold in 1992.

Figure skating, even more than gymnastics, blinds parents and athletes with the glittering possibilities, and for good reason. Peggy Fleming and Dorothy Hamill are still living off gold medals won decades ago. Nancy Kerrigan landed endorsements with Reebok, Evian, Seiko, and Campbell's soup with only a bronze medal in 1992. With glamorous and feminine stars like Kerrigan and Kristi Yamaguchi to lead the way, the United States Figure Skating Association has seen the influx of corporate sponsorship climb 2000 percent in just five years. Money that used to go to tennis is now being shifted to figure skating and gymnastics as their popularity grows. The payoff in money and fame now looms large enough to be seen from a distance, sparkling like the Emerald City, driving parents and children to extremes to reach its doors.

I'm not suggesting that all elite gymnasts and figure skaters emerge from their sports unhealthy and poorly adjusted. Many prove that they can thrive under intense pressure and physical demands and thus are stronger for the experience. But too many can't. There are no studies that establish what percentage of elite gymnasts and figure skaters are damaged by their sports and in what ways. So the evidence I've gathered for this book is anecdotal, the result of nearly a hundred interviews and more than a decade of covering both sports as a journalist.

The bottom line is clear. There have been enough suicide attempts, enough eating disorders, enough broken bodies, enough regretful parents, and enough bitter young women to warrant a serious reevaluation of what we're doing in this country to produce Olympic champions. Those who work in these sports know this. They know the tragedies all too well. If the federations and coaches truly care about the athletes and not simply about the fame and prestige that come from trotting tough little champions up to the medal stand, they know it is past time to lay the problems on the table, examine them, and figure out a way to keep their sports from damaging so many young lives. But since those charged with protecting young athletes so often fail in their responsibility, it is time the government drops the fantasy that certain sports are merely games and takes a hard look at legislation aimed at protecting elite child athletes.

It is also my hope that by dramatizing the particularly intense subculture of female gymnastics and figure skating, we can better understand something of our own nature as a country bent on adulating, and in some cases sacrificing, girls and young women in a quest to fit them into our pretty little boxes.

13

Bench the Parents

Buzz Bissinger

Like just about every father of good intentions gone wild, I coached a youth baseball team once for kids between the ages of 10 and 12. It was in the mid-'90s, and I was determined to do it the right way: victory with honor, you might say.

I bought a little clipboard to keep track of all the players so everybody played equal amounts. I encouraged and I clapped. I treated strikeouts as home runs, giving my little minions a pat on the rump just like the big boys do, whispering such clever motivational bromides as, "You'll get 'em next time!" I really did want to do it the right way. I really did want to place sportsmanship ahead of winning. I really did want to involve all the kids, even the ones who were perfectly content to sit at the end of the bench and pick their noses and hold the bat as if it were a toxic waste stick. When my son came in to pitch, I promised not to grimace, or show disappointment when he got a case of the yips with the bases loaded and acted as if home plate were located in Canada. I promised not to get into screaming fights with other coaches, some of whom acted as if they were the vituperative worst of Bobby Cox and Tommy Lasorda rolled into one.

Promises. . . . Promises. . . . Promises. . . .

As a coach, I was a minor disaster at times. Sportsmanship? Forget sportsmanship. I wanted to win! Not showing negative emotion when my son walked in what seemed like a billion batters with the bases loaded? Forget that. Not getting into fights with other coaches? Definitely forget that.

Source: Buzz Bissinger, "Bench the Parents," *New York Times* (August 23, 2008).

I stopped coaching after several years. I could see the pathology that was overcoming me, the sickness of winning and having my stomach ache when we didn't win. The sickness of five-minute car rides home with my son that seemed like five hours, as I went through the litany of all the things he had done wrong. The sickness of seeing the frustration and tears in his eyes as he was forced to listen to my addled concept of what I thought it meant to be a coaching parent.

And this was not some high-pressure youth baseball organization we were competing in. It was set in a leafy corner of northwest Philadelphia called Chestnut Hill and was sweetly named The Chestnut Hill Fathers Club. Most coaches did make an effort to act with sanity. But still there was excess. There were moments of surrealism, reaching a peak before the start of the season, when we sometimes drafted players on the basis of the size of their feet (the assumption: the bigger the feet, the bigger a kid might grow and hit down the line for power). Not to mention how we talked about them as if we were conducting the Major League draft—brutally, bluntly, without any of the innocent beauty that should be youth sports in America.

Need some examples of what the landscape is like out there in the country?

Take the under-14 soccer tournament in San Juan Capistrano, Calif., in 2001, where about 30 parents were involved in a post-game melee including one man biting and swinging a metal rod. The apparent cause: an assistant coach for the winning team trying to pick a fight with a player.

Take the 13-year-old who three years ago killed a 15-year-old player with a bat after a Pony League baseball game in Palmdale, Calif., because the 15-year-old had apparently teased and taunted him.

Take the T-ball coach in Dunbar, Penn., who the same year paid one of his own players $25 to hit an autistic teammate in the head with a baseball so he would not have to use him during a game.

Take the fans at a little league game at Concord, N.H., last year, who, upset with the calls made by umpires, threw pizza at them and descended on them to the point where the umps found themselves cornered in a room.

The incidents are legion—parents out of control like blithering idiots, coaches out of control like blithering idiots, young players supposedly being taught sportsmanship watching their blithering idiot parents and blithering idiot coaches and learning the very opposite. It all reflects a culture of youth sports in our country that is berserk.

"The biggest problem that referees have had with bad behavior has been at the youth level," Barry Mano, the president of the National Association of Sports Officials, told me. "It consistently has been a problem."

He added: "You have an intersection of the least skilled players and least skilled parents and the least skilled referees. By and large, things are pretty good, but there is this overarching problem."

How much of a problem? Enough of one that Mr. Mano's organization has helped get legislation passed in 23 states making assault of an official more than a simple misdemeanor charge. "That's a sad commentary," he said.

How much of a problem? In a survey conducted by *Sports Illustrated for Kids,* 74 percent said they had seen out-of-control adults at games and 43 percent said there was too much violence in youth sports. And *SportingKids* magazine, in a survey of more than 3,000 parents, coaches, sports administrators, and players, reported that a whopping 80 percent believed inappropriate behavior was destroying what youth sports are supposedly meant to be.

Which leads to one of the more boneheaded decisions in the recent annals of Sportsworld—the move by officials of Little League International to allow the use of instant replay during this year's Little League World Series.

On paper, at least, the reasons don't sound too terribly ridiculous. Because all the World Series games are televised on ESPN, the technology available for instant replay is already there, Stephen Keener, the president of Little League International, told me. It will be exclusively confined to balls that have left the field of play in the outfield and may have done something unseen to the naked eye of an umpire, such as hit the top of the fence or the foul pole.

The impetus for it stems from a game in the 2005 Little League World Series when a fly ball, instead of being properly ruled a home run because it had hit the left field foul pole and then bounced back onto the field, was incorrectly deemed by the umpire to have ricocheted off the top of the fence. The ruling meant a double instead of a three-run homer that would have put the team from Maitland, Fla., ahead, 3-2. "I had a chance to talk to the umpire and my heart broke for the guy because he felt so badly," said Mr. Keener. "He spent the rest of his time here apologizing to anyone who would listen." Maitland ended up losing the game, 6-2.

But apologies aside, this is still Little League. It is still young kids who should be playing for fun, not do-or-die stakes, and not with bated breath waiting to see if the umpire blew it. And all instant replay will do is create an atmosphere that is already too professional and slick, given the insidious influence of ESPN, not America's leader when it comes to youth sports but America's greatest instigator of dangerous overemphasis.

"I think this makes it too much of a professional sports atmosphere," Dr. E. Lyle Cain, the fellowship director of the American Sports Medicine Institute at the Andrews Sports Medicine and Orthopaedic Center in Birmingham, Ala., told me. "Little league is meant to be fun. Nobody wants a bad call, but to introduce instant replay makes it too much high-stakes."

Dr. Cain doesn't come at this as some idle observer. In July, he co-authored a revelatory study in which an alarming increase was discovered in the number of pitchers 18 and under requiring so-called "Tommy John" surgery, in which a damaged elbow ligament has to be reconstructed often because of throwing overuse. The incidence of the surgery, Dr. Cain found, is as much as 10 times greater than it was a decade ago. And one of the primary reasons for that, in his estimation, is pure and simple: "As a society we are getting away from the fact that sports are meant to be fun for the kids. They are not meant to be competitive for the parents. A lot of kids and parents and coaches are trying to make it into professional sports. [We have] gotten so aggressive with sports that we've lost sight of what it is to some degree."

The age threshold for Tommy John surgery is 15. But younger pitchers are not immune from overuse. Because they are still generally growing, a growth plate can literally pull off the elbow when a pitcher throws too much. The telltale sign is arm soreness. But as orthopedist Damon Petty points out, that issue is moot for coaches intent on winning at all costs. "A coach who has a 12-year-old who can throw 80 miles an hour is going to have ear plugs in his ears even if the kid is sore," Dr. Petty told me.

And Dr. Cain, in a previous study he did of high school athletes who had Tommy John surgery, discovered something even more appalling—previous to the surgery, most had had only two weeks off from throwing a year. "The only time they weren't throwing was between Christmas and New Year's," he said.

Dr. Cain, and other orthopedists, have practical solutions to the problem. Young pitchers, he says, should take at least three months off from throwing each year. Participation in multiple leagues should be limited. Year-round baseball, which is played in some areas of the country, should be curtailed as well. Pitch counts should be strictly enforced; the Little League World Series, to its credit, has done that through a rule change that was enacted last year.

But far too many coaches care about winning far more than they care about the kids trying to do the winning for them. Too many parents in general, with fanciful visions of college scholarships and seven-figure major league salaries dangling in their delusional heads, are maniacal in their silly dreams of glory. Instead of setting examples for their children, they live through them, pathetically feed off them. And I know. Because, to some degree, I used to be one of them.

And that was before instant replay.

14

Harm to Children in Youth Sports

Mark Hyman

Rachel didn't want her real name used for reasons that, as she told me about her nightmare, I understood completely. She grew up in a large family in south Florida; of all her brothers and sisters, she had been the best athlete. She had talent and especially loved softball, which she began playing when she was in the third grade. Her father, a lawyer, took a close interest in her sports life. From the moment she started playing, he was her tutor, coach, and, she explained, tormentor. Softball practices were like boot camp, she told me. Mistakes were not acceptable. When she was nine years old, the penalty for an errant throw was to run around the school where the team worked out. "There were entire practices when all I did was cry," she recalls. The older she got, the more intense her father's behavior became. And scary. As he left the field one day, her brooding father swung a metal bat at a wooden post "with every bit of force in his body." Turning to his daughter, he said, "That's what I feel like doing right now *to you*."

The drumbeat of criticism drained whatever fun was left in the sport for Rachel. When she'd started playing, she had dreamed of becoming a softball player in the Olympics. But before her senior year in high school, she decided to quit the sport. Breaking the news to her father was one of the hardest things she'd ever done. He was furious. For the next five months he shunned her, refusing to speak to her about her decision or anything else. "He told me I was making the biggest mistake of my life. He'd spent all that time and money so I could amount to a professional softball

---

Source: Mark Hyman, *Until It Hurts: America's Obsession with Youth Sports and How It Harms Our Kids.* Boston: Beacon Press, 2009, excerpts pp. 57–58, 97–99, 101–102.

player, at least play in college, and get a free ride to some great school. He meant it was the biggest mistake of *his* life," she says. That was about five years ago. Rachel and her father still aren't close, but an emotional talk initiated by Rachel has begun the healing. She says he was startled to learn how his behavior had left such scars. "He felt terrible. He wanted us to go to group therapy."

* * * *

Kimiko Hirai is open about her past. As a college student and Olympic diver, she suffered from bulimia, a debilitating eating disorder in which sufferers are caught in an endless cycle of binge eating followed by behavior referred to as purging. Typically, they get rid of food by vomiting. Sometimes, bulimics resort to laxatives, enemas, and even fasting.

For almost two years, Hirai lived through hell. She was controlled by thoughts of food, of when to eat and how to purge what she'd eaten. Like other bulimics, wherever she was going, she knew exactly where to buy laxatives and the location of the bathrooms. She plotted strategy about slipping away from friends and coaches so that she could empty her stomach. Fears about gaining weight were all-consuming. In a shopping mall, she chose stairs instead of escalators, thinking, "Maybe I can burn one more calorie." She could not put a stick of gum in her mouth without worrying about the five calories she would be ingesting.

A member of the 2004 U.S. Olympic team, Hirai traces her eating ordeal to her first days as a college athlete at Indiana University. She was at risk, she believes, for the same reasons so many female athletes are. She was driven to succeed in her sport, and she was a self-described pleaser. She craved approval from her teammates and her coaches. Especially her coaches. She recalls a brief exchange with a coach the summer before she began classes at Indiana. She asked the coach what she could do to prepare for the start of diving workouts in the fall. Hirai has no trouble remembering the coach's response: "Don't get fat." Later, after school had begun and Hirai had slipped into a cycle of eating and purging, the coach raised the issue of food again. During a meeting with the entire team, the subject of eating disorders came up, and, Hirai recalls, the coach turned to her. "I still don't know whether it was tongue-in-cheek. But he said, 'You're not doing any of that crap, are you?'" The incident left her feeling shamed and more isolated than ever. "I decided right there I was never going to tell him what I was doing."

For the next eighteen months, she purged almost everything. Her weight plunged from 130 pounds to 100, a precipitous loss. She sought help for her eating disorder only after graduating from Indiana and, she says, pulling away from negative influences there. From a distance of more than a decade, Hirai sees her experience with a clarity that escaped her in her diving days. She accepts responsibility for her bulimia, for what she did to her body, and why. "It's easy to point and blame. I won't do that," she says. Yet the attitudes of coaches "absolutely contributed" to her eating disorders, Hirai told me. "Coaches carry tremendous power, whether they realize it or not, whether they like it or not," she says. "People with eating disorders are people pleasers. When you tell me, 'Don't get fat,' when that's your number one thing, I'm going to do everything I can to make you happy. Not only that, I'm going to lose twenty pounds, and you're going to be more pleased and really like me."

In the high-stakes world of youth sports, the most troubling and least understood injuries may be the ones that are self-inflicted. The list is a compendium of disorders, syndromes, and risky behaviors that target our children, often the most talented and driven. The list is scary: anabolic steroids that build astonishing muscle mass but leave users with damaging lifelong health effects; brain injuries resulting from multiple concussions; and eating disorders that shrink some young athletes and dangerously bulk up others. Why are children literally putting their lives at risk in pursuit of sports glory? Many reasons, of course. Pressure from peers. A child's inborn curiosity, even recklessness. Too often, youth athletes have unwitting accomplices—coaches and parents.

* * * *

For boys, the pressure to shed weight, and to shed it quickly, may be most intense in wrestling. Training often focuses on "dropping down," shorthand for doing whatever is necessary to slip into a lower, more advantageous, weight class. The most ambitious wrestlers can lose ten to fifteen pounds in a matter of days, sticking to a maniacal regimen, which includes restricting food and drink, loading up on laxatives, and sweating it out in saunas. The risk was never more evident than in 1997. In little more than a month, three college wrestlers died while on crash weight-loss programs. Within a few months, the NCAA had issued stringent rules regarding weight loss, banning the use of rubber suits, diuretics for any reason, and saunas for water loss.

The deprivation that typifies the fatal cases is hard to fathom. One of those who died, Jeffrey Reese, a junior at the University of Michigan, had set a goal of losing twenty-two pounds in just four days. To accomplish it, he put himself through pure torture. Reese limited his diet to fruit and water-based foods. All the while, he exercised relentlessly and insanely, riding a stationary bicycle in a sauna while wearing a rubber suit. At the moment Reese's heart stopped, almost unbelievably, the wrestler had been checking his weight on a scale, according to the *Michigan Daily*, the campus newspaper.

The risky mindset isn't limited to college wrestling, where scholarships and campus glory are at stake, or even high school wrestling. Sometimes the young athletes skipping breakfast and lunch are kindergarteners. Yes, five-year olds are "cutting weight," with the encouragement of parents.

Young Bennie was a spunky wrestler from a family steeped in wrestling tradition. His story was documented by two Ohio physicians, Randy Sansone and Robert Sawyer, and published in the *British Journal of Sports Medicine* in 2005. Bennie's father had been modestly successful during his days on the mat, and an older son, fifteen, had followed his dad's footsteps in the sport, even winning recognition on the national level. The father clearly had a deep emotional investment in his sons' wrestling activities and attended every one of their matches.

Bennie was preparing for the season finale, a little-guy wrestling championship on which much was riding for the boy and, apparently, much more for his father. On the day of weigh-ins—when wrestlers step on scales to determine their wrestling classification—the team coach heard the boy chiding teammates about their food intake. As the coach listened, Bennie went on, telling other wrestlers, "I'll bet that I was the only one in the sauna last night. I haven't had anything to eat today, or yesterday."

The astonished coach couldn't believe he was listening to a five-year-old. As he thought about the boy, his father, and the upcoming match, the pieces fit together. The boy had been on the cusp of wrestling in a weight class lower than his usual class, and there were reasons for the highly ambitious father to push his son. Bennie had been victorious in all but one of his matches during the season. If he were able to compete at the lower weight in the final match, he would avoid a rematch against the only tyke who'd beaten him. When the coach contacted the father, he admitted he'd gone too far but explained his reasons: He was helping his son uphold the family's wrestling reputation.

15

Missed Opportunities

Boston's Student-Athletes Face a Sports Program in Distress

Bob Hohler

They feel like the forgotten ones: Football teams training on hazardous turf, soccer teams practicing on fields without goals, track teams running in school hallways for lack of access to training facilities.

They are players who share uniforms because there are too few to go around, players who yearn for more qualified coaches on the sidelines and a few fans in the empty stands, players who never make it to the field because of academic woes and the scourge of deadly street violence.

In a golden age of professional sports in Boston, they are portraits of a bleak reality for student-athletes in the city's public schools.

Consider the baseball players at Burke High School in Dorchester who were forced this spring to practice in an alley strewn with broken glass three days before their season opener because their field—a mile-plus walk from school through one of the city's most dangerous neighborhoods—had yet to be prepared. Outfielder Augusto Ceron spoke for many of his fellow athletes when he said of city leaders, "They treat us like second-class citizens. It's like nobody cares."

City leaders point to a few splendid new fields and facilities and offer promises of better days. But as students like Ceron know all too well, Boston's high school

Source: Bob Hohler, "Missed Opportunities: Boston's Student-Athletes Face a Sports Program in Distress." *Boston Globe* (June 21, 2009).

athletic program languishes in chronic distress. A system that could inspire greater achievement on the field and in the classroom while providing a vital alternative to the hazards of the streets is failing because of inadequacies in funding, facilities, equipment, coaching, oversight, and vision, according to a nine-month review by the *Globe*.

Mayor Thomas M. Menino has trumpeted "the true value of sport" for Boston's youth and frequently appears at neighborhood sports events. But by many measures, the educational system the mayor oversees has severely shortchanged children in the schools who long for a chance to play, to compete, to succeed.

The first measure of failure is financial. City leaders allocated just under $4 million this year for athletics, less than one-half percent of the total budget of $833 million. That's far less than the statewide average of 3 to 4 percent, according to the Massachusetts Interscholastic Athletic Association. The national average is 1 to 3 percent, according to the National Federation of State High School Associations.

Boston dedicates a smaller percentage of its school budget to athletics than neighboring cities such as Cambridge and Somerville and similarly sized urban centers, including San Francisco and Atlanta. Boston's athletic budget has not increased in more than six years.

"The inequality is stark," said Stanley Pollack, executive director of the Boston-based Center for Teen Empowerment. "There is a real dearth of athletic opportunities in the city schools, and it contributes to a persistent achievement gap and much higher dropout rates."

The second measure is opportunity. Only about 3,000 students participate in Boston's struggling sports system, as countless others are effectively deprived of the opportunity to play because the programs are not available to them. While 68 percent of students statewide play interscholastic sports, a mere 28 percent participate in the Boston Public Schools, according to an MIAA survey last year.

SCARCER OPPORTUNITIES

It's not that many Boston students don't want to play. It's because, for a host of reasons, they can't. At Charlestown High School, for instance, girls have the option of playing only five sports all year—volleyball, basketball, softball, and indoor and outdoor track—and they turn out in small numbers to participate. By comparison, girls in neighboring Everett enjoy many more sports options, including field hockey, ice hockey, soccer, tennis, and swimming, and they participate at much higher levels.

In Boston, many sports are delivered in a two-tier system that disenfranchises the 14,000 students who cannot gain entry to the city's three exam schools: Boston Latin, Latin Academy, and O'Bryant School of Mathematics and Science. Only Boston Latin students can compete in sailing and crew. Only students at the two Latin schools can participate in girls' ice hockey and girls' varsity soccer.

And though the city claims to offer every athlete access to interscholastic tennis, golf, and cross-country through co-op programs at exam schools, only one of the 14,000 students outside the exam schools—a female tennis player—opted to participate.

Of the 18,000 public high school students in Boston, none have access to the fast-growing sport of lacrosse. Nor can they compete in field hockey or gymnastics, which are offered in neighboring communities.

The situation is even bleaker at Boston's 22 middle schools. The only interscholastic sports available to those children are basketball and spring track.

Other *Globe* findings underscore the scope of the problem:

- The city employs only one athletic director to oversee 18 high schools that field teams, and he is chronically overwhelmed. The vast majority of other athletic directors in the state oversee a single high school.
- Boston has just one part-time athletic trainer under contract for all of its schools, which results, coaches say, in some players competing with undiagnosed or inadequately treated injuries.
- The city faces a shortage of qualified coaches, even though its coaching stipends rank among the highest in the state. Boston's contract with its teachers union also makes it hard to root out lackluster or incompetent coaches because it renders the athletic director powerless to hire and fire coaches.
- The coaching shortage also deprives some student-athletes of proper instruction and increases their risk of injury. Coed track teams with 50 or more athletes, for instance, are led by a single coach, making it impossible for the coach to monitor players competing in track's multiple disciplines.
- The athletic department's limited equipment budget has stagnated for years, while the cost of necessities such as football helmets has ballooned. Boston, for example, spends $1,700 a year to equip each high school football team, compared with $4,800 in Lincoln-Sudbury.
- Widespread academic ineligibility contributed to low participation levels in many sports. Five teams with too few players for various reasons were shut down during their seasons, and more than 30 other games were forfeited for reasons ranging from ineligible players to transportation snafus.
- With Boston largely considered a wasteland by college recruiters, only two of the city's 3,500 graduating seniors—a distance runner at Charlestown and a boys basketball player at English—received full Division 1 college athletic scholarships, though English catcher Nelfi Zapata was the first Massachusetts high school player selected in this year's Major League Baseball draft, in the 19th round by the New York Mets.
- By comparison, more than 20 students in the smaller Atlanta school district received full athletic scholarships this year.
- Boston is an under-recruited league at every level," said Juan Figueroa, O'Bryant's boys basketball coach. "The perception, unfortunately, is that kids in Boston can't qualify academically."
- Other than the Charlestown boys winning a Division 2 indoor track title, the Boston schools were so overmatched by suburban opponents that 39 of the city's 52 teams that qualified for postseason tournaments failed to win a game. (Boston's baseball and softball teams were outscored in the playoffs, 158-25.)

PLEAS FOR ASSISTANCE

In a city where school spirit, neighborhood pride in athletics, and a sense of personal security among students have plummeted, it's no wonder that most of Boston's best athletes have abandoned the public schools for private and parochial schools, and that others have enrolled in suburban schools through the Metco program, according to many coaches, parents, and advocates.

"I know people want to be optimistic," said Latin football coach John McDonough, "but if you look at the situation and think about whether the glass is half-full or half-empty, I want to say, 'It's half-empty. Fill the damn thing, would you?' "

A city whose high school teams once were envied by suburban rivals now fosters a system that inspires little more than pity.

"My heart goes out to those folks," said Nancy O'Neil, the athletic director at Lincoln-Sudbury High School, which competes against Latin in the Dual County League. "There's no question that across Massachusetts you have the haves and the have-nots, and the Boston schools clearly fall into the category of the have-nots. It's such a tragedy."

Menino said he is committed to improving the city's high school athletic system.

"Can we do better? We sure can," the mayor said. "It's a work in progress. We're making some gains, but the issue is resources. We need to find a way to do more in these difficult financial times."

Boston School Superintendent Carol R. Johnson said she is strongly committed to building an athletic system that provides excellence, access, and equity for every student.

"We're not there yet, but we're working toward that goal," she said. "Because of the challenges we have with our budget, we have not expanded as rapidly as we would like, but we do consider sports part of our effort to reduce the dropout rate, and we understand how important athletics are in helping students learn about teamwork and sportsmanship."

Johnson said she has dedicated a $20,000 donation from Red Sox pitcher Manny Delcarmen, who graduated from West Roxbury High in 2000, to help pay a new administrator to upgrade athletics in middle schools. She said Boston Public Schools athletic director Ken Still is working with Boston University to provide more athletic trainers. The city also has funded six artificial turf fields for Boston schools and built a new gym as part of a $49.5 million project at Burke.

But with a proposed 2.5 percent cut in Boston's school budget, the prospects of upgrading athletics appear grim. Unlike most communities in the state, Boston does not charge students a user fee to play sports. The fee to play football at Hamilton-Wenham, for example, was $969.

Meanwhile, the state of Boston school athletics is such that maintaining the status quo is viewed as unthinkable by numerous coaches, students, and advocates.

"Things are bad enough already," said Dennis Wilson, the boys basketball coach at Madison Park Technical Vocational High School. "We need to get the word to the bigwig politicians that they need to add to the sports budget. We need more equipment, more resources, more opportunities for students to participate."

In Hyde Park, the football team dodges manhole covers on its practice field. In West Roxbury, the football team practices on a field so rutted that players regularly injure ankles. The Brighton team works out on an uneven field so littered with dog feces and goose droppings that players call it "the toilet bowl."

In South Boston, football coach Sean Guthrie turned away nearly 20 players because he lacked enough equipment. A shortage of uniforms forced members of Charlestown's champion track team to swap sweat-soaked jerseys during meets. Guthrie and other coaches scavenged for equipment and reached into their pockets for thousands of dollars to outfit their teams.

Stranded on the sidelines were scores of students who hanker to compete in lacrosse, field hockey, tennis, golf, cross-country, and gymnastics but have little or no chance to pursue them in the Boston schools.

"You need to offer these activities if you want to keep kids engaged in the classroom," said Matt Knapp, who persuaded administrators to let him launch a wrestling program last winter at Burke. "A lot of kids are quitting the Boston schools because the schools offer nothing to them."

ALTERNATIVE TO CRIME

The need for a vibrant high school athletic system has never been greater, according to administrators, coaches, and advocates who said experience has shown that students who participate in sports are more likely to stay out of trouble and achieve better grades.

"When I step on the field, it's the one place where I don't think about all the craziness," said Alex Munoz, a Dorchester High baseball player. For him, the "craziness" is this: a lender threatening to foreclose on his mother's home, a personal dilemma involving his girlfriend, the shooting deaths of several friends, the escalating gang violence in his Roxbury neighborhood.

Many student-athletes in Boston this year were victims of crimes, from assault and armed robbery to murder. Others were perpetrators.

"The way things are going, probation and parole officers are the new guidance counselors," said Guthrie, who teaches math at South Boston's Monument High.

Numerous students said that, but for sports, they might well have succumbed to the lure of the streets. Boston Police Superintendent Paul Joyce, who helped secure wrestling mats for the Burke team and volunteered as an assistant coach for the Charlestown boys basketball team, said high school sports are crucial in the fight against crime, particularly gang violence.

"There's nothing easy about playing sports in the city schools," Joyce said. "There's a lot these kids have to endure, but we've found that sports can help them gain the confidence and self-esteem they need to say no to picking up a gun."

Boston's struggle to sustain competitive athletic programs is also made more difficult by the city's surge of immigrant students who have never been exposed to numerous sports, most notably football and hockey. Coaches in those sports routinely struggle to recruit enough athletes to field teams.

The challenge is particularly acute at Burke, which has a large number of Cape Verdean immigrants; Hyde Park, which enrolls an abundance of newcomers from Haiti; and Madison Park, where English is a second language for 51 percent of the students. Coaches often rely on bilingual players to translate their instructions.

"The nationalities of our players go from A to Z," said Madison Park football coach Roosevelt Robinson. "When I ask everybody who is American to stand up, nobody does."

Shortcomings in the system are less extreme at the exam schools, particularly Latin, which enjoys most of the privileges of its suburban counterparts thanks to generous financial support from alumni. But coaches and students in the non-exam schools consider the disparity between Latin's programs and theirs a form of de facto discrimination.

"The city treats the big three exam schools like real schools," Robinson said. "They get special privileges. It's a shame the rest of the schools aren't treated that way."

Latin's McDonough could do little more than express sympathy.

"I know what some of my peers have to deal with to make ends meet," he said. "It's extremely difficult for them. I wish it could be better. Unfortunately, it's not right now."

* FOR FURTHER STUDY *

Adler, Patricia, and Peter Adler. 1998. *Peer Power: Preadolescent Culture and Identity.*

Anderson, Sally. 2001. "Practicing Children: Consuming and Being Consumed by Sports." *Journal of Sport and Social Issues* 25 (August): 229–250.

Bissinger, Buzz. 2008. "Creep Show." *New York Times,* August 9. Available at http://www.nytimes.com/2008/08/09/opinion/09bissinger.html.

Coakley, Jay. 2006. "The Good Father: Parental Expectations and Youth Sports." *Leisure Studies* 25 (2).

———. 2007. *Sports in Society: Issues and Controversies.* 9th ed. New York: McGraw-Hill.

Eitzen, D. Stanley. 2009. *Fair and Foul: Beyond the Myths and Paradoxes of Sport.* Lanham, MD: Rowman and Littlefield.

Eitzen, D. Stanley, and George H. Sage. 2009. *Sociology of North American Sport.* 8th ed. Boulder, CO: Paradigm.

King, Kelley. 2002. "High School Sports: The Ultimate Jock School." *Sports Illustrated* (November 25): 49–54.

Fejgin, Naomi, and Ronit Hanegby. 2001. "Gender and Cultural Bias in Perceptions of Sexual Harassment in Sport." *International Review for the Sociology of Sport* 36 (December): 459–478.

Sokolove, Michael. 2004. "The Thoroughly Designed American Childhood: Constructing a Teen Phenom." *New York Times Magazine,* section 6 (November 28): 80.

Watts, Jay. 2002. "Perspectives on Sport Specialization." *JOPERD* 73 (October): 33–37, 50.

PART SIX

Problems of Excess: Sport and Deviance

Sport and *deviance* would appear on the surface to be antithetical terms. After all, sports contests are bound by rules, school athletes must meet rigid grade and behavior standards in order to compete, and there is a constant monitoring of athletes' behavior because they are public figures. Moreover, sport is assumed by many to promote those character traits deemed desirable by most in society: fair play, sportsmanship, obedience to authority, hard work, and commitment to excellence.

The selections in this part show, to the contrary, that deviance is not only prevalent in sport but that the structure of sport in American society actually promotes deviance. Players and coaches sometimes cheat to gain an advantage over an opponent. Some players engage in criminal violence on and off the playing field. Some players use performance-enhancing drugs. Some players are sexually promiscuous.

The first selection, by D. Stanley Eitzen, provides an overview of deviance by looking at the dark side of competition in society as well as sport. This is an important consideration because the value Americans place on competition is at the heart of much deviance.

The second selection, by Richard E. Lapchick, counters the implications of the preceding chapter that athletes are prone toward sexual violence. He argues that male athletes are unfairly stereotyped as being more likely than others their age to be violent and, especially, gender violent. He concludes that "the distortions about our athletes and the crimes that a few of them commit need to be put in their real social context. The misleading perceptions need to be corrected so we can focus on the truth and what is really necessary."

16

Ethical Dilemmas in American Sport

The Dark Side of Competition

D. Stanley Eitzen

Although there are a number of prominent American values, I am going to focus on the consequences of the two that I consider the most central—achievement and competition. We Americans glorify individual achievement in competitive situations. A recent book, *The Winner-Take-All Society*, shows how we heap incredible rewards on winners and barely reward others in a number of markets including sport.

The values we promote throughout American society are believed to be good. They motivate. They promote excellence. They make individuals and society productive. They fit with capitalism. And, they make life interesting.

We believe that sports participation for children and youth prepares them for success in a competitive society. According to folk wisdom, these young people will take on a number of desirable character traits from sport. They will learn to persevere, to sacrifice, to work hard, to follow orders, to work together with others, and to be self-disciplined. Assuming that these traits are learned through sport, what else is learned through the sports experience? This is the central question I wish to discuss. I will focus on the dark side of competition, emphasizing ethical dilemmas.

Now I want you to know that while I am going to be critical of sport, much of the time I celebrate sport. I was an athlete in high school and college. I have coached youth sports and several high school sports. My children participated from youth

Source: D. Stanley Eitzen, "Ethical Dilemmas in American Sport: The Dark Side of Competition," *Vital Speeches of the Day* (January 1, 1996): 182–185.

sports through college sport. The last 25 years I have been an active researcher and teacher in the sociology of sport. I am energized by sport. Going to sports events and watching them on television adds zest to my existence. I savor the great moments of sport, when my favorite team and athletes overcome great odds to defeat superior opponents. I am transfixed by the excellence of athletes. I am moved by the genuine camaraderie among teammates. Of course, I suffer when these same athletes make mistakes and fall short of expectations. The key is that I genuinely love sport. I want you to place my critical analysis of sport within the context of my great affection for sport. I love sport, and in criticizing it, I hope to improve it.

Sport has a dark side. It is plagued with problems. Big-time sport has corrupted academe. Coaches sometimes engage in outrageous behaviors, but if they win, they are rewarded handsomely. Gratuitous violence is glorified in the media. Some athletes take drugs. Some athletes are found guilty of gang rape and spouse abuse. Many athletes cheat to achieve a competitive edge. Sports organizations take advantage of athletes. In the view of many, these problems result from bad people. I believe that stems from a morally distorted sports world—a world where winning supersedes all other considerations, where moral values have become confused with the bottom line. And winning-at-any-price has become the prevailing code of conduct in much of sport.

This chapter is divided into three parts: (1) a brief examination of the high value placed on success in sport; (2) the ethical dilemmas in sport that can be traced to this emphasis on success; and (3) the consequences of unethical practices in sport.

SUCCESS: WINNING IS EVERYTHING

My thesis is that American values are responsible for many of the ethical problems found in sport. We glorify winners and forget losers. As Charles Schulz, the creator of the Peanuts comic strip, puts it: "Nobody remembers who came in second." Let me quote a few famous coaches on the importance of winning:

- "Winning isn't everything, it is the only thing." (Vince Lombardi)
- "Defeat is worse than death because you have to live with defeat." (Bill Musselman)
- "In our society, in my profession, there is only one measure of success, and that is winning. Not just any game, not just the big game, but the last one." (John Madden)
- "There are only two things in this league, winning and misery." (Pat Riley)
- "Our expectations are to play for and win the national championship every year … second, third, fourth, and fifth don't do you any good in this business." (Dennis Erickson, when he was head football coach at the University of Miami)

Americans want winners, whether winning is in school or in business or in politics or in sport. In sport, we demand winners. Coaches are fired if they are not successful; teams are booed if they play for ties. The team that does not win the

Super Bowl in a given year is a loser. My team, the Denver Broncos, has made it to the Super Bowl three times and lost that big game each time. In the minds of the Bronco coaches, players, fans, as well as others across the United States, the Broncos were losers in each of those years even though they were second out of twenty-eight teams, which, if you think about it, is not too shabby an accomplishment.

One other example shows how we exalt first place and debase second place. A football team composed of fifth graders was undefeated going into the Florida state championship game. They lost that game in a close contest. At a banquet for these boys following that season, each player was given a plaque on which was inscribed a quote from Vince Lombardi: "There is no room for second place. I have finished second twice at Green Bay and I never want to finish second again. There is a second place bowl game but it is a game for losers played by losers. It is and always has been an American zeal to be first in anything we do and to win and to win and to win."

In other words, the parents and coaches of these boys wanted them to not be satisfied with being second. Second is losing. The only acceptable placement is first.

If second is unacceptable and all the rewards go to the winners, then some will do whatever it takes to be first. It may require using steroids, or trying to injure a competitor, or altering the transcript of a recruit so that he or she can play illegally. These, of course, are unethical practices in sport, the topic of this chapter.

ETHICAL DILEMMAS

This section points to some questionable practices in sport that need to be examined more closely for their ethical meaning and consequences.

The Culture of Certain Sports

The essence of sport is competition. The goal is to win. But to be ethical this quest to win must be done in a spirit of fairness. Fairness tends to prevail in certain sports such as golf and tennis but in other sports the prevalent mood is to achieve an unfair advantage over an opponent. Getting such a competitive edge unfairly is viewed by many in these sports as "strategy" rather than cheating. In these sports some illegal acts are accepted as part of the game. Coaches encourage them or look the other way, as in the case of steroid use. Rule enforcers such as referees and league commissioners rarely discourage them, impose minimal penalties, or ignore them altogether.

The forms of normative cheating are interesting and important to consider because they are more widespread and they clearly violate ethical principles. Nevertheless, they are accepted by many. In basketball, for example, it is common for a player to pretend to be fouled in order to receive an undeserved free throw and give the opponent an undeserved foul. In football players are typically coached to use illegal techniques to hold or trip opponents without detection. The practice is common in baseball for the home team to "doctor" its field to suit its strengths and minimize the strengths of a particular opponent. A fast team can be neutralized, for example, by slowing down the base paths with water or sand.

Home teams have been known to gain an edge by increasing the heat by several degrees from normal in the visitors' dressing room to make the athletes sluggish. At my school the visiting football team's dressing room is painted pink. This upset the coach of Hawaii because the color pink, he argued, reduces strength and makes people less aggressive.

Let's look at sportspersonship in sport, using three examples. First, in a state championship basketball game in Colorado, Agate was playing Stratton. Agate because of a mix-up over keys could not dress in time. The referees called a technical foul, allowing Stratton to begin the game with two free throws. The Stratton coach, however, told his player to miss the shots.

A second example involves a football game between Dartmouth and Cornell a number of years ago, with Dartmouth winning. Later, after reviewing the films, it was established that Dartmouth had received a fifth down on its winning drive. The Dartmouth president forfeited the win.

As a third example, consider the case of a basketball team in Alabama a few years ago that won the state championship—the first ever for the school. A month or so later, the coach found that he had unknowingly used an ineligible player. No one else knew of the problem. Moreover, the player in question was in the game only a minute or two and had not scored. The coach notified the state high school activities association and, as a result, the only state championship in the school's history was forfeited.

Each of these examples has an unusual resolution. They represent acts of true sportspersonship. Usually, we hear of the opposite situations, a team scoring with a fifth down as the University of Colorado did to defeat Missouri in the year Colorado won the national championship but refused to forfeit (not only did this school accept the victory, so, too, did its coach, the very religious Bill McCartney). In 1995, Stanford and Northwestern played to a 41–41 tie. After reviewing the films, the referees admitted that they gave Stanford an undeserved touchdown, yet Stanford did not forfeit. What did the fans of these offending schools say? What did the media outlets say? What did the school administrations say? At my school, Colorado State, the football team upset LSU in 1992. On CSU's winning drive there was a fumble. A LSU player fell on the ball, but in the ensuing pile up, a CSU player ended up with the ball illegally. The player, Geoff Grenier, was quoted in the newspaper that he elbowed and kicked a player in the pile to get the ball. The referees did not see this action and awarded the ball to CSU. CSU's coach, Earle Bruce, said: "One player who should get credit for the victory is Geoff Grenier. If we had lost the ball, the game was over. Geoff found a way to get the ball." The point: the coaches, players, and fans of the "winning" teams accepted these ill-gotten gains as victories. Isn't this strange behavior in an activity that pretends to be built on a foundation of rules and sportspersonship. To the contrary. Such activities involved "normative cheating"—acts to achieve an unfair advantage that are accepted as part of the game. The culture of most sports is to get a competitive advantage over the opponent even if it means taking an unfair advantage. When this occurs, I argue, sport is sending a message—winning is more important than being fair. In this way, sport is a microcosm of society where the bottom line is more important than how you got there. That, my friends, is a consequence of the huge importance we put on success in our society.

Violence

Another area of ethical concern has to do with normative violence in sport. Many popular sports encourage player aggression. These sports demand body checking, blocking, and tackling. But the culture of these sports sometimes goes beyond what is needed. Players are taught to deliver a blow to the opponent, not just to block or tackle him. They are taught to gang tackle, to make the ball carrier "pay the price." The assumption is that physically punishing the other player will increase the probability of the opponent fumbling, losing his concentration, and executing poorly the next time, or having to be replaced by a less talented substitute. Coaches often reward athletes for extra hard hits. In this regard, let me cite several examples from a few years ago:

- At the University of Florida a football player received a "dead roach" decal for his helmet when he hit an opponent so hard that he lay prone with his legs and arms up in the air.
- Similarly, University of Miami football players were awarded a "slobber knocker" decal for their helmets if they hit an opposing player so hard that it knocked the slobber out of his mouth.
- The Denver Broncos coaching staff, similar to other NFL teams yet contrary to league rules, gave monetary awards each week to the players who hit their opponents the hardest.

To show the assumption of unethical violence by opponents in football, in a 1993 playoff game, a player from the Buffalo Bills put a splint on the outside of his good leg so that opponents would concentrate on that leg rather than on his bad leg.

This emphasis on intimidating violence is almost universally held among football and hockey coaches, their players, and their fans. The object is not to just hit, but to hit to punish, and even to injure. The unfortunate result is a much higher injury rate than necessary. Clearly, these behaviors are unethical. John Underwood, a writer for *Sports Illustrated,* has said this about these practices: "Brutality is its own fertilizer. From 'get by with what you can' it is a short hop to the deviations that poison sport.... But it is not just the acts that border on criminal that are intolerable, it is the permissive atmosphere they spring from. The 'lesser' evils that are given tacit approval as 'techniques' of the game, even within the rules."

Player Behavior

Players engage in a number of acts that are unethical but are considered part of their sport. These include: (a) use of intimidation (physical aggression, verbal aggression such as taunting and "trash talking," physical threats, and racial insults); (b) use of drugs to enhance performance (steroids, amphetamines, blood doping); (c) use of illegal equipment (changing a baseball with a "foreign" substance, or roughing one side, a "corked" bat, and a hockey stick curved beyond the legal limits); and (d) use of unethical tactics (e.g., a punter acting as if he had been hit by a defender).

The Behavior of Coaches

Coaches are rewarded handsomely if they win. In addition to generous salary raises, successful college coaches receive lucrative contracts from shoe companies and for other endorsements, media deals, summer camps, speaking engagements, country club memberships, insurance annuities, and the like. With potential income of college coaches approaching $1 million at the highest levels, the temptations are great to offer illegal inducements to prospective athletes or to find illicit ways to keep them eligible (phantom courses, surrogate test takers, altered transcripts). Because winning is so important, some coaches drive their athletes too hard, take them out of the classroom too much, and encourage them to use performance-enhancing drugs. They may also abuse their athletes physically. Verbal assaults by coaches are routine.

Coaches may encourage violence in their players. Vince Lombardi, the famous football coach, once said that "to play this game, you have to have that fire within you, and nothing stokes that fire like hate." Let me cite two examples of how coaches have tried to whip their players into a frenzy that could lead to violence: (1) you'll likely remember that Jackie Sherrill, the coach at Mississippi State, at the end of the last practice before they were to play the Texas Longhorns, had a bull castrated in front of his players. (2) In a less celebrated case, a high school coach in Iowa playing a team called the "Golden Eagles" spray-painted a chicken gold and had his players stomp it to death in the locker room before the contest.

Are these actions by coaches in educational settings appropriate? What lesson is being taught to athletes when their coaches blatantly ask the players to cheat? Consider, for example, the situation when a high school football coach in Portland sent a player into the game on a very foggy night. The player asked: "Who am I going in for?" "No one," the coach replied, "the fog is so thick the ref will never notice you."

Is it all right for coaches to crush the opposition? This is the case in college football this season, as it is imperative to be ranked in the top two at season's end, so your team can play in the Fiesta Bowl for the national championship (and, by the way, each team receives $12 million). But this happens at other levels as well. A Laramie, Wyoming, girls' junior high school basketball team won a game by a score of 81–1, using a full-court press the entire game. Is that OK?

In general it appears coaches condone cheating, whether it be an offensive lineman holding his opponent or a pitcher loading a baseball so that it is more difficult to hit. For example, consider this statement by Sparky Anderson, the former manager of the Detroit Tigers: "I never teach cheating to any of my players but I admire the guys who get away with it. The object of the game is to win and if you can cheat and win, I give you all the credit in the world."

Spectator Behavior

Spectator behavior such as rioting and throwing objects at players and officials is excessive. The question is how are we to evaluate other common but unsportspersonlike practices? Spectators not only tolerate violence, they sometimes encourage it. They do so, when they cheer an opponent's injury, or with bloodlust cheers such as:

> Kill, Kill!
> Hate, Hate,
> Murder, Murder!
> Mutilate!

What about those unethical instances where fans try to distract opponents by yelling racial slurs, or as in the case of Arizona State fans several years ago chanting "P-L-O" to Arizona's Steve Kerr, whose father had been killed by terrorists in Beirut?

Athletic Directors and Other Administrators

The administrators of sport have the overall responsibility to see that the athletic programs abide by the spirit of the rules and that their coaches behave ethically. They must provide safe conditions for play, properly maintained equipment, and appropriate medical attention. Are they showing an adequate concern for their players, for example, when they choose artificial turf over grass, knowing that the rate and severity of injuries are higher with artificial turf?

There are several other areas where athletic directors and administrators may be involved in questionable ethics. They are not ethical when they "drag their feet" in providing equal facilities, equipment, and budgets for women's athletic programs. Clearly, athletic directors are not ethical when they schedule teams that are an obvious mismatch. The especially strong often schedule the especially weak to enhance their record and maintain a high ranking while the weak are enticed to schedule the strong for a good pay day, a practice, 1 suggest, that is akin to prostitution.

Finally, college administrators are not ethical when they make decisions regarding the hiring and firing of coaches strictly on the won-lost record. For the most part school administrators do not fire coaches guilty of shady transgressions if they win. As John Underwood has characterized it, "We've told them it doesn't matter how clean they keep their program. It doesn't matter what percentage of their athletes graduate or take a useful place in society. It doesn't even matter how well the coaches teach the sport. All that matters are the flashing scoreboard lights."

The Behavior of Parents

Parents may push their children too far, too fast. Is it appropriate to involve children as young as five in triathlons, marathons, and tackle football? Should one-year-olds be trying to set records as was the case in 1972 when the national record for the mile run for a one-year-old was set by Steve Parsons of Normal, Illinois, at 24:16.6 (one day short of his second birthday). Is such a practice appropriate or is it a form of child abuse? Is it all right to send ten-year-old children away from home to work out eight hours a day with a gymnastics coach in Houston, a swimming coach in Mission Viejo, California, or a tennis coach in Florida?

Parents may encourage their child to use drugs (diuretics for weight control, drugs to retard puberty, growth hormones, or steroids).

Parents sometimes are too critical of their children's play, other players, coaches, and referees. Some parents are never satisfied. They may have unrealistic expectations for their children and in doing so may rob them of their childhood and their self-esteem.

The Behaviors of Team Doctors and Trainers

There are essentially two ethical issues facing those involved in sports medicine, especially those employed by schools or professional teams. Most fundamentally these team doctors and trainers often face a dilemma resulting from their ultimate allegiance—is it to their employer or to the injured athlete? The employer wants athletes on the field not in the training room. Thus, the ethical question—should pain-killing drugs be administered to an injured player so that he or she can return to action sooner than is prudent for the long-term health of the athlete?

A second ethical issue for those in sports medicine is whether they should dispense performance-enhancing drugs and the related issue of whether or not they should help drug-using athletes pass a drug test.

Organizational Behavior

Immorality is not just a matter of rule breaking or bending the rules—the rules themselves may be immoral. Powerful organizations such as universities, leagues, Little League baseball, and the U.S. Olympic Committee have had sexist rules and they exploit athletes. The rules of the NCAA are consistently unfair to college athletes. For example, the NCAA rules require that athletes commit to a four-year agreement with a school, yet schools only have to abide by a year by year commitment to the athlete. Moreover, the compensation of athletes is severely limited while the schools and the NCAA make millions.

This listing of areas of ethical concern for various aspects of sport is not meant to be exhaustive but rather to highlight the many ethical dimensions present in the sports world. I now turn to the consequences of unethical practices.

THE ETHICAL CONSEQUENCES OF UNETHICAL PRACTICES IN SPORT

A widely held assumption of parents, educators, banquet speakers, and editorial writers is that sport is a primary vehicle by which youth are socialized to adopt the values and morals of society. The ultimate irony is, however, that sport as it is presently conducted in youth leagues, schools, and at the professional level does not enhance positive character traits. As philosopher Charles Banham has said, many do benefit from the sports experience but for many others sport "encourages selfishness, envy, conceit, hostility, and bad temper. Far from ventilating the mind, it stifles it. Good sportsmanship may be a product of sport, but so is bad sportsmanship."

The "winning-at-all-costs" philosophy pervades sport at every level and this leads to cheating by coaches and athletes. It leads to the dehumanization of athletes and to their alienation from themselves and from their competitors. Under these conditions, it is not surprising that research reveals consistently that sport stifles moral reasoning and moral development. For example, from 1987 to the present physical educators Sharon Stoll and Jennifer Beller have studied over 10,000 athletes from the ninth grade through college. Among their findings:

1. Athletes score lower than their non-athlete peers on moral development.
2. Male athletes score lower than female athletes in moral development.
3. Moral reasoning scores for athletic populations steadily decline from the ninth grade through university age, whereas scores for non-athletes tend to increase.

This last point is very significant: the longer an individual participates in sport, the less able they are to reason morally. Stoll and Beller say: "While sport does build character if defined as loyalty, dedication, sacrifice, and teamwork, it does not build moral character in the sense of honesty, responsibility, and justice." Thus, I believe the unethical practices so common in sport have negative consequences for the participants. Gresham's law would seem to apply to sport—bad morality tends to defeat good morality; unfairness tends to encourage unfairness. Sociologist Melvin Tumin's principle of "least significant morality" also makes this point: "In any social group, the moral behavior of the group as an average will tend to sink to that of the least moral participant, and the least moral participant will, in that sense, control the group unless he is otherwise restrained and/or expelled.... Bad money may not always drive out good money, though it almost always does. But 'bad' conduct surely drives out 'good' conduct with predictable vigor and speed."

The irony, as sport psychologists Brenda Jo Bredemeir and David Shields have pointed out, is that often "to be good in sports, you have to be bad." You must, as we have seen, take unfair advantage and be overly aggressive if you want to win. The implications of this are significant. Moral development theorists agree that the fundamental structure of moral reasoning remains relatively stable from situation to situation. Thus, when coaches and athletes in their zeal to succeed corrupt the ideals of sportspersonship and fair play, they are likely to employ or condone similar tactics outside sport. They might accept the necessity of dirty tricks in politics, the manipulation of foreign governments for our benefit, and business practices that include using misleading advertising and selling shoddy and/or harmful products. The ultimate goal in politics, business, and sport, after all, is to win. And winning may require moving outside the established rules. Unfortunately, this lesson is learned all too often in sport.

Sport has the potential to ennoble its participants and society. Athletes strain, strive, and sacrifice to excel. But if sport is to exalt the human spirit, it must be practiced within a context guided by fairness and humane considerations. Competition is great but it can go too far. Personally, I know that my competitive drive has gone too far when:

1. The activity is no longer enjoyable—i.e., there is too much emphasis on the outcome and not enough on the process.
2. I treat my opponents with disrespect.
3. I am tempted to gain an unfair advantage.
4. I cannot accept being less than the best even when I have done my best.

I believe that many times those intimately involved in sport have stepped over these lines. When they make those choices, when the goal of winning supersedes other goals, they and sport are diminished. Sport, then, rather than achieving its ennobling potential has the contrary effect. Rather than making the best of our American emphasis on success and competition, unethical sport perverts these values.

It is time we who care about sport recognize the dangers in what sport has become and strive to change it. Above all, we must realize, to win by going outside the rules and the spirit of the rules is not really to win at all.

17

Crime and Athletes

New Racial Stereotypes

Richard E. Lapchick

It is ironic that as we begin a new millennium, hopeful that change will end the ills such as racism that have plagued our society throughout past centuries, more subtle forms of racism in sport may be infecting American culture.

Polite white society can no longer safely express the stereotypes that so many believe about African Americans. Nonetheless, surveys show that the majority of whites still believe that most African Americans are less intelligent, are more likely to use drugs and be violent, and are more inclined to be violent against women.

However, sport as it is currently being interpreted, now provides whites with the chance to talk about athletes in a way that reinforces those stereotypes about African Americans. With African Americans dominating the sports we watch most often (77 percent of the players in the National Basketball Association, 65 percent in the National Football League, 15 percent in Major League Baseball—another 25 percent are Latino). African Americans comprise 57 percent of the students playing National Collegiate Athletic Association (NCAA) Division I basketball and 47 percent of those playing NCAA Division IA football. Whites tend to "think black" when they think about the major sports.

Many athletes and community leaders believe that the public has been unfairly stereotyping athletes all across America. The latest, and perhaps most dangerous,

Source: Richard E. Lapchick, "Crime and Athletes: New Racial Stereotypes," *Society* 37 (March–April 2000): 14–20.

stereotype, is that playing sport makes athletes more prone to being violent and, especially, gender violent.

Rosalyn Dunlap, an eight-time All-American sprinter who now works on social issues involving athletes, including gender violence prevention, said, "perpetrators are not limited to any category or occupation. The difference is that athletes who rape or batter will end up on TV or in the newspapers. Such images of athletes in trouble create a false and dangerous mindset with heavy racial overtones. Most other perpetrators will be known only to the victims, their families, the police and the courts."

On our predominantly white college campuses, student athletes are being characterized by overwhelmingly white student bodies and faculties while they are being written about by a mostly white male media for a preponderance of white fans.

At an elite academic institution, I asked members of the audience to write down five words they would use to describe American athletes. In addition to listing positive adjectives, not one missed including one of the following words: dumb, violent, rapist, or drug user!

In the past two years, I have met with NBA and NFL players as well as college-student athletes on more than a dozen campuses. There are a lot of angry athletes who are convinced the public is characterizing them because of the criminal acts of a few.

Tom "Satch" Sanders helped the Boston Celtics win eight world championships. Sanders noted, "If they aren't angry about their broad brush depiction, they should be. The spotlight is extremely bright on athletes; their skills have made them both famous and vulnerable. Their prominence means they will take much more heat from the media and the public for similar situations that befall other people with normal lives."

He is now vice president for player programs for the NBA. That office helps guide players off the court to finish their education, prepares them for careers after basketball, and helps those that may have problems adjusting to all the attention that goes to NBA stars.

Many American men have grown to dislike athletes. Given the choice, a typical man might want the money and the fame but knows it is unattainable for him. After reading all the negative stories about athletes, he doesn't want to read about Mike Tyson complaining about being treated unfairly when Tyson has made a reported $100 million in his post-release rehabilitation program; or about the large number of professional athletes signing contracts worth more than $10 million a year.

The anger of some white men extends to people who look or act differently than themselves. They are a mini-thought away from making egregious stereotypes about the "other groups" they perceive as stealing their part of the American pie.

Big-time athletes fit the "other groups." Whether it is an African American athlete or coach, or a white coach of African American athletes, when something goes wrong with a player, the national consequences are likely to be immediate.

Sanders expanded on this. "Everyone feels that athletes have to take the good with the bad, the glory with the negative publicity. However, no one appreciates the broad brush application that is applied in so many instances. Of the few thousand that play sport on the highest level, if four or five individuals in each sport—particularly if they are black—have problems with the law, people won't have long to wait before some media people are talking about all those athletes."

Here is the equation we are dealing with as stereotypes of our athletes are built. Fans, who are mostly white, observe sport through a media filter which is overwhelmingly made up of white men. There are 1,600 daily newspapers in America. There are only four African American sports editors in a city where there are professional franchises and 19 African American columnists. Both numbers, as reported at the recent conference of the National Association of Black Journalists, have almost doubled since 1998 and represent a positive sign. Nonetheless, there are no African American sports writers on 90 percent of the 1,600 papers!

I do not, nor would I ever, suggest that most or even many of the white writers are racist. However, they were raised in a culture in which many white people have strong beliefs about what it means to be African American.

The obvious result is the *reinforcement* of white stereotypes of athletes, who are mostly African American in our major sports.

According to the National Opinion Research Center Survey, sponsored by the National Science Foundation for the University of Chicago, whites share the following attitudes:

- 56 percent of whites think African Americans are more violent;
- 62 percent think African Americans are not as hard working as whites;
- 77 percent of whites think most African Americans live off welfare;
- 53 percent think African Americans are less intelligent.

It can be expected that some white writers learned these stereotypes in their own upbringing. When they read about an individual or several athletes who have a problem, it becomes easy to leap to the conclusion that fits the stereotype. Sanders said, "Blacks in general have been stereotyped for having drugs in the community as well as for being more prone to violence. However, now more than ever before, young black athletes are more individualistic and they resist the 'broad brush.' They insist on being judged as individuals for everything." But even that resistance can be misinterpreted by the public and writers as merely being off-the-court trash-talking.

SPORTS' SPECIFIC PROBLEMS

There are, of course, problems in college and professional sports. For the purposes of this chapter, I will only deal with those that involve problems and perceptions of athletes.

Our athletes are coming from a generation of despairing youth cut adrift from the American dream. When the Center for the Study of Sport in Society started in 1984, one of its primary missions was helping youth balance academics and athletics. Now, the issue for youth is balancing life and death.

We are recruiting athletes:

- who have increasingly witnessed violent death. If one American child under the age of 16 is killed every two hours with a handgun, then there is a good chance that our athletes will have a fallen family member or friend. More American children have died from handguns in the last ten years than all the American soldiers who died in Vietnam. Tragedies in places like Paducah, Kentucky, and Littleton, Colorado, have shown us that violent deaths are not limited to our cities.
- who are mothers and fathers when they get to our schools. There are boys who helped 900,000 teenage girls get pregnant each year so we are increasingly getting student-athletes who will leave our colleges after four years with one or more children who are 4–5 years old.
- who have seen friends or family members devastated by drugs.
- who have seen battering in their home.
- who were victims of racism in school. Three-quarters (75 percent) of all students surveyed by Lou Harris reported seeing or hearing about racially or religiously motivated confrontations with overtones of violence very or somewhat often.
- who come home alone: 57 percent of all American families, black and white alike, are headed by either a single parent or two working parents.

We desperately need professionals on our campuses who can deal with these nightmarish factors. The reality is that few campuses or athletic departments have the right people to help guide these young men and women into the 21st century. So what are our problems?

ACADEMIC ISSUES IN COLLEGE SPORT

Academically, we get athletes who have literacy problems. The press discusses that student-athletes have literacy problems extensively throughout the year as if it were a problem unique to athletes. However, it is rarely reported—and never in the sports pages—that 30 percent of *all entering freshmen* must take remedial English or math.

Academically, we get athletes who will not graduate. It is—and always should be—an issue for college athletics to increase the percentages of those who graduate from our colleges. However, the demographics of college have now changed to the point where only 14 percent of entering freshmen graduate in four years. If an athlete does not graduate in four years, some call him dumb; others say the school failed him. Few note that he may be typical of college students.

Don McPherson nearly led Syracuse to a national championship when he was their quarterback in the 1980s. After seven years in the NFL and CFL, McPherson worked until recently directing the Mentors in Violence Prevention (MVP) Program.

MVP is the nation's biggest program using athletes as leaders to address the issue of men's violence against women.

McPherson reflected on the image of intelligence and athletes. "When whites meet an uneducated black athlete who blew opportunities in college or high school, they think he is dumb. They don't question what kind of school he may have had to attend if he was poor, or how time pressures from sport may have affected him. If they don't make it as a professional athlete, they're through without a miracle.

"I met lots of 'Trust Fund Babies' at Syracuse. They blew opportunities. No one called them dumb, just rich. We knew they would not need a miracle to get a second chance.

"I played at Syracuse at a time when being a black quarterback had become more acceptable. But the stereotypes still remained. As a player, people still remember me as a great runner and scrambler. I had not dented their image of the physical vs. intelligent black athlete."

This was in spite of the fact that McPherson led the nation in passing efficiency over Troy Aikman and won the Maxwell Award. He won many awards but Don McPherson was most proud of being the nation's passing efficiency leader. "I should have shattered the image of the athletic and mobile black quarterback and replaced it with the intelligent black quarterback. Unfortunately, stereotypes of football players, mostly black, still prevail. They make me as angry as all the stereotypes of black people in general when I was growing up."

McPherson wore a suit to class and carried the *New York Times* under his arm. He was trying to break other images of African American men and athletes. But McPherson said that those whites who recognized his style were both "surprised and said I was 'a good black man' as if I was different from other black men. Most students assumed I was poor and that football was going to make me rich. Like many other blacks on campus, I was middle class. My father was a detective and my mother was a nurse."

There is a common belief that student-athletes, especially those in the revenue sports, have lower graduation rates than students who are not athletes. The facts do not bear this out. Yet it is difficult to get accurate reporting.

- Irrespective of color or gender, student-athletes graduate at higher rate than non-student-athletes.
- White male Division I student-athletes graduate at a rate of 58 percent vs. 57 percent for white male nonathletes. African American male Division I student-athletes graduate at a rate of 42 percent vs. 34 percent for African American male nonathletes.
- White female Division I student-athletes graduate at a rate of 70 percent while 61 percent of white female nonathletes graduate. African American female Division I student-athletes graduate at a rate of 58 versus only 43 percent of the African American female nonathletes.

The disparities, however, remain when we compare white to African American student athletes:

- White male Division I basketball student-athletes graduate at a rate of 52 percent versus a 38 percent graduation rate for African American male Division I basketball student-athletes, still higher than the 34 percent grad rate for African American male nonathletes.
- White female Division I basketball student athletes graduate at a rate of 71 percent while only 57 percent of African American female Division I basketball student-athletes graduate.

College sport does not own these problems. They belong to higher education in general and its inheritance of the near bankruptcy of secondary education in some communities. The publication of graduation rates, long feared by athletic administrators, at once revealed those scandalous rates, but also showed what poor graduation rates there were for all students of color. It turned out that our predominantly white campuses were unwelcoming environments for all people of color.

African American student-athletes arrive on most campuses and see that only seven percent of the student body, three percent of the faculty, and less than five percent of top athletics administrators and coaches look like them. Unless there is a Martin Luther King Center or Boulevard, all of the buildings and streets are named after white people.

In many ways, the publication of graduation rates for student-athletes helped to push the issue of diversity to the forefront of campus-wide discussions of issues of race, ethnicity, and gender. Educators finally recognized what a poor job they were doing at graduating all students of color.

DRUGS AND ALCOHOL IN SPORT

We will get athletes who use drugs. CNN Headline News will understandably run footage of every name athlete who is arrested with drugs. It has become a common belief that athletes have a particular problem with drug and alcohol abuse. Reoccurring problems of athletes like Darryl Strawberry reinforce this image but facts do not bear this out.

According to an extensive *Los Angeles Times* survey of athletes and crime committed in 1995, a total of 22 athletes and three coaches were accused of a drug related crime in 1995. That means that, on average, we read about a new sports figure with a drug problem every two weeks! Anecdotally, those numbers have seemed to continue in succeeding years. Each new story reinforces the image from the last one.

Their stories are and surely should be disturbing. But those stories are rarely, if ever, put in the context of the 1.9 million Americans who use cocaine each month or the 2.1 million who use heroin throughout their lives. A total of 13 million people (or a staggering 6 percent of the American population) use some illicit drug each month. When you look at the 18–25 male age group in general, the percentage leaps to 17 percent. Twenty-two athletes represent a small fraction of a single percent of the more than 400,000 who play college and professional sports in America.

The NBA's drug policy with the potential of a lifetime ban is generally recognized as a model for sports. The policy may have stopped a substance abuse problem that existed before its inception.

Now players recognize that using so-called "recreational" drugs can seriously hurt their professional abilities in one of America's most competitive professions. Don McPherson emphasized the point that "our personal and professional lives have to be clean and sharp. We cannot afford to lose the competitive edge or our careers will be cut short. There are too many talented young men waiting to step in our shoes."

The NBA's Sanders insists that African American athletes are still being stereotyped as drug users because "blacks in general have been stereotyped for having drugs in the community.... I know they [athletes] are hurt by the broad brush" used by the public when it come to African American athletes.

In the same *Los Angeles Times* survey, 28 athletes and 4 coaches had charges related to alcohol. None of these 32 cases were put in the context of the 13 million Americans who engage in binge drinking at least 5 times per month. Yet we read about a new athlete with an alcohol problem every 11 days. Such images can surely create a building sense of problems in athletics if they are not viewed in the context of society.

McPherson remembered being "shocked" when he arrived on Syracuse's campus to see how much drinking went on each night among students in general. He felt compelled to call football players he knew on other campuses. "It was the same everywhere. Now when I go to speak on college campuses I always ask. It is worse today. Athletes are also part of that culture, but insist that practice and academics crowd their schedules too much to be in bars as often as other students."

ATHLETES AND VIOLENCE

We are getting athletes who have fights during games, in bars, and on campus. Is there a link between the violence of a sport and one's actions away from that sport? There is certainly a growing body of public opinion that assumes that there is. Media reports regularly imply that the violence of sport makes its participants more violent in society.

Are sports any more violent today than 20 years ago when no one would have made such an assertion? Or is it the fact that our streets and our schools surely are more violent. According to the National Education Association, there are 2,000 assaults *in our schools every hour of every day!* It is an ugly phenomenon that is neither bound by race, class, geography, nor by athlete vs. nonathlete.

We do have athletes who are the perpetrators in cases of gender violence. In the wake of the O.J. Simpson case, any incident involving an athlete assaulting a woman has received extraordinary publicity. The individual cases add up to the mindset stereotype of 1999: athletes, especially basketball and football players, are more inclined to be violent towards women than nonathletes.

Joyce Williams-Mitchell is the executive director of the Massachusetts Coalition of Battered Women's Service Groups. As an African American woman, she abhors the imagery of athletes being more prone to be violent against women. "It is a myth. The facts do not bear this out. All the studies of patterns of batterers; defined by occupation point to men who control women through their profession. We hear about police, clergy, dentists, and judges. I only hear about athletes as batterers when I read the paper. They are in the public's eye. Men from every profession have the potential to [be] batterers."

There have been, of course, too many cases of athletes committing assaults on girls and women.

However, there has never been a thorough, scientific study conclusively showing that athletes are more inclined than others to commit assaults. The only study that comes close was written by Jeffrey Benedict, Todd Crossett, and Mark McDonald. It was based on 65 cases of assault against women over three years on 10 Division I campuses. Thirteen of the cases involved athletes; seven were basketball or football players.

In spite of the authors pointing out the limitations of both the small numbers and the fact that they did not control for use of alcohol, tobacco, and the man's attitude toward women (the three main predictors of a male's inclination to gender violence), the press regularly quotes their study without qualification. Media reports never state that it is a study that came up with 13 athletes over three years. They simply say that the study concluded that nearly 20 percent of all campus assaults are committed by student-athletes and most are committed by basketball or football players. Rosalyn Dunlap underlines that "This is a racially loaded conclusion. When I was a student-athlete at the University of Missouri, I never thought of keeping myself safe from a 260-pound football player anymore than any other man on the street. In fact, male athletes on campus protected me."

Here is some critical data usually missing in the debate about athletes and violence against women.

- In 1994, 1,400 men killed their significant others. O.J. Simpson was the only athlete accused of murder.
- In 1998, an estimated three million women were battered and close to one million were raped. According to various reports in the press over the past five years, between 70 and 100 athletes and coaches have been accused of assault against a woman each year.
- In data released in 1999 in *The Chronicle of Higher Education*'s annual campus crime survey, there were 1,053 forcible sex offenses in 1997. Less than 35 student-athletes were arrested.

Gender violence is a serious problem of men in America. The cost of crime to America is pegged at $500 billion per year according to a National Institute for Justice research report for the Justice Department released in March 1996. Gender assault and child abuse account for $165 billion—more than one-third of that total! Men who beat their significant others are statistically also likely to beat their children.

Dunlap, who works with McPherson to create more awareness about the issue, said, "There are no men who should be exempted from being educated about the issue of gender violence although many believe they are. It is a problem for naval commanders, day care providers, fraternities, guys at a bar, in corporations, in halls of higher education and, yes, on athletic teams. But no more so on athletic teams."

There have been numerous cases in corporations in which women brought suits against the corporation for harassment and/or assault. The *Boston Globe* gave extensive coverage to the case in which there were 16 formal legal complaints for incidents from sexual harassment to rape at Astra USA, Inc., a chemical company. Mitsubishi had a suit against it placed by 29 women for the same reasons. No stories about Astra suggested that working in a chemical company produced this climate. At Mitsubishi, no one suggested that any relationship to the manufacturing process is a link to gender assault. So why do stories about athletes imply such a linkage to athletics? Does it fit white America's racial imagery?

McPherson believes it does.

> Football and basketball mean black. When the public talks about gender violence and athletes, it talks black. No one discusses the problems of golfer John Dailey or Braves manager Bobby Cox. Warren Moon was another story altogether.
>
> Problems about athletes hit the papers and people think they detect a pattern because of the seeming frequency. But no one else's problems get in the papers. How do we make legitimate comparisons?
>
> With Astra and Mitsubishi, we look at the corporate climate and don't generalize about individuals. But with athletes, especially black athletes, we look at players and look for patterns to add up.

Some observers say athletes are trained to be violent and we can expect that to carry over into our homes. If this is true about training, then what about the training we give to police, the Army, Air Force, Navy, and Marines to use lethal force. Will they come home and kill? McPherson adds, "There is no logic to connect these cases but we do fit our stereotypes of African Americans with such images when we carry through the implication for athletes."

With all the recent publicity about the horrors of gender violence, it would be easy to forget that it was America's big, dirty secret until the notoriety surrounding the O.J. Simpson case. Few were willing to talk about gender violence. But we can never change if we do not confront this disease that is devouring our communities. The same unwillingness to confront racism diminishes society's ability to eradicate it.

Neither were being realistically discussed on college campuses nor in corporate board rooms. We are paying a horrible human price as we realize that society rarely told men that their dominating and controlling actions against women have helped create a climate in which there is a seemingly uncontrollable tidal wave of men's brutality against women.

Athletes should take a leadership role on this, just as they have on drug abuse and educational opportunities. In 1990, Louis Harris completed a landmark study which showed that our children desire to participate in changing their society and viewed athletes as their first choice in terms of who they wanted to give them socially relevant messages.

The MVP Program, organized in 1992 by Northeastern University's Center for the Study of Sport in Society, has been on more than 55 campuses over the last seven years training male athletes to be spokespeople on the issue of gender violence. Each of those schools has become proactive on an issue that has hurt so many women and their families. Don McPherson worked full-time for MVP for several years.

Our society is unraveling at a breakneck pace and McPherson insists "we have to do more to help our youth survive by including our athletes rather than excluding them in helping our youth. The stereotyping of our athletes does not help. We need to be ready with facts to dispute the easy labels."

McPherson and Sanders both argue vigorously that America's athletes not only don't fit the emerging stereotypes about athletes and crime but that the vast majority of professional athletes are extremely positive individuals. Sanders said, "When I look at the many NBA players who have their own foundations and who are very involved with giving back to the communities where they play and where they came from, I know they are hurt by the stereotypes." McPherson asserts that "most of the players in the NFL are deeply religious, family-centered men who are constantly giving back to their communities with time and money."

Rosalyn Dunlap wonders when the public and the media will stop being cynical about athletes.

> I hear so many people say that if athletes do some thing in the community that they do it for publicity. Why can't we accept that athletes want to help?
>
> Sport and those who play it can help educate us and sensitize us. While we can't ignore the bad news, we should also focus on the overwhelming good news of what athletes do to make this a better world.

What is the power of sport? Lin Dawson, a ten-year NFL veteran who has spent much his post-playing career in efforts to improve race relations, said,

> Sports can bring good news that can lift the weight of the world. That is a powerful gift to possess, one we all share when we use it in the most noble way we can—to lift the spiritual poverty that hovers over our children. That spirit is the antidote to the loneliness and the feeling of being unwanted that so many young people are burdened with.
>
> We can give them the richness of spirit that comes with being part of a real team, being interdependent and being able to count on a brother or a sister in a time of need.

Sports figures are in a unique position to affect change. Among them are a few who have dramatically hurt the image of the vast majority. Dawson, who is now the chief operating officer of the National Consortium for Academics and Sport, added, "the community needs positive role models now more than ever. They can help young people to believe in what they cannot yet see. Our children need faith considering what they do see in their communities."

The distortions about our athletes and the crimes that a few of them commit need to be put in their real social context. The misleading perceptions need to be corrected so we can focus on the truth and what is really necessary. In that way, we can help America live up to the dream that Jackie Robinson created for us more than 50 years ago.

* FOR FURTHER STUDY *

Benedict, Jeff. 2004. *Out of Bounds: Inside the NBA's culture of Rape, Violence, and Crime.* New York: HarperCollins.

Coakley, Jay. 2007. *Sports in Society: Issues and Controversies.* 9th ed. New York: McGraw-Hill.

Eitzen, D. Stanley. 2000. "Sport and Social Control." Pp. 370–381 in Jay Coakley and Eric Dunning, eds., *Handbook of Sport Studies.* London: Sage.

Eitzen, D. Stanley, and George H. Sage. 2009. *Sociology of North American Sport.* 8th ed. Boulder, CO: Paradigm.

Horrow, Rick. 2006. "You Can Still Bet on It: Gambling and March Madness." Available at http://cbs.sportsline.com (September 26).

Nack, William, and Don Yaeger. 1999. "Every Parent's Nightmare." *Sports Illustrated* (September 13): 40–53.

Nixon, Howard L. II. 2008. *Sport in a Changing World.* Boulder, CO: Paradigm.

Palmer, Catherine. 2001. "Outside the Imagined Community: Basque Terrorism, Political Activism, and the Tour de France." *Sociology of Sport Journal* 18 (2): 143–161.

Young, Kevin. 2000. "Sport and Violence." Pp. 382–407 in Jay Coakley and Eric Dunning, eds., *Handbook of Sport Studies.* London: Sage.

Zaichkowsky, Leonard D. 2000. "The Dark Side of Youth Sports: Coaches Sexually Abusing Children." *USA Today* 128 (January): 56–58.

Zimniuch, Fran. 2009. *Crooked: A History of Cheating in Sports.* Lanham, MD: Taylor Trade Publishing.

PART SEVEN

Problems of Excess: Performance-Enhancing Drugs in Sports

Athletes have long used artificial means to enhance performance. These practices raise many questions: Is it fair to have competitions where some athletes compete against those who have used artificial means to improve upon their natural abilities? If you feel that it is unfair, then where do you draw the line? Should any athlete that uses a stimulant be disqualified? Then what about the caffeine in coffee? Should athletes who sleep in parabolic chambers to simulate the conditions of high altitude be disqualified but not those endurance athletes who train at high altitudes? What about vitamins? Bee pollen? Is it all right for wrestlers and boxers to use over-the-counter diuretics to lose weight in order to compete at lower weight classes? Should access to the wonders of the pharmaceutical world trump training, hard work, and strategy? Or is that cheating?

The first selection in this section examines the drug culture in sports. Selection 19 looks to the future of performance enhancement—gene doping. The final essay, by sportswriter Robert Lipsyte, shows the role of drugs in society to athletes and nonathletes alike. The issues and contradictions are complex. So, too, are the answers.

18

Creating the Frankenstein Athlete

The Drug Culture in Sports

Fran Zimniuch

> "The use of performance-enhancing drugs like steroids in baseball, football and other sports is dangerous, and it sends the wrong message—that there are shortcuts to accomplishment, and that performance is more important than character."
> —President George W. Bush, State of the Union address, January 20, 2004

As sure as the sports section in every morning newspaper across the country reviews sporting events from the previous day, an increasingly troublesome trend in the world of sports is that the morning paper also often includes news of yet another athlete's involvement in the use of illegal drugs. For many outside the sports spotlight, their only experiences with illegal drugs is the occasional use of the recreational kind. But in the high-powered world of sports, where fortune and fame can be decided by a millisecond, any means by which one athlete can gain even the slimmest edge has become acceptable. The drug culture in sports has reached such a crescendo that we've gone well beyond jocks doping to win events. Now, many are doping just trying to keep up with their competitors. It is a vicious circle that has fans doubting the validity of just about every outstanding athletic achievement.

If a big, powerful home run hitter like Ryan Howard hits a gargantuan tater, fans will whisper—even though most players are just like Ryan Howard: honest,

Source: Fran Zimniuch, "Creating the Frankenstein Athlete: The Drug Culture in Sports," *Crooked: The History of Cheating in Sports.* Lanham, MD: Taylor Trade Publishing, 2009, pp. 113–119.

hardworking, nondoping athletes who strive to be the best they can be the old-fashioned way. It's just not fair.

Most fans, who live their lives out of the spotlight and who have been so disappointed by so many athletes, are certainly against the use of performance-enhancing drugs—particularly when that use filters down to local college and high school athletes trying to ensure their piece of the pie. That's when it gets dangerous—and hits home.

The amateur and professional sports world has reacted—albeit a day late and a dollar short—in an attempt to put an end to the widespread use of illegal drugs on every level. But when confronted by talented, aggressive, extremely competitive athletes surrounded by throngs of enablers who also want *their* piece of the pie, the recipe for dishonest disaster is always percolating.

Unless our culture decides that it wants überleagues of doped-up, 'roided jocks with watermelon-sized heads and pea-sized testicles performing their sport as if there was no such thing as gravity, then stringent measures need to be taken.

We're only human, and many of us have opinions about issues we really don't understand. Just look at the wide variety of—sometimes underinformed—opinions about any political campaign or particularly controversial topic. So it seems prudent to take a step back and try to get a better understanding of just what we're dealing with.

Before talking about the use of steroids, particularly in baseball, history dictates that we should discuss greenies, otherwise known as peptos. Greenies are an amphetamine—speed—which helps a player boost his effort. But a clear distinction should be made between greenies and present-day steroids. Decades ago, players might pop a few greenies prior to a game or sip from a special pot of "hot" coffee in the clubhouse, which was for players only. Greenies helped players to get loose more quickly and play through stretches of the long season when they just weren't able to get up for the game. But greenies, unlike steroids and human growth hormone, did not enable a ballplayer to do things he was normally unable to do. Instead, they gave him what amounted to an extreme caffeine rush to get his ass in gear, loosen up, and play through pain or fatigue. But they never allowed anyone to play beyond his natural ability.

"You have to distinguish greenies, or peptos, as they were called, from steroids," says former pitcher Jim Bouton, who authored what might be the greatest book ever on baseball, *Ball Four.* "Greenies only allowed you to play up to your ability. If you didn't get a good night's sleep, or you had a hangover, it would allow you to play up to your ability, or at least some players thought that. It did not create a different human being. It did not change your physical makeup. It did not allow you to play beyond your ability, your normal ability, as steroids do and human growth hormone does.

"Greenies were performance *enablers,* not enhancers."

Greenies, named for the color of the pills, were introduced to the game in the 1940s. Amphetamines speed up the heart rate and have been proven to fight fatigue, increase alertness, and sharpen reaction time. They were actually considered harmless pep pills until 1970, when they were made illegal without a prescription. They have since been found to be addictive and can cause heart attacks and strokes.

Baseball's love affair with greenies officially ended before the start of the 2006 season, when Major League Baseball began testing players for them. Now, a player who fails the test once is sent to counseling. The second strike results in a twenty-five-game suspension.

The pharmaceutical industry—and baseball—have come a long way since the days of greenies, with the introduction of steroids. While everyone has an opinion about steroids, not as many people understand just what they are. What do steroids do to make the long-term health risks so acceptable to so many of today's athletes?

According to the National Institute on Drug Abuse, anabolic-androgenic steroids are man-made substances related to male sex hormones. "Anabolic" refers to muscle building and "androgenic" refers to increased masculine characteristics. "Steroids" is the name of the class of drug. These types of drugs are available legally only by prescription, to treat conditions that occur when the body produces abnormally low amounts of testosterone, such as in delayed puberty and some types of impotence. They can also be prescribed to treat body wasting in patients with AIDS and other diseases that result in loss of lean muscle mass. Abuse of anabolic steroids can lead to serious health issues, some of which are irreversible.

Today, athletes and others abuse anabolic steroids to enhance performance and improve physical appearance. Anabolic steroids can be taken orally or injected, and are used in cycles of weeks or months, rather than continuously, in a practice known as cycling. Users often combine several different types of steroids to maximize their effectiveness while minimizing negative effects. This is known as stacking.

The major side effects of anabolic steroid abuse include a litany of serious health issues, including liver tumors and cancer, jaundice (the yellowish color of skin, tissues, and body fluids), fluid retention, high blood pressure, and an increase in bad cholesterol and decrease in good cholesterol. Abusers may also suffer from kidney tumors, severe acne, and trembling.

Men who abuse steroids often suffer from gender-specific side effects such as shrinking of the testicles, reduced sperm count, infertility, baldness, development of breasts, and increased risk for prostate cancer. For women, side effects can include the growth of facial hair, male-pattern baldness, changes in or cessation of the menstrual cycle, enlargement of the clitoris, and a deepened voice.

And for adolescents who make the misguided decision to abuse steroids, side effects include permanently halted growth as a result of premature skeletal maturation and accelerated puberty changes. So adolescents risk being shorter than they would normally have been for the remainder of their lives.

"We have a guy in our book, Tim Montgomery, who said that if he could break the 100-meter record, he didn't care if he dropped dead after he crossed the finish line," says Lance Williams, coauthor of *Game of Shadows*. "In *Ball Four* by Jim Bouton, they have guys sitting in the bullpen talking about if you would take a pill that could make you become a twenty-game winner, even if it took five years off your life. Athletes are young men and women and they don't have the perspective that an older person—even in their thirties and forties—has. They think they'll never die. They think the future will never come. The rewards are so incredible. Financially, it's a tremendous temptation."

A 2005 report by the President's Council on Physical Fitness and Sports titled *Anabolic-Androgenic Steroids: Incidence of Use and Health Implications* treated the subject of steroid use and abuse in great detail. The report concludes: "Although anabolic steroids are illegal, and their use is banned by virtually every sport's governing body, survey and drug-testing data indicate continued use by competitive athletes at all levels. That fact that the level of steroid use appears to have increased significantly over the past three decades among adolescents, women, and recreational athletes is also of growing concern. The use of anabolic steroids presents an interesting public health challenge. While these drugs are associated with deleterious physical and psychological outcomes, they are being used to achieve what many consider socially desirable ends: being physically attractive and being a winner."

But, as so many sports fans have learned over the past decade, steroids are not the only synthetic drugs of choice by today's injectors. Human growth hormone is another well-known performance-enhancing drug that many don't understand. The difference between steroids and HGH can be described as follows: steroids are like heroin while HGH is like marijuana. Unlike steroids, HGH has not been proven to increase weight-lifting ability and it has a greater effect on muscle definition than it does on muscle strength.

So why would an athlete risk suspension and suspicion by using HGH? On the surface, it makes no sense. A baseball player can beef up on steroids and improve his performance as a result. HGH, on the other hand, is often used to attempt to reverse the effects of aging. What's the connection?

"One possibility is that the drug really does enhance performance but that the effect is too subtle to measure in a controlled setting," according to Daniel Engber in "The Growth Hormone Myth: What Athletes, Fans and the Sports Media Don't Understand about HGH," at *Slate.* "An elite athlete might be able to detect very slight improvements in strength and agility that would be invisible to lab scientists or statistical tests. At the highest levels of sport, a tiny edge can make a big difference. Athletes might also derive some added benefit by mixing HGH with other drugs—anti-aging doctors often prescribe growth hormone in combination with testosterone.

"It's also possible that baseball players aren't using HGH to beef up at all. Almost everyone who gets caught red-handed claims they were using the drug to recover from an injury. This might be more than a ploy to win sympathy: Some doctors believe that growth hormone can speed up tissue repair. There isn't much clinical work to support this idea, however.

"The most likely reason that athletes use HGH, though, is superstition. A ballplayer might shoot up with HGH for the same reason we take vitamin C when we have a cold: There's no good reason to think it does anything, but we're willing to give it a try. The fact that the major sports leagues have banned growth hormone only encourages the idea that the drug has tangible benefits. Why would they ban something unless it worked?

"This mentality has put doping officials and athletes into a feedback loop of added hysteria. The World Anti-Doping Agency (WADA) will ban any drug that athletes use, whether or not it has an effect. The WADA code points out that the use of substances, 'based on the mistaken belief they enhance performance is clearly contradictory to the spirit of sport.' In other words, it doesn't matter if HGH gives athletes an unfair advantage. If Jerry Hairston believes he's cheating, then he really is cheating."

According to the Mitchell Report, which investigated and reported on the use of illegal steroids and human growth hormone in professional baseball, it seems that many of the players implicated for the use of HGH were actually trying to recover from an injury. Whether the drug actually does speed up tissue repair, thus enabling players to recover and return sooner from injury, is not known for certain. What is known is that growth hormone stimulates the synthesis of collagen, which is necessary for strengthening cartilage, bones, tendons, and ligaments.

Jason Grimsley reportedly used the drug in combination with the anabolic steroid Deca-Durabolin to recover from ligament replacement in just nine months—half the usual estimated recovery time for pitchers.

When you combine anabolic steroids and HGH, the result is apparently very conducive and potent—sort of like combining a triple espresso martini with a double shot of Jägermeister. The stronger connective tissues developed through the use of HGH not only work better and heal faster, but they are better equipped to handle the oversized muscles often associated with steroid use.

HGH also increases red blood cell count, boosts heart function, and makes more energy available by stimulating the breakdown of fat. Users also have noticed improved eyesight, better sleep, and better sex.

HGH users can sometimes be identified by the characteristic side effects of the hormone. Use of HGH can cause acromegaly, a condition characterized by excessive growth of the head, feet, and hands. In people with acromegaly, the lips, nose, tongue, jaw, and forehead increase in size, and fingers and toes can widen. Excessive use of HGH can also lead to diabetes.

Another drug that has made the rounds among athletes is andro, short for androstenedione, which was manufactured as a dietary supplement. Andro—a hormone produced in the adrenal glands that increases testosterone production and protein synthesis, resulting in increased lean body mass and strength during training—was commonly used by MLB players, including Mark McGwire, throughout the 1990s.

On March 12, 2004, the Anabolic Steroid Control Act of 2004 was introduced into the United States Senate. It amended the Controlled Substances Act of 1970, placing both anabolic steroids and prohormones on a list of controlled substances and making possession of the banned substances a federal crime. The law took effect on January 20, 2005.

When McGwire was attacking record home run seasons, he openly admitted to taking andro, which was, at the time, a legal over-the-counter muscle enhancement product. So when he took andro, McGwire was not breaking any rules—either those of baseball or those of society.

But the abuse of such dangerous substances by athletes did not just begin with steroids and other performance-enhancing drugs. They are simply the latest of an ever-growing list of dangerous man-made substances used to help create the Frankenstein Athlete. The history goes well beyond even the historical period where Mary Shelley wrote *Frankenstein* in 1831.

We've seen the impact of pharmaceuticals on performance on the field, but it will be interesting and perhaps tragic to see what health-related ramifications drug use will have on these athletes later in life. They may have raised the bar significantly on the playing field. What happens in their future is a crapshoot, because this past generation of performance-enhanced athletes are also guinea pigs who may very well pay a huge price for their athletic achievements.

Has our society become aware of the problem soon enough? Will the risks of such behavior preclude future jocks from crossing over the line? The United States has yet to experience the long-term effect of the use of steroids and performance-enhancing substances, but the same cannot be said of other countries.

19

Finding the Golden Genes

Patrick Barry

In early August—8/8/08, to be precise—the curtain will rise on what many experts believe could prove to be the first genetically modified Olympics.

For the unscrupulous or overdriven Olympic athlete, the banned practice of "doping" by taking hormones or other drugs to enhance athletic prowess may seem so last century. The next thing in doping is more profound *and* more dangerous. It's called gene doping: permanently inserting strength- or endurance-boosting genes into DNA.

"Once you put that gene in, it's there for the rest of that person's life," says Larry Bowers, a clinical chemist at the U.S. Anti-Doping Agency in Colorado Springs, Colorado. "You can't go back and fish it out."

Scientists developed the technology behind gene doping as a promising way to treat genetic diseases such as sickle-cell anemia and the "bubble boy" immune deficiency syndrome. This experimental medical technology—called gene therapy—has begun to emerge from the pall of early failures and fatalities in clinical trials. As gene therapy begins to enjoy some preliminary successes, scientists at the World Anti-Doping Agency, which oversees drug testing for the Olympics, have started to worry that dopers might now see abuse of gene therapy in sport as a viable option, though the practice was banned by WADA in 2003.

"Gene therapy has now broken out from what seemed to be too little progress and has now shown real therapies for a couple diseases, and more coming," says

Source: Patrick Barry, "Finding the Golden Genes," *Science News* (August 2, 2008): 16, 18, 20–21.

Theodore Friedmann, a gene therapy expert at the University of California, San Diego and chairman of WADA's panel on gene doping.

While gene therapy research has begun making great strides, the science of detecting illicit use of gene therapy in sport is only now finding its legs. To confront the perceived inevitability of gene doping, Friedmann and other scientists have started in recent years to explore the problem of detecting whether an athlete has inserted a foreign gene—an extra copy that may be indistinguishable from the natural genes—into his or her DNA.

It's proving to be a formidable challenge. Genetic makeup varies from person to person, and world-class athletes are bound to have some natural genetic endowments that other people lack. Somehow, gene-doping tests must distinguish between natural genetic variation among individuals and genes inserted artificially—and the distinction must stand up in court.

Scientists are fighting genetics with genetics, so to speak, enlisting the latest technologies for gene sequencing or for profiling the activity of proteins to find the telltale signs of gene doping. Some techniques attempt the daunting search for the foreign gene itself, like looking for a strand of hay in an enormous haystack.

But new research could also lead to an easier and more foolproof approach: detecting the characteristic ways that an inserted gene affects an athlete's body as a whole.

RESURGENCE OF GENE THERAPY

In 1999, 18-year-old Jesse Gelsinger died during a gene therapy trial for a rare liver disease. Investigators later attributed his death to a violent immune reaction to the delivery virus rather than to the therapeutic gene. His death was a major setback for the field. It also may have scared away early would-be gene dopers.

In recent years, safety and efficacy of gene therapy have shown signs of progress in numerous clinical trials for conditions ranging from early-onset vision loss to erectile dysfunction. As scientists develop ways to use safer, weaker viruses for delivery, and as gene therapies wind their way through clinical trials, athletes and coaches might start to see gene doping as even more viable than they already do.

In the courtroom during the 2006 trial of Thomas Springstein, a German track coach accused of giving performance-enhancing drugs to high-school-age female runners, prosecutors read aloud an e-mail Springstein had written that would shock the sports world.

"The new Repoxygen is hard to get," the e-mail read, according to press reports. "Please give me new instructions soon so that I can order the product before Christmas."

Repoxygen isn't merely another doping drug such as a hormone or the latest designer steroid—it's an experimental virus designed to deliver a therapeutic gene and insert it into a person's DNA.

British pharmaceutical company Oxford BioMedica developed Repoxygen in 2002 as a treatment for severe anemia. The therapy "infects" patients with a harmless virus carrying a modified gene that encodes erythropoietin, a protein that boosts red blood cell production. This protein, often called EPO, is itself a favorite among dopers seeking to increase their oxygen capacity, and hence their endurance.

Viruses have the natural ability to inject genetic material into their host's DNA. The host's cells can translate that gene into active proteins as if the foreign gene were the cells' own. So by delivering the gene for EPO within a virus, Repoxygen could potentially increase the amounts of EPO protein—and the change would be permanent.

Athletes might also be tempted by perhaps the most tantalizing gene therapy experiment of all: the "mighty mouse." In 1998, H. Lee Sweeney and his colleagues at the University of Pennsylvania School of Medicine injected mice with a virus carrying a gene that boosted production of insulin-like growth factor 1, or IGF-1, a protein that regulates muscle growth. As a result, the mice had 15 percent more muscle mass and were 14 percent stronger than untreated mice—without ever having exercised. The treatment also prevented the decline of muscle mass as the mice grew older.

Other genetic paths to increase muscle strength and volume could include the gene for human growth hormone or segments of DNA that block a protein called myostatin, which normally limits muscle growth.

Endurance might also be boosted by the gene encoding a protein called peroxisome proliferator-activated receptor delta, or PPAR-delta. Mice engineered to have extra copies of this gene hopped onto a treadmill and, without ever having trained, ran about twice as far as unaltered mice. The extra PPAR-delta improved the ability of the mice's muscles to use fat molecules for energy, and it shifted the animals' ratio of muscle fiber types from fast-twitch toward slow-twitch fibers—a change that would improve muscle endurance in people as well. Ronald Evans and his colleagues at the Salk Institute for Biological Studies in La Jolla, Calif., published the research in 2004.

Since then, Evans says, he has been routinely approached by curious coaches and athletes. "I've had athletes come to my lectures and go to the microphone and say, 'If I took this drug, would it work with EPO and growth hormone?' I mean, they would ask this publicly," Evans says.

"Based on athletes I've talked with, I'd say that it's a reasonable possibility that gene doping will be used in this Olympics, and I think there's a very high probability that it will be used in the next Olympics," he says.

ELUSIVE SIGNS

Around the time that Evans was announcing his "marathon mouse" results, WADA kicked off a funding program to focus scientific research on strategies for detecting gene doping.

"A key part of our project is to try to define what we call signatures of doping," says Olivier Rabin, a biomedical engineer and director of science for WADA. "We are looking at the impact of those kinds of genetic manipulations at different levels."

The first and most obvious approach is simply to look for the inserted gene among the roughly 6 billion "letters" of genetic code in both sets of a person's chromosomes.

For clinical gene therapy trials, finding the inserted gene is fairly easy. Scientists know the exact sequence of the gene they inserted, and often they know where on the person's chromosomes the gene should have ended up. Standard DNA sequencing techniques can reveal the genetic code for that region on the chromosomes, and the unique sequence of the inserted gene will be in plain view. With gene doping, the situation is much trickier.

"In sport, you don't know where that gene will be put, what virus was used or even what particular variety of gene was used," Friedmann says. "You don't have the advantage of knowing where to look and for what, so the argument is to look everywhere."

Another difficulty is that copies of the foreign gene wouldn't be in all of a person's cells. The gene-carrying viruses selectively target certain tissues such as muscle or liver (the liver helps to regulate muscle metabolism). Some blood cells might also take in the viruses' genetic payloads, but it's questionable whether a standard blood sample from an athlete would contain the gene. Instead, anti-doping officials would have to sample muscle tissue directly using punch biopsies, a procedure that is mildly painful.

"No one's expecting that an athlete will agree to a muscle biopsy," Friedmann says. "That's a nonstarter."

Still, direct detection of inserted genes could work in some cases. Evans points out that an artificially inserted gene for PPAR-delta would be much smaller than the natural gene. That's because the natural gene is far too big to hitch a ride on the carrier virus. Fitting the gene onto a virus means only a trimmed down version of the gene can be used. This distinctive genetic pattern would only exist in a person who had undergone gene doping.

In other cases, genes would end up in tissues where they're not normally active, making detection more straightforward. For example, the liver and kidneys normally produce the protein EPO, which makes red blood cells, but gene doping could deliver the EPO-coding gene directly to muscle tissues. The trick, then, is to find a noninvasive way to detect where EPO production is occurring inside the body.

One solution is to use medical imaging techniques such as PET scans. In research funded by WADA, Jordi Segura and his colleagues at the Municipal Institute for Medical Research in Barcelona, Spain, attached slightly radioactive "flags" to molecules made during EPO production. A standard PET scan can spot this radioactivity, revealing where EPO was being made in the bodies of mice injected with gene-doping viruses, the team reported in the October 2007 *Therapeutic Drug Monitoring*. The researchers showed that production of EPO in muscle tissue was a telltale sign of gene doping.

With radioactivity that is relatively mild, the labels are routinely used in medical imaging to diagnose diseases and don't pose a significant hazard. But Friedmann notes that asking athletes to undergo such a procedure could be controversial.

DETECTION BY PROXY

Another approach is to look for signs of the viral "infection," rather than for the gene itself. Even a weakened virus could trigger a mild, and specific, immune reaction that might show up in a blood test.

Perhaps the greatest challenge facing this method is that viruses aren't the only way to deliver a gene into a doper's body. "The reality is that you can just inject naked DNA directly into tissues" with a syringe, Evans says. "Direct injection could be more local and harder to detect."

This relatively crude way to insert a gene won't spread the gene as widely through a person's body as viruses injected into the bloodstream would. But many cells near the site of injection could take in the gene, perhaps enough to improve athletic performance.

Microscopic, synthetic spheres of fat molecules called liposomes can also shuttle doping genes into the body.

To prevent dopers from evading detection by simply changing delivery vehicles, scientists are also exploring a third approach to developing tests: proteomics, the detailed study of all the proteins in the human body.

Regardless of the vehicle used, adding a new gene to the body's tightly woven web of interacting genes and proteins will cause ripples of change to spread throughout that web. "There will be a body-wide response no matter what gene you use or where in the body you put it," Friedmann says, "and those changes can be used as a signature of doping."

Painful biopsies wouldn't be required. Because the cascade of changes in protein activity would be widespread, anti-doping officials could test using blood, urine, hair or even sweat. Tools developed for the burgeoning fields of genomics and proteomics allow scientists to see the activity levels of thousands of genes or proteins simultaneously.

In preliminary unpublished experiments, Friedmann and his colleagues injected a type of muscle cell with the gene for IGF-1. Activity of hundreds of genes changed as a result, including a boost in the activity of genes that control production of cholesterol, steroids and fatty acids. All of these changes might be detectable with simple blood tests.

WADA is funding half a dozen or so ongoing studies on this proteome-based detection strategy, but research in this area is still at an early stage. "There's good reason to think that's likely to work, and a number of labs are having some nice results," Friedmann says.

As for whether any tests for gene doping will be ready in time for the Beijing Olympics, anti-doping authorities aren't giving away many hints that might help dopers evade detection. "We never say when our tests are going to be in place," WADA's Rabin says.

Even if detection methods do lag behind the games, dopers may want to think twice before assuming they're in the clear, Friedmann notes. "With stored [blood and urine] samples, one always has the option of going back some months or years later and checking again with the newest tests."

Just in case the dangers of tampering with a person's genetic makeup weren't enough of a disincentive.

EXPLORE MORE

National Institutes of Health Handbook on Gene Therapy: ghr.nlm.nih.gov/hand book/therapy/genetherapy.

Gene Therapy, Athletes, and Doping

1928
IAAF, the International Association of Athletics Federations, becomes the first international sport federation to ban doping, the use of performance-enhancing substances.

1968
The International Olympic Committee approves a ban on doping, a year after British cyclist Tom Simpson collapsed and died during the Tour de France. His autopsy revealed high levels of methamphetamine.

1998
Mighty mouse: injecting mice with a virus carrying the gene for IGF-1 makes the animals 14 percent stronger, even without the benefit of exercise. This mouse is shown climbing a ladder while carrying weights.

1999
18-year-old Jesse Gelsinger becomes the first person to die during a gene therapy clinical trial, apparently because of a massive immune response to the virus used to deliver the genes.

2004
The World Anti-Doping Agency begins a program to fund scientific research on ways to detect gene doping.

2006
The first public evidence of a coach seeking gene doping substances for his athletes emerges in court during the trial of German coach Thomas Springstein.

June 10–11, 2008
The World Anti-Doping Agency holds the third Gene Doping Symposium, in Saint Petersburg, Russia.

Gene therapy could help an athlete change production of ...	And the result could be ...
Erythropoietin	Enhanced red blood cell production, thus greater oxygen delivery for endurance
Human growth factor	Increased muscle size, power and recovery from fatigue
Insulin-like growth factor	Increased number of muscle regulator cells, thus size, power and recovery from fatigue
PPAR-delta	More fat metabolism and increased muscle endurance
Myostatin	Greater muscle growth due to the inhibition of myostatin production

20

Outraged over the Steroids Outrage

Robert Lipsyte

As a longtime steroid user, I'm confused by the frenzied reaction to the juicy news coming out of baseball these days.

Why should we care what those players do, as long as they entertain us? Who wouldn't expect pro athletes, like the rest of us, to try to be the best they could be? And how has this become a chance for yet more face time for flabby moralists instead of an opportunity to gather some necessary information?

Here's what I want to know: Exactly which performances are enhanced—and how—by which anabolic steroids, androgens, human growth hormone, and whatever else athletes shoot, swallow, and sniff? What are the long-term and short-term effects? Are those enhancements and side effects different for adolescents and adults, men and women?

I have ethical questions, too. How different is steroid use from cosmetic surgery for the male TV newsies reporting these stories, from Botox for actresses, beta blockers for public speakers and all the new psychological drugs for well people with the willies—the shy, the anxious, the fidgety, and the sexually apprehensive?

Speaking of which, consider the tomcat fight between two of baseball's best-known sluggers and congressional testifiers, Jose Canseco and his childhood pal, Rafael Palmeiro. In his best seller, *Juiced,* Canseco claims he personally injected steroids

Source: Robert Lipsyte, "Outraged over the Steroids Outrage," *USA Today. The Magazine of the American Scene,* March 22, 2005. Used with permission. See http://www.robertlipsyte.com.

into Palmeiro when they both played for George W. Bush's Texas Rangers. Palmeiro denies it. Of course, Palmeiro, as baseball's most famous pitchman for Viagra, is no stranger to performance-enhancing drugs.

"Performance-enhancement is in a gray area," says Robert Klitzman, codirector of Columbia University's Center for Bioethics. "Would you include new technologies to improve cognitive abilities? How about access to SAT prep coaching? Assisted pregnancies?"

Meanwhile, athletes certainly have no ethical dilemma about using steroids, says Michael Miletic, a psychiatrist whose Detroit-based practice includes high school, college, and professional athletes. "Steroids are totally embedded in the sports culture. We need to get past the finger-pointing. There's been a wholesale abandonment of critical analysis."

MY STEROID USE

Analyze this: I've been shooting steroids for almost 15 years, since a third cancer operation left me unable to produce testosterone naturally. Once a month, I nail one of my quadriceps with a 22-gauge needle and pump in the oily yellow fluid. Without it, my prescribing surgeon tells me, I would be physically fatigued and mentally sluggish, lose my sex drive, be achy and depressed. No question, I'm taking a performance-enhancing drug.

Yet, even with it, I can't hit a major-league fastball, sack a moving NFL quarterback, or bench-press 500 pounds. Using steroids, most people can train harder and recover more quickly from breakdown and injury. But to reach all-pro you have to be what athletes call a "freak" with those potentially all-pro genes to tweak.

But chemicals also help high school boys pump themselves into beach studs, put on extra pounds for the football team, and gain strength and stamina for the campaign to win a college scholarship and a pro contract. This is the danger zone, says Miletic, who is far less concerned with the middle-aged Barry Bonds's possible career choices than with unsupervised drug use by kids.

"This is where we should be paying attention," Miletic says. "First of all, there is adult complicity here. Some parents and coaches are actively helping kids get drugs, others are looking the other way. How could you not notice the dramatic changes in your child's body?

"I don't believe kids are taking steroids because they think it helped Mark McGwire. They're taking it because teammates, opponents, a strength coach, a gym owner is telling them it will make them better," he says.

Performance-enhancers have been around for a long time, and as our games, from Little League to Super Bowl, became less classrooms for character building and more stages for spectaculars, the pressure to enhance performance swelled like Popeye's biceps (his drug was spinach, remember?). We expect our sports heroes to do anything to win for us, to find the edge, to take risks, even to play hurt. If they don't, they're replaced by those who will.

"WHERE DOES CHEATING BEGIN?"

At the same time, the self-help movement made the concept of improvement, of reinvention, of taking charge of body and psyche, a kind of mandate for everybody. To refuse to at least try to find a way to feel better, look better, do better was regarded as almost a crime. Is self-help from a mind-numbing mantra more moral than self-help from the tip of a needle?

"It's going to get even more complicated," says Klitzman, the Columbia bioethicist, "as techniques for screening embryos and scanning brains become more sophisticated. Scientists will be looking for stupidity genes and smart pills. Cosmetic psycho-pharmacology is an area where people with money will have advantages over people who don't. Is that fair? In an ideal world, there would be a level playing field. Exactly where does cheating begin?"

I'll be watching baseball this season for guys who look less bulked-up than they did last season. How many are using newer, riskier, test-proof drugs? That's probably not fair.

The pundits and politicians will declare a moral victory and move on, leaving our questions unanswered. That's cheating.

* FOR FURTHER STUDY *

Bee, Peta. 2005. "This One Will Help Me Run and Run: The World of Sport Is Full of Performance-Enhancing Fads." *Guardian,* August 30. Available at http://sport.guardian.co.uk/news/story/0,10488,1558931.00.html.

Begley, Sharon, and Martha Brant. 1999. "The Real Scandal in International Sport: Doping." *Newsweek* (February 15): 48–54.

Bjerklie, David, and Alice Park. 2004. "How Doctors Help the Dopers." *Time* (August 16): 58–62.

Dixon, Patrick. 2006. "Steroids: The Truth about Steroids." *Global Change* (January 3). Available at http://www.globalchange.com/steroids/htm.

Hoberman, John M. 2004. *Testosterone Dreams: Rejuvenation, Aphrodisia, Doping.* Berkeley: University of California Press.

Jendrick, Nathan. 2006. *Dunks, Doubles, Doping: How Steroids Are Killing American Athletes.* Guilford, CT: Lyons.

Mehlman, Maxwell J. 2004. "What's Wrong with Using Drugs in Sports? Nothing." *USA Today* (August 11). Available at http://www.usatoday.com/news/opinion/editorials/2004-08-11-mehlman_w.htm.

Pound, Richard W. 2006. *Inside Dope: How Drugs Are the Biggest Threat to Sports, Why You Should Care, and What Can Be Done about Them.* New York: Wiley.

PART EIGHT

Problems of Excess: Big-Time College Sport

Interschool sports are found in almost all American schools and at all levels. There are many reasons for this universality. Sports unite all segments of a school and the community or neighborhood they represent. School sports remind constituents of the school, which may lead to monetary and other forms of support. School administrators can use sport as a useful tool for social control. But the most important reason for the universality of school sports is the widespread belief that the educational goals are accomplished through sport. There is much merit to this view; sports do contribute to physical fitness, to learning the value of hard work and perseverance, and to being goal-oriented. There is some evidence that sports participation leads to better grades, higher academic aspirations, and positive self-concept.

However, there also is a negative side to school sports. They are elitist, since only the gifted participate. Sports often overshadow academic endeavors (e.g., athletes are disproportionately rewarded and schools devote too much time and money to athletics that could be diverted to academic activities). Where winning is paramount—and where is this not the case?—the pressure becomes intense. This pressure has several negative consequences, the most important of which is that participants are prevented from fully enjoying sport. The pressure is too great for many youngsters. The game is work. It is a business.

The pressure to win also contributes to abuse by coaches, poor sportsmanship, dislike of opponents, intolerance of losers, and cheating. Most significant, although not usually considered so, is that while sport is a success-oriented activity, it is fraught with failure (losing teams, bench warmers, would-be participants cut from teams, the humiliation of letting down your teammates and school, and so on). For every ego enhanced by sport, how many have been bruised?

While this description fits all types of schools, big-time college sports deserve special attention, for they have unique problems. Athletes in these settings are athletes first and students second; thus they are robbed of a first-class education. They are robbed by the tremendous demands on their time and energy. This problem is further enhanced by athletes being segregated from the student body (in classes, majors, and in eating and living arrangements); thus they are deprived of a variety of influences that college normally facilitates.

Another problem of college sports is that they tend to be ultraelitist. The money and facilities go disproportionately to the male athletes in the revenue-producing sports rather than to intramurals, minor sports, and club sports.

The greatest scandal involving college sports is the illegal and immoral behavior of overzealous coaches, school authorities, and alumni in recruiting athletes. In the quest to bring the best athletes to a school, players have been given monetary inducements, sexual favors, forged transcripts, and surrogates to take their entrance exams. In addition to the illegality of these acts, two fundamental problems exist with these recruiting violations: (1) Such behaviors have no place in an educational setting, yet they are done by some educators and condoned by others, and (2) these illicit practices by so-called respected authorities transmit two major lessons—that greed is the ultimate value and that winning supersedes how one wins.

Finally, the win-at-any-cost ethic that prevails in many of America's institutions of higher learning puts undue pressure on coaches. They must win to keep their jobs. Hence, some drive their athletes too hard or too brutally. Some demand total control over their players on and off the field. Some use illegal tactics to gain advantage (not only in recruiting but also in breaking the rules regarding the allowed number of practices, ineligible players, and unfair techniques). But coaches are not the problem. They represent a symptom of the process by which school sports are big business and where winning is the only avenue to achieve success.

The selections of Part Eight reflect on these problems. The first is a summary by the Knight Commission on Intercollegiate Athletics of the problem areas of big-time college sports. The second concentrates on one issue—the admissions exemptions that favor athletes. This is followed by Duke professor of public policy, economics, and law, Charles T. Clotfelter, who addresses the fundamental question of whether big-time college sports are compatible with the educational goals of colleges and universities. The final selection in Part Eight, by D. Stanley Eitzen, uses the metaphor of slavery to show how big-time college athletes are exploited.

21

College Sports 101

A Primer on Money, Athletics, and Higher Education in the 21st Century

The Knight Commission on Intercollegiate Athletics

INTRODUCTION

Intercollegiate athletics at the country's most prominent colleges and universities has become a multi-billion dollar enterprise. It involves not only institutions of higher education, but also television networks, apparel manufacturers, advertisers from all sectors, and above all, millions of fans and donors. Now, almost all state flagship universities, many regional institutions, and some private research universities maintain teams in the Football Bowl Subdivision (FBS) of the National Collegiate Athletic Association (NCAA), formerly Division I-A.

At these institutions, athletics are a focal point for universities and their communities. Tens of thousands of fans (and at a few institutions, over a hundred thousand) come to cheer on football teams, with smaller numbers flocking to men's basketball and other sports. Team logos and nicknames are recognized coast-to-coast, branding their institutions for people who could not find the university on a map. Donors give munificent sums to fund athletic scholarships or construct stadiums.

A handful of the most visible athletics programs can afford to spend more than $80 million annually on their operations, thanks to such donations as well as ticket

Source: The Knight Commission on Intercollegiate Athletics, "College Sports 101: A Primer on Money, Athletics, and Higher Education in the 21st Century." Miami: John S. and James L. Knight Foundation, 2009.

revenue, royalties from championship events, licensing and sponsorship revenue, and broadcast rights. Indeed, most fans and observers of college sports believe that the majority of athletics departments generate large net sums of money for their institutions. A 2006 survey sponsored by the Knight Commission on Intercollegiate Athletics found that 78 percent of Americans polled believed athletics programs were profitable (Knight Commission on Intercollegiate Athletics, 2006).

In fact, the vast majority of athletics programs reap far less money from external sources than they need to function. Virtually all universities subsidize athletics departments through general fund allocations, student fees, and state appropriations, and the NCAA estimates in a given year that only 20 to 30 athletics programs actually generate enough external revenue to cover operating expenses. Institutional subsidies to athletics can exceed $11 million, according to data provided by the NCAA. With costs in athletics rising faster than in other areas of university operations, it is not clear how many institutions can continue to underwrite athletics at their current level without allocating significant funds that could be used for teaching, research, service, student services, or other core functions.

The economic downturn has exacerbated these financial pressures, but the problems with the economic structure of big-time intercollegiate athletics go much deeper than the current circumstances. Among the primary issues:

- The wide gap between wealthy conferences and struggling conferences is growing wider, deepening a class structure even within the ostensible "big time." Among the eleven conferences with teams in the bowl subdivision, the richest league's members generated approximately fourteen times as much revenue as those programs in the poorest conference in 2007, according to data provided by the NCAA.
- No matter the size of an athletic department's budget, over the past decade expenditures have been rising dramatically every year and much faster than revenue is growing.
- At many institutions, athletics budgets are rising more quickly than educational budgets, and the subsidies provided by institutions to their athletics budgets are rising more quickly than both.

The finances of intercollegiate athletics always have been one of the core concerns for the Knight Commission on Intercollegiate Athletics. In its 1991 report *Keeping Faith with the Student-Athlete,* the Commission called for the development of a "one-plus-three" model for the governance of college sports—the "one" being presidential control, and the "three" being academic integrity, fiscal soundness, and a system of accountability (Knight Commission on Intercollegiate Athletics, 1991).

In most of these areas, there are notable signs of progress. Presidents now act as directors of the NCAA's Division I and the organization as a whole. There are metrics for academics designed to hold individuals, teams, and institutions accountable for retention and graduation rates. A detailed certification process for athletics that has served as a quiet accountability mechanism on individual campuses is now in its third cycle of institutional reviews. Obviously, there are problems remaining in each of these areas, but on the whole, the landscape has changed considerably since 1991.

However, finances remain an intractable problem, particularly given the growth of athletics expenses in big-time sports. As this report will show, this intractability has many roots. One of the key ones may be a lack of a common understanding or willingness to address the national dynamics that lead to decisions that exacerbate the economic problems in intercollegiate athletics, and the goal of this primer is to provide that common ground in the hopes of engaging academic leaders and policymakers.

This report is focused on intercollegiate athletics. However, policymakers must recognize that the challenges and trends in college sports, particularly at the nation's top universities, mirror situations across campus. Universities subsidize all manner of programs, both academic and auxiliary, that do not generate revenue. Costs have been rising inexorably at all institutions, to the dismay of state legislators, federal officials, and tuition-paying parents. Observers of higher education have raised concerns about institutional investments in areas such as applied research focused more on technology transfer than on the production of basic knowledge, as well as about programs designed to drive higher margins of tuition revenues, such as executive MBA programs.

In such circumstances, the question of what is and isn't appropriate must be answered by the institution's administration, faculty, governing board, and to some extent its accrediting agency. With regard to athletics, the extraordinary visibility of big-time programs and the pressure applied by all of the agents involved in college sports require a heightened level of vigilance on the part of institutional decisionmakers and policymakers with an interest in higher education.

This report is organized into the following chapters:

Background: How has the business of college sports evolved over the century and a half since colleges first fielded teams?

Expenses: Where do big-time athletics programs spend money? How much of a department's budget does coaches' compensation represent? Are expenses growing more quickly than revenue?

Revenue: Where do athletics departments get the funds they need to operate? How do these sources vary from institution to institution, or conference to conference? Which revenue streams are growing most quickly, and at which universities? How much are universities paying to subsidize their athletics programs?

Construction in college sports: Is there an "arms race" among programs that spend more on facilities in hopes of increasing revenue and attracting top-flight high school athletes?

Cost-containment: What are colleges doing to cut costs? Are such cuts window dressing, or do they fundamentally affect the nature of college athletics? What roles do leaders such as college presidents, conference commissioners, and NCAA officials play in this process?

Title IX and Olympic sports: As budgets get tighter, how will the business model of big-time athletics address gender equity and the maintenance of non-revenue sports?

Myths and intangibles: How do intercollegiate athletics really affect donations, prospective student applications and the quality of prospective students? Does more spending lead to greater athletics success and increased revenue?

Commercialism: Where are universities blurring the line between collegiate and professional sports to keep their programs viable?

Conclusion: What will happen to athletics departments and their universities if the business model of big-time intercollegiate athletics persists in its current form? What are the biggest threats?

To assist in the preparation of this report, the NCAA provided a report on financial data compiled from member institutions. The 119 member institutions in the Bowl Subdivision in 2007 were ranked by total athletic expenditures that year and divided into ten groups of 11 to 12 members. From these deciles, median values for a wide range of revenues and expenses were calculated. The results demonstrate the wide range between the "haves" and the "have-nots."

Intercollegiate athletics arouse the passions of millions of Americans, particularly during the football and basketball seasons. In its consideration of the issues outlined here, the Knight Commission's goal is to help develop a model of college sports that is sustainable at the top rank of American colleges and universities without compromising their core missions or exploiting the student-athletes who participate in them. This is a complicated and daunting goal, but the intent of this primer is to help those who care about college sports to understand the challenges facing the enterprise, especially at this critical moment.

CHAPTER 1: BACKGROUND

At present, more than 2,000 colleges and universities field intercollegiate athletic teams. There are a few small collections of institutions, such as the National Small College Athletic Association and the United College Athletic Association, but the three primary organizations are the National Association of Intercollegiate Athletics (287 members), the National Junior College Athletic Association (roughly 527 members), and the NCAA, which has 1,075 active and provisional member institutions. The NCAA is divided into three divisions—I (336 active and provisional members), II (294), and III (445). Each division has its own rules for institutional eligibility and requirements for teams and programs.

Division I itself has three subdivisions. The top level, the Football Bowl Subdivision, consists of 120 institutions competing in big-time football, where colleges award up to 85 full grants-in-aid to football players, must have minimum attendance standards, and must field teams in football and at least 15 other sports. This report is primarily concerned with this group. The next level, the Football Championship Subdivision, has 118 members, and is distinguished from the Bowl Subdivision primarily because its members compete in a 16-team football championship playoff, while the Bowl Subdivision members compete for slots in more than 30 bowl games.

The third group, known simply as Division I, consists of 98 active and provisional members that do not field football teams.

In addition to sponsoring championships and maintaining rulebooks for its sports, the NCAA mandates an extensive system of rules and regulations governing ethics and conduct for athletes, coaches, athletics administrators, and institutions. Enforcement of these rules happens through self-reporting and, in significant situations, an NCAA investigative group. Additions and changes to the rules must undergo a complex legislative process that differs from division to division.

As will become evident later in this report, even the top level, the Bowl Subdivision, has its own pecking order, and this has significant implications for its members.

This complex hierarchy got its start in 1852 in a race between crews from Harvard and Yale on Lake Winnepesaukee in New Hampshire, and business considerations were present from the start. The event was designed to promote the Boston, Concord, and Montreal railroad and a new resort built on the lake, and it attracted a crowd of spectators from Boston and New York. (Harvard won.) (For more information, please consult Mendhall's *The Harvard-Yale Boat Race, 1852–1924, and the Coming of Sport to the American College* [1993]). Baseball, track and field, and, somewhat later, basketball and football got their start as student clubs that were eventually taken over by university administrations desirous of regulating sometimes-dangerous events, promote events that would interest alumni, and, of course, win. The National Collegiate Athletic Association was formed in 1906 and began sponsoring national championships in 1925.

College athletic events became massively popular in the last two decades of the 19th century and only continued to grow, particularly in the Northeast, but also in the Midwest and the South. Despite the enthusiasm of crowds that often equaled the largest of those today, criticisms of the enterprise also came early. What we now know as the Ivy League was the biggest of the big time in those days, and, for example, the University of Pennsylvania's student-run Athletic Association was $6,600 in debt by 1894, turning to the university's alumni to bail it out. By 1906, the Athletic Association had an administrative staff that reported to no one and a budget of $141,000. In 1922, in debt from a trip to the Rose Bowl, the university tore down Franklin Field and built a new, 54,000-seat stadium in its place. Four years later, the university added an upper deck. Penn financed the expansion and a new basketball arena with a bond issue that raised $4 million.

The salaries of football coaches were seen as a particularly egregious expense; a survey of 96 coaches in 1929 found that the highest paid salary was $14,000 per year while the median salary was $6,000 (taking inflation into account, that $14,000 would be worth about $175,000 in 2009 dollars). Both salary figures then were higher than comparable figures for full professors, and roughly equivalent to those of deans. Additionally, alumni often schemed to pay players under the table for their services, according to a report published by the Carnegie Foundation for the Advancement of Teaching (Savage, 1929).

The commercial enterprise of intercollegiate athletics continued to expand over the course of the 20th century. The NCAA began sponsoring championship events in 1925, with the men's basketball tournament commencing in 1939. By the 1960s, the NCAA controlled regular-season football television broadcasts, doling out proceeds on a broad basis to universities from "Game of the Week" contracts. In the 1980s, however, the football powerhouses challenged the association's monopoly on televised regular-season football. The Board of Regents of the Universities of Georgia and Oklahoma sued the NCAA and in 1984 won a landmark case that gave colleges control over regular-season television contracts, and by extension other revenue not tied to NCAA-sponsored events.

Live, televised college football, the court ruled, was a unique product that consumers desired, just like professional football on television. The NCAA could pass and enforce some rules that were noncommercial in nature, such as scholarship limits and requirements that athletes were amateurs, but it had no right to restrict its members' opportunities to make money from televising football games.

Since this decision, the financial stakes have grown enormously, both for regular-season contests and for championship events, driven in part by the growth of the television market for college athletics, both on cable and the major networks. The Southeastern Conference divided $16 million in revenue among its members in 1990; in 2008–09, the league distributed more than $130 million (Southeastern Conference, 2009). In pursuit of similar opportunities, nearly all of the athletics programs and conferences in the top tier have been rearranged over the past two decades as colleges have tried to make the best television deals: The SEC grew from 10 to 12 teams; the Big Eight acquired four members of the Southwest Conference to form the Big 12; the ACC reached far beyond its Tobacco Road roots to create a league stretching from Boston to Miami; and most recently the Big East reached out to acquire the University of Cincinnati, DePaul University, University of Louisville, Marquette University, and the University of South Florida in 2005–06.

The NCAA has maintained control over the logistics and revenue for its championship events, and specifically uses money from the Division I men's basketball tournament to fund the majority of its operations, other championships in all three divisions, and a large payout to its membership based on various formulas. The NCAA has signed contracts that exceeded $16 million a year in 1981 for rights to the tournament, $140 million per year in 1989, $216 million per year in 1994, and $545 million per year on average under the current contract with CBS.

In the 2000s, two groups have emerged among Bowl Subdivision institutions. The top group is the true "big time," and consists of universities belonging to the conferences whose football teams are granted automatic access to the Bowl Championship Series, which consists of the BCS championship game as well as the Fiesta, Orange, Rose, and Sugar Bowls. These conferences are the Atlantic Coast, Big East, Big Ten, Big 12, Southeastern, and Pacific-10 Conferences. The champions of these six leagues are granted automatic and lucrative slots in this top tier of bowl games, and four at-large teams are selected from these conferences as well as the others, Conference USA and the Mid-American, Mountain West, Sun Belt, and Western Athletic Conferences. The conferences with automatic BCS access have guaranteed annual revenue from these games, while the other leagues receive revenue contingent on their teams qualifying according to a complex formula.

The differences between the universities in the conferences with automatic BCS bids and other leagues go far beyond this formulaic distinction. Most of the institutions in the "have" conferences have historically been the most prominent in their states or regions, enjoy deep and wide fan bases, and can command television contracts, bowl-game agreements, and ticket prices to support vast enterprises. Particularly in the Northeast, Midwest, and West, they have maintained large athletics departments with gymnastics, lacrosse, rowing, and soccer teams in addition to more-traditional sports like baseball, basketball, swimming, tennis, track and field, and wrestling. The "have-not" conferences tend to consist of newer, smaller, and more regional institutions that lack these resources and opportunities. Nonetheless, their leaders and constituents desire the visibility and the prestige associated with big-time college sports, and must supplement the revenue they can generate from athletics with substantial internal funds to "keep up with the Joneses" in the elite leagues.

To the reality of burgeoning budgets and growing deficits, of heightened commercialism and aggressive marketing, add the layer of the global recession of 2008–09, which has affected state appropriations, private giving, and enrollment at most colleges and universities. This has put big-time college sports in the eye of a perfect storm of economic challenges.

CHAPTER 2: EXPENSES

As noted above, universities in the Football Bowl Subdivision sponsor football and also must fund at least 15 others sports, and most universities actually sponsor significantly more. Some athletic departments have more than 250 employees, including coaches, administrators, academic advisers, marketing and ticket sales personnel, videographers, and sports medicine staff. Some have as many as 900 student-athletes on their men's and women's teams, with an average of 493 per institution.

One of the primary ways in which university athletic programs are distinct from professional sports is that the labor cost of the athletes involved is largely fixed. An athlete participating in football, basketball, women's gymnastics, women's tennis, or women's volleyball receives a scholarship equivalent to tuition, room, board, books, and mandatory fees. Athletes in most other sports receive partial scholarships. Universities are not required to award all the scholarships permitted in a given sport, and most do not fully fund grants in all the sports they offer. There are no requirements for facilities, spending, or any other expense category as it relates to a particular sport.

Division I athletic programs operate as semiautonomous units within the university enterprise, but they share commonalities with both academic and auxiliary enterprises. Attached to their universities, they report to their central administrations. Some athletic "associations" are separately-incorporated 501(c)(3) not-for-profit corporations. They offer academic services to student-athletes, much as academic units do to students as a whole. They simultaneously serve student-athletes and also mandate their participation in particular activities without compensation beyond a grant-in-aid. This is not dissimilar in form to on-campus jobs such as those of residence hall assistants or graduate assistants, but is different enough to prompt debates about whether student-athletes constitute an unpaid labor force.

The median budget for athletics programs in the Football Bowl Subdivision is about $40 million, but that number is deceiving. There is a wide gap in spending from the very top programs to the bottom. If we split big-time athletics programs into 10 deciles of 12 institutions based on expenses, the median budget for the lowest decile was $14 million in 2007 and the median budget for the top decile was $83 million. The highest spending categories for the average athletics program includes the following:

- Salaries and benefits, especially coaches' salaries (32 percent of total expenses);
- Tuition-driven grants-in-aid—or sports scholarships (16 percent);
- Facilities maintenance and rental (14 percent);
- Team travel, recruiting and equipment and supplies (12 percent combined);
- Fund-raising costs, guaranteed payments to opponents, game-day expenses, medical costs, conducting sports camps and other miscellaneous costs (12 percent).

The greatest challenge facing universities and their athletics departments today is dealing with the rapid rise of expenses. Athletics expenses are growing at an annual rate approaching 7 percent, according to a variety of studies (For more information, see references to Cheslock, Fulks, and Orszag and Israel at the end of this report.)

At the same time, revenues are not keeping up. In 2009, the National Collegiate Athletic Association published a report that found median operating spending for athletics increased 43 percent between 2004 and 2008, but median revenue generated by athletics programs grew only 33 percent over the same time period (Fulks, 2008). In another telltale spending reality a few years earlier, the NCAA reported in 2005 that athletic expenses rose as much as four times faster than overall institutional spending between 2001 and 2003 (Orszag & Orszag, 2005).

There are two key challenges facing athletics programs when it comes to cost reduction. First, athletic programs cannot control university tuition and fees, which determine the cost of scholarships. Second, they have not controlled salaries, particularly coaches' salaries. Between 2005 and 2007, total coaches' salaries in the top decile of big-time programs increased by 25 percent, according to the data supplied by the NCAA. A separate study from the NCAA found that for head football coaches alone, in the period from 2004–2006, the median salary across the top tier of major athletic programs increased by 47 percent, by 20 percent for head women's basketball coaches, and 15 percent for head men's basketball coaches (Fulks, 2006). *The Chronicle of Higher Education* reported that University of Southern California football coach Pete Carroll, at more than $4 million per year, was the highest-paid employee of any kind at any private university in the nation in 2007 (Brainard, 2009).

In an article on coaches' compensation, *USA Today* found that at public universities, the salaries are comparable: Bob Stoops at the University of Oklahoma received a raise early in 2009 to $3.7 million, plus an $800,000 bonus should he remain at his job through 2011. The University of Florida's Urban Meyer received a raise of $750,000 weeks before the start of the 2009 season, lifting his annual salary to $4 million.

The University of Alabama's Nick Saban, Louisiana State University's Les Miles, Ohio State University's Jim Tressel, and the University of Iowa's Kirk Ferentz are all being paid more than $3 million per year. While they are among the highest-profile university employees and may have multi-year contracts, coaches can be fired for not winning enough games despite meeting or exceeding other expectations, such as leading teams with high graduation rates. Coaches can also break their contracts and jump to another university for massive pay raises, leading to the proliferation of buyout clauses in coaches' contracts. While the competition among top universities for elite faculty members and administrators can be intense, it tends not to be as public as the battle for coaches.

An example of this process is the story of the University of Memphis men's basketball coach John Calipari jumping to the University of Kentucky. Calipari, who was being paid a reported $2.5 million in 2008–09 at Memphis, jumped to Kentucky for a reported eight-year, $31.5 million contract. As with many coaches' deals, Calipari was also guaranteed, among other things, two "late model, quality automobiles," a country club membership, income from basketball camps at university facilities and hundreds of thousands of dollars in performance incentives. Kentucky paid Memphis $200,000, the amount Calipari was required to compensate his former institution for voiding his contract.

"We're the pre-eminent basketball program in the country," Kentucky athletics director Mitch Barnhart told the *Memphis Commercial Appeal,* "and if we want a premier coach, then that's what it takes to get it done" (McMurray, 2009).

Calipari's contract was negotiated weeks before the state of Kentucky, facing a statewide budget deficit, cut back funding to the university by 2 percent, according to published reports. As part of the cuts, about 20 faculty positions were eliminated or remained unfilled.

Football and men's basketball make enough operating revenue to cover their operating expenses at more than half of the elite athletics programs, including salaries of their head and assistant coaches and additional personnel. During the period from 2004–2006, 54 percent of those football programs reported external revenue (i.e., that from ticket sales, television contracts, and other sources outside the university) that exceeded operating expenses for their football teams, according to the NCAA (Fulks, 2006). Men's basketball programs achieved greater financial success, with 57 percent producing net revenue during the same three-year period.

With few exceptions, however, reported operating surpluses from the two marquee sports were not enough to cover the costs of an athletic department's other sports offerings, whether it be 14 or 24 squads. The myth of the business model—that football and men's basketball cover their own expenses and fully support non-revenue sports—is put to rest by an NCAA study finding that 93 institutions ran a deficit for the 2007–08 school year, averaging losses of $9.9 million. That was more than twice as large as the average net revenue ($3.9 million) for the 25 programs that reported an operating surplus in 2008.

Even so, this may understate the true cost of intercollegiate athletics at any given institution. Data produced by NCAA member institutions suffer from varying methods of accounting; for instance, the major item of capital costs for facilities, the projected costs of maintaining an athletic department's infrastructure, the time spent on athletics issues by the central administration, and other factors generally are not fully included in athletic departments' financial statements or reports to the NCAA. Also, colleges have different ways of accounting for the cost of athletes' grants-in-aid: Many big-time programs pay the full cost of tuition to the institution, but sometimes colleges forego such revenue by, for instance, placing athletes on in-state tuition.

Overall, spending on athletics appears to have created a so-called "arms race" between competing athletic programs and institutions. Economists Jonathan Orszag and Mark Israel (2009) define an arms race as "a situation in which the athletic expenditures by a given school tend to increase along with expenditures by other schools in the same conference." In their analysis of the college sports business, using data from 2004–2007, Orszag and Israel (2009) found evidence to support such a dynamic; one university spends an additional dollar in operations costs in Conference X and a rival in the same conference spends an increased 60 cents, and the spending continues among those who can afford it and even those who cannot.

In 2007, two of the nation's most watched conferences, with some of the most popular college sports brands among its members, posted some of the largest financial deficits of the 11 top-tier football-playing conferences. The median net revenue for one league's member athletic departments was negative $7.2 million; for another it was negative $10.4 million. For the former, its red ink had grown by 44 percent since 2005. Meanwhile, every athletic program in three less prosperous conferences relied on more dollars from their central administrations than they were able to generate on their own.

Consider these disparities. The University of Alabama, one of the nation's most prestigious football powers, is paying salaries of nearly $6.6 million to its head football coach and his nine assistants for the 2009 season. That's more than 32 bowl-subdivision programs spend on football as a whole, according to an analysis by the *Orlando Sentinel* (Limon, 2009). The "have-not" institutions within each conference cannot compete revenue-wise with some of their "have" peers because of stadium capacity, fan demographics and other factors. Some athletic directors believe these intraconference disparities are as much of a threat to financial stability as the differences among conferences. It is, said one athletic director, similar to the disparities in Major League Baseball, in which the Pittsburgh Pirates and Kansas City Royals must try to compete for players in the same market as the New York Yankees and Los Angeles Dodgers.

Iowa State University of the Big 12 is an example of a have-not school in a big-time conference. It brings in a respectable $17 million per year in football revenue. Among its competitors are Texas, with $73 million in football revenue, and Nebraska, with $49 million in football revenue. But Iowa State's fans and boosters expect its program to retain coaches and build facilities at the same level as their richer Big 12 colleagues. Keeping up with the Joneses is increasingly difficult, if not impossible.

CHAPTER 3: REVENUES

While universities and even the biggest athletics programs are not-for-profit organizations, some can generate significant sums from ticket sales, television contracts, and other sources. Most, however, depend on institutional transfers from general funds, student fees, and state appropriations to cover the expenses discussed in the previous section. The NCAA has begun to make this distinction in its reports as one between "generated" revenue—or that coming from external sources—and "allocated" revenue, which consists of intrainstitutional transfers.

External sources of athletics department revenue stand, generally, in this order:

- Cash contributions from alumni and others (30 percent);
- Ticket sales (28 percent);
- Payments from conferences, which include revenue from regular-season television contracts, royalties from the NCAA's basketball tournament contract, and football bowl game payouts (17 percent);
- Local marketing income, such as in-stadium signs and payments from corporate sponsors, local radio-TV rights fees, etc. (10 percent).

The remainder comes from food and program sales at games, sports camp income, guarantees paid out by opponents for road games, and payouts from athletics department scholarship endowments.

While these are overall f gures, breaking them down yields a much clearer picture of disparities among institutions. At the bottom of the revenue-producing rankings among FBS programs, ticket sales—driven, of course, by far lower attendance and cheaper prices—account for less than 10 percent of their total revenue. At the top-revenue producers, ticket sales in large stadiums at high prices generate about 30 percent of all revenue. In 2007, half of big-time programs sold less than $5 million in tickets to all contests. But the other half sold more than $10 million in tickets, with the top 20 percent of programs exceeding $20 million in ticket sales, most of that attributable to football.

This is separate from the donations from fans. Most of these take the form of contributions to "ticket priorities." Especially at major institutions, ticketholders make annual donations on top of the price of a season ticket to secure prime seating or luxury boxes. These donations are 80% tax-deductible under Internal Revenue Service guidelines. The University of Georgia received some publicity in 2008 when, on the eve of a season in which its football team was ranked No. 1 in early polls, a first-time season-ticket buyer would have had to donate $10,651 for the right to purchase tickets. There is some evidence that this and other forms of fundraising in athletics may compete with overall university fundraising for gifts, according to a recent study by *The Chronicle of Higher Education* (Wolverton, 2007).

On top of revenues generated from ticket sales, universities belonging to the BCS conferences receive significant funds from television contracts through complex arrangements. Essentially, the major television networks sign contracts with the NCAA to televise championship events, including men's basketball, the primary money generator. They also sign deals with the conferences to broadcast regular-season contests in football, men's basketball, and occasionally other sports. Finally, they sign contracts to broadcast the assortment of football bowl games and pay royalties to the conferences whose teams are involved. All of these funds are distributed to conferences, which then have their own revenue-sharing arrangements with member institutions. Conferences also reap revenue from their own conference championship events, both from ticket sales and broadcast rights. The television networks then sell advertising and marketing rights to make good their revenue commitments in these broadcasting agreements. (For a more-thorough description of this process, particularly with relevance to bowl, games visit ESPN. For more data on the finances of college football, visit the NCAA.)

The end result may or may not be of significant benefit for the institutions involved. For example, the Big Ten Conference distributed $154 million to its 11 members in 2006–07; at the other end of the scale, the Sun Belt Conference distributed roughly $1.2 million to its nine members. This disparity reflects, once more, the gap between the "haves" and "have-nots."

Whether or not they earn significant revenue from these sources, virtually all athletics programs receive some form of institutional subsidy. According to 2007 NCAA financial data, half of all top-flight athletic programs rely on at least $9 million in institutional and governmental subsidies to balance their budgets. Even in the most prosperous conference, its members received a median subsidy of $3.4 million.

Such allocations come from student fees, support from a university's general fund (covering indirect costs such as utilities), state support, staffing or facilities maintenance. In 2006, that average subsidy from central funds stood at 20 percent of total revenue for bowl subdivision programs (Fulks, 2006).

As financial burdens on typical college students have increased, the rise in student fees to fund athletics has stirred debate and controversy. At all levels of big-time college sports, students are funding their campuses' athletics programs with mandatory fees; NCAA data shows that, generally speaking, programs at the lower end of expenses and revenues rankings tend to rely more heavily on student fees than financially successful programs.

In 2007, FBS programs with median expenses of $19.7 million saw students pay a median of $4.7 million, or nearly 24 percent of those athletics budgets. On the other end, in the top decile of programs with budgets in the $83 million range, students typically paid for less than two percent of their universities' sports costs. In 2006, Fulks found that, across the board, six percent of total revenues at bowl-subdivision institutions were paid by student fees. At universities without football and, so, without substantial revenue-generating opportunities, students bore a higher burden; 18 percent of athletics budgets came from student fees (Fulks, 2006).

Battles over fees have triggered campus-wide referenda. In 2008, at California State University, Fresno, students voted against an increase from $7 to $50 per semester; the university president overrode that result and upped the fee to subsidize athletics to $32 per semester. At Utah State University, about 53 percent of students voting approved a 100 percent increase from $113 to $243 annually to help lift the university's athletics department out of debt. In 2009, students at the University of New Orleans, a non-footballplaying Division I institution, soundly rejected a doubling of student fees for athletics from about $200 per year to nearly $400.

Student fees often subsidize all or part of ticket prices for events; a typical arrangement is for such fees to cover admission to games for nonrevenue teams and enable students to buy lower-cost season tickets to men's basketball and football games. While such fees generally are mandatory for full-time students, the number of students who attend such games or purchase tickets varies from campus to campus.

CHAPTER 4: CONSTRUCTION IN COLLEGE SPORTS: AN ARMS RACE?

As with the rest of higher education, which has engaged in an "amenities race" for new laboratory facilities, student unions, residence halls, and other projects, a construction boom has echoed throughout intercollegiate athletics as programs have upgraded existing and created new facilities. Many football stadiums have been refurbished, adding capacity, luxury suites and other premium amenities at a cost often exceeding $100 million. Basketball arenas have been built or renovated, as state-of-the-art practice, strength training, and tutoring facilities have proliferated.

Most such facilities are financed through private fundraising and selling bonds. The annual expenses of repaying these bonds have become a significant proportion of many athletics departments' budgets. For instance, Ohio State had a reported $197 million facilities debt burden in 2007, with an annual debt service payment of $17 million. With a sold-out 105,000-seat football stadium, Ohio State officials imposed a ticket surcharge on their fans to pay down facilities debt. Overall, *Street & Smith's Sports Business Journal* reported that spending on intercollegiate athletic facilities reached $15.2 billion between 1995 and 2005 (King, 2005).

In 2005, the NCAA's Presidential Task Force on the Future of Intercollegiate Athletics reported that nearly 20 percent of current spending on average is tied to facility expansion and capital debt. The task force warned that "higher education has monetized the anticipated growth potential of athletics for near-term benefits while mortgaging the long-term financial security of the university, if there is a downturn in the fortunes of college sports."

Recruiting costs remain a relatively small item in most budgets, accounting for only two percent of total departmental costs, according to the latest NCAA Revenue and Expenditures Report (Fulks, 2008). However, some argue that facilities construction should be considered a recruiting expense as different athletics programs woo 17- or 18-year-old high school seniors with the most lavish practice facility, shiniest academic study center or snazziest arena.

The University of Kentucky opened a $30 million basketball practice facility in 2007. Georgia opened a $31 million practice and weightlifting facility soon after for men's and women's basketball and gymnastics. Texas Tech University spent $4 million four years ago for a student-athlete center, and Texas A&M University topped that with a $27 million academic center and a $22 million basketball practice gym.

CHAPTER 5: TITLE IX AND OLYMPIC SPORTS

Most of this report focuses on revenue, expenses, facilities, and other trends primarily associated with football and men's basketball, for a simple reason: Those sports are where the money is. However, big-time athletics programs maintain a variety of other teams for a variety of reasons. Among them are institutional history, local differences, and NCAA membership requirements. But an undeniable reason for a large number of athletics programs is the law forbidding colleges from discriminating on the basis of gender: Title IX of the Education Amendments of 1972. Between 1981 and 2007, the number of Division I women's teams sponsored jumped from 2,011 in 1981–82 to 3,339 in 2006–07, according to NCAA records; the number of women student-athletes in big-time programs more than doubled. Much of this growth was triggered by lawsuits in the mid-1990s forcing colleges and universities to adhere to Title IX guidelines.

Despite these gains, far more men than women are still participating in sports at the Division I level. The NCAA's study found that even though 53 percent of full-time students at Division I institutions in 2007–08 were female, only 45 percent of scholarship athletes were (DeHass, 2004).

Virtually no women's teams attract enough fans to make money, and few have the kind of marketing deals from corporate sponsors that enable men's teams to generate net operating revenue. In fact, the NCAA reported that in 2006, universities in the Football Bowl Subdivision ran a median annual deficit of just under $5 million on women's sports. They were hardly alone: 49 percent of universities also ran a deficit on men's sports, with a median loss of $4.4 million.

In recent years, athletics directors, faced with rising costs and the decision to spend more on revenue-producing sports, have faced a dilemma: Do they cut costs (or eliminate increases) evenly across all sports, even if it makes some teams uncompetitive? Or do they choose to eliminate a sport altogether to concentrate cost-cutting there? Teams in the so-called Olympic sports—such as track and field or swimming—have fallen prey to the budgetary knife when athletic departments need to cut back. Such teams are easy targets, but because most athletics departments are not in compliance with Title IX's requirements for women's participation, colleges risk expensive legal battles if they cut women's sports. That leaves cuts to, or finding efficiencies for, men's sports as the only options.

Proponents for men's sports have long said that sports opportunities for men have been reduced as slots for women have grown because of Title IX, but many studies have found otherwise. A Women's Sports Foundation study found that between 1992–93 and 2000–01, women's participation increased annually by 4.5% and men's participation increased annually by 0.3% (Cheslock, 2008). The corresponding figures are 2.5% and 0.2% for the periods 1981–82 to 1992–93 and 2000–01 to 2004–05.

However, out of all the NCAA's divisions, only in Football Bowl Subdivision programs have there been a decline in men's opportunities; "slight" in the conferences with automatic bids to the BCS—but larger decline in the other FBS conferences, according to the Women's Sports Foundation study.

CHAPTER 6: COST CONTAINMENT, THEN AND NOW

Just about every athletics program, no matter what its budget, has been in cost-containment and budget-cutting modes over the past year. Such budget trimming has intensified as the national recession deepened. A day does not go by, it seems, when an athletics department or conference is not laying off staff members, reducing travel costs, or rethinking how to conduct postseason tournaments with fewer dollars.

Few in academe will be sympathetic, as the downturn has caused layoffs at institutions of all sizes and missions, as well as furloughs and delays in new projects and cutbacks in old ones. Notably, neither in academics nor in athletics are many institutions stepping back to look at enterprise-level changes that would make the cost structure more manageable.

This is not to say that athletics programs have not made significant cuts. According to various media reports: Rice University trimmed its athletic budget 10 percent; Conference USA reduced the number of football players on its traveling squads; Iowa State cut a chartered flight to a football game, downsizing to bus travel and an international men's basketball excursion was eliminated (Cross, 2009); Florida State cut its men's basketball travel budget by $256,000 (Carter, 2009); Stanford, among the nation's richest institutions with the broadest sports offerings, must cut more than $7 million from its athletics budget over the next two years (Schlabach, 2009).

Nationwide, athletic administration jobs are being eliminated or left unfilled; printed media relations materials are being abandoned for less-expensive Web-based sports information. In some cases, such as the University of Cincinnati and the University of Washington (Belson, 2009), non-revenue sports have lost scholarship support or been dropped completely. At the beginning of the 2009 football season, the sports budget trims continued nationwide with no end in sight.

To a certain extent, history is repeating itself. "N.C.A.A. Seeking Way to Cut Budget" reads a headline from the April 29, 1975, *New York Times* (White, 1975). It was about a "Special Meeting on Economy in Intercollegiate Athletics" convened by the NCAA. Cost-cutting legislation and the need to do something "severe" and not "cosmetic" were on the agenda. Among the cuts then: A limit on 105 football scholarships per university was reduced to 95.

Fifteen years later, in 1990, the NCAA convened a "Special Committee on Cost Reduction" that led to trimming men's scholarships in all sports by 10 percent, dropping football to 85 scholarships. A limit on the salaries of the fourth assistant basketball coach at Division I programs also was approved (NCAA News, 1990). (Later, that was ruled a violation of federal antitrust laws, and a jury awarded a class of coaches $54.5 million to be paid by the NCAA.)

The reason for the national moves in 1975 and 1990 was the reluctance of individual athletics programs to contain their costs unilaterally. Andy Geiger, who served as athletics director at the University of Pennsylvania, Maryland, Stanford and Ohio State, was a member of the 1990 NCAA cost-containment task force. He said recently that efforts then to reduce costs were done "collectively, which is the only way this effort of cost reduction could happen. We all have to agree and figure out a way to do it."

In 2009, conferences have taken the lead on promoting cost containment, creating new travel arrangements, eliminating in-person "media days" for coaches and athletes, and promoting other policies to reduce costs without putting member teams at competitive disadvantages with one another. However, there appear to have been few, if any, substantive changes to the way college athletic programs do business in the current climate. The two exception might be Birmingham-Southern College and Centenary College of Louisiana, whose boards voted to drop from Division I to Division III. Neither was a member of the Football Bowl Subdivision, but other universities have pondered a similar move in recent years.

CHAPTER 7: COMMERCIALISM

As with universities as a whole, athletics programs are trying to find new sources of revenue to keep up with expanding costs and are looking to the commercial world for assistance. The fast-evolving world of sports business includes event promoters, television networks, marketing firms, ticket brokers and sponsors from all sectors of the corporate world, creating new questions about intellectual property for both the institution and the student-athlete, the appropriate distance between athletes and commercial presence, and the ability to maintain amateur athletics in a commercial marketplace.

Ticket sales and donations aside, television revenue and marketing dollars are the largest paths to sizable revenue. The Southeastern Conference (SEC) is an example of success on the broadcast front. In 2009, as noted earlier, the SEC's 12 member institutions shared $132.5 million in conference-generated revenue, or about a four percent increase over 2008 (Southeastern Conference, 2009). Each school received an average of $11 million. The key sources of revenue within the $132.5 million were $52 million from football television; $25.4 million from football bowls; $14.3 million from the SEC football championship game; $13.6 million from basketball television; $4.1 million from the SEC men's basketball tournament; and $23.1 million from NCAA championships. With its most recent contract in place, the SEC is expected to distribute upwards of $200 million annually to its institutions in future years.

Recently, a major trend among big-time institutions is the outsourcing of marketing, promotions, and sales to professional agencies. Those agencies, including IMG College, Learfield Sports, and ISP, guarantee athletics departments millions of dollars, and then sell a university's sports marketing inventory to corporate sponsors and broadcast partners. Even in this widespread commercial practice, the "haves" and "have-nots" benefit at different orders of magnitude. According to *USA Today,* in 2009, Ohio State University signed a deal with IMG guaranteeing the Buckeyes' athletics department $11 million a year for 10 years in marketing revenue; for that $110 million, IMG will then perform all the work selling in-stadium signs, coaches' radio and TV shows, and other corporate sponsorships (Perez & Berkowitz, 2009). By comparison, Utah State University recently signed a 10-year deal with Learfield for a total of $7.7 million. Utah State will receive less money over a period of 10 years than Ohio State will each year.

As athletics programs seek more commercial funding, they must balance that objective with the principle of protecting athletes from commercial exploitation. This tightrope act has become more difficult with legal challenges that allege current commercial products licensed by the NCAA violate athletes' publicity rights. Recently, athletes and former student-athletes have sued the NCAA and its commercial partners claiming their names and likenesses are being exploited without permission and compensation. As reported in the *New York Times,* college quarterbacks' jerseys numbers, height, weight, hair color, passing styles, home towns and other characteristics appear in EA Sports' *NCAA Football 2009* video game, although their names are omitted (Thomas, 2009). In the suits brought by current and former football and men's basketball athletes, players charge they are being exploited; their likenesses are generating revenue for the NCAA and the game manufacturer, but not for the student-athlete himself.

The lawsuits raise critical questions at a time when the NCAA is considering changes to its rules that could allow for greater use of athletes' images and names by commercial partners. The NCAA's governance group regulating amateurism recently has examined the effects of new media issues—such as webcasts and statistics distributed on mobile devices—on the commercialization of student-athletes. Legislation is expected to be introduced to NCAA members that could deregulate in some ways the use of athletes' likenesses and names. A "Commercial Activities Oversight Committee" has been proposed to track and make decisions in this area (Hosick, 2009).

The NCAA has attempted to frame the issue by proposing a bright-line distinction between the "amateur" model of intercollegiate athletics and the professional model used by big-league sports. NCAA vice president Wallace I. Renfro noted in 2008 that for years, colleges and universities "have encouraged intercollegiate athletics to seek outside sources of revenue as a means of diminishing institutional subsidization.... The problem is that we mistakenly extend the concept of amateurism to the enterprise itself. To be clear, student-athletes are amateurs. Intercollegiate athletics is not."

CHAPTER 8: MYTHS AND INTANGIBLES

NCAA data from a February 2009 study authored by economists Jonathan Orszag and Mark Israel shows athletics budgets amount to 6 percent of most universities' total institutional spending (Orszag & Israel, 2009). Despite that relatively thin slice of a campus' budget, athletics events where thousands of students, faculty, administrators and alums gather are often the visible "front porch" for a university. Contests can be community builders. Logos, nicknames, and television appearances brand institutions locally and nationally. Even if athletics programs do not generate net revenue, they surely stimulate alumni giving and increase prospective student applications. This is known as the "Flutie effect," on the exaggerated notion that Doug Flutie put Boston College on the map with his Hail Mary pass in a 1984 football game against the University of Miami.

Rigorous studies of the subject, however, suggest that there is no significant institutional benefit to athletic success. In a 2004 report for the Knight Commission, Cornell University economist Robert H. Frank, after reviewing the extant scholarly literature, concluded any links to football and men's basketball victories and increased applications and the SAT scores of the applicants "is small and not significantly different from zero" (Frank, 2004). A 2009 study by Devin G. Pope of the University of Pennsylvania's Wharton School and Jaren C. Pope of Virginia Tech finds applications do rise from two to eight percent after football and men's basketball success, but "the impact is often short-lived" (Pope & Pope, 2008).

As for donations, while winning records do not necessarily increase gifts, football bowl game appearances do, Frank wrote, to the tune of $6.50 per alumnus at public universities and $40 per year per alumnus at private schools. "The empirical literature seems to say that if the overall net effect of athletic success on alumni giving is positive, it is likely to be small," wrote Frank (2004).

Indeed, donations to athletics departments may cannibalize contributions to academic programs. As an April 2007 study in the *Journal of Sport Management* revealed, athletics departments between 1998 and 2003 received an increased share of gifts—from 14.7 percent to 26 percent—from university supporters even as overall giving to institutions was flat (Humphreys & Mondello, 2007). Even so, a Knight Commission survey of university presidents finds that they "do not view fundraising for athletics and academics a zero-sum game, in which financial gains for athletics programs are made at the expense of the academic side of the house."

There are two other myths to be dispelled. First, there is no correlation between spending more on athletics and winning more, according to an NCAA report titled, "The Empirical Effects of Collegiate Athletics: An Interim Report" (Litan, Orszag, & Orszag, 2005). Second, increased spending on coaches' salaries has no significant relationship to success or increased revenue, according to a follow-up study.

Given increased expenses demanded by elite programs, the question is: At what cost would a winning athletic program increase the size and quality of applicants and the donations of boosters? Frank wrote: "A big-time athletic program might be a cost-effective means of expanding the applicant pool if a highly visible winning program could be launched at moderate expense. But . . . even the cost of fielding a losing program is extremely high and growing rapidly" (Frank, 2004).

Another trend has been for athletics programs to reclassify from the Football Championship Subdivision to the Football Bowl Subdivision or from Division II to Division I. Division II sports programs offer fewer athletic grants-in-aid, fewer teams, and little media exposure for their athletes, teams and institutions. When Division II schools jump to Division I and, for some, eventually, to the highest FBS status, there is an educational aspiration component to it. "You are who you play," one official said.

"Our alumni tell us, 'We look at the ticker at the bottom of CNN and [our scores] aren't there,'" Joseph Chapman, president of North Dakota State University, told the Minneapolis *Star Tribune* before NDSU's program leaped to Division I in 2004. "Your athletic status is wrapped in your image and visibility as an institution."

However, elevation to the higher competitive classification rarely lifts net revenue. In a report on about 50 university programs that reclassified from Division II to some subset of Division I, the authors found that:

- Programs that stepped up from Division II to Division I spent more than they took in, experiencing "an average deterioration in net operating revenue" of more than $1 million each;
- Schools that switched divisions did not generally tend to experience a significant increase in enrollment, although some did;
- Student fees—and, so, institutional subsidies—increased considerably as programs moved from Division II to Division I;
- Switching to Division I increased alumni giving earmarked for athletics, but there was no evidence it helped general alumni donations (Orszag & Orszag, 2005).

CHAPTER 9: CONCLUSION

Concerns about the expenses of college sports are nothing new, and the current economic crisis only exacerbates a long-term trend. The NCAA's Presidential Task Force on the Future of Intercollegiate Athletics concluded in 2006 that while there was no "imminent financial crisis in intercollegiate athletics … [t]he rate of growth combined with the rapid rise in capital costs has the current system under stress."

The rate of spending is a concern because of the risk it poses to athletics programs, universities, and student-athletes themselves. The success of major conferences and their institutions in the media marketplace may render second-tier conferences and their institutions invisible, destroying the investment such universities have made in "big-time" athletics. As for universities, the run-up in athletics costs comes at a time when other costs are rising faster than inflation in the broad economy and states are reducing appropriations for higher education. Thus, it is plausible to think that a regional university in any of the major conferences may find itself having to choose between funding an academic department and subsidizing athletics. And student-athletes, particularly in non-revenue sports, may be at risk of their teams being cut or funding reduced to meet other needs, such as those of revenue sports.

Second, the structure of intercollegiate athletics is changing rapidly. Intercollegiate athletics programs have become heavily dependent on revenue from media and other corporations with no vested interest in higher education. This already has led to tension over game scheduling and marketing presence at events, but it also creates an internal danger for athletics departments: As one official put it, "I just hope that ESPN and CBS are too big to fail." If the economy takes another turn, or technology threatens traditional television and media corporations are not able to make good on their contract obligations, the effects in college sports would be seismic.

More immediately, there is a concern among athletic administrators that costs will continue to rise, but there are no more pots of gold to find. As University of Minnesota athletic director Joel Maturi put it recently, major athletics programs may be running out of that "next somehow," even as their parent institutions are reeling from an overarching funding dilemma. The future may not be about more revenue. University of Arizona athletics director Jim Livengood told ESPN.com recently, "The old adage of 'just make more money' through better development and fundraising won't help. The problems are too big to just be able to fix on the revenue side."

Penn State's athletics director Tim Curley, who currently oversees 29 intercollegiate sports, told the Knight Commission in 2009: "I believe the economic realities and conditions facing athletics will have a major impact on sponsorship [of teams] and participation in the years ahead. I remain concerned that, if adjustments are not made, we will see a reduction of both men and women's programs in the next three to five years" (Knight Commission on Intercollegiate Athletics, 2009). He warned that non-revenue men's sports will be hardest hit and reduced to club or intramural status.

Moreover, on average, institutional subsidies to athletics are rising faster than educational subsidies for the student body. This means that colleges will have to expend a greater percentage on athletics than ever before.

These kinds of concerns are by no means exclusive to athletics. Colleges and universities across the country are under attack for an economic structure that contains few if any incentives to mitigate expenses, and instead rewards institutions for pursuing high-cost research and building programs. Tuition and fees have been rising more quickly than inflation while colleges have had difficulty providing metrics to demonstrate that they are meeting their students' educational needs. And the expansion of universities in the face of declining state support has created the need to seek funds through corporate partnerships and other arrangements that have prompted ethical questions about the ability of institutions to conduct impartial academic inquiry.

As such, it is incumbent upon colleges and universities to make sure that they and their athletic programs are functioning efficiently to fulfill their missions. In terms of athletics, this means that it is time for a serious examination of the structure of intercollegiate athletics to find ways to brake the runaway train of athletic expenses.

REFERENCES

Austin American-Statesman. (2007, September 20.) A Texas-Size Building Boom.

Belson, K. (2009, May 3). Universities cutting teams as they trim their budgets. *New York Times.*

Bernstein, M. F. (2001). *Football: The Ivy League Origins of an American Obsession,* Illinois: University of Illinois Press.

Blumenstyk, G. (2009, May 1). In a time a crisis, colleges ought to be making history. *Chronicle of Higher Education,* 55 (34), A1.

Brainard, J. (2009, February 27). The biggest campus paycheck may not be the president's. *Chronicle of Higher Education,* A1.

Carter, A. (2009, June 24). FSU AD Randy Spetman: Proposed budget cut less drastic than anticipated. *Orlando Sentinel.*

Centenary College. (2009, July 29). Centenary Board Votes to Reposition Centenary Athletics.

Cheslock, J. (2008). *Who's playing college sports? Money, race, and gender.* New York: NY, Women's Sports Foundation.

Cheslock, J. (2009). Maintaining Broad-Based Athletic Programs in an Era of Rapid Expenditure Growth. Presented to the Knight Commission on Intercollegiate Athletics, January 2009, Washington, D.C.

Conference USA. (2009, May 14). Conference USA Concludes 2009 Spring Meetings.

Cross, M. (2009, June 17). Athletic budget cut update #34. *Ultimate Sports Insider.*

Crowley, J. N. (2006). In the Arena: The NCAA's First Century. Indianapolis, Ind: National Collegiate Athletic Association.

Deford, F. (2007, January 10). Birmingham Southern Chose Students Over Athletes. *SI.com.*

DeHass, D. (2004) 2003–04 Race and Gender Demographics of NCAA Member Institutions' Athletics Personnel. Indianapolis, IN: National Collegiate Athletic Association.

Frank, R. H. (2004). *Challenging the myth: A review of the links among college athletic success, student quality, and donations.* Miami, FL: John S. and James L. Knight Foundation Commission on Intercollegiate Athletics.

Fulks, D. L. (2006). *Revenues and Expenses, Profits and Losses of Division I-A Intercollegiate Athletics Programs Aggregated by Conference—2003 Fiscal Year.* Indianapolis, IN: National Collegiate Athletic Association.

Fulks, D. L. (2008). *2004–06 NCAA Revenue and Expenses of Division I Intercollegiate Athletics Programs Report.* Indianapolis, IN: National Collegiate Athletic Association.

Gerrard, J. (1989, November 22). In $1 Billion Deal, CBS Locks Up N.C.A.A. Basketball Tournament. *New York Times.*

Hosick, M. B. (2009, March 26). Commercialism project enters legislative phase. *NCAA News.*

Humphreys, B. R., & Mondello, M. (2007). Intercollegiate athletic success and donations at NCAA Division I institutions, *Journal of Sport Management,* 21 (5), 265–280.

King, B. (2005, December 5). Race for Recruits. *Sports Business Journal,* 8(31), 19–25.

Knight Commission on Intercollegiate Athletics (1991). *Keeping faith with the student-athlete: A new model for intercollegiate athletics.* Miami, FL: John S. and James L. Knight Foundation Commission on Intercollegiate Athletics.

Knight Commission on Intercollegiate Athletics (2006). *Public Opinion Poll.* Miami, FL: John S. and James L. Knight Foundation Commission on Intercollegiate Athletics.

Knight Commission on Intercollegiate Athletics (2009). Quantitative and Qualitative Research with Football Bowl Subdivision University Presidents on the Cost and Financing of Intercollegiate Athletics. Miami, FL: John S. and James L. Knight Foundation Commission on Intercollegiate Athletics.

Limon, L. (2009, July 29). Come on Down: College football coaches still lining up for rising pay. *Orlando Sentinel.*

Litan, R. E., Orszag, J. M., & Orszag, P. R. (2005). *The Empirical Effects of Collegiate Athletics: An Update.* Indianapolis, IN: National Collegiate Athletic Association.

Longman, J. (2009, May 29). As Costs of Sports Rise, Students Balk at Fees. *New York Times.*

McMurray, J. (2009, April 2), Perks sweeten Calipari's Kentucky contract: Cars, country clubs, game tickets included in the deal. *Associated Press.*

Mendenhall, T. C. (1993). *The Harvard-Yale Boat Race, 1852–1924, and the Coming of Sport to the American College.* Mystic, Conn.: Mystic Seaport Museum

NCAA v. Board of Regents of the University of Oklahoma et al., 468 US 85 (1984).

NCAA News (1990, August 15). Council agrees to sponsor most reform proposals. *NCAA News,* 27(29).

Orszag, J. M., & Israel, M. (2009). *The Empirical Effects of Collegiate Athletics: An Update Based on 2004–2007 Data.* Indianapolis, IN: National Collegiate Athletic Association.

Orszag, J. M., & Orszag, P. R. (2005). *The Physical Capital Stock Used in Collegiate Athletics.* Indianapolis, IN: National Collegiate Athletic Association.

Perez, A. J., & Berkowitz, S. (2009). Multimedia marketing deals at NCAA schools. *USA Today.*

Pope, J., & Pope, D. (2009). The impact of college sports success on the quantity and quality of student applications. *Southern Economic Journal.*

Sandomir, R. (1994, December 7). March Madness Stays on CBS's Calendar. *New York Times.*

Sandomir, R. (1999, November 19). CBS Will Pay $6 Billion for Men's N.C.A.A. Tournament. *New York Times.*

Savage, W. H. (1929). *American college athletics.* New York: Carnegie Foundation for the Advancement of Teaching.

Schlabach, M. (2009, July 13). Programs struggle to balance budget. *ESPN.*

Shelman, J. (2007, March). Questions & Answer: Joel Maturi, University of Minnesota Athletics Director. *Minnesota Star Tribune.*

Smith, M., & Ourand, J. (2008, August 25). ESPN pays $2.25B for SEC rights. *Sports Business Journal,* Page 01.

Southeastern Conference (2009, May 29). 2008–09 SEC Revenue Distribution. *SEC in the Community.*

Suggs, W. (2005). *A Place on the Team: The Triumph and Tragedy of Title IX.* Princeton, N.J.: Princeton University Press.

Suggs, W. (2006). "Historical Overview: At Play in America's Colleges," in Lapchick, R. E. (ed.). *A New Game Plan for College Sport.* Westport, Conn.: Praeger Publishers.

Suggs, W. (2007). "Heroines As Well As Heroes," in Zimbalist, A. and Hogshead-Makar (eds.). *Equal Play: Title IX and Social Change.* Philadelphia: Temple University Press.

Thomas, K. (2009, July 3). College starts sue over likenesses in video games. *New York Times.*

Title IX of the Education Amendments of 1972, 20 U.S.C. § 1681 (2000).

United States Government Accountability Office. (2007). *Intercollegiate Athletics: Trends by Sport in National Collegiate Athletic Association Sports.* GAO–07–744SP. Washington, D.C.

University of Georgia Sports Communications. (2008, July 15). Score Requirements Announced for Hartman Fund Contributors.

University of Kentucky. (n.d.). Joe Craft Center.

USA Today. (2003). *I-A conference expansion timeline.* Retrieved July 23, 2009 from http:// www.usatoday.com/sports/college/football/ expansion-timeline. htm

USA Today. (2007). *Compensation for Div. 1-A. college football coaches: An in-depth analysis of total income and how it is complied.*

USA Today. (2007). *Compensation for Division I men's basketball coaches: What the coaches earn at the 65 schools that played in the 2006 NCAA Tournament.*

Utah State University. (2009, March 24). Utah State University Students Vote To Support Athletic Fee Increase.

White, G. S. (1975, April 29). N.C.A.A. seeking way to cut budget. *New York Times.*

White, G. S. (1981, March 5). N.C.A.A. Title Basketball Sold to CBS for $48 Million. *New York Times.*

Wolverton, B. (2007, October 5). Growth in Sports Gifts May Mean Fewer Academic Donations. *Chronicle of Higher Education.*

Zimbalist, A. (1999). *Unpaid Professionals.* Princeton: Princeton University Press.

Zwerneman, B. (2009, June 23). Schools now keep score on balance sheets. *Houston Chronicle.*

22

Admissions Exemptions Benefit Athletes

Alan Scher Zagier

If grades make you a long shot for college, you're much more likely to get a break if you can play ball.

An Associated Press review of admissions data submitted to the NCAA by most of the 120 schools in college football's top tier shows that athletes enjoy strikingly better odds of having admission requirements bent on their behalf.

The notion that college athletes' talents give them a leg up in the admissions game isn't a surprise. But in what NCAA officials called the most extensive review to date, the AP found the practice is widespread and can be found in every major conference.

The review identified at least 27 schools where athletes were at least 10 times more likely to benefit from special admission programs than students in the general population.

That group includes 2009 Bowl Championship Series teams Oregon, Georgia Tech and Alabama, which is playing Texas for the national title Jan. 7.

At Alabama, 19 football players got in as part of a special admissions program from 2004 to 2006, the most recent years available in the NCAA report. The school tightened its standards for "special admits" in both 2004 and 2007, but from 2004 through 2006, Crimson Tide athletes were still more than 43 times more likely to benefit from such exemptions.

Source: Alan Scher Zagier, "Admissions Exemptions Benefit Athletes," Associated Press (December 30, 2009).

Alabama coach Nick Saban offered no apologies.

"Some people have ability and they have work ethic and really never get an opportunity," he said. "I am really pleased and happy with the job that we do and how we manage our students here, and the responsibility and accountability they have toward academics and the success that they've had in academics."

The NCAA defines special admissions programs as those designed for students who don't meet "standard or normal entrance requirements." The NCAA says such exceptions are fine as long as schools offer the same opportunities to everyone from dancers, French horn players and underrepresented minorities as they do to fleet-footed wide receivers and 300-pound offensive linemen.

Texas was one of seven schools that reported no use of special admissions, instead describing "holistic" standards that consider each applicant individually rather than relying on minimum test scores and grade-point averages.

But the school also acknowledged in its NCAA report that athletic recruits overall are less prepared. At Texas, the average SAT score for a freshman football player from 2003 to 2005 was 945—or 320 points lower than the typical first-year student's score on the entrance exam.

School officials did not make coach Mack Brown or athletic director DeLoss Dodds available to comment.

In all, 77 of the 92 Football Bowl Subdivision schools that provided information to the AP reported using special admissions waivers to land athletes and other students with particular talents. The AP spent three months obtaining and reviewing the reports through state public records laws.

Ten schools did not respond to the AP's request and 18 other schools, including Notre Dame, Pittsburgh and Southern California, declined to release their reports. The reports do not identify specific students who benefited from admissions waivers, but they are identified by sport in many cases.

The NCAA sets minimum eligibility standards to compete once a student is in college, but leaves admissions decisions to individual schools and does not compare "special admits" across schools.

Kevin Lennon, NCAA vice president for academic and membership affairs, noted that NCAA schools face penalties, including losing scholarships, if athletes' graduation rates are too low or if they fail to show adequate progress toward a degree.

"While it's an institution's decision on who they bring in, we're most interested in what they do once they get there," he said. "And if they're not successful, there are consequences."

At California, one of the country's most selective public universities, Golden Bear football players were 43 times more likely to gain special admissions than non-athletes from 2002–04.

"It doesn't matter to us if that student is a junior Olympian in tae kwondo or the best oboe player in the United States or someone who can really run fast and jump high," said Walter Robinson, admissions director at Cal. "We still look at that student with the same consideration: can that student be successful at Berkeley if admitted?"

While schools can tout the high graduation rates of athletes, they are not required to track the academic performance of special admits—and few do.

The AP review also found wide variance in how schools compile admissions data for NCAA review.

The NCAA asks schools to provide the annual percentages of special admits for all freshmen and all freshmen student-athletes on scholarship as well as a breakdown by individual sports.

But some schools only supply raw numbers, not percentages. Other schools, such as Florida, say they don't track special admissions outside athletics.

And several schools report no special admissions but describe in great detail remedial efforts and other programs that adhere to the NCAA's definition of special admissions.

Gerald Gurney, incoming president of the National Association of Academic Advisers for Athletics, favors a return by the NCAA to the minimum test score requirement abandoned several years ago. He said the NCAA's "virtually open admissions standards" threaten academic integrity.

"Special admissions, in and of itself, isn't something to be ashamed of. It does add value to a university," said Gurney, senior associate athletic director for academics and student life at Oklahoma. "However, when you have students who need such a great deal of remediation, it jeopardizes the very essence of the university."

Six schools besides Texas reported no use of special admissions on campus: Air Force, Connecticut, Kansas State, Purdue, Tennessee and Virginia.

The AP review also identified eight schools where athletes were no more likely than other students to get a break with special admissions: Arizona State, Arkansas State, Boise State, Iowa, Kent State, Mississippi State, New Mexico and West Virginia.

At South Carolina, All-American linebacker Eric Norwood recently graduated early with a bachelor's degree in criminal justice.

Norwood was twice denied admission to South Carolina before being accepted as a special admit. The school softened special admission standards in 2007 after coach Steve Spurrier threatened to quit when two recruits who met NCAA eligibility requirements were turned down.

"When I got here I applied myself," Norwood said. "I had great support from the academic staff, great support from the football staff. And my teammates, they held me accountable."

South Carolina athletic director Eric Hyman dismissed critics who call special admissions simply a way to land athletes.

"It's also a way to get better artists, better musicians," he said. "It's not all athletes. If you graduate, if your people are successful, there's going to be more flexibility. And that's what we've done."

23

Is Sports in Your Mission Statement?

Charles T. Clotfelter

As we enter the thick of college football season, with its abundance of televised games, I am reminded every Saturday of an important but seldom acknowledged fact about several hundred prominent American universities: They are members in good standing of the commercial entertainment industry. But the academic world's unwillingness to admit that rather obvious fact stands in the way of what should be an honest recognition—perhaps even appreciation—of some of the surprising benefits of big-time, commercialized college sports.

The evidence of this commercialization begins with ubiquitous TV coverage. This season's second week featured 23 nationally televised games on Saturday, plus three on Thursday and another on Friday, not counting the dozens of games covered regionally and those on the Big Ten's own cable network. It also shows up in mushrooming athletic budgets, lucrative contracts with shoe and apparel companies, hefty sales of logo-embossed gear, and, of course, outsized pay packages for celebrity coaches. The head football coaches at several dozen public universities earned an average of $2 million last year, more than 14 times the average pay for full professors and several multiples of what their presidents made.

For reasons that are peculiarly American, universities here have developed commercial-sports enterprises that have no counterpart anywhere else in the world. With clear-eyed rationality, they nourish their sports enterprises year after year because, contrary to their official pronouncements, intercollegiate athletic competition

Source: Charles T. Clotfelter, "Is Sports in Your Mission Statement?" *The Chronicle of Higher Education* (October 24, 2010). Online: http://chronicle.com/article/is-Sports-in-your-mission/125038/.

is actually one of their core functions. Entrusting the operation of such enterprises to administrators entirely distinct from those who run the academic operations, these universities seek commercial opportunities because they must have income to buy what is necessary to keep their teams competitive.

This need for revenue has existed for a century. What is new today, thanks to cable television and three decades of growing incomes among the affluent, is the breathtaking amount of money to be earned from big-time college sports. The number of televised college football games on a typical fall weekend rose from just two in 1983 to 29 last year. And the NCAA's take from TV for its annual men's basketball tournament last year, $571 million, was 15 times, in inflation-adjusted dollars, what it made in 1983.

Is it an overstatement to claim that athletics is a core function of these universities? My fellow faculty members would no doubt shrink from that view, for few of us relish the thought that we work in the entertainment business. Most of us would prefer to believe the words of our universities' official mission statements, which are more likely to mention our law schools, our schools of social work, our agricultural extension services, or a host of other administrative units, than they are to mention intercollegiate athletics.

Nor do most scholars of higher education acknowledge the actual importance of big-time college sports. Entire books covering a wide variety of topics related to American higher education have been published in recent years without a single mention of commercial sports. The same goes for journals devoted to higher education. Although there are some books devoted just to college sports, most of those who speak for or study American universities write as if big-time sports either do not exist or are just too inconsequential to mention.

When practiced by university administrators, this unwillingness to acknowledge the outsized importance of college sports might be dismissed as nothing more than the spin one expects to find in any advertising. But for us faculty members, our blindness to the significance of big-time sports amounts to operating in a parallel universe. The evidence is all around us, so commonplace that sometimes only visitors from abroad can see it. Football games close down entire campuses. Sports schedules routinely dictate when university meetings can and cannot be held. Wholly separate admissions criteria are applied to recruits in the revenue sports. The University of Alabama even delayed the start of its spring semester in January because of a bowl game in California.

For universities with big-time sports enterprises, sports dominate their media coverage, even by the country's self-styled newspaper of record. In 2007, more than six out of every seven articles in the *New York Times* about universities in one of the nation's top college football conferences were sports stories. Google the names of your university's president and the head football coach, and you will see who gets more coverage.

For many Americans, sports represent by far a university's most significant activity. Marketing surveys show that a sizable share of Americans either attend college football games or watch them on TV. Even practice games attract fans. Last year's spring scrimmage at Alabama drew an astounding 91,000 spectators. People care, and care deeply. In a recent survey taken in Lexington, Ky., a third of those responding agreed with the statement, "I live and die with the Wildcats. I'm happy if they win and sad if they lose."

Not only does this devotion provide college sports with commercial value, but it also represents an authentic but unheralded social benefit: the sheer enjoyment and pride that citizen-fans feel. Economists call it consumer surplus. The everyday term is "happiness."

Another social benefit of big-time college sports is its potential to teach by example civic values like meritocracy and productive interracial cooperation. One of the forces that opposed many Southerners' fierce embrace of segregation was another cherished tradition: college football. Coaches who treated their players equally and interracial teams that worked together provided much-needed models for the region and the country. This teaching by example continues today, as racially diverse college teams play together with harmony enough for high fives and fist bumps.

And let's not forget the potential for real benefit to the academic enterprise. Although most athletic departments fail to earn enough to cover the cost of all their university's teams, the evidence suggests that successful big-time programs help to attract applicants and raise contributions.

Whether the benefits of big-time college sports programs are worth the costs may still be a subject worthy of robust debate. But faculty members and administrators do a disservice to themselves and their institutions by pretending that the sports-entertainment complex is no more significant to a university's functioning than are its dining halls or art museums. Such lack of candor is out of step with the imperative we teach in classrooms and practice in laboratories—to seek and speak the truth.

24

The Big-Time College Sports Plantation and the Slaves Who Drive It

D. Stanley Eitzen

> "The plantation owner of old couldn't stay in business were he to divest himself of slaves. Slaves were the production engines of production."
>
> —Walter Mosley in *Workin' on the Chain Gang*

Many youths dream of playing football or basketball for a university with a big-time sports program. They want to be part of the pageantry, glory, excitement of intense competition, shared sacrifice, commitment to excellence, bonding with teammates, and to be the object of adoring fans. Not incidentally, they would also receive an all-expenses-paid college education, which, if a professional sports career does not work out, will open other lucrative career opportunities. Many observers of big-time college sports accept this idealized version, but just how glamorous is participation in athletics at this level? Are the athletes as privileged as it appears?

There is a dark side to big-time college sports. To show this, let me use the metaphor of big-time college sports as a plantation system. I admit at the outset that this metaphor is overdrawn. Big-time college sports is not the same as the brutalizing, inhumane, degrading, and repressive institution of slavery found in the antebellum South. Nevertheless, there are significant parallels with slavery that highlight the

Source: This is a revised and updated version of D. Stanley Eitzen, "Slaves of Big-Time College Sports," *USA Today: The Magazine of the American Scene* 120 (September 2000), pp. 26–30. Revised in 2010.

serious problems plaguing collegiate athletics. Thus, the plantation/slavery metaphor is useful to understand the reality of the big-time college sports world.

There is the organization—the National Collegiate Athletic Association (NCAA)—that preserves the plantation system, making and enforcing the rules to protect the interest of the individual plantation owners. The plantations are the football and men's basketball factories within the universities with big-time programs. The overseers are the coaches who extract the labor from the workers. The workers are owned by the plantation and, much like the slaves of the antebellum South, produce riches for their masters while receiving a meager return on the plantation's profits.

Many observers of big-time college sports, most certainly the coaches and players, would argue vehemently with this assertion that big-time college athletes are slaves in a plantation environment. After all, the athletes not only choose to participate, they want desperately to be part of big-time sport. Moreover, they have special privileges that separate them from other students (much like what house slaves received, when compared to field slaves of the Old South), such as more and better food, special housing arrangements, favorable handling in registration for classes, and, sometimes, generous treatment when they break the rules. Also, the athletes, unlike slaves, can leave the program if they wish.

If participation is voluntary and the athletes want to be part of the system, what is the problem? My argument that these athletes are slaves in a plantation system, whether they realize it or not, involves several dimensions: (1) The athletes (slaves) are exploited economically, making millions for their masters but provided only with a subsistence wage of room, board, tuition, and books; (2) they are controlled with restricted freedoms; (3) they are subject to physical and mental abuse by overseers; and (4) the master-slave relationship is accepted by the athletes as legitimate. I begin my argument with demonstrating that big-time college football and men's basketball bring in large sums to the "plantations" while severely limiting the wages of the workers.

THE PLANTATION PROFITS FROM THE WORK OF SLAVES

The governing body of big-time college sports, the NCAA, is caught in a huge contradiction—trying to reconcile a multibillion-dollar industry while claiming that it is really an amateur activity. That it is a huge money-making industry is beyond dispute.

- The major conferences have a four-year package (ending in 2012) worth $500 million.
- The NCAA has signed a $6.2 billion, 11-year deal giving CBS the rights to televise its men's basketball championship (that's $545 million a year). The NCAA also, of course, makes money from advertising and gate receipts for this tournament. To enhance gate receipts the finals are always scheduled in huge arenas with seating capacities of at least 30,000, rather than normal basketball-sized venues.

- Universities sell sponsorships to various enterprises for advertising. The athletic department of the University of Colorado, for example, has 50 corporate sponsors. Its major sponsor is Coors Brewing Company, which has a $300,000 advertising package for scoreboard, radio and TV advertising, and a sign on the mascot's trailer. That university also named its basketball arena the Coors Events Center in return for a $5 million gift.
- Several football and basketball coaches are paid in excess of $4 million in overall compensation (base salary, television and radio, shoe company stipends). An estimated $2.5 billion a year in college merchandise is sold under license, generating about $100 million to the schools in royalties.
- The dominant schools have lucrative deals with shoe companies (Nike, Reebok, Adidas) worth millions to each school in shoes, apparel, and cash. For example, in 2001 the University of North Carolina at Chapel Hill signed an eight-year agreement with Nike worth about $3.2 million annually. The University of Texas had an annual athletic budget of $125 million in 2009.

Obviously, big-time athletic programs are commercial enterprises. The irony is that while the sports events generate millions for each school, the workers are not paid. Economist Andrew Zimbalist has written that: "Big-time intercollegiate athletics is a unique industry. No other industry in the United States manages not to pay its principal producers a wage or a salary." The universities and the NCAA claim that their athletes in big-time sports programs are amateurs and that, despite the money generated, the NCAA and its member schools are amateur organizations promoting an educational mission. This amateur status is vitally important to the plantation owners in two regards. First, by schools *not* paying the athletes what they are worth their expenses are minimized, thus making the enterprises more profitable. And, second, since athletic departments and the NCAA are considered part of the educational mission, they do not pay taxes on their millions from television, sponsorships, licensing, the sale of skyboxes and season tickets, and gate receipts. Moreover, contributions by individuals and corporations to athletic departments are tax deductible.

THE INJUSTICE OF AMATEURISM

To keep big-time college sports "amateur," the NCAA has devised a number of rules that eliminate all economic benefits to the athletes: They may receive only educational benefits (i.e., room, board, tuition, fees, and books); cannot sign with an agent and retain their eligibility; cannot do commercials; cannot receive meals, clothing, transportation, or other gifts by individuals other than family members; and their relatives cannot receive gifts of travel to attend games or other forms of remuneration.

These rules reek with injustice. Athletes can make money for others, but not for themselves. Their coaches have agents as may students engaged in other extracurricular activities, but the athletes cannot. Athletes are forbidden to engage in advertising, but their coaches can readily endorse products for generous compensation. Corporate advertisements are displayed in the arenas where they play but with no payoff to the athletes. The shoes and equipment worn by the athletes bear very visible corporate logos, for which the schools are compensated handsomely. The athletes make public appearances for their schools and their photographs are used to publicize the athletic department and sell tickets but they cannot benefit. The schools sell memorabilia and paraphernalia that incorporate the athletes' likenesses, yet only the schools pocket the royalties. The athletes cannot receive gifts but coaches and other athletic department personnel receive the free use of automobiles, country club memberships, housing subsidies, and the like.

Most significantly, coaches receive huge deals from shoe companies (e.g., Duke coach Mike Krzyzewski has a fifteen-year shoe endorsement deal with Adidas, which includes a $1 million bonus plus $375,000 annually) while the players are limited to wearing that corporation's shoes and apparel. An open market operates when it comes to the pay for coaches resulting in huge pay packages for the glamour coaches but not so for star players. When a coach is fired or resigns he often receives a "golden parachute," which sometimes is in the multimillion dollar category, while players who leave a program early receive nothing but vilification for being disloyal. When a team is invited to a bowl game it means an extra month of practice for the athletes while head coaches, depending on the bowl venue, receive generous bonuses. A university entourage of administrators and their spouses accompany the team to the bowl game with all expenses paid while the parents and spouses of the athletes have to pay their own way.

As an example of the discrepancy in pay for college athletes, an analysis of the economic impact of premium Division I-A football players showed they generated more than $400,000 for their school and basketball players more than $1 million.

What exactly are the wages of average college athletes in the big-time sports? The answer is a bit complicated since athletes who do not graduate have not taken advantage of their tuition, so they have played only for their room and board. Also, there is a significant difference in tuition costs between state and private universities. Economist Richard G. Sheehan has calculated the hourly wage of big-time college players taking these considerations into account and assuming a work load of 1,000 hours per year. The best pay received, he found, occurred at private schools with high graduation rates for the athletes; the lowest pay at state schools with low graduation rates. Duke, for example, paid an equivalent of $20.37 an hour for its football players, while Texas-El Paso paid $3.51. The median wage at all big-time schools for basketball players was $6.82 an hour and $7.69 an hour for football players. Now compare these wages with their coaches, assuming they also work 1,000 hours annually. A coach with a $1 million package makes $1,000 an hour; a coach with a $250,000 package only $250 an hour. Meanwhile, the workers—whose health is jeopardized by participation in hazardous sports—make a relative pittance and even then not in the form of money but in "free" room, board, and tuition. So it is, that the work of the big-time college athletes, just like the slaves on the antebellum plantations, allows the masters to accumulate wealth at their expense.

RESTRICTIONS ON THE RIGHTS AND FREEDOMS OF THE SLAVES

Slaves, by definition, are not free. The slaves of the antebellum era did not have the right to assemble or to petition. They did not have the right to speak out or to freedom of movement. Those conditions characterize today's college athletes as well. The NCAA, the schools, and the coaches restrict the freedom of the athletes in many ways. By NCAA fiat, once athletes sign a contract to play for a school, they are bound to that school. They make a four-year commitment to that college, yet the school makes only a one-year commitment to them. If an athlete wishes to play for another big-time school, he is ineligible for one year (two years if their former coach refuses to release the athlete from his contract). Yet if a coach wants to get rid of an athlete, the school is only bound to provide the scholarship for the remainder of that academic year. Coaches, on the other hand, can break their contracts, and immediately coach another school. Richard Sheehan illustrates how unfair this rule is for athletes, when they are compared with nonathlete students: "Suppose you accept a scholarship from Harvard to study under a Nobel laureate who then takes a position at Yale. Are you under any obligation to attend Harvard and not attempt to matriculate at Yale? This NCAA regulation, like many others, gives schools options and gives athletes nothing."

The right to privacy is invaded routinely when it comes to athletes. College athletes—but not their coaches, teachers, administrators, or other students—are subject to mandatory drug testing. Personnel from the athletic department watch athletes in their dorms and locker rooms, either in person or on closed-circuit television, for "deviant behaviors." Bed checks are not uncommon. Sometimes there are "spies" who watch and report on the behaviors of athletes in local bars and other places of amusement.

Freedom of choice is violated when athletes are red-shirted (i.e., held from play for a year) without their consent. Athletes may have little or no choice in what position they play. They may be told to gain or lose weight, with penalties for noncompliance. Coaches may demand mandatory study halls. They may determine what courses the athletes will take and their majors. Robert Smith, formerly a running back for the Minnesota Vikings, was a premed student and star athlete at Ohio State University. To meet his premed requirements Smith needed a laboratory course that conflicted with football practices twice a week. The coaches insisted that football take precedence and that he must drop the course. To Smith's credit, he took the course and did not play football that year.

A number of coaches insist that their athletes avoid political protest. Some paternalistic coaches prohibit their athletes from associating with individuals or groups that they feel will have a negative influence on their players. Certain coaches demand dress codes and may even organize leisure-time activities that everyone must attend. Former University of Colorado basketball coach Ricardo Patton, for example, included among his mandatory team activities: touring a prison, attending church services, sleeping together on cots in the gym for a week, and practicing at six in the morning. During slavery, the masters imposed their religious beliefs onto their slaves. In today's sportsworld, team chaplains, chapel services, bible study, and team prayers are commonplace. Ricardo Patton concluded each practice with the players holding hands in a circle while Patton or a player he called upon led the team in prayer. He claims that participation was voluntary. Sportswriter Mike Littwin of the *Denver Rocky Mountain News* argues that the practice is anything but voluntary: "According to the argument, players, whose playing time and scholarship are dependent upon the coach's whim, are free to pray or not to pray with him. Here's what I believe: Anyone who thinks that when the coach says it's time to pray that it's somehow voluntary ought to pray for more wisdom. It is inherently coercive. It's about as voluntary as when the coach tells you to run laps. You're not the coach for 60 minutes of practice and then not the coach once you kneel on the floor.

OPPRESSION, BRUTALITY, AND TERROR: KEEPING SLAVES IN THEIR PLACE

Although not a universal trait of coaches, instances of physical and mental cruelty toward players occur all too frequently. Bob Knight, the highly successful basketball coach at Indiana University and Texas Tech once stopped the videotape of a game to say to one of his players: "Daryl, look at that. You don't even run back down the floor hard. That's all I need to know about you Daryl. All you want to be out there is comfortable. You don't work, you don't sprint back. Look at that! You never push yourself. You know what you are Daryl? You are the worst f——— pussy I've ever seen play basketball at this school. The absolute worst pussy ever. You have more goddamn ability than 95 percent of the players we've had here but you are pussy from the top of your head to the bottom of your feet. An absolute f——— pussy."

When football coach Lou Holtz was at Notre Dame University, one of his players, Chet Lacheta, made several mistakes in practice. In Lacheta's words: "[Holtz] started yelling at me. He said that I was a coward. He said that I should find a different sport to play and that I shouldn't come back in the fall. He was pretty rough.... First he grabbed me by my face mask and shook it. Then he spit on me."

On the return trip from a road game coaches may punish their players by having the bus driver let them off several miles from the school. Another tactic is to schedule practices at inconvenient times such as 2 a.m. or on holidays. Coach Bob Knight schedules some holiday practices, without telling the players when to report for the next practice. Consequently, they must wait by their phones to hear from the manager about the practice schedule. If not, they will incur the wrath of their autocratic boss. These acts of control are similar to those used by the military to train recruits. As sociologist Philip Slater has observed: "Exposure to random punishment, stress, fatigue, personal degradation and abuse, irrational authority, and constant assertions of one's worthlessness as a human being [are] all tried-and-true techniques of 'reeducation' used by totalitarian regimes. . . ." In effect, these are powerful means to create and maintain obedient slaves.

THE SLAVE MENTALITY

Historians George Fredrickson and Christopher Lasch have stated that the real horror of slavery was that many of the slaves "mentally identified with the system that bound and confined them." This is an especially troubling aspect of the plantation system that is big-time college sport. Jerry Farber's description of students in his classic 1960s critique of higher education, "The Student as Nigger," aptly describes athletes as well: "They're pathetically eager to be pushed around. They're like those old greyheaded house niggers you can still find in the South who don't see what all the fuss is about because Mr. Charlie 'treats us real good.' "

Sport sociologist George H. Sage provides some of the reasons why athletes rarely resist the authoritarian and unjust regime: "A question may be raised about the lack of protest from intercollegiate athletes about the prevailing conditions under which they labor. In one way it can be expected that the athletes would not find anything to question: they have been thoroughly conditioned by many years of organized sport involvement to obey athletic authorities. Indeed, most college athletes are faithful servants and spokespersons for the system of college sport. They tend to take the existing order for granted, not questioning the status quo because they are preoccupied with their own jobs or making the team and perhaps gaining national recognition. As a group, athletes tend to be politically passive and apathetic, resigned to domination from above because, at least partly, the institutional structure of athletics is essentially hostile to independence of mind. Hence, athletes are willing victims whose self-worth and self-esteem have largely become synonymous with their athletic prowess. Their main impulse is to mind their own business while striving to be successful as athletes."

Another reason for the docility and submissiveness of athletes is that they are politically disenfranchised. Athletes who challenge the athletic power structure risk losing their scholarships and eligibility. Athletes who have a grievance are on their own. They have no union and no arbitration board. The coaches, athletic directors, and ultimately the NCAA have the power over them as long as they are scholarship athletes. Their only option is to leave the plantation. If they do quit, they are often viewed by others as the problem. After all, most accept the system. Those who quit are not seen as victims but as losers. So powerful is the socialization of athletes, even those who quit are likely to turn their anger inward, regarding themselves as the problem.

Others may tolerate the oppressive system because they see it as the only vehicle to become a professional athlete. If they were to become professional athletes, the rewards are substantial. However, except for the most-talented few, making it to the pros is just a dream. Of the thousands of players eligible for the National Football League draft each year, only 336 are drafted and about 160 actually make a final roster. Fewer than one-half of one percent of all Division I male basketball players make it to the National Basketball Association.

DISMAL GRADUATION RATES

Since most college athletes never play at the professional level, the attainment of a college degree is a crucial determinant for their upward mobility and thus a rationale for tolerating the unjust plantation system. But graduation from college, while not the long shot of becoming a professional athlete, is not a sure thing, especially for African American male athletes in revenue-producing sports.

In 2010 the NCAA declared that the college player graduation rate was 69 percent. That is, almost seven out of ten athletes entering college in 2003 had graduated within six years. These data inflate the graduation rate for athletes in the big-time revenue-producing sports of football and men's basketball because they include the graduate rates for *all* athletes (female athletes and athletes in the non-revenue sports graduate at a higher rate than their revenue-producing peers). Clearly, the sports of men's basketball, football, and baseball lag behind the other sports in producing graduates.

- More than a quarter of the 320 Division I basketball schools graduated fewer than 50 percent of their players.
- All 31 NCAA Division I basketball conferences have men's basketball player graduation rates that are less than the full-time male student body rate.
- The overall graduation rate for Division I football players was 13.9 percentage points below the male student body rate.
- One in six Division I baseball programs were at less than 50 percent graduation, including the last six national champions.
- Of the teams that reached the Sweet 16 in the NCAA men's basketball championship, four graduated less than 50 percent of their players with the University of Arizona only graduating 20 percent. On the women's side, in sharp contrast, all 16 teams had graduated at least two-thirds of their players, including four teams with a 100 percent graduation rate.

There are several reasons for the relatively low graduation rates for big-time college athletes. Compared to nonathletes they are less prepared for college. On average, they enter college in the bottom quarter of the freshman class (based on SAT scores). Football and men's basketball players in big-time sports programs are more than six times as likely as other students to receive special treatment in the admissions process; that is, they are admitted *below* the standard requirements for their universities. Second, athletes spend 30 to 40 hours a week on their sport, which is demanding as well as physically and mentally fatiguing. Third, an anti-intellectual atmosphere is common within the jock subculture. Finally, some athletes attend college not for the education but because they believe it will lead to a professional career. In this regard, former Iowa State football coach Jim Walden has said: "Not more than 20 percent of the football players go to college for an education."

Not only do typical athletes in big-time sports enter at an educational disadvantage, they often encounter a diluted educational experience while attending their schools. Coaches, under the intense pressure to win, tend to diminish the student side of their athletes by counseling them to take easy courses, to choose easy majors, and to enroll in easy courses from professors friendly to the athletic department. Some of the more unscrupulous have altered transcripts, given athletes answers to tests, staged phantom courses, and hired surrogate test takers. In one infamous case of academic fraud, a tutor for the University of Minnesota athletic department wrote more than 400 papers for basketball players over five years. Even with that help only 23 percent of the players recruited since 1986 to play basketball at that university have graduated, the worst rate of any Big Ten basketball team during that period.

Some ill-prepared and/or unmotivated athletes manage to stay eligible without being educated. Dexter Manley, for example, testified before a Senate committee that he had played football four years at Oklahoma State University only to leave illiterate. As Cynthia Tucker, editor of the *Atlanta Constitution* editorial page, writing about exploited basketball players but applicable to football players as well, said: "So those college basketball players you're watching on the court desperately need to earn degrees. If they don't, they'll be left with little more than shattered 'hoop dreams.'" The uneducated have been exploited by their schools and when used up, the schools turn to another crop to exploit. As columnist George Will has argued: "College football and basketball are, for many players, vocations, not avocations, and academics are unsubstantiated rumors."

Reexamining the plantation/slave metaphor, athletes voluntarily enter into an unjust arrangement. Nevertheless, there are important similarities that college sport shares with slavery. The plantation system as represented by the NCAA and the individual (school) plantations benefit handsomely from the work of the athletes. The athletes, meanwhile, like slaves, are bound to the plantation by the plantation's rules. They are dominated, managed, and controlled. They take orders. They do not receive a wage commensurate with their contribution to the economic return. They are sometimes mistreated physically and mentally by their overseers. They are denied the rights and freedoms of other citizens and they have no real democratic recourse to right an unjust system.

CHANGING THE PLANTATION SYSTEM

The obvious starting point for changing the "plantation" system is to pay athletes in the revenue-producing sports fair compensation for the revenues they generate. Athletes should receive a monthly stipend for living expenses, insurance coverage, and paid trips home during holidays and for family emergencies. Media basketball commentator Dick Vitale suggests a modest plan to make the system somewhat more fair. He says that the NCAA should invest a billion of its $6.2 billion deal to broadcast the NCAA men's basketball tournament and pay the athletes $250 a month. *Sports Illustrated* writer E. M. Swift responded: "Is Vitale right on the money? You make the call. For now, as the NCAA continues to treat its athletes with supercilious contempt while reaping GNP-sized windfalls from their labor, you can at least say this for scholarship athletes: They're getting a free education in no-holds-barred capitalism."

The time has come to end the pretense that players in big-time college sports are amateurs. They are paid through a scholarship but far from a just or living wage in this world of big-time sports megabucks.

Second, maximize the probability that athletes receive a legitimate education and graduate. The late Ernest L. Boyer, former president of the Carnegie Foundation for the Advancement of Teaching, said: "I believe that the college sports system is one of the most corrupting and destructive influences on higher education. It is obscene, and there is no way to put an educational gloss on this enterprise." In short, as currently structured, big-time sports are not compatible with education.

To emphasize education and replace athlete-student with student-athlete, I suggest the following: Do not admit athletes who do not meet the minimum entrance requirements for admission and retention. Eliminate freshman eligibility so that incoming students have time to adjust to the demanding and competitive academic environment. Provide remedial classes and tutoring as needed. Reduce the time demands on athletes by eliminating spring football practice, starting the basketball season at the beginning of second semester, and holding the weekly time devoted to sport at 20 hours. Include among the criteria for evaluating coaches, the humane treatment of players, and, most critically, the proportion of their athletes who graduate in six years.

Third, establish a comprehensive athletes' Bill of Rights to ensure a nonexploitive context. At a minimum these "Rights" should include:

- The right to transfer schools. Athletes who transfer should be eligible to play the next school year, eliminating the current stipulation that they must wait a year with no athletic scholarship aid.
- The right to a four-year scholarship, not the one-year renewable at the option of the coach as is the current NCAA policy. Those athletes who compete for three years should be given an open ended scholarship guaranteeing that they will receive aid as long as it takes to graduate.
- The rights that other college students have (freedom of speech, privacy rights, protections from the physical and mental abuse of authorities, and the fair redress of grievances). There should be an impartial committee on each college campus, separate from the athletic department, that monitors the behavior of coaches and the rules imposed by them on athletes to ensure that individual rights are guaranteed.
- The right of athletes to consult with agents concerning sports career choices.
- The right of athletes to make money from endorsements, speeches, and the like. Walter Byers, former executive director of the NCAA, has stated that

> athletes should have the same financial opportunities as other students, arguing that "The athlete may access the marketplace just as other students exploit their own special talents, whether they are musicians playing on weekends, journalism students working piecemeal for newspapers, or announcers for the college radio station filing reports for CNN radio."

Big-time college sport presents us with a fundamental dilemma. We like the festival, pageantry, exuberance, excitement, and the excellence, but are we then willing to accept the hypocrisy, scandal, and exploitation that goes with them? To date, the plantation system is not challenged as the college presidents and various NCAA committees make timid and tepid cosmetic changes. As a beginning to the real reform of the oppressive system, we need to understand who benefits and who is exploited. The plantation/slave metaphor illuminates the injustices of the system in stark reality. Seeing it this way should create an urgency among educators to make real changes. The time is ripe for bold action to transform big-time college athletics so that it can be part of the educational vision of the university *without* the shame and the sham that characterize it now.

* FOR FURTHER STUDY *

Armstrong, Ken, and Nick Perry. 2010. *Scoreboard, Baby: A Story of College Football, Crime, and Complicity*. Lincoln, NE: Bison Books.

Bower, William G., and Sarah A. Levin. 2003. *Reclaiming the Game: College Sports and Educational Values*. Princeton, NJ: Princeton University Press.

Burke, Monte. 2008. "The Most Powerful Coach in Sports." *Forbes* (September 1): 92–96.

Coakley, Jay. 2007. *Sports in Society: Issues and Controversies*. 9th ed. New York: McGraw-Hill.

Eitzen, D. Stanley. 2007. "Sport, College." Pp. 4665–4668 in *Blackwell Encyclopedia of Sport*. Vol. 9.

Eitzen, D. Stanley. 2009. *Fair and Foul: Beyond the Myths and Paradoxes of Sport*. 4th ed. Lanham, MD: Rowman and Littlefield.

Eitzen, D. Stanley, and George H. Sage. 2009. *Sociology of North American Sport*. 8th ed. Boulder, CO: Paradigm.

Feldman, Bruce. 2007. *Meat Market: Inside the Smash-Mouth World of College Football Recruiting*. New York: ESPN Books.

Gerdy, John R. 2006. *Air Ball: American Education's Failed Experiment with Elite Athletics*. Jackson: University Press of Mississippi.

Lewis, Michael. 2007. *The Blind Side*. New York: W. W. Norton.

Mandel, Stewart. 2007. *Bowls, Polls & Tattered Souls: Tackling the Chaos and Controversy that Reign over College Football*. Hoboken, NJ: John Wiley & Sons.

Meggyesy, David. 2000. "Athletes in Big-Time College Sports." *Society* 37 (March–April): 24–28.

Shulman, James L., and William G. Bowen. 2001. *The Game of Life: College Sports and Educational Values*. Princeton, NJ: Princeton University Press.

Sokolove, Michael. 2002. "Football Is a Sucker's Game." *New York Times Magazine* (December 22): 36–41, 64, 68–71.

Solomon, Alisa. 2002. "Guys and Dollars: Women Still Trail the Greed Game of College Sports." *Village Voice* (April 11). Available at http://villagevoice.com/issues/0215/solomon.php.

Walton, Teresa. 2001. "The Sprewell/Carlesimo Episode: Unacceptable Violence or Unacceptable Victim?" *Sociology of Sport Journal* 18 (3): 345–357.

Young, Kevin. 2002. "Standard Deviations: An Update on North American Sports Crowd Disorder." *Sociology of Sport Journal* 19 (3): 237–275.

Zimbalist, Andrew. 1999. *Unpaid Professionals: Commercialism and Big-Time College Sports*. Princeton, NJ: Princeton University Press.

PART NINE

Problems of Excess: Sport and Money

A dilemma that characterizes professional sport and much of what is called amateur sport in the United States has been described by journalist Roger Kahn: "Sport is too much a game to be a business and too much a business to be a game."[1] The evidence indicating a strong relationship between sport and money is overwhelming. Some recent facts demonstrate this relationship in the United States:

- The estimated size of the entire sports industry in 2010 was $444 billion.
- In the 1960s, the prize money for the entire Professional Golf Association (PGA) tour was about $7 million. In 2009 it was $275 million.
- The National Football League (NFL) had total revenues of $9.2 billion in 2010.
- In 2009, Tiger Woods became the first athlete worth more than $1 billion.
- More than $8 billion is bet illegally on the annual Super Bowl. Another $100 million is bet legally in Nevada on this game.
- Sports video games represent a $1 billion industry, accounting for more than 30 percent of all video game sales.

There is no longer any question that corporate sport is a business, although the owners and certainly big-time sport universities would like to perpetuate the myth that it is not. In this part of the book we will examine the intimate interrelationship between money and sport and the consequences of this trend.

Money is often the key motivator of athletes. Players and owners give their primary allegiance to money rather than to the sport or to the fans. Modern sport, whether professional, big-time college, or Olympic, is "corporate sport." The original purpose of sport—pleasure in the activity—has been lost in the process. Sport has become work. Sport has become the product of publicity agents using superhype methods. Money has superseded the content as the ultimate goal. Illicit tactics are commonplace, because winning translates into more revenues. In short, U.S. sport is a microcosm of the values of U.S. society. Journalist Roger Angell has said of baseball what is applicable to all forms of corporate sport. "Professional sports now form a noisy and substantial, if irrelevant and distracting, part of the world, and it seems as if baseball games taken entirely—off the field as well as on it, in the courts and in the front offices as well as down on the diamonds—may now tell us more about ourselves than they ever did before."[2]

The selections in Part Nine illustrate the problems and issues involving the impact of money on sports. The first, by journalist Sally Jenkins, asks the question, "Does Football Cost Too Much?" She attends a Dallas Cowboys game in their new stadium and finds going to a game very expensive and very entertaining. She wonders how long NFL teams will be able to keep working-class fans attending and spending. The second selection is a chapter from journalist Dave Zirin's book *Bad Sports: How Owners Are Ruining the Games We Love.* Zirin focuses on how the public is ripped off by publicly funding stadiums that subsidize wealthy professional team owners. Selection 27, by journalist Geoff Dembicki, provides a history of the creeping commercialization and the ever-increasing intrusion of corporations in the Olympic Games and the World Cup.

NOTES

1. Roger Kahn, quoted in CBS Reports, "The Baseball Business," television documentary narrated by Bill Moyers (1977).

2. Roger Angell, "The Sporting Scene: In the Counting House," *New Yorker* (May 10, 1976): 107.

25

Does Football Cost Too Much?

Sally Jenkins

I'm in Arlington, Tex., standing outside the NFL's newest stadium, the state-of-the-art home of the Dallas Cowboys. With its $1.15 billion price tag, Cowboys Stadium represents the best and worst of today's NFL experience. The arena itself is a technological marvel of glass and steel. But in order to enjoy it, fans need to dig deep into their wallets—make that bank accounts. While the average cost of attending an NFL game for a family of four is $412.64, it's a staggering $758.58 to watch the Cowboys. (That figure includes tickets and drinks for four people, as well as a couple of caps.)

Has the NFL gotten so overpriced that it's inaccessible to most fans? And is seeing a game in person worth the trouble and expense, or is it just as good to stay home with a satellite hook-up and a big TV?

I decided to find out by going to a game. My natural choice was "America's Team," the Cowboys, playing their first season in a facility that is likely to become the NFL standard. I went to Ticketmaster and clicked on "Cheapest available" seats for the Nov. 1 contest between the Cowboys and the Seattle Seahawks. I was offered the uppermost deck in the end zone at $129. Then I clicked on "Best available," which found me a seat in the second-highest tier (25 rows from the top), with a view of the 10-yard line, for $239. I purchased that ticket.

By contrast, many spectators at the first pro-football games in the U.S. went for free. The early stadiums had open end zones where people could watch without

Source: Sally Jenkins, "Does Football Cost Too Much?" *Parade* (November 29, 2009), pp. 14–16. Reprinted by permission of International Creative Management, Inc.

tickets, and often the "deadheads"—the nickname for those fans—outnumbered the paying audiences. With 10 franchises in cities like St. Louis and Detroit, the modern NFL began to take shape in 1934. The sport gradually won Americans' hearts, and by 1965, a Harris Poll found that football had surpassed baseball in popularity.

"The NFL became successful by becoming the people's game," says historian Michael Oriard, author of *Brand NFL*. "It built on a working-class population and expanded into the middle class until it achieved respectability."

In keeping with the game's humble origins, I searched for public transportation to go from Dallas to the Cowboys game. There was none. Fortunately, parking is plentiful, so I drove in. A space in Lot B, around a quarter mile from the stadium, ran $50. Lot A, closer by the distance of a first down, was $60. I chose the $50 spot and took a pleasant 10-minute stroll to the game.

On my first view of the arena, it seemed worth the money I'd spent. Truly awe-inspiring, Cowboys Stadium is the NFL's largest dome, with a capacity of 110,000. Two steel arches lunge into the sky over massive blocks of white stone and green glass. Thanks to the arches, the roof floats high above, free of columns, offering every seat a panoramic view. The centerpiece is the world's largest high-def jumbotron—a screen that is 160 feet wide and 72 feet high.

By the time I made it to my seat, I was out almost $100. A sweatshirt was $50, a T-shirt $22, a chicken sandwich $8, french fries $5, and a soda $6. However, I opted to skip the $14 margarita (called a Cowboyrita) and $10 bucket of popcorn.

Ticket prices for a Cowboys game run from $59 seats located in the arena's uppermost reaches to $500,000 luxury boxes. Between the two extremes are season tickets. Their holders shell out for "personal seat licenses," multiyear commitments that go for $2000 to $150,000. David, a contractor who lives in Maryland, sat next to me. He had paid $24,000 for 30-year rights to two seats in the upper tier and an additional $2500 per season for the seats themselves. And he was glad to do it. "My son will have them," he said. "Not only can you see everything, but it's clean and family-oriented."

The team really tried to deliver a thrilling time to its customers. By kickoff, flames shot from 3000 flat-screen TVs until the entire venue seemed alive. We saw music videos, pregame interviews, and highlights from past games. A locker-room cam showed players chatting and warming up. The sound was immense and intergalactic. Many of the seats, including mine, were padded and had drink holders. The floors had been polished to a skating-rink sheen and were swept perpetually by armies of attendants.

There is one genuinely cheap seat in the house—although it isn't really a seat. I spoke to Gary, a Houston engineer, who was at the game with his daughter. He'd gone to the box office that morning and asked, "What are the cheapest seats left between the 20-yard lines?" The vendor said $239, but he also explained the party-pass option—$29 for standing room on platforms in the end zone. Gary took two and parked at a remote lot for $15.

He called it a good deal, even as he sipped an $8 beer. "I like the experience," he said. "It's as close as you can get to going to a concert." The drawback, he added, was that they had to stand right at the railing to see and were afraid to leave their spots and lose them.

In return for our efforts, all of us ended up getting an exultant afternoon of football. After country star Jessie James sang the national anthem, we watched the Cowboys beat the Seahawks 38-17.

A game at Cowboys Stadium attempts to please its entire audience, from the people with party passes to the affluent in their windowed boxes. But how long and in how many cities can the NFL retain both? If Cowboys Stadium is the trendsetter, the NFL is moving toward a day when only the wealthiest fans can afford to watch in person.

For now, the league seems to be maintaining its mass appeal. While pro-basketball and -baseball games are cheaper to attend, football remains the most popular sport in North America. And NFL officials state that they have no intention of turning their backs on their supporters. "Those working-class people who helped build the game have to be able to go to games," says Mark Waller, chief marketing officer for the NFL. "We can't ever lose sight of the fans who made us what we are."

When I walked out of Cowboys Stadium that evening, the crowd was still being enthusiastically entertained. Postgame interviews were piped over loudspeakers, and attendants handed out coupons for free french fries and tacos from local fast-food chains. A live band serenaded the plaza with a version of the Jackson 5's "I Want You Back" that was so energetic it started a dance party. As hard as I looked, I couldn't see a single dissatisfied face.

26

When Domes Attack

Dave Zirin

In August 2005, when Hurricane Katrina flattened New Orleans and the world saw the levees rupture, the only safe harbor for poor residents was in the Louisiana Superdome. When the Mississippi River bridge collapsed in Minneapolis, Minnesota, the new Twins stadium was to break ground that very week. In spring of 2009, when a Washington, D.C., Metro train went off the tracks, a publicly funded $1 billion stadium had just opened its doors the previous year.

There is no Montgomery Burns or Bond villain celebrating this state of affairs. No one in the owner's box is maniacally chortling as our cities rot (at least I hope not). There are finite resources in a given city budget in the best of times, and these are anything but the salad days and these are the results when stadiums come first.

The landscape is made worse by the fact that during the economic boom of the 1990s, the longest period of economic expansion in U.S. history, publicly funded stadiums became the substitute for anything resembling an urban policy in this country. These stadiums, ballparks, arenas, and domes were presented as a microwave-instant solution to the problems of crumbling schools, urban decay, and suburban flight. They are now the excrement of the urban neoliberalism of the 1990s, sporting shrines to the dogma of trickle-down economics. In the past twenty-five years, more than $30 billion of the public's money has been spent for stadium construction and upkeep from coast to coast.[1] Though many cities now resist paying the full tab, any kind of subsidy is a fool's investment, ending up being little more than monuments

---

to corporate greed: $500 million welfare hotels for America's billionaires built with funds that could have been spent more wisely on just about anything else.

And the dollar amount keeps growing. We are perhaps extorted from most visibly when our communities cover a stadium's price tag. But this isn't the only method the sports bosses use to stick us with the bill. A college football bowl game might be brought to us by GMAC, but the only reason GMAC still has a pulse is the more than $10 billion it has received in the taxpayer bailout funds. Last year, a proposed ban on federal stimulus dollars going to stadiums was also dropped.

As Neil deMause, coauthor of the book *Field of Schemes,* said to me, "The history of the stadium game is the story of how, by slowly refining their blackmail skills, sports owners learned how to turn their industry from one based on selling tickets to one based on extracting public subsidies. It's been a bit like watching a four-year-old learn how to manipulate his parents into buying him the new toy that he saw on TV; the question now is how long it takes our elected officials to learn to say 'no.'"[2]

But our elected officials have been more like the children in this scenario, as sports owners tousle their hair and set the budget agendas for municipalities around the country with a simple credo: stadiums first and people last.

Polls show that consistent majorities don't want public funds spent on stadiums.[3] That means a bulk of sports fans oppose the stadium glut as well. We may love baseball. We may love football. We may bleed our team's colors on game day. But that doesn't mean we should have to pay a billionaire millions of dollars for the privilege to watch. The counterargument is job creation. But employment opportunities created by the domes are the kinds of irregular poverty wage jobs that expand the gap between rich and poor. "They're parking garage attendants, they are hot dog salespeople, they are waiters and waitresses, sometimes cooks, people who do maintenance work and repair work and cleaning;" said Cleveland union activist John Ryan during that city's stadium battles. "And none of them are jobs that the mayor hugs his kids and says, 'I hope you can get one of those jobs someday.'"[4]

We've now seen the extreme results of these kinds of priorities. In cities as politically, ethnically, and geographically diverse as New Orleans, Minneapolis, and Washington, D.C., the results are like a horror movie: *When Domes Attack.*

NOLA

After Hurricane Katrina flattened the Gulf Coast, the Louisiana Superdome morphed into a homeless shelter from hell, inhabited yet uninhabitable for an estimated thirty thousand of New Orleans's poorest residents.[5]

It took Hurricane Katrina for them to actually see the inside of the Superdome, a stadium whose ticket prices make entry an exclusive affair. At the time of the hurricane, game tickets cost $90, season seats went for $1,300, and luxury boxes for eight home games ran more than $100,000 a year. But the Katrina refugees' tickets were courtesy of the federal and local government's malignant neglect.

It was only fitting, because these thirty thousand people helped pay for the stadium in the first place. The Superdome was built entirely on the public dime in 1975, as a part of efforts to create a "New New Orleans" business district.[6] New Orleans leaders have a history of elevating political graft to a finely honed art, and in this case they did not disappoint. Much of jazz legend Louis Armstrong's historic old neighborhood was ripped up for extra stadium parking,[7] and, in an instance of brutal foreshadowing that would shame Wes Craven, an old, aboveground cemetery was eradicated to make space for the end zones.[8] As a Saints fan said to me, "New Orleans's football team is nicknamed 'the Saints,' their brand is the fleur-de-lis, and the owner, Tom Benson, makes no bones about dancing on other people's graves. Oh, yeah, the fleur-de-lis was also the emblem viciously branded on enslaved Africans to identify them as being from Louisiana. Talk about ownership."[9]

New Orleans officials decided that building the largest domed stadium on the planet was in everyone's best interests. Even coming in years late, and at triple the expected budget, the Superdome was ready for business in August 1975.[10] And business it has brought. It has been the site of six Super Bowls, four Final Fours, and the 1988 Republican National Convention.[11] It is now the home of the 2010 Super Bowl champion Saints. It also launched a thirty-year path toward destruction for the Big Easy: a path that has seen investment for the tourist industry and the accompanying minimum-wage jobs, but no stable industry; a path that's seen money for the stadium but not for levees; money for the stadium but not for relief following an all-too-predictable disaster.

The tragedy of Katrina then became a farce when the Superdome's inhabitants were finally moved: not to government housing, public shelters, or even another location in the area, but to the Houston Astrodome. Ladies and gentlemen, in a moment when charity and irony collided, we had the March of Domes. Houston was a fitting destination. This was a place that stood up to the NFL's Houston Oilers when they demanded a new stadium. The mayor, Bob Lanier, said at the time, "The subsidy they get is totally disproportionate to the economic benefit they bring.... It would shame Jay Gould and his fellow robber barons of the nineteenth century. Even Genghis Khan got sated after a while."[12] Lanier, it should be pointed out, then caved, in 1998, when a new baseball stadium was demanded by Houston Astros' owner Drayton McLane. The city then funded the infamously named Enron Field. Lanier said, "The result [of not using public funds] is that we won't have any pro sports in Houston. Things might change someday, but the reality is that if you say [no to public subsidies] in today's market, you're below any market."[13] And if nothing else, you get an extra mass shelter for the next natural disaster.

Houston is now a city that suffers in silence, with two new stadiums (the expansion NFL team, the Houston Texans, also found a home), and according to 2007 data, more than a third of children living below the poverty line.[14] If Houston suffers in silence from these priorities, New Orleans, even four years after Katrina, still makes a sane person want to holler.

When the city was ready to begin the rebuilding, it was as if nothing had been learned. The first major renovation in New Orleans, the symbol of deliverance, was the $185 million overhaul of the Louisiana Superdome," $94 million of which came from FEMA.[16] Never mind that the Dome's adjoining mall and hotel were still shuttered or that the city hasn't seen that kind of money spent on low-income housing destroyed by Hurricane Katrina. The road back for the Big Easy began in the Dome. As one ESPN talking head solemnly told us, "The most daunting task is to scrub away memories of the Superdome as a cesspool of human misery."[17]

These memories shouldn't be scrubbed away but remembered, so we don't repeat the same damn mistakes. The stadium was overhauled and rehabilitated. Public housing wasn't. If you move beyond Bourbon Street, you can still witness the houses of worship that are still half sunk in the water or see homes with marks on them to show where dead bodies were found. You can also see the locations where the B. W. Cooper, C. J. Peete, Lafitte, and St. Bernard housing projects used to rest.

These four "developments," which housed 4,584 families, have been demolished.[18] Many of these families haven't even come back since the levees broke, unable to reclaim their homes and advocate for their communities.

New Orleans is crying out for grand acts of daring and leadership. Nothing grand is coming from Washington, D.C. When the Super Bowl–winning Saints visit the White House, it might be the first time President Barack Obama says the words "New Orleans" in a public setting. The answer begins not with "scrub[bing] away memories of the Superdome" but in amplifying those memories so they fuel a movement to bring back not only the city but also every last resident who wants to return.

As New Orleans resident and commentator Harry Shearer wrote in 2009, "The farther we get into [the Obama] administration, the clearer it becomes that New Orleans is now enjoying its second consecutive federal administration which, far from offering to fix what it broke, far from offering a hand of support, is merely offering one finger."[19] This is particularly poignant as quarterback Drew Brees and the New Orleans Saints hold the Lombardi trophy. Team success is not an express train ride to solvency or recovery.

MINNESOTA

For too many years stadiums were exalted as the difference between a cutting-edge city ready for the globalized world of tomorrow, and a sleepy town left behind in the dust. The stadium pushers ask the question with the aggressive posture of a corner evangelist. Do you want your city left behind? Do you want to be trapped in a Thornton Wilder play or be featured in *Condé Nast Traveler*?

When the late Minnesota Twins' owner Carl Pohlad failed to fleece the locals in a stadium referendum, one of his minions bemoaned that the Twin Cities—the birthplace of Prince, Morris Day, and Husker Dü-would become (heaven forbid) "another Bismarck, North Dakota:" Pohlad died at age ninety-three in January 2009 with the title "the richest owner in baseball."[20] He first made his money by foreclosing on the land of Minnesota farmers during the Great Depression.[21] As an owner, he is perhaps best known for trying to contract his own team.[22] He's the only sports boss who could be comfortably profiled by both John Steinbeck and John Feinstein.

Pohlad found himself repeatedly frustrated in his quest for stadium manna. The multibillionaire spent the last two decades of his life trying to get the taxpayers of his home state to give him $522 million for a state-of-the-art megadome.[23] It seemed that Minneapolis–St. Paul, with its social democratic traditions, wouldn't go the way of Houston, Texas. This is a state where the Democrats call themselves Democrat Farm and Labor (DFL) and Republicans are in fact named the Independent Republicans (IR). Of course, it's also the state that gave us Governor Jesse Ventura, so anything is possible.

Granted, the old home of the Twins, the Hubert H. Humphrey Metrodome, isn't the most attractive of stadiums. It's like watching a game inside a condom. The late, great Billy Martin, who managed the Twins in 1969, once said, "How could Hubert Humphrey's parents name him after this dump?"[24] The solution seemed obvious. Either continue to enjoy the latex charms of the Metrodome or have the billionaire Pohlad finance and build his own stadium. Pohlad, however, insisted that the state pick up at least half the tab.[25] The people in numerous referendums were polite and firm that the Pohlad way was not the Minnesota way.[26]

They even voted it down when the Minnesota Twins ran a TV commercial featuring a ballplayer visiting a boy in the hospital. A voice-over solemnly announced, "If the Twins leave Minnesota, an eight-year-old from Willmar [Minnesota] undergoing chemotherapy will never get a visit from [Twins infielder] Marty Cordova."[27]

It turned out that the boy had already died by the time the commercial aired.

Pohlad was undeterred, saying, "Sports is a way of life, like eating. People say, 'You should pay to feed the homeless.' But the world doesn't work that way."[28]

He couldn't win even with then-governor Arne Carlson in his pocket. Carlson described himself as "the state's number one booster" for the team.[29] When he was asked why the multibillionaire Pohlad couldn't buy his own stadium, Carlson said, "That's irrelevant," and lashed out at stadium critics, saying that they were fomenting "class warfare."[30] Carlson, that old honeydripper, then tried a romantic tack, saying, "When you call up a hot tootsie for a date, you're not going to go to the water treatment plant."[31] It still didn't work. Carlson's stadium scheme for Pohlad was opposed by 69 percent of the electorate.[32] Even a majority of self-identified Twins fans opposed the deal.[33]

But you don't get to be ninety-three without some serious stubbornness pulsing through your veins. Pohlad continued to fight for his fair share of the public trough. "I don't know if you'd call me evil," he said. "I've been put into an impossible situation."[34] The impossible situation was that no matter how many politicians were in his pocket, no matter how many commercials he funded, no matter how many times he sent former players—such as team icon Kirby Puckett—to shill around the state, a significant majority of the people simply opposed the stadium.

Eventually he came around to the puckish wisdom of former New York mayor Rudolph Giuliani. Giuliani once said that the problem with stadium referendums is that people won't vote for them. Pohlad took the Giuliani gospel to heart. His people worked it behind the scenes, giving hundreds of thousands of dollars to politicians in both parties, eventually making a mockery of the Farm and Labor label on the Democrats and the Independent label on the Republicans.[35, 36] Governor and presidential aspirant Tim Pawlenty, who has vetoed every effort to raise taxes to refurbish the state's infrastructure, became a born-again stadium supporter. Others also got religion and began to worship at the altar of "revenue streams," "naming rights," and "luxury boxes." As the Minnesota-based *City Pages* put it, "After a long string of public relations disasters that have entrenched his reputation as a miserly, something-for-nothing businessman, Carl Pohlad—the richest owner in major league baseball—has finally learned his political lesson. This time all the hardball haggling occurred behind closed doors."[37]

Groundbreaking for Pohlad's monument to corporate greed and political graft was supposed to be on Thursday, August 2, 2007. Unfortunately for all concerned parties, earlier that week, the I-35W Mississippi River bridge (officially known as Bridge 9340) collapsed, killing 13 and injuring 145.[38] Celebrations, complete with ceremonial shovels, were hastily scuttled. The irony was simply too much: to celebrate the fleecing of the public to the tune of half a billion dollars—more than $300 out of the pockets of every taxpayer—while bodies had still yet to be recovered from the river, would have been monstrous, even for the congenitally shameless Pawlenty.[39]

WASHINGTON, D.C.

The U.S. capital is more than a tale of two cities; it's also a tale of two worlds. First we have Washington, home of the White House, the Capitol Building, and the Washington Monument. This city is the province of fat-cat power brokers and slick-talking lobbyists oozing from one five-star steak house to the next. Then we have D.C., a majority African-American city with some of the highest poverty, infant mortality, and HIV rates in the nation. This city is where residents taste a cold reality where services have been cut to the bone and 50 percent of young black men are in prison or on parole.[40] The only public hospital was shut down, the schools creak in buildings that predate Prohibition, and the roads have potholes cavernous enough to provide safe harbor for the rats that contend for power after dusk.

Former mayor Anthony Williams looked at this urban environment in desperate need of reinvestment and saw the answer as clear as his ubiquitous bow tie in the mirror: a new baseball stadium. A $611 million tax hike was jammed through the D.C. City Council to build the new park.[41] Cost overruns would take the project to more than $1 billion.[42] The park was built even though the team, the Washington Nationals—having just made the journey from being the Montreal Expos—didn't have an owner. They were the foster child of Major League Baseball, run by the office of Commissioner Bud Selig. But after D.C. put together this "ultimate sweetheart deal," it was only a matter of time before prospective owners began to line up. The wretched Montreal Expos got to move from a decrepit near-empty stadium built in celebration of the 1976 Summer Olympics, to a brand-spanking-new near-empty stadium in Southeast Washington, D.C.

How a couple dozen of the richest men in the United States—major league owners—got one of the most impoverished cities in the Western Hemisphere to give them $1 billion is still a mystery. It was a heist so audacious that all the Sopranos still must be shaking their heads in admiration. Just to compare, the St. Louis Cardinals' franchise paid for *77* percent of their new $387 million stadium.[43] The Detroit Tigers paid for 62 percent of their $327 million stadium, Comerica Park.[44] In D.C., the city picked up every penny.[45]

Williams gurgled with glee at the press conference announcing this exercise in corporate welfare. He boasted that because the stadium would be funded by business taxes, "the people in D.C. won't pay one dime."[46]

But Mayor Williams didn't mention the rise in the cost of living, as businesses pass on these new taxes to consumers. (Numerous D.C. neighborhoods have since become case studies of gentrification.) He didn't mention that cost overruns have nowhere to hide except in regressive taxes on the backs of D.C. residents. He didn't mention the city's willingness to take people's homes and bulldoze them to the ground if they live on the proposed stadium site and don't want to sell. (This they call "eminent domain.") He also said that the stadium would create jobs. He didn't say that this could be a case of robbing Peter to kill Paul.

Roger Noll, coauthor of the book *Sports, Jobs, and Taxes: The Economic Impact of Sports Teams and Stadiums,* wrote, "Any independent study shows that as an investment, it's silly. If they're trying to sell it on the grounds of actually contributing to economic growth and employment in D.C., that's wrong. There's never been a publicly subsidized stadium anywhere in the United States that had the effect of increasing employment and economic growth in the city in which it was built."[47]

In the end, Mayor Williams's plan was pushed through without the pretense of referendum, even though the great majority of the people of D.C. wanted no part of it. A poll released by the Service Employees International Union found that 70 percent of the city opposed public funding, and more than half strongly opposed it.[48] These numbers crossed all ethnic and racial lines. But the mayor insisted on giving D.C. a new baseball stadium the same way a dog gets medicine at the vet: held down, pried open, and force-fed. But still, as residents squirmed, Williams had his media-offensive line drive-blocking ahead.

Tom Boswell of the *Washington Post* played his part selling the stadium by expounding about how "revitalized" stadium-blessed cities such as Cleveland are in the wake of Major League Baseball's noblesse oblige.[49] He neglected to mention that Cleveland had just been named the poorest city in the United States, with the poverty rate hitting 30 percent.[50]

Sally Jenkins, also of the *Post,* captured the true dynamic perfectly, writing, "If we strip away all the pastoral nonsense, and the nostalgia, and the exuberant projections about urban redevelopment, doesn't it look like the nation's capital is being extorted by Commissioner Bud Selig?"[51]

But Mayor Williams wasn't done. Proving once again that inflicting injury is no fun without a sweet insult, he wanted the team to be named the Grays. "Grays" is neither a self-aggrandizing nod toward the former mayor's less than sparkling personality nor his favorite color. It was, in Williams's words, "a tribute" to the area's old Negro National League team the Homestead Grays, which featured Hall of Fame legends Josh Gibson and Buck Leonard. (The name Grays was eventually passed over for the Nationals.)

The mayor's nostalgia for the Negro Leagues and his touching olive branch to this majority African-American city was somewhat dulled by his battle plan to build this $1 billion lemon in the overwhelmingly black Southeast neighborhood of Anacostia.

It was a stunning act of chutzpah. Williams wanted to gentrify the most historic black neighborhood in the city in the name of honoring the Negro Leagues. Not since the production of the 1992 pornographic film *Malcolm XXX* has a symbol of African-American pride been so abused. But the stadium was pushed through with fawning help from the local press. Rarely has the coverage of an event been so pandering, so utterly absent of objectivity than the *Washington Post*'s coverage of the debut of the Washington Nationals' new stadium.

The *Post* reported on the ballpark's grand opening with hard-hitting articles such as "Lapping Up a Major Victory, and Luxuries, at New Stadium."[52] Without even a raised eyebrow, the article quoted people from the suburbs of Maryland and Virginia about how much fun they were having on stadium grounds playing *Guitar Hero* and eating authentic D.C. half smokes from Ben's Chili Bowl before the big game. The column should have come with coupons for the Make Your Own Teddy Bear booth.

But that was nothing compared to Tom Boswell. Some Boswell gems from opening night included, "Imagine 25,000 people all smiling at once. Not for a few seconds, but continuously for hours. You won't see it at a tense World Series. But when a brand-new ballpark opens, especially in a city that hasn't had such an experience for 46 years, people can't help themselves."[53]

In a nod to actual journalism, Boswell did manage to raise a few questions. "Are they worth the money? Has MLB mastered civic extortion, playing one city against another?" But have no fear. He had no answers. "That's a different story, a different day."[54] Unfortunately, it's a story over the past three years he has never written. He did quote another suburban game-tripper making the trek into the big bad city who said, "Sometimes you got to spend money to make money." Of course, it's not his money, but why quibble?

Boswell was actually a model of restraint compared to *Post* city columnist Marc Fisher. In a piece titled "The City Opens the Ballpark, and the Fans Come Up Winner," Fisher wrote, "An investment in granite, concrete and steel buys a new retail, residential and office neighborhood. It buys the president of the United States throwing out the first ball. And it buys a son showing his father what his boy has become."[55] (I don't even understand that last line. A son shows his father . . . his boy? So the father is a grandfather? Is this some sort of southern Gothic goes to the ballpark? Maybe Fisher was just blissed out on $8 beers and making his own teddy bears.)

While Boswell and Fisher were given prime column real estate to gush, columnist Sally Jenkins didn't even get a corner of the comics page. Her absence was conspicuous, but it's very understandable why Jenkins, the 2002 Associated Press sports columnist of the year, didn't get to play. Four years ago, she refused to gush over prospects for a new stadium. "While you're celebrating the deal to bring baseball back to Washington, understand just what it is you're getting: a large publicly financed stadium and potential sinkhole to house a team that's not very good, both of which may cost you more than you bargained for and be of questionable benefit to anybody except the wealthy owners and players. But tell that to baseball romantics, or the mayor and his people, and they act like you just called their baby ugly. It's lovely to have baseball in Washington again. But the deal that brings the Montreal Expos to Washington is an ugly baby."[56]

Jenkins's words have come to pass. But this isn't just an "ugly baby," its Rosemary's baby. It's $1 billion of taxpayer money in a city that has become a ground zero of economic segregation and gentrification; $1 billion in a city set to close down a staggering twenty-four public schools. That's $1 billion, rammed through a mere five months after a mayor-commissioned study found that the district's poverty rate was the highest it had been in a decade and African-American unemployment was 51 percent.

That's $1 billion in a city where the libraries shut down early and the Metro rusts over. That's a living, throbbing reminder that the vote-deprived District of Columbia doesn't even rest on the pretense of democracy. This isn't just taxation without representation. This is sports as ethnic and economic cleansing. Fittingly, when the stadium opened, President George W. Bush came out to throw the first pitch. Fittingly, he was roundly booed. He stood on the mound, proudly oblivious, taking center stage yet again in what can only be described as occupied territory.

Many in D.C. were relieved when after a seventeen-month search, the Nationals finally found ownership in the Lerner family. The Lerners are a clan of real estate tycoons building the grandest minimalls in the D.C. area. They have one-stop-shopped their way to a fortune estimated at $3.5 billion.[57]

The family's eighty-year-old patriarch, Theodore Lerner, gushed in an interview, "We're delighted to receive the opportunity to own this franchise. It's something I've been thinking about all my life, from the time I used to pay 25 cents to sit in the bleachers at Griffith Stadium," the former home of the Washington Senators.[58] He also said, "I plan on doing everything I can do to make sure this franchise becomes an international jewel for Major League Baseball, the nation, D.C., and its wonderful fans." But unless Lerner was referring to that prized jewel known as "the cubic zirconium," this simply has not been the case. Last-place finishes, meager attendance (even in that new stadium), and boredom have been the hallmarks of the club under the Lerners. There is a very good reason why the Washington Nationals are referred to as "the Gnats."

In addition to putting out a product that has stymied any goodwill the city was feeling about the return of baseball, the Lerners stonewalled for months on the $3.5 million they owed the city in back rent on the taxpayer-funded stadium.[59] In October 2008, the Lerners finally announced that they would happily pay the millions, but only in exchange for $4 million more in taxpayer-funded concessions.[60] This was the move that put the public cost of the stadium at more than $1 billion.

As Dave McKenna, sports columnist for the *Washington City Paper*, wrote, "All year, they hit more wrong notes than a grade-school cellist. The Lerners, after all, had responded to the initial reports about the unpaid rent not by apologizing but by threatening to dock the city $100,000 a day until the stadium they'd been using for months was, to their way of thinking, 'finished.' The Nationals had played nearly 50 home games in the allegedly unfinished stadium by that point."[61]

The Lerners also held two large fan events at hotels outside Washington, D.C., in the Maryland suburbs. It probably shouldn't surprise us that the midwives of the area's minimalls were more comfortable in the 'burbs. But while the local politicians were furious, they were all bark and no bite. The attitude of the Lerner family should have emboldened the city to take the team and the stadium back and run it in the public interest. Instead, the City Council howled a bit and then rolled over, hoping for a tummy scratch. Not surprisingly, the expected economic development hasn't been there, either.

Fan Steve Guzowski said to me, "As a current D.C. resident, I (along with every other district citizen) have a daily reminder about our great civic investment that is Nationals Park. A year and half after the stadium's opening, Half Street still remains a giant bowl of mud, while the Lerner family reaps the in-stadium markup on concessions without any up-front investment on the facility they call home."[62]

Meanwhile, as the city has fallen further and further into disrepair, the chickens of corporate welfare came home to roost. On June 22, 2009, two Washington, D.C., Metro trains collided, killing nine and sending more than seventy-five to the hospital.[63] The accident took place a ten-minute walk from my house, and, like many others, I spent most of that day on the phone, either assuring people that my family was safe, or checking on friends to make sure no one was in the hospital or worse. Everyone I knew was fine, although several had been on the trains involved, shaken but not grievously injured. The relief was palpable, even physical. But then the stories started to be released in small doses, and relief turned to horror.

There were the families of the dead on television: the inconsolable loved ones of train operator Jeanice McMillan, forty-two; David and Ann Wherley, both sixty-two; Mary Doolittle, fifty-nine; LaVonda King, twenty-three; Veronica DuBose, twenty-nine; Cameron Williams, thirty-seven; Dennis Hawkins, sixty-four; and Ana Fernandez, forty. A teacher, a young mother, a retired National Guard major general, a woman who cleaned office buildings while raising six children—all gone.

The wreckage near my house was not an accident site. Essentially, it was a crime scene. The subsequent investigation revealed that the trains and the tracks were rife with problems—the lead train car was one of the original 1000-Series, which dates back to the Carter administration. Train maintenance was overdue. Metro's crash avoidance system had experienced repeated problems and failures. Safety recommendations had gone ignored.

The Metro became our broken levee: an utterly preventable tragedy if only people in government had the will to do the public good.

Our current D.C. mayor, Adrian Fenty, stepped up to the cameras after the crash, ready to have his "Giuliani moment" of a mayor in control of a crisis. But he didn't have to explain why the District of Columbia is on the hook for a $1 billion ballpark, where the city's last-place team toils in front of their dozen or so biggest fans. No one asked, "Why, under your watch, does the D.C. government own sky boxes at all sporting venues? Why are you in discussion for more stadium spending—on soccer, hoops, and the mother of all stadium deals, the possible return of the Washington Redskins from suburban Maryland to the district?"

Every billionaire sports owner has his hand out because Fenty has shown that he will turn his pockets inside out for them—this despite the fact that Fenty became mayor on the strength of standing up to the Nationals' stadium deal when he was on the City Council.

It is a question of priorities, plain and simple.

I spoke to former Major League Baseball All-Star and *Ball Four* author Jim Bouton about the publicly financed "doming" of America. He said:

> It's such a misapplication of the public's money.... You've got towns turning out streetlights, they're closing firehouses, they're cutting back on school supplies, they're having classrooms in stairwells, and we've got a nation full of kids who don't have any health insurance. I mean, it's disgraceful. The limited things that our government does for the people with the people's money, to spend even a dime or a penny of it on ballparks is just a crime.
>
> It's going to be seen historically as an awful folly, and it's starting to be seen that way now, but historically that will go down as one of the real crimes of American government, national and local, to allow the funneling of people's money directly into the pockets of a handful of very wealthy individuals who could build these stadiums on their own if it made financial sense. If they don't make financial sense, then they shouldn't be building them.[64]

Bouton went on to say, "If I was a team owner today, asking for public money, I'd be ashamed of myself. But we've gone beyond shame. There's no such thing as shame anymore. People aren't embarrassed to take—to do these awful things."[65]

Bouton is absolutely correct. When it comes to fleecing our cities, some of the richest people in this country have shown a complete absence of shame. The question is whether we are going to finally stand up and impose our priorities on them, instead of continually taking it on the chin. Every time a publicly funded stadium is considered in your hometown, New Orleans, Minneapolis, and Washington, D.C., need to be part of the conversation and debate. Stadiums aren't built out of thin air. They're built on our backs.

NOTES

1. Dave Zirin, "Football in L.A.: If There's No Team: It's Bonkers to Build a Stadium," *Los Angeles Times,* October 29, 2009, http://www.latimes .com/2009/oct/29/opinion/oe-zirin29.
2. Neil deMause, personal correspondence, April 13, 2007.
3. Neil deMause and Joanna Cagan, *Field of Schemes: How the Great Stadium Swindle Turns Public Money into Private Profit* (Lincoln, Neb.: Bison Books, 2008), 209.
4. Ibid., 36.

5. "New Orleans Mayor Orders Mandatory Evacuation as 'Catastrophic' Hurricane Gustav Roars over Cuba," *London Evening Standard,* http://www.thisislondon.co.uk/news/article-23546267-new-orleans-mayor-orders-mandatory-evacuation-as-catastrophic-hurricane-gustav-roars-over-cuba.do.

6. Michael N. Danielson, *Home Team: Professional Sports and the American Metropolis* (Princeton, N.J.: Princeton University Press, 2001), 279.

7. Alecia P. Long, "Poverty Is the New Prostitution: Race, Poverty, and Public Housing in Post-Katrina New Orleans," *Journal of American History* (December 2007).

8. "Archie Manning: Saints Must be Wary of Winless Lions," *USA Today,* http://www.usatoday.com/sports/football/nfl/saints/2008-12-18-lionssaints_N.htm.

9. Saints fan, personal correspondence, August 31, 2009.

10. Richard Campanella, *New Orleans Then and Now* (Gretna, La.: Pelican Publishing, 1999), 26.

11. Arthur Q. Davis and J. Richard Gruber, *It Happened by Design: The Life and Work of Arthur Q. Davis* (Jackson: University of Mississippi Press, 2009), 50.

12. DeMause and Cagan, *Field of Schemes,* 62.

13. Ibid.

14. "StreetAdvisor: Houston, Texas," http://www.streetadvisor.com/texas/ houston/demographics.

15. "Tulane—Louisiana Superdome," http://ncaafootball.com/index.php?s =&url_channel_id=348curl_article_id=12775.Scchange_well_id=2.

16. "FEMA Public Assistance Division Still Busy One Year After Katrina," http://www.fema.gov/news/newsrelease.fema?id=29068.

17. ESPN's *Monday Night Football,* September 25, 2006.

18. Katy Reckdahl, "Hurricane Disaster Program Not Quite as Busy: Fewer Applying for Food-Stamp Aid," *Times-Picayune,* September 3, 2009, http://www.nola.com/hurricane/index.ssf/2009/09/disaster_program_ not_quite_as.html.

19. Harry Shearer, "Obama to New Orleans: Drop Dead?," May 18, 2009, http://www.huffingtonpost.com/harry-shearer/obama-to-new-orleansdrop_b_204796.html.

20. Steven A. Riess, *Encyclopedia of Major League Baseball Clubs* (Westport, Conn.: Greenwood Publishing Group, 2006), vol. 1, 695.

21. Jonah Keri, "The Owners We Love to Hate," September 24, 2007, http://sports.espn.go.com/espn/page2/story?page=keri/owners/070924.

22. "Minnesota Twins Owner, Pohlad Dies at 93," *USA Today, January* 6, 2009, http://www.usatoday.com/sports/baseball/al/twins/2009-01-05-pohladobit_N.htm.

23. "Twins Owner Carl Pohlad Dies," *Minneapolis/St. Paul Business Journal,* January 5, 2009, http://twincities.bizjournals.com/twincities/stories/ 2009/01/05/daily8.html.

24. "Why Your Stadium Sucks: Hubert H. Humphrey Metrodome," http://newshaven.org/sports/why-your-stadium-sucks-hubert-h-humphreymetrodome/.

25. Joe Christensen and Jim Souhan, "Legacy, Loyalty, Finances Defined Twins Owner," *Star Tribune,* January 5, 2009, http://www.startribune.com/sports/twins/37110909.html?elr=KArksLckD8EQDUoaEyqyP40:DW3ckUiD3aPc:_Yyc:aUycaEacyU.

26. "Citizens Campaigning Against Renegade Legislators," http://www.ccarl.com/.

27. "Scott Miller's Bull Pennings: Carl Pohlad: 1915–2009," January 5, 2009, http://scott-miller.blogs.cbssports.com/mcc/blogs/entry/6270335/12742055.

28. deMause and Cagan, *Field of Schemes,* 160.

29. Ibid., 169.

30. Ibid.

31. Peter Finley and Laura L. Finley, *The Sports Industry's War on Athletes* (Westpoint, Conn.: Praeger Security International, 2006), 133.

32. deMause and Cagan, *Field of Schemes,* 170.

33. Ibid.

34. Jay Weiner, *Stadium Games: Fifty Years of Big League Greed and Bush League Boondoggles* (Minneapolis: University of Minnesota Press, 2000), 116.

35. Kenneth P. Vogel and Matthew Lindsey, "Sports Owners Fund McCain, Shun Obama," August 15, 2008, http://dyn.politico.com/printstory.cfm?uuid=C5A22B4A-18FE-70B2-A8B408A4049C60F3.

36. "Carl Pohlad: Political Campaign Contributions 2008 Election Cycle," http://www.campaignmoney.com/political/contributions/carl-pohlad .asp?cycle=08.

37. Dave Zirin, "Even in Minnesota," August 4, 2007, www.counterpunch.org/zirin08042007.html.

38. "Engineering Expert to Discuss I-35W Bridge Collapse," http://www.sdstate.edu/news/articles/khani-sahebjam.cfm.

39. Dennis Coates and Brad R. Humphrey, "The Stadium Gambit and Local Economic Development," *Cato Institute: Economic Development Policy* 23, no. 2.

40. Thomas G. Blomberg and Stanley Cohen, *Punishment and Social Control* (Hawthorne, N.Y.: Aldine de Gruyter, 2003), 404.

41. Richard Lapchick, "Do the Right Thing in D.C.," http://sports.espn.go.com/espn/page2/story?page=lapchick/060209&num=0.

42. Michael Neibauer, "Fenty Plans to Raid Ballpark Tax," *Washington Examiner,* July 26, 2009, http://www.washingtonexaminercom/local/Fentyplans-to-raid-ballpark-tax-51747192.html.

43. Tom Sullivan and Fred Lindecke, "What the Public Paid for the Cardinals' Stadium: The Media Never Told the Whole Story," *St. Louis Journalism Review,* June 2003, http://findarticles.com/p/articles/mi_hb6666/is_296_37/ai_n29355249/.

44. "Baseball Statistics: Comerica Park," http://www.baseball-statistics.com/Ballparks/Det/index.htm.

45. "Study: Publicly Funded Stadium in Washington, D.C., Amounts to Reverse Commuter Tax on Residents," November 8, 2004, http://www.ntu.org/main/press_release.php?PressID=6688corg_name=NTUF.

46. "Reverse Robin Hood: D.C. Mayor Williams Mulcts from Taxpayers, to the Profit of Sports-Franchise Multimillionaires," November 30, 2004, http://www.nationalreview.com/comment/bandow200411300826.asp.

47. Roger G. Noll and Andrew S. Zimbalist, *Sports, Jobs, and Taxes: The Economic Impact of Sports Teams and Stadiums* (Washington, D.C.: Brookings Institute, 1997), 168.

48. Lori Montgomery, "Baseball Proposal Losing in D.C. Poll: Public Financing Plan Would Build Stadium," *Washington Post,* August 26, 2004, http://www.washingtonpost.com/wp-dyn/articles/A33715-2004Aug25.html.

49. Tom Boswell, "A Thing of Beauty," *Washington Post,* November 14, 2007, http://www.washingtonpost.com/wp—dyn/content/article/2007/11/13/AR2007111302361.html?nav=emailpage.

50. Rich Exner, "Data Central: Cleveland Ohio Statistics, Demographics & Census," September 29, 2009, http://www.cleveland.com/datacentral/ index.ssf/2009/09/find_povertydata_for_us_citie.html.

51. Sally Jenkins, "Badly Fooled by the Pitch," *Washington Post,* September 24, 2004, http://www.washingtonpost.com/wp-dyn/articles/A48793-2004Sep24.html.

52. David Nakamura, "Lapping Up a Major Victory, and Luxuries, at New Stadium; Fans Giddy After Storybook Ending (and the Occasional Cocktail)," *Washington Post,* March 31, 2008, http://www.washingtonpost.com/wp-dyn/content/article/2008/03/30/AR2008033001584.html.

53. Thomas Boswell, "Upon Inspection, New Home Has Some Sweet Aspects to It," *Washington Post,* March 30, 2008, http://www.washingtonpost.com/wp-dyn/content/article/2008/03/29/AR2008032902217.html.

54. Ibid.

55. Marc Fisher, "What Do You Get for Your $611 Million?," *Washington Post,* http://voices.washingtonpost.com/rawfisher/2008/03/what_do_you_get_ for_your_611_m.html.

56. Sally Jenkins, "Is the District Being Sold a Bill of Goods?," *Washington Post,* September 30, 2004, http://www.washingtonpost.com/wp-dyn/articles/A60832-2004Sep29.html.

57. "The Business of Baseball: #14 Washington Nationals," *Forbes,* April 22, 2009, http://www.forbes.com/lists/2009/33/baseball-values-09_Washington-Nationals_337401.htm1.

58. Thomas Heath and David Nakamura, "After 17 Months, Baseball Introduces Nats' Owner: Lerner Group Pledges to Work Closely on Stadium," *Washington Post,* May 4, 2006, http://www.washingtonpost.com/wp-dyn/content/article/2006/05/03/AR2006050301121.html.

59. Tierney Plumb, "Washington Nationals to Pay Overdue Rent," *Washington Business Journal,* October 28, 2008, http://washington.bizjournals.com/washington/stories/2008/10/20/daily8.html.

60. Ibid.

61. Dave McKenna, "Unsportsmen of the Year: In 2008, the Lerners Taught Us the Meaning of Ingratitude," *Washington City Paper,* December 17, 2008, http://www.washingtoncitypaper.com/display.php?id=36612.

62. Steve Guzowski, personal correspondence, August 29, 2009.

63. Lena H. Sun and Lyndsey Laytner, "Red Line Train Operator Used Brakes in Failed Bid to Stop Six-Car Train," *Washington Post,* June 24, 2009, http://www.washingtonpost.com/wp-dyn/content/article/2009/06/23/AR2009062300653.html.

64. Jim Bouton, personal correspondence, January 9, 2007.

65. Ibid.

27

Corporate Titans Competing for Olympic Gold

How Ad Wars Have Hijacked the Games

Geoff Dembicki

On June 16, 2006, 1,000 Dutch soccer fans were forced to strip to their underwear in Stuttgart, Germany. They'd waited in 25-minute lines, shuffling step by step towards the Gottlieb-Daimler-Stadion. At the door, stern FIFA World Cup officials ordered them to remove their bright orange lederhosen.

One Dutch man threw his over a fence. A stadium steward approached his waiting friends, likely tossing the confiscated pants into a rubbish-filled storage bin with all the others. Bare-legged Dutch fans ambled to their seats, leg hairs bristling from the draft.

Absurd? Not in the bloodied-nose arena of international sports marketing, where no punches are held and most are below the belt. FIFA was merely protecting the $1.1 billion investment of official World Cup sponsor Budweiser. Dutch brewery Bavaria had circulated thousands of branded orange trousers to beer-loving soccer fans.

Despite the best efforts of FIFA's pants-police, Budweiser's dollar signs couldn't match the simple ingenuity of its rival. Worldwide media exposure meant everyone was talking about Bavaria's crazy stunt. And FIFA and its sponsors looked profoundly uncool.

Source: Geoff Dembicki, "Corporate Titans Competing for Olympic Gold: How Ad Wars Have Hijacked the Games." *AfterNet* (January 16, 2010). Online: http://www.alternet.org/story/145204/.

Now jump three years into the future. In October 2009, two well-known Olympics critics sued the city of Vancouver. New bylaws, passed partly to protect the rights of official 2010 Winter Games sponsors, would trample local civil liberties, the pair believed.

It sounds like a bad joke: What do bare Dutch legs and litigious activists have in common? A lot, as it turns out.

Both crown a story as old as the modern Olympics. A tale of financial need and corporate hunger, culminating in crisis in the late 1970s. With the very future of the Olympics movement at stake, a logo-covered phoenix took flight. Its journey is far from over.

This February, get ready for a 21st-century Games, where the big spending battles of corporate titans could overshadow the rivalries of the ice rink and ski slope. And the supreme prize is the eyes, minds and ultimately, pocketbooks of the entire world.

START OF A MOVEMENT

It wasn't always like this. The modern Olympics began as the idealistic vision of a romantic dreamer. His name was Pierre de Coubertin. The moustachioed French aristocrat grew up during his country's humiliating defeat in the 1870–71 Franco-Prussian war.

He spent most of his young adult years campaigning for better physical education. Sports could instill positive values, he believed. And possibly prepare a new generation of French youth for combat.

Coubertin adored ancient Greece. There had been modest Olympics revivals before him. None had the benefit of his superb political connections. He proposed an international celebration of youth, culture, tolerance and peace. It was a convincing sell in a tumultuous era.

Athens was the test run. Its 1896 Olympics were largely funded by the private donations of patriotic Greek businessmen scattered across the planet. At least 60,000 spectators and dignitaries attended. By all accounts, the festival was a complete success. Yet Coubertin's fledgling International Olympic Committee (IOC) soon ran into a recurring problem: Who would pay for future Games?

The world of big business showed little interest. For instance, readers of the official race programme at London's 1908 Games would have perused full-page advertisements for Wawkphar's Antiseptic Military Foot Powder and Vaughton's Medal and Badge Makers.

Each new Olympics begat more athletes, dignitaries and spectators. Costs got higher and riskier. The 1920 Antwerp Games handed a 625,000 franc deficit to its Belgium hosts. Four years later, the first Winter Olympics in Chamonix, France, became the financial equivalent of a 30-skier pile-up, leaving organizers two million francs in debt.

Still, cities continued to host. "I don't think the expectation was there in terms of profit," said Stephen Wenn, co-author of *Selling the Five Rings: The International*

Olympic Committee and the Rise of Olympic Commercialism. "But whether you're talking the 1900s or 21st century, you're always going to find civic leaders who see these as something beneficial for their city—not to mention their own reputation."

Coubertin died in 1937. His heart was buried at the ancient ruins of Olympia, according to orders in his will. The movement he'd fathered was growing fast, but headed for an identity crisis. No one would exemplify it better than a millionaire businessman from Chicago named Avery Brundage.

CRUSADE AGAINST COMMERCIALISM

Brundage's own dream of Olympic gold died at the 1912 Stockholm Games, where he competed and finished well back in the pentathlon and decathlon. The failures haunted him as he went on to amass a fortune in the world of heavy construction. When he eventually did return to the world of athletics, it was in the role of administrator. By 1938, Brundage was head of the United States Olympic Association (USOA).

Brundage began a protracted crusade against Helms Bakeries that year. The Californian company sold lucrative "Olympic Bread" branded with the five-rings logo. It'd registered the word "Olympic" and all accompanying insignia in nearly every U.S. state. Essentially, a private company had scooped the USOA.

Brundage huffed and fumed. There was little else he could do. "You cannot imagine how many attempts there are to capitalize on the Olympic Games and the difficulty we have in preventing promoters to use the Olympic Movement for their own personal gain," he wrote to a colleague in 1938.

The most frustrating part was Helms Bakeries had every legal right on its side. None of the threatening letters Brundage wrote for 12 years could change that. Yet Helms Bakeries did let go of control of the Olympic brand in 1950. As a big supporter of American athletes, the company probably tired of so much ill will. Federal legislation soon granted the USOA wide jurisdiction over Olympics trademarks. It was official recognition of an obvious fact: the five rings had become a marketing goldmine.

That worried Brundage. He feared corporate dollars would destroy the ideals at the heart of the movement—or at least, his version of them. He adhered to an unyielding belief in amateurism, the concept that athletes shouldn't be paid professionals.

Brundage assumed the IOC presidency in 1952. He was stubborn and dictatorial. International controversy followed his decision to ban Austrian skier Karl Schranz from the 1972 Winter Olympics for receiving sponsorship dollars. There were many like it.

"Let's be blunt," said David Wallechinsky, vice-president of the International Society of Olympic Historians. "He was quite a tyrant. He was a very wealthy man who had no tolerance for athletes trying to make money."

It wasn't just athletes. With the first major television rights deals and the advent of satellite technology in the early 1960s, a perpetually broke IOC was suddenly awestruck by wealth.

Brundage could see the huge benefits of TV coverage, as marketing tool and revenue stream. It still made him uneasy. "I'm not sure we should ever get into [the

TV] business," he declared in 1955. "But on the other hand certainly we should not give millions of dollars away."

FINANCIAL DISASTERS AND TERRORIST ATTACKS

The value of TV rights deals shot skyward. The 1960 Squaw Valley, U.S.A. Winter Games brought US$50,000. Four years later, Innsbruck, Austria Olympics organizers sold rights worth US$936,667. Televised broadcasts let millions identify with the universal ideals and ancient symbolism at the heart of the Olympic movement.

That kind of exposure helped create the perfect consumer, ready to buy anything linked to the Games. Indeed, organizers at Tokyo's 1964 Olympics licensed official cigarettes with a five-ring logo stamped on every package.

Yet greater interest meant bigger spectacles. And new revenue streams couldn't necessarily pay the bills. In 1970, financial worries prompted Colorado voters to reject Denver's successful bid to host the 1976 Games. A flustered IOC pleaded with fourth-ranked bidder Whistler to take over. The resort didn't want them either. They were finally given to Innsbruck, three years later.

More crises followed. In 1972, Palestinian radicals in black track suits took 11 Israeli athletes hostage. Sniper bullets, machinegun rounds and grenade explosions left 17 dead, forever linking the Munich Games to politically-motivated violence. Brundage stepped down as IOC president that year.

Montreal's 1976 Games were no less calamitous. Mayor Jean Drapeau famously promised the spectacle "can no more have a deficit than a man can have a baby." He was only half right. Montreal finally settled its $1.5 billion tab in 2006.

Only months before the 1980 Moscow Games, Soviet tanks ploughed into Afghanistan. U.S. President Jimmy Carter retaliated with a full American boycott, the largest in Olympics history.

"A lot of people were questioning the Olympic movement," Wenn said. "There was a chill in municipal councils all around the world—whether there was any viable reason for going ahead with the Games."

Was Coubertin's movement in jeopardy? Would the flaming ideals of the five rings be snuffed out by warring political ideologies and financial fears?

FIRST COMMERCIAL OLYMPICS

When Los Angeles won its bid to host the 1984 Summer Olympics, nobody was surprised. It was the only serious contender. Peter Ueberroth, head of the Los Angeles organizing committee, told a reluctant city council not to worry. He was going to raise all the operating money himself.

At Montreal's 1976 Olympics, organizers had sold sponsorship rights to anyone who asked. The result was 628 "official" partners clamouring for attention at the least exclusive party in town.

Ueberroth in effect kicked out the riffraff. He sold sponsorship rights to a small cadre of multinational corporations. Everybody won. Companies such as Converse projected their brands through the global Olympics lens. Organizers were left with a record US$225 million surplus. Even a Soviet boycott went largely unnoticed.

The IOC launched TOP, its worldwide sponsorship program, the next year. Nine corporations paid huge sums for global marketing rights. It was a wild success. The first four years alone generated revenues of US$96 million. (The program brought US$866 million in 2005–08.)

It appeared the financial disaster of Montreal was largely forgotten. Six cities jostled to host the 1992 Summer Olympics. Five battled for the next. "Once Peter Ueberroth demonstrated a way to carry off the enterprise on the backs of the private sector, there was renewed interest," Wenn said.

But the model was vulnerable. Converse had paid millions to partner with the 1984 Olympics. Its rival Nike plastered huge murals of swoosh-wearing athletes all over Los Angeles. Forty-two percent of Americans confused Nike as an official partner.

"If you sponsor a big [sporting event], people will ultimately buy more of your products," said Simon Chadwick, founder and director of the Centre for the International Business of Sport at Coventry University. "Ambush marketing is about creating a misperception in the minds of consumers."

Nike's brazen murals were only the beginning. Each Games saw bigger and more sophisticated branding battles. When Visa sponsored the 1992 Barcelona Olympics, American Express retaliated with a simple slogan: "You don't need a Visa to visit Spain." Host cities—and countries—were becoming corporate war zones.

For the Olympics movement, the stakes were high. Unregulated ambush campaigns threatened a now vital revenue base. Why would sponsors invest tens of millions of dollars when their rivals could win the same market exposure for way less?

"DRACONIAN" MEASURES

The IOC wasn't the only one worried. In 1996, Nike ambushed the UEFA European Football Championship, snatching all outdoor ad space in and around London's Wembley Park tube station. Official sponsor Umbro was incensed.

Yet maybe Nike was on to something. UEFA decided to rent every advertising property within a one to three kilometre radius of soccer venues at future competitions. With the IOC's urging, local Olympics committees began to go even further. Organizers of the 2004 Athens Games literally reserved every outdoor ad space in the city. The billboards they couldn't sell sat blank.

The Vancouver 2010 organizing committee (VANOC) spent $38 million to give official partners the same protection, snapping up every outdoor ad property in the Lower Mainland. (Selling the inventory has been tough. And organizers freely admit they probably won't unload it all.)

Over the past decade, ad monopolies have been fortified with tougher trademark legislation. Legal guarantees are now a vital part of any successful Games bid.

"The Olympic Symbol and the terms 'Olympic' and 'Olympiad' and the Olympic motto" must be defended, the Manual for Candidate Cities for the XXI Olympic Winter Games 2010 stated. All bidders promised to "obtain from their government and/or their competent national authorities, adequate and continuing legal protection to the satisfaction of the IOC."

VANOC gained "considerable powers" from legislation passed by the Canadian government in 2007. Organizers could now seek lightning-fast court injunctions against unauthorized attempts to profit off the Olympic brand. For instance, a local jewellery store holding an "Olympics sale."

Did recent Vancouver bylaws go too far? Anti-Games activists Chris Shaw and Alissa Westergard-Thorpe sued the city in Oct. 2009. Temporary new rules imposed maximum $10,000 fines for unauthorized signs during the Games. The activists saw a blatant attack on their right to protest.

Vancouver relented in late November. The city promised to clearly distinguish between political and commercial signs. Yet most temporary powers remain. If someone were to hang a Pepsi banner from their balcony, bylaw officers could legally enter the residence within 24 hours to remove it. (The same rules apply to signs of official sponsors.)

During the 2010 Games, a team of 60 city inspectors will patrol Olympics corridors, venue zones and local celebration sites. VANOC is deploying about nine personnel to keep venues commercial-free. Their mandate could include taping over "blatant" logos on the shoes of volunteers.

The team will also monitor the city. "We'll hop on the Skytrain and ride out to Metrotown mall and go out around Vancouver to see how the brand is being used," said Bill Cooper, VANOC's director of commercial rights management.

It's worth mentioning domestic and international sponsorship revenue pays for about $1 billion of VANOC's $1.75 billion operating budget. Also notable are the billions of provincial and federal dollars necessary to widen the Sea-to-Sky highway, tunnel a new rapid transit line, construct the official media centre and secure the Games.

The United Kingdom just passed legislation protecting official sponsors during London's 2012 Olympics. And South Africa has done the same for the 2010 World Cup. Chadwick sees an escalating trend with some troubling implications.

"Some of the legal rights it gives the authorities are becoming increasingly draconian," he said. "So inevitably there has been a natural rise in concerns about people's civil liberties."

ARE CRACKDOWNS EFFECTIVE?

Let's return to Germany's 2006 World Cup, home of the rubbish bins overflowing with bright orange lederhosen. Bavaria's ambush became one of the most famous of all time. Nike's innovative use of social media was no less effective.

In the months leading up to the World Cup, the apparel giant told people to video themselves juggling a soccer ball. The only rule was the ball had to enter from the left of the screen, and leave on the right.

Thousands of amateur directors uploaded content to Nike's official site. The company spliced the best clips. A soccer ball got bounced, kicked and head-butted across entire continents.

"This became a real phenomenon, particularly in Europe," Chadwick said. "In the end, more people were talking about Nike in 2006 than Adidas, even though Adidas was the official sponsor."

And there's the problem, according to Chadwick. New rules to control ambush marketing are getting stricter all the time. But cities, event organizers and the international committees that direct them may be in a perpetual game of catch-up.

Last December saw Lululemon and Pepsi launch inventive ambush-style campaigns.

The same month, Vancouver police seized a million dollars worth of illegal goods that brazenly displayed the Olympics logo without official permission. The product? More than *100,000 ecstasy pills.*

Who knows what branding battles await Vancouver next month?

* FOR FURTHER STUDY *

Armstrong, Jim. 1999. "Money Makes the Sports Go 'Round,'" *Denver Post,* July 25, 1C, 12C.

Atkinson, Michael. 2002. "Fifty Million Viewers Can't Be Wrong: Professional Wrestling, Sports-Entertainment, and Mimesis." *Sociology of Sport Journal* 19 (1): 1–24.

Badenhausen, Kurt. 2008. "Where the Money Is." *Forbes* (June 30): 114.

Barney, Robert K., Stephen R. Wenn, and Scott G. Martyn. 2002. *Selling the Five Rings: The International Olympic Committee and the Rise of Olympic Commercialism.* Salt Lake City: University of Utah Press.

Beamish, Rob. 2007. "Sport and Capitalism." Pp. 4660–4662 in *Blackwell Encyclopedia of Sociology.* Vol. 9.

Brown, Clyde, and David M. Paul. 2002. "The Political Scorecard of Professional Sports Facility Referendums in the United States, 1984–2000." *Journal of Sport and Social Issues* 26 (August): 248–267.

Coakley, Jay. 2007. *Sports in Society: Issues and Controversies.* 9th ed. New York: McGraw-Hill.

Crapeau, Richard. 2007. "The *Flood* Case." *Journal of Sport History* 34 (Summer): 183–191.

Delaney, Kevin J., and Rick Eckstein. 2003. *Public Dollars, Private Stadiums: The Battle over Building Sports Stadiums.* New Brunswick, NJ: Rutgers University Press.

Eckstein, Rick, and Kevin Delaney. 2002. "New Sports Stadiums, Community Self-Esteem, and Community Collective Conscience." *Journal of Sport and Social Issues* 26 (August): 235–247.

Eitzen, D. Stanley. 2009. *Fair and Foul: Beyond the Myths and Paradoxes of Sport.* 4th ed. Lanham, MD: Rowman and Littlefield.

Eitzen, D. Stanley, and George H. Sage. 2009. *Sociology of North American Sport.* 8th ed. Boulder, CO: Paradigm.

Harvey, Jean, Alan Law, and Michael Cantelon. 2001. "North American Professional Sport Franchises Ownership Patterns and Global Entertainment Conglomerates." *Sociology of Sport Journal* 18 (4): 435–457.

Hudson, Ian. 2001. "The Use and Misuse of Economic Impact Analysis: The Case of Professional Sports." *Journal of Sport and Social Issues* 25 (February): 20–39.

Lewis, Michael. 2001. "Franchise Relocation and Fan Allegiance." *Journal of Sport and Social Issues* 25 (February): 6–19.

Malcolm, Dominic. 2007. "Sports Industry." Pp. 4713–4717 in *Blackwell Encyclopedia of Sport.* Vol. 9.

Nixon, Howard L. II. 2008. *Sport in a Changing World.* Boulder, CO: Paradigm.

Zimbalist, Andrew. 2006. *The Bottom Line: Observations and Arguments on the Sports Business.* Philadelphia, PA: Temple University Press.

Zimmer, Martha Hill, and Michael Zimmer. 2001. "Athletes as Entertainers: A Comparative Study of Earnings Profiles." *Journal of Sport and Social Issues* 25 (May): 202–215.

PART TEN

Structured Inequality: Sport and Race/Ethnicity

By definition, a minority group is one that (1) is relatively powerless compared with the majority group, (2) possesses traits that make it different from others, (3) is systematically condemned by negative stereotyped beliefs, and (4) is singled out for differential and unfair treatment (that is, discrimination). Race (a socially defined category on the basis of a presumed genetic heritage resulting in distinguishing social characteristics) and ethnicity (the condition of being culturally distinct on the basis of race, religion, or national origin) are two traditional bases for minority group status and the resulting social inequality. Sociologists of sport are interested in the question: Is sport an area of social life where performance counts and race or ethnicity is irrelevant? The three selections in this section examine four racial or ethnic minorities—Native Americans, Asian Americans, Latinos, and African Americans—to answer this question.

The first selection, by journalist Kevin Simpson, seeks an answer to the dilemma posed by the typical behaviors of excellent Native American athletes from reservations: Why do so many who are given scholarships either refuse them or return quickly to the reservation? These responses do not make sense to Anglos because the reservation has high unemployment, a life of dependency, and disproportionate alcohol abuse. Simpson points to these young men being "pulled" by the familiar, by the strong bonds of family, and by their unique culture. They are also "pushed" back to the reservation by social isolation, discrimination, poor high school preparation for college, and little hope for a return on their investment in a college education.

The second selection (29) provides a brief account of the surge in Latinos in Major League Baseball along with various issues of discrimination. The third selection in Part Ten is an excerpt from the *2010 Racial and Gender Report Card* by Richard Lapchick and his associates at the Institute for Diversity and Ethics in Sport. It summarizes and evaluates various dimensions of inequality in the National Football League, and provides recent data on stacking in professional football. The final selection shifts our attention to the examination of racism and discrimination of migrants and minorities in sport.

28

Sporting Dreams Die on the "Rez"

Kevin Simpson

Last season, basketball fans followed Willie White everywhere through the unforgiving South Dakota winter. Mesmerized by smooth moves, and spectacular dunks, they watched the most celebrated product of the state's hoop-crazy Indian tribes secure his status as local legend by leading his high school to an undefeated season and state championship.

They would mob him after games in an almost frightening scene of mass adulation, press scraps of paper toward him, and beg for an autograph preferably scribbled beneath some short personal message. White would oblige by scrawling short, illegible phrases before signing. He made certain they were illegible for fear someone would discover that the best prep basketball player in South Dakota could barely read or write.

As the resident basketball hero on the impoverished Pine Ridge Reservation, where there was precious little to cheer about before the state title rekindled embers of Indian pride, White was allowed to slip undisturbed through the reservation school system, until, by his senior year, he could read at only the sixth-grade level. Ironically, the same hero status moved him to admit his problem and seek help. The constant humiliation at the hands of autograph-seekers proved more than he could take.

"I had to face up to it," says White, a soft-spoken 6-foot–4 Sioux who looks almost scholarly behind his wire-rimmed glasses. "I couldn't go on forever like that. In school I didn't study. I cheated on every test they gave me. I couldn't read good enough to answer the questions."

Source: Kevin Simpson, "Sporting Dreams Die on the 'Rez,'" *Denver Post,* September 6, 1987, 1C, 19C.

After some intense individual help with his reading and writing, this fall White enrolled at Huron (South Dakota) College, where he intends to continue his basketball career and take remedial reading courses. If he manages to play four years and complete his degree, he'll be the first schoolboy athlete from Pine Ridge to do so.

Other than his close friends, nobody thinks he stands a chance. Indians usually don't.

Every year, all over the western United States, promising native American athletes excel in high school sports only to abandon dreams of college, return to economically depressed reservations, and survive on their per capita checks, welfare-like payments from the tribal government, or the goodwill of more fortunate relatives. They waste away quietly, victims of alcohol, victims of inadequate education, victims of boredom, victims of poverty, but nearly always victims of their own ambivalence, caught between a burning desire to leave the reservation and an irresistible instinct to stay.

"We've had two or three kids get scholarships in the eight years I've been here," says Roland Bradford, athletic director and basketball coach at Red Cloud High School, just a few miles down the highway from Pine Ridge. "None have lasted. It's kind of a fantasy thing. In high school they talk about going to college, but it's not a reality. They have no goals set. They start out, things get tough and they come home."

At 6-foot–7 and 280 pounds, Red Cloud's Dave Brings Plenty inspired enough comparisons to the Refrigerator to lure a photographer from *People* magazine out to the reservation. He went to Dakota Wesleyan to pursue his football career, but returned home after suffering a mild concussion in practice. He never played a game. Brings Plenty says he might enroll at a different school sometime in the future, but his plans are vague. For now, he's content to hang out on the reservation and work as a security guard at a bingo parlor.

Some of the athlete-dropouts have squandered mind-boggling potential. Jeff Turning Heart, a long-distance legend on South Dakota's Cheyenne River Reservation, enrolled at Black Hills State College in Spearfish, South Dakota, on a Bureau of Indian Affairs grant in 1980 amid great expectations. He left eight days later.

In 1982, he wound up at Adams State College in Alamosa, Colorado. Longtime Adams State coach Joe Vigil, the U.S. men's distance coach for the 1988 Olympics, says that as a freshman Turning Heart was far more physically gifted than even Pat Porter, the Adams State graduate who now ranks as the premier U.S. runner at 10,000 meters. Both Porter and Vigil figured Turning Heart was on a course to win the national cross-country title—until he left school, supposedly to tend to his gravely ill father in North Dakota. He promised to return in a few days. The story was bogus and Turning Heart never went back.

At Black Hills State, where in 19 years as athletic director and track coach, David Little has seen only one Indian track athlete graduate, Turning Heart wasn't the first world-class, Native American runner to jilt him. Myron Young Dog, a distance man from Pine Ridge who once won 22 straight cross-country races in high school, came to Black Hills after dropping out of Ellendale (North Dakota) Junior College in 1969. Although he was academically ineligible for varsity sports and hadn't trained, Young

Dog stepped onto the track during a physical conditioning class and ran two miles in 9:30 "like it was a Sunday jog," according to Little. Three weeks later he entered a 15-km road race and ran away from all the collegiate competition.

It was a tantalizing glimpse of talent ultimately wasted. Little still rates Young Dog as one of the top 10 athletes ever to come out of South Dakota, but in the spring of 1970 he returned to the reservation, never to run competitively again.

It doesn't take many heartbreaks before the college coaches catch on to the risky business of recruiting off the reservations. Although Indian athletes often are immensely talented and given financial backing from the tribe and the BIA—a budgetary boon to small schools short on scholarship funds—they suffer from a widespread reputation as high-risk recruits who probably won't stick around for more than a few weeks.

That's part of the reason so many schools backed off Willie White—that and his reading deficiency. Huron College coach Fred Paulsen, who made White his first in-state recruit in four years, thought the youngster's potential made him worth the risk.

"I hate to stereotype," says Paulsen, "but is he the typical Indian? If Willie comes and doesn't make it, nobody will be surprised. My concern is that he'll go home for the weekend and say he'll be back on Monday. Which Monday?"

Talented Indians are diverted from their academic and athletic career courses for many reasons, but often they are sucked back to subsistence-level life on the reservation by the vacuum created by inadequate education and readily available escapes like drugs and alcohol.

Ted Little Moon, an all-state basketball player for Pine Ridge High School in 1984 and '85, still dominates the asphalt slab outside the school. At 6-foot–6, he roams from baseline to baseline jamming in rebounds, swatting away opponents' shots, and threading blind passes to teammates beneath the basket. He is unmistakable small-college talent.

But Little Moon missed his first opportunity to play ball in college when he failed to graduate from high school. By the following August, though, he had passed his high school equivalency exam and committed to attend Huron College. But when the basketball coach showed up at his house to pick him up and drive him to school, Little Moon said he couldn't go because he had gotten his girlfriend pregnant and had to take care of a newborn son.

He played independent basketball, a large-scale Indian intramural network, until last fall, when he planned to enroll at Haskell Junior College, an all-Indian school in Lawrence, Kansas. He and some friends drank heavily the night before he was to take the bus to Kansas. Little Moon was a passenger in a friend's car when they ran a stop sign and hit another vehicle. He spent four days in jail, missed his bus, and missed out on enrolling at Haskell.

Now he talks of going back to school, of playing basketball again, but there's ambivalence in his voice. He has become accustomed to cashing his biweekly per capita check for $28.50, drinking beer, and growing his own marijuana at a secret location on the reservation. He distributes it free to his friends.

"I guess I'm scared to get away," Little Moon admits. "But also I'm afraid I'll be stuck here and be another statistic. You grow old fast here. If I get away, I have a chance. But I'm used to what I'm doing now. Here, your mom takes care of you, the BIA takes care of you. You wait for your $28.50 and then party. It's something to look forward to.

"I started drinking as a freshman in high school, smoking dope as a sophomore. I used to get high before practice, after practice. I still do it, on the average, maybe every other day. After I play, I smoke some. It makes you forget what you're doing on the reservation."

At home, alcohol offers whatever false comfort family ties cannot. Then it kills. Two years ago, Red Cloud's Bradford tallied all the alcohol-related deaths he had known personally and came up with some sobering statistics. In 13 years of teaching, 18 of his former students have died in alcohol-related tragedies. Aside from students, he has known an incredible 61 people under the age of 22 who have lost their lives in one way or another to the bottle.

Many died along a two-mile stretch of Highway 407 that connects Pine Ridge with Whiteclay, Nebraska, a depressing cluster of bars and liquor stores that do a land-office business. Three years ago, South Dakota's highway department began erecting metal markers at the site of each alcohol-related fatality. Locals say that if they'd started 10 years ago, the signs would form an unbroken chain along the road. They'd have run out of signs before they ran out of death.

Among Indians nationwide, four of the top 10 causes of death are alcohol-related: accidents, suicides, cirrhosis of the liver, and homicide. Alcohol mortality is nearly five times higher among Indians, at 30 per 100,000 population, than for all other races. According to Dr. Eva Smith of the Indian Health Service in Washington, D.C., between 80 and 90 percent of all Indian accidents, suicides, and homicides are alcohol-related.

Fred Beauvais, a research scientist at Colorado State University, points out that Indians not only start using drugs and alcohol earlier than the general population, but the rate of use also tends to be higher. According to a 1987 study of 2,400 subjects in eight western tribes Beauvais conducted with funding from the National Institute on Drug Abuse, 50 percent of Indian high school seniors were classified as "at risk" of serious harm because of drug and alcohol use. An amazing 43 percent are at risk by the seventh grade. The figure for seniors probably is too low, Beauvais explains, because by 12th grade many Indian students already have dropped out.

He attributes these phenomena not to racial or cultural idiosyncrasies, but to socioeconomic conditions on the reservations.

"Once it becomes socially ingrained, it's a vicious cycle," Beauvais says. "The kids see the adults doing it and they see no alternatives. It's a real trap. For some Indian kids to choose not to drink means to deny their Indianness. That can be a powerful factor."

Even those athletes who excel in the classroom are not necessarily immune to the magnetic pull of alcohol. Beau LeBeau, a 4.0 student at Red Cloud High who has started for the varsity basketball team since he was in eighth grade, recognizes the dangers but speaks of them as if they are elements quite out of his control. He estimates that 90 percent of his friends abuse alcohol.

"I'm going to the best academic school on the reservation," he says. "I should get a good education if I don't turn to drugs and alcohol in the next few years and ruin it for myself. In my room before I go to sleep I think, 'Is this how I'm going to spend the rest of my life? On the reservation?' I hope not."

For all the roadside signs that stand as chilling monuments to death around Pine Ridge, the drinking continues, a false and addictive cure for boredom and futility.

"If they win they want to celebrate," offers Bryan Brewer, athletic director at Pine Ridge High School. "If they lose, that's another excuse to drink. People who didn't make it want to drag the good athletes down with them."

Consequently, the road to a college athletic career sometimes ends before it even begins.

"I'm not opposed to recruiting the Indian athlete," offers Black Hills State athletic director Little. "I'm selective about who I recruit, though. I don't have the answer to the problem and don't know [if] I totally understand the situation. I do know that what's going on now is not working."

Something definitely isn't working in Towoac (pronounced TOI-ahk), in southwestern Colorado, where Indian athletes don't even wait until after high school to see their careers disintegrate. There, on the Ute Mountain Reservation, a multitude of Indian athletes compete and excel up to eighth grade and then quit rather than pursue sports at Montezuma-Cortez High, a mixed-race school 17 miles north of the reservation in the town of Cortez.

They drop out at the varsity level sometimes for academic reasons but often because of racial tension—or what they feel is bias on the part of white coaches. Pressed for particulars, current and former athletes make only vague accusations of negative attitudes and rarely cite specific instances. But how much of the discrimination is real and how much imagined is academic. The perception of discrimination remains, passed down among the athletes almost as an oral tradition.

For instance, today's athletes hear stories like those told by former Cortez High athlete Hanley Frost, who in the mid-1970s felt the wrath of the school administration when he was a sophomore on the basketball team and insisted on wearing his hair long, braided in traditional Indian style. He played four games with it tucked into his jersey but then was told school policy demanded that he cut it off. Eventually, he quit the team and began experimenting with drugs and alcohol.

Frost stated, "Really, it was the townspeople who didn't enjoy having a long-haired Indian on the team. There were a lot of people out there who would rather see their kids in a position on the team an Indian kid has."

"There's something about Towoac that just doesn't sit right." Adds reservation athletic director Doug Call, a Mormon who came to the Ute Mountain Reservation from Brigham Young University. "I don't know if people are afraid or what, but there's a stigma if you live out here."

Those Indians who do participate in sports at the high school level tend to live in Cortez, not on the reservation. An invisible wall of distrust seems to surround

Towoac, where most of the young athletes play what is known on reservations as "independent ball," a loosely organized kind of intramural basketball.

"They feel they're not getting a fair chance, I know they do," says Gary Gellatly, the Cortez High School athletic director who once served as recreation director on the reservation. "And I'm sure they have been discriminated against, directly or indirectly. It's tough to get them to compete. Yet you go out there on any weekend and watch those independent tournaments—you'll see kids playing basketball that you've never seen before. But I'm afraid if we start an overt effort to get them to participate you crowd them into a tighter corner. In a sense, not participating because they think they might be discriminated against is a cop-out, but it's been perpetuated by circumstances. Somewhere, something happened that wasn't good."

After massive turnover in the school's coaching staff, some new hires have expressed a desire to see more Indians become involved in the school's sports programs. Bill Moore, the new head football coach, heard the rumors that Indian kids wouldn't even try out for the squad and mailed tryout invitations to much of the student body including as many Indian boys as he could find addresses for. Even so, the turnout hasn't been markedly different from previous years.

"The solution," says varsity basketball coach Gordon Shepherd, "is that something has to give. Cultural groups that remain within themselves don't succeed. For Indians to succeed in white society terms, they have to give up some cultural ethnicity."

Ethnic idiosyncrasies present a whole range of problems—from students' inclination or ability to perform in the classroom to conflicts such as the one currently under way at Jemez Pueblo, a small reservation north of Albuquerque, New Mexico. There, in a hotbed of mountain running, a cross-country coach at a mixed-race school has struggled with athletes who reject modern training techniques for the less formal but highly traditional ways of their ancestors.

On some reservations, Indian student-athletes are merely ill-prepared to cope with the stringent academic demands of college. According to BIA statistics, the average Indian high school senior reads at the ninth-grade level. Of the 20 percent of high school seniors who go on to attempt college, 40 percent drop out.

And with some reservations approaching economic welfare states, students considering college confront a serious question about the value of an education: Why spend four years pursuing a college degree only to return to a reservation that has few or no private sector jobs?

Indians often find themselves without any real ethnic support system in college and become homesick for reservation life and the exceptionally strong bonds of an extended family in which aunts, uncles, and grandparents often live under the same roof. In some tribal cultures, 18- or 19-year olds still are considered mere children and haven't been pressed to formulate long-term goals. It's no coincidence, says an education administrator for the Arapahoe tribe on central Wyoming's Wind River Reservation, that most successful Indian students are in their mid- to late 20s—when, incidentally, athletic eligibility has gone by the board.

Even the basic incentive of athletics tends to evaporate in a more intense competitive climate far removed from the reservation.

Myron "The Magician" Chavez, a four-time all-state guard from Wyoming Indian High School on the Wind River Reservation, enrolled at Sheridan (Wyoming) College last fall but left school during preseason workouts when he was asked to redshirt. He felt he had failed because he didn't step immediately into a starting position. Jeff Brown, who preceded Chavez at WIHS, had a scholarship offer from the University of Kansas in 1982 but turned it down because he feared he would fail—academically if not athletically.

Dave Archambault, a Sioux who started the athletic program at United Tribes Junior College in Bismarck, North Dakota, has found the fear of failure to be a familiar theme among talented Indian athletes. On the reservations, he points out, athletes become heroes, modern extensions of the old warrior society that disappeared after defeat at the hands of the white man.

"They're kicking butt on the reservation," Archambault explains, "and then all of the sudden they're working out with juniors and seniors in college and getting their butts kicked. They're not held in that high regard and esteem. But they can go back to the reservation any time and get it."

They recapture their high school glory through independent ball, the intramural network among reservations that quenches an insatiable thirst for basketball competition among all age groups. There are tournaments nearly every weekend and an all-Indian national tournament each spring, where the best teams often recruit talent from a wide area by offering modest incentives like cash and expenses. At most levels, though, independent ball resembles extremely organized pickup basketball.

For most Indian athletes, it represents the outer limits of achievement, caught though it is in a void between the reservation and the outside world. It's in that limbo—socially as well as athletically—that most Indians play out their careers.

"There's no way to return to the old way, spiritually and economically," observes Billy Mills, the 1964 Olympic gold medalist at 10,000 meters who grew up on the Pine Ridge Reservation. "It's like walking death—no goals, no commitment, no accomplishment. If you go too far into society, there's a fear of losing your Indianness. There's a spiritual factor that comes into play. To become part of white society you give up half your soul. Society wants us to walk in one world with one spirit. But we have to walk in two worlds with one spirit."

29

Say It Ain't So, Big Leagues

The Downside for Latin American Players

Dave Zirin

In early October 30-year-old Mario Encarnación was found dead in his Taipei, Taiwan, apartment from causes unknown. His lonely death, with the lights on and refrigerator door open, ended a tragic journey that began in the dirt-poor town of Bani in the Dominican Republic and concluded on the other side of the world. In between, Encarnación, or "Super Mario," as he was known on the baseball diamond, was the most highly touted prospect in the Oakland A's organization, considered better than future American League Most Valuable Player Miguel Tejada. Tejada, also from Bani, paid the freight to bring his friend home from Taiwan. It's hard to imagine who else from their barrio could have managed to foot the bill.

Encarnación's death was not even a sidebar in the sports pages of the United States. A 30-year-old playing out his last days in East Asia might as well be invisible.

But he shouldn't be. As Major League Baseball celebrates its annual fall classic, the World Series, it is increasingly dependent on talent born and bred in Latin America. Twenty-six percent of all players in the major leagues now hail from Latin America, including some of the game's most popular stars, like David Ortiz, Pedro Martinez and Sammy Sosa. Leading the way is the tiny nation of the Dominican Republic. Just five years ago there were sixty-six Dominican-born players on baseball's Opening Day rosters. This year, there were more than 100. This means roughly one

Source: Dave Zirin, "Say It Ain't So, Big Leagues: The Downside for Latin American Players," *Nation* (November 14, 2005).

out of every seven major league players was born in the DR, by far the highest number from any country outside the United States. In addition, 30 percent of players in the US minor leagues hail from this tiny Latin American nation, which shares an island with Haiti and has a population roughly the size of New York City's.

All thirty teams now scout what baseball owners commonly call "the Republic of Baseball," and a number of teams have elaborate multimillion-dollar "baseball academies." The teams trumpet these academies. (One executive said, "We have made Fields of Dreams out of the jungle.") But unmentioned is that for every Tejada there are 100 Encarnacións. And for every Encarnación toiling on the margins of the pro baseball circuit, there are thousands of Dominican players cast aside by a Major League Baseball system that is strip-mining the Dominican Republic for talent. Unmentioned is the overarching relationship Major League Baseball has with the Dominican Republic, harvesting talent on the cheap with no responsibility for who gets left behind. Unmentioned is what Major League Baseball is doing—or is not doing—for a country with 60 percent of its population living below the poverty line. As American sports agent Joe Kehoskie says in *Stealing Home,* a PBS documentary, "Traditionally in the Latin market, I would say players sign for about 5 to 10 cents on the dollar compared to their US counterparts." He also points out that "a lot of times kids just quit school at 10, 11, 12, and play baseball full-time. It's great, it's great for the kids that make it because they become superstars and get millions of dollars in the big leagues. But for ninety-eight kids out of 100, it results in a kid that is 18, 19, with no education."

Considering both the poverty rate and the endless trumpeting of rags-to-riches stories of those like Sosa and Tejada, it's no wonder the academies are so attractive to young Dominicans. Most young athletes in the DR play without shoes, using cut-out milk cartons for gloves, rolled-up cloth for balls, and sticks and branches for bats. The academies offer good equipment, nice uniforms and the dream of a better life.

Sacramento Bee sportswriter Marcos Breton's book *Home Is Everything: The Latino Baseball Story* highlights the appeal of the academies: "Teams house their players in dormitories and feed their prospects balanced meals. Often it's the first time these boys will sleep under clean sheets or eat nutritious meals. The firsts don't stop there: Some of these boys encounter a toilet for the first time. Or an indoor shower. They are taught discipline, the importance of being on time, of following instructions."

The competition to get into the "baseball factories," as they are often referred to, is fierce. Sports anthropologist Alan Klein describes, in *Stealing Home,* the scene in front of one of the academies:

> Every morning you would drive to the Academy, you would see fifteen, twenty kids out there, not one of them had a uniform, they all had pieces of one uniform or another, poor equipment, they would be right at the gate waiting for the security people to open up the gates and they would go in for their tryout. If they got signed, they were happy. If they didn't get signed, it didn't even deter them for a minute; they would be on the road hitchhiking to the next location. And they would eventually find one of those 20-some clubs that would eventually pick them up. And if not, then they might return to amateur baseball.

Yet even the ones who make it through the academy doors often find themselves little more than supporting players in a system designed to help pro teams ferret out the few potential stars. As Roberto González Echevarría, a Cuban baseball historian who also appears in the documentary, says, "I take a dim view of what the major leagues are doing in the Dominican Republic with these so-called baseball academies, where children are being signed at a very early age and not being cared for. Most of them are providing the context for the stars to emerge; if you take 100 baseball players in those academies, or 100 baseball players anywhere, only one of them will play even an inning in the major leagues. The others are there as a supporting cast."

And little is done for those very select few who make it into a major league farm system to protect them from the likely fall to the hard concrete floor of failure.

Brendan Sullivan III, a pitcher who played five seasons for the San Diego Padres, told author Colman McCarthy, "Sure, they were thrilled to have gone from dirt lots to playing in a US stadium before fans and getting paychecks every two weeks. But once a team decides a Dominican won't make it to the big leagues, he is discarded as an unprofitable resource. That's true for US players, but at least they have a high school diploma, and often college, and thus have fallback skills. Most Dominicans don't. They go home to the poverty they came from or try to eke out an existence at menial labor in the States, with nothing left over except tales of their playing days chasing the dream."

Major League Baseball seems unconcerned and uninterested in the situation it has a central role in shaping. Boston Red Sox owner John Henry speaks of the "special relationship Major League Baseball has with the people of the Dominican Republic," but it's unclear whether he believes the Bosox and Major League Baseball have any responsibilities regarding the players they employ and the families left behind.

Al Avila, assistant general manager of the Detroit Tigers, whose father, Ralph, operated the Los Angeles Dodgers' Dominican academy for decades, told ESPN .com, "Baseball is the best way out of poverty for most of these kids and their families. They see on television and read in the newspapers how many of their countrymen have made it. For parents that have kids, they have them playing from early on. The numbers show that the dream is within reach. And even if they don't make it, these Dominican academies house, feed and educate these kids in English. They become acclimated to a new culture, which is always positive. At the very least, even if they don't make it as a player, they could get different doors opened, like becoming a coach."

The question we need to ask is, Does baseball have a broader responsibility to the Dominican Republic and these 10- and 11-year-old kids who think they have a better chance of emerging from desperately poor conditions with a stick and a milk-carton glove than by staying in school? Does the highly profitable Major League Baseball have any responsibility to cushion the crash landing that awaits 99.9 percent of DR kids with big-league dreams, or the 95 percent of players who are good enough to be chosen for the academy but are summarily discarded with nothing but a kick out the door? We can probably surmise where the family and friends of Mario Encarnación fall on this question.

The death of "Super Mario" went unnoticed in the US press with one exception, a heart-wrenching column on October 6 in the *Sacramento Bee* by his friend Marcos Breton, who wrote, "Mario wasn't a warped athlete like we've come to expect in most ballplayers. He was big-hearted, fun-loving, a good friend.... The pressure of succeeding and lifting his family out of poverty was a weight that soon stooped Encarnación's massive shoulders."

Should it have been his responsibility alone to shoulder such a burden?

30

The 2010 Racial and Gender Report Card

National Football League

Richard Lapchick with
Jamile M. Kitnurse and Austin Moss II

EXECUTIVE SUMMARY

Orlando, Fla.—Sept. 29, 2010 . . . The National Football League achieved an **A** grade on racial hiring practices and a **C** on gender hiring practices in the 2010 NFL Racial and Gender Report Card, released by The Institute for Diversity and Ethics in Sport (TIDES) at the University of Central Florida. This gave the NFL a combined **B** grade. In the history of the NFL Racial and Gender Report Card, that is the best grade ever received on racial hiring practices by the NFL.

This was the NFL's first full **A** grade for racial hiring practices after the NFL's score for race improved slightly from 89.2 in the previous report to 90.6 points out of 100. This moved the 2009 **A–** grade to a full **A**. The score for gender decreased slightly from 71.5 to 69.5.

Using data from the 2009 season, The Institute conducted an analysis of racial breakdowns of the players, managers and coaches. In addition, the Report includes a racial and gender breakdown of top team management, senior administration, profes-

Source: Richard Lapchick with Jamile M. Kitnurse and Austin Moss II, *The 2010 Racial and Gender Report Card: National Football League*. Orlando, Florida: The Institute for University and Ethics in Sport, University of Central Florida, 2010.

sional administration, physicians, head trainers and broadcasters. Coaches, general managers, presidents and owners were updated as of August 1, 2010.

For the fourth consecutive year, African-Americans played a significant role in the Super Bowl when Indianapolis' first-year head coach Jim Caldwell helped lead his team to the Super Bowl against the New Orleans Saints. In 2007, two African-American head coaches faced each other in the Super Bowl for the first time, and an African-American general manager helped lead his team to a win in the 2008 Super Bowl. In 2009, head coach Mike Tomlin helped Pittsburgh win the Super Bowl. The Report shows sustained progress in the key positions of head coach (seven in 2006 and six in 2007, 2008, 2009 and 2010) and general manager (four in 2006 and five in 2007, 2008, 2009 and 2010).

The NFL's League Office recently hired Robert Gulliver as EVP for Human Resources and Chief Diversity Officer. Over the past few years, the League Office has had a substantial package of programs that have focused on diversity and inclusion initiatives....

From the 2008 to 2009 season, the percentages for people of color increased for team vice presidents, players and physicians, remained constant for League Office management positions, head coaches, general managers and trainers and decreased by one percentage point at the team level for professional administrators, senior administrators, and assistant coaches.

The percentage of women increased for team vice-presidents while decreasing slightly for League Office management positions, team professional administrators and senior administrators. The opportunities for women continue to lag significantly behind the progress on race....

It is imperative that sports teams play the best athletes they have available to win games. The Institute for Diversity and Ethics in Sport (TIDES) strives to emphasize the value of diversity to sports organizations when they choose their team on the field and in the office. Diversity initiatives such as diversity management training can help change attitudes and increase the applicant pool for open positions. It is clearly the choice of the organization regarding which applicant is the best fit for its ballclub, but The Institute wants to illustrate how important it is to have a diverse organization involving individuals who happen to be of a different race or gender. This element of diversity can provide a different perspective and possibly a competitive advantage for a win in the boardroom as well as on the field.

The Report Card asks, "Are we playing fair when it comes to sports? Does everyone, regardless of race or gender, have a chance to score a touchdown or operate the business of professional football?"

The Institute for Diversity and Ethics in Sport (TIDES), located at the University of Central Florida, publishes the *Racial and Gender Report Card* annually to indicate areas of improvement, stagnation and regression in the racial and gender composition of professional and college sports personnel and to contribute to the improvement of integration in front office and college athletic department positions. The publication of the 2010 NFL Racial and Gender Report Card follows the publication of the reports on MLB, the NBA and the WNBA. The remaining reports for this year will be for Major League Soccer and college sport.

REPORT HIGHLIGHTS

- The NFL received its highest grade for racial hiring practices in the history of the NFL Racial and Gender Report Card.
- During the 2009 NFL season, the percentage of white players decreased slightly from 31 to 30 percent, while the percentage of African-American players remained constant at 67 percent.
- In the League Office, almost 25 percent of management was African-American, Latino, Asian, Native American and "other" during the 2010 season. Over 27 percent of the professionals were women.
- No person of color has ever held majority ownership of an NFL team.
- The six African-American head coaches at the start of the 2009 season remained in their capacity at the start of the 2010 season.
- The NFL started the 2010 season with five African-American general managers, just as it had started the 2007, 2008 and 2009 seasons. One of the five, Jerry Reese, became the first African-American general manager to win a Super Bowl when the New York Giants won in 2008.
- Amy Trask of the Oakland Raiders remained the only female president/CEO of a team in the NFL, a position she has held since 2005. There has never been a person of color serving as president or CEO in the history of the NFL.
- When Pittsburgh won the 2009 Super Bowl, Mike Tomlin became the second African-American head coach in three years to lead his team to a Super Bowl championship.
- Six out of the last eight Super Bowl teams have had either an African-American head coach or general manager: coaches Tony Dungy (Colts), Lovie Smith (Bears), Mike Tomlin (Steelers) and Jim Caldwell (Colts) and GMs Jerry Reese (Giants) and Rod Graves (Cardinals).
- The number of female vice presidents on NFL teams increased by five from 2008 to 2009 to a total of 25. Pamela Browner-Crawley of the Philadelphia Eagles became the first minority woman to hold a vice president position in the NFL.
- People of color held more than 17 percent of senior administrator positions on NFL teams in the 2009 season. Seventeen percent of the total senior administrator positions were held by women.
- In 2009, the percentage of women in professional administrative positions on NFL teams dropped one percentage point to 28 percent.
- Latino radio and television broadcasters decreased two percentage points from 18 percent during the 2008 season to 16 percent at the beginning of 2009 season.
- The 2009 and 2010 Super Bowls each had two African-American officials.

OVERALL GRADES

The National Football League achieved an **A** grade on racial hiring practices. The NFL's score for race improved from the previous report from 89.2 to 90.6 points out of 100. The grade for gender decreased slightly from 71.5 to 69.5 and remained a **C**.

This gave the NFL a combined **B** with 80.1 points out of 100.

In the history of the NFL Racial and Gender Report Card, the **A** for race was its first while the **C** for gender and **B** for the combined grade equaled the 2009 marks, which at the time were the best grades ever received in those categories for the NFL.

For race, the NFL received an **A+** for players and assistant coaches, an **A** for the League Office and NFL Diversity Initiatives and a **B+** for head coaches, general managers and team senior and professional administrators. The only grade below a **B+** was a **B–** for team vice-presidents.

For gender, the NFL received a **C** for the heavily weighted (50 percent) category of team professional administrators and a **C** for the League Office. It received an **F** for team vice-presidents and team senior administrators although the percentages for women VPs increased. . . .

STACKING

Most observers agree that the issue of stacking in the NFL is no longer a major concern. In the 2009 NFL season, African-Americans held 16 percent of the quarterback positions. Quarterback is football's central "thinking" position. Historically, the positions of running back, wide receiver, cornerback and safety have had disproportionately high percentages of African-Americans. The latter positions rely a great deal on speed and reactive ability. The quarterback position was the primary concern since it was so central to the game, and now that African-Americans have broken down that barrier, concern about stacking has greatly diminished.

The breakdown of all positions for African-Americans and whites is listed in Tables 30-1, 30-2 and 30-3.

Table 30-1 NFL Offense

Year	QB	RB	WR	TE	OT	OG	C
2009							
White	81%	11%	11%	57%	45%	51%	75%
African-American	16%	87%	87%	41%	54%	42%	18%
2008							
White	82%	14%	10%	58%	47%	53%	74%
African-American	17%	85%	89%	39%	51%	42%	20%
2007							
White	76%	9%	10%	56%	49%	59%	77%
African-American	19%	89%	89%	42%	49%	35%	18%
2006							
White	82%	10%	8%	54%	43%	53%	70%
African-American	16%	88%	91%	43%	57%	42%	26%
2005							
White	82%	9%	9%	57%	44%	54%	69%
African-American	16%	89%	91%	40%	55%	39%	24%
2003							
White	77%	13%	14%	55%	44%	56%	85%
African-American	22%	86%	86%	42%	55%	41%	12%
2002							
White	76%	16%	12%	56%	45%	56%	83%
African-American	24%	82%	88%	41%	53%	41%	14%
2000							
White	78%	13%	10%	56%	48%	48%	70%
African-American	21%	86%	90%	41%	30%	50%	25%
1999							
White	81%	13%	9%	55%	42%	55%	75%
African-American	18%	86%	91%	42%	55%	42%	20%
1998							
White	91%	13%	8%	55%	39%	67%	83%
African-American	8%	87%	92%	42%	55%	29%	17%

Table 30-2 NFL Defense

Year	CB	S	LB	DE	DT
2009					
White	2%	16%	24%	21%	16%
African-American	98%	81%	72%	76%	79%
2008					
White	2%	14%	24%	20%	18%
African-American	97%	84%	73%	77%	77%
2007					
White	2%	13%	26%	21%	18%
African-American	97%	84%	71%	73%	76%
2006					
White	4%	14%	24%	24%	18%
African-American	96%	85%	73%	75%	75%
2005					
White	5%	14%	26%	24%	20%
African-American	95%	83%	71%	75%	75%
2003					
White	2%	19%	17%	22%	20%
African-American	98%	81%	80%	77%	76%
2002					
White	1%	13%	19%	20%	23%
African-American	98%	87%	78%	78%	78%
2000					
White	7%	13%	22%	25%	26%
African-American	93%	87%	76%	73%	73%
1999					
White	4%	10%	23%	21%	20%
African-American	96%	90%	74%	77%	68%
1998					
White	1%	9%	24%	19%	31%
African-American	99%	91%	75%	79%	63%

Table 30-3 NFL Special Teams

Year	K/P
2009	
White	97%
African-American	1%
Latino	2%
International	8%

31

Racism, Ethnic Discrimination, and Exclusion of Migrants and Minorities in Sport

A Comparative Overview of the Situation in the European Union

European Union Agency for Fundamental Rights

FOREWORD

Sport brings together millions of people, regardless of their sex, colour, gender, age, nationality or religion, and has thus the potential to play an important role in creating an inclusive society. Sports activities ranging from the local to the national and international level, embracing leisure as well as competitive sport, can support the integration of migrants and persons belonging to minorities into society as whole. In other words, sport events could be an ideal platform to foster inclusion, acceptance of diversity and mutual respect while combating racism, discrimination and exclusion.

This potential of sports to convey human values is of increasing interest for the European Union. With the entry into force of the Treaty of Lisbon in December 2009, the European Union holds now an explicit competence in the field of sport. Union actions shall aim to develop "the European dimension in sport, by promoting fairness and openness in sporting competitions and cooperation between bodies

Source: European Union Agency for Fundamental Rights, "Racism, Ethnic Discrimination, and Exclusion of Migrants and Minorities in Sport." (October 2010).

responsible for sports, and by protecting the physical and moral integrity of sportsmen and sportswomen, especially the youngest sportsmen and sportswomen." The new Treaty also introduces a horizontal clause that obliges the Union to combat discrimination on the grounds of sex, racial or ethnic origin, religion or belief, disability, age or sexual orientation in all contexts—that is, whenever the Union is "defining and implementing its policies and activities."

Against this background, the European Union Agency for Fundamental Rights (FRA) has carried out research on racism, discrimination and exclusion in sport, focusing on different sports and levels of practice. The findings show that despite significant progress made in past years, sport continues to face a number of challenges related to racism and ethnic discrimination. Incidences of racism and ethnic discrimination affect sport at professional as well as at amateur level. Particularly at amateur level, there is reluctance to recognise such incidents. Moreover, few Member States have established effective monitoring systems to record racism and racial discrimination in sport.

Policy makers are increasingly interested in the role of sport in combating racism and discrimination. This report provides some useful assistance in their efforts to explore the rich potential of sport for promoting equality.

—Morten Kjaerum
Director

EXECUTIVE SUMMARY

This report provides data and information on the occurrence and different forms of racism, ethnic discrimination and exclusionary practices in sports in the European Union (EU). While the focus of the research is on ethnic minorities and migrants, attention is also paid to gender and age in relation to sport. The report draws on the findings of 27 studies conducted in all EU Member States by the National Focal Points (NFPs) of the RAXEN network of the European Union Agency for Fundamental Rights (FRA). These studies were based on interviews with relevant experts and stakeholders, and on secondary data and information covering the period 2003–2008. In addition, input was provided by stakeholders at European and national level including national sport federations. The research examined professional and amateur sports engaging men, women and children or youth. Football and athletics were examined in all Member State; in addition, a third sport, different for each Member State depending on its national popularity, was also covered.

MAIN FINDINGS

Racist Incidents

Incidents of racism, anti-Semitism and anti-Gypsyism were identified in football and basketball across the EU. In particular in Germany and Italy, experts warn that rightwing extremists are becoming active in amateur leagues. No data were available for athletics and almost no data for the various sports examined within the national context of each Member State, with the exception of basketball. Only 10 EU Member States monitor systematically incidents of racism in sports and mainly relating to men's professional football, although racist incidents also occur frequently in men's amateur football.

In football, fans are primarily the perpetrators of racist incidents in men's professional and amateur football. However, a considerable number of racist incidents concerned children's and youth football. Racist incidents were also recorded among players, particularly in amateur football, but there is a tendency to ignore them in amateur sports. Referees and club officials were involved in some racist incidents. No data were available for women's amateur and professional sport.

Regulations and Sanctions

Beyond the general legal provisions against racist crime and discrimination on grounds of racial or ethnic origin that exist in all EU Member States, some Member States have introduced specific legal provisions regarding sport. In at least 16 Member States, equality bodies and other institutions, such as National Human Rights Institutions (NHRIs), take action in cases of racist incidents and ethnic discrimination in sport.

European football federations include anti-racist clauses or provisions in their statutes as well as disciplinary regulations and two thirds of European football federations specifically penalise racist incidents, for example racist abuse and abusive spectator behaviour. However, only two athletics federations explicitly address the issue of racism or related intolerance in their statutes or regulations. The number of racist incidents where action was taken by football federations was very low in the reference period 2003–2008.

Barriers to Equal Participation in Sports

Little attention is paid to the issue of underrepresentation of persons belonging to minority ethnic groups. Relevant data are available only in five EU Member States showing that minorities and migrants and, in particular, of women and girls with minority or migrant background, are generally underrepresented in sport. In some countries social exclusion, as well as geographical isolation, can affect Roma and Travellers participation in sport.

The research also found some evidence suggesting that in several Member States the participation rate of youth belonging to ethnic minorities—especially second generation youth—in some sports is lower at youth and amateur level than in professional sports.

Quota regulations limiting the access of non-nationals to professional and amateur sports leagues and competitions in combination with restrictive citizenship laws can negatively impact the participation of permanent residents, who do not have citizenship, in both amateur and professional sports. Although such restrictions do not constitute discrimination in a legal sense, they could affect perceptions of social exclusion.

Anti-racist Provisions among Sports Organisations

Statutes or similar documents of European and international sports organisations include references to anti-racism or anti-discrimination provisions, but few follow the example of football and cricket organisations that have clear disciplinary procedures against racist or discriminatory behaviour. In this regard it is worth noting the excellent practices of the Union of European Football Associations (UEFA) in combating racism and ethnic discrimination. Further good practice at EU level can be found in several other initiatives, for example, the fan network Football Supporters Europe (FSE), the anti-racism network Football Against Racism in Europe (FARE) and the International Federation of Professional Footballers' Associations (FIFPro).

Considerations for Policy Development

The research shows that a number of measures could be useful in the fight against racism and discrimination on grounds of racial or ethnic origin in sport. Such measures that also enhance the potential of sport for the social inclusion and integration of migrants and minorities could, for example, include awareness-raising campaigns, initiatives to increase diversity in sports, identifying barriers to equal participation in sport, and encouraging athletes, players, officials and fans to take a stance against racism and intolerance. In addition, a more effective monitoring of racist incidents would provide valuable information to authorities and sports bodies for improving their policies.

European Union institutions, in particular the European Parliament and the European Commission, could explore the possibilities provided by the Lisbon Treaty to reinforce their role in fighting racism and discrimination in sport. In this respect guidelines are provided in General Policy Recommendation No. 12 of the Council of Europe (European Commission against Racism and Intolerance, ECRI).

* FOR FURTHER STUDY *

Beton, Maracos, and Jose Luis Villegas. 2003. *Home Is Everything: The Latino Baseball Story from the Barrio to the Major Leagues.* El Paso, TX: Cinco Puntos Press.

Boeck, Greg. 2007. "The Native American Barrier: Group Culture and Individualism." *USA Today* (February 22): 1C-2C.

Brown, Tony N., James S. Jackson, Kendrick T. Brown, Robert M. Sellers, Shelley Keiper, and Warde J. Manuel. 2003. " 'There's No Race on the Playing Field': Perceptions of Racial Discrimination among White and Black Athletes." *Journal of Sport and Social Issues* 27 (May): 162–183.

Bryant, Howard. 2002. *Shut Out: A Story of Race and Baseball in Boston.* New York: Routledge.

Carrington, Ben. 2007. "Sport and Race" Pp. 4686–4690 in *Blackwell Encyclopedia of Sport.* Vol. 9.

Coakley, Jay. 2007. *Sports in Society: Issues and Controversies.* 9th ed. New York: McGraw-Hill.

Edwards, Harry. 1998. "An End of the Golden Age of Black Participation in Sport?" *Civil Rights Journal* 3 (Fall): 19–24.

———. 2000. "Crisis of Black Athletes on the Eve of the 21st Century." *Society* 37 (March–April): 9–13.

Eitzen, D. Stanley. 2009. *Fair and Foul: Beyond the Myths and Paradoxes of Sport.* 4th ed. Lanham, MD: Rowman and Littlefield.

Eitzen, D. Stanley, and George H. Sage. *Sociology of North American Sport.* 8th ed. Boulder, CO: Paradigm.

Goldsmith, Pat Antonio. 2003. "Race Relations and Racial Patterns in School Sports Participation." *Sociology of Sport Journal* 20 (2): 147–171.

Hanson, Sandra L. 2005. "Hidden Dragons: Asian American Women and Sports." *Journal of Sport and Social Issues* 29 (August): 259–265.

Harrison, C. Keith. 2000. "Black Athletes at the Millennium." *Society* 37 (March–April): 35–39.

Hoberman, John. 2000. "The Price of 'Black Dominance.' " *Society* 37 (March–April): 35–39.

Jamieson, Katherine M. 2003. "Occupying a Middle Space: Toward a Mestiza Sport Studies." *Sociology of Sport Journal* 20 (1): 1–16.

Jones, Robyn L. 2002. "The Black Experience within English Semiprofessional Soccer." *Journal of Sport and Social Issues* 26 (February): 47–64.

Juffer, Jane. 2002. "Who's the Man? Sammy Sosa, Latinos, and Televisual Redefinitions of the 'American' Pastime." *Journal of Sport and Social Issues* 26 (November): 337–359.

King, C. Richard. 2007. "Sport and Ethnicity." Pp. 4681–4684 in *Blackwell Encyclopedia of Sport.* Vol. 9.

King, C. Richard, and Charles Fruehling Springwood. 2001. *Beyond the Cheers: Race as Spectacle in College Sport.* Albany: State University of New York Press.

Lapchick, Richard E. 2008. "Games Could Have Lasting Impact on Asian-Americans." *Sports Business Journal* (August 25). Available at rlapchick@bus.ucf.edu.

Lapchick, Richard E. Annual Report. *Racial and Gender Report Card.* Institute for Diversity and Ethics in Sport, University of Central Florida–Orlando.

Leonard, David J., and C. Richard King. 2011. *Commodified and Criminalized: New Racism and African Americans in Contemporary Sports.* Lanham, MD: Rowman & Littlefield.

McDonald, Mary G. 2005. "Special Issue: Whiteness and Sport." *Sociology of Sport Journal* 22 (September).

Nixon, Howard L. II. 2008. *Sport in a Changing World.* Boulder, CO: Paradigm.

Prior, Anthony E. 2006. *The Slave Side of Sunday.* Charleston, SC: BookSurge.

Rhoden, William C. *Forty-Million-Dollar Slaves: The Rise, Fall, and Redemption of the Black Athlete.* New York: Crown.

Segura, Melissa. 2008. "The Latino Athlete Now." *Sports Illustrated* (October 6, 2008): 52–55.

Verducci, Tom. 2003. "Blackout: The African-American Baseball Player Is Vanishing. Does He Have a Future?" *Sports Illustrated* (July 7): 56–66.

PART ELEVEN

Structured Inequality: Sport and Gender

Traditionally, gender role expectations have encouraged girls and women to be passive, gentle, delicate, and submissive. These cultural expectations clashed with those traits often associated with sport, such as assertiveness, competitiveness, physical endurance, ruggedness, and dominance. Thus, young women past puberty were encouraged to bypass sports unless the sport retained the femininity of participants. These "allowable" sports had three characteristics: (1) they were aesthetically pleasing (e.g., ice skating, diving, and gymnastics); (2) they did not involve bodily contact with opponents (e.g., bowling, archery, badminton, volleyball, tennis, golf, swimming, and running; and (3) the action was controlled to protect the athletes from overexertion (e.g., running short races, basketball where the offense and defense did not cross half-court).

In effect, these traditional expectations for the sexes denied women equal access to opportunities, not only to sports participation but also to college and to various occupations. Obviously, girls were discriminated against in schools by woefully inadequate facilities—compare the "girls' gym" with the "boys' gym" in any school—and in the budgets. The consequences of sexual discrimination in sport were that: (1) the femininity of those who defied the cultural expectations was often questioned, giving them marginal status; (2) approximately one-half of the population was denied the benefits of sports participation; (3) young women learned their "proper" societal role (i.e., to be on the sidelines supporting men who do the actual achieving); and (4) women were denied a major source of college scholarships.

Currently, quite rapid changes are occurring. Unquestionably, the greatest change in contemporary sport is the dramatic increase in and general acceptance of sports participation by women. These swift changes have occurred for several related reasons. Most prominent is the societal-wide women's movement that has gained increasing momentum since the mid-1960s. Because of the consciousness raising resulting from the movement and the organized efforts to break down the cultural tyranny of gender roles, court cases were initiated to end sexual discrimination in a number of areas. In athletics, legal suits were successfully brought against various school districts, universities, and even the Little League.

In 1972 Congress passed Title IX of the Education Amendments Act. The essence of this law, which has had the greatest single impact on the move toward sexual equality in all aspects of schools, is: "No person in the United States shall, on the basis of sex, be excluded from taking part in, be denied the benefits of, or be subjected to discrimination in any educational program or activity receiving federal financial assistance."

Although the passage of Title IX and other pressures have led to massive changes, discrimination continues, as noted in selection 32 by R. Vivian Acosta and Linda Jean Carpenter. The next selection, by the Women's Sports Foundation, documents the health benefits of sport and physical activity for girls and women. The final selection, by sociologist Michael A. Messner, answers the question "What is the relationship between participation in organized sports and a young male's developing sense of himself as a success or failure?"

32

Are We There Yet? Thirty-Seven Years Later, Title IX Hasn't Fixed It All

R. Vivian Acosta and Linda Jean Carpenter

Some trips seem endless. On the road, the call "Are we there yet, are we there yet?" from the back seat is both a sign and a cause of frustration. Implementation of the federal anti-sex-discrimination legislation known as Title IX is akin to an aggravating trip that seems to take forever to arrive at its destination. The journey has lasted almost thirty-seven years so far. Measured in student lifetimes, that's equal to more than nine generations of students. Measured against our personal professional lives, it has gone on for our entire careers.[1]

When the Title IX road trip began, we were young, freshly tenured professors with few wrinkles and fewer aches and pains. Our own collegiate athletic experiences a few years earlier had included varsity team memberships coached by female physical education teachers who carried full-time teaching loads and even fuller community service loads. Our competitive seasons were short; at the time, women were thought to lack the stamina for lengthier competitive experiences. For one of us, short seasons were good, because athletic mediocrity was left undiscovered by the time the season ended. For the other, short seasons terminated dreams of exploring the limits of athletic talents; the seasons ended before boundaries could be discovered.

Our experience was typical of the times. We were not alone in having short seasons, women physical educators as coaches, a woman faculty member as athletic

Source: R. Vivian Acosta and Linda Jean Carpenter, "Are We There Yet? Thirty-Seven Years Later, Title IX Hasn't Fixed It All," *Academe* 95 (July/August 2009), pp. 22–24. Reprinted with permission from the July–August 2009 issue of *Academe: Magazine of the American Association of University Professors.*

director of women's programs, and little or no financial support. (We provided our own uniforms, traveled on converted yellow school buses, and paid our own lodging and food bills.) But we had a grand time and competed with intensity. We learned a lot about ourselves, forged lifelong friendships, and understood the worth of trying to excel in both the gym and the classroom. Our success in the classroom related to our future; our success in the gym related to our sense of self.

THE JOURNEY BEGINS

As soon as the Title IX road trip began with the law's enactment in 1972, the scenery passing the window began to change dramatically—even though the regulations that would come to define and refine the meaning of the thirty-eight words of Title IX's statutory language were not yet penned. This uncertainty did not dampen the remarkable expansion of new women's teams created to meet pent-up demand for participation opportunities. With explosive growth came the need to find additional coaches for women's teams and to start paying them at least a token salary. Men who coached men's teams had been paid for years. It seemed reasonable to assume that Title IX would require more equitable treatment of coaches of women's teams.

Men who had no interest in coaching women for free, or who had been barred by the unwritten but generally followed road sign "only females need apply," quickly began filling the coaching ranks in women's athletics. Programmatic leadership also changed. Separate departments of athletics were merged, typically with a former men's athletics director becoming director of a combined program. The former female director took a step down and became an assistant director or, like one of us, decided to spend more time on teaching and research.

ON THE ROAD

The Title IX road trip continued. Progress slowed now and then for court challenges, reinterpretations, and sometimes simple recalcitrance. At times, detours threatened the entire enterprise. Yet from where the trip started to mile marker 2009, great progress has been made. This progress can be measured in the positive benefits of enhanced self-knowledge, more widely opened doors, and less fettered dreams.

When we were young professionals, our students often found that wearing athletic attire outside the gym was met with labels of "tomboy" or worse. At mile marker 2009, opportunities for both men and women continue to increase, and women's participation in athletics less often involves negative labels. More female high school and intercollegiate athletes participate than ever before. In 2008, more than 9,100 women's intercollegiate teams competed. Almost 15,000 women are employed in intercollegiate athletics (as athletics directors, assistant or associate directors, coaches, trainers, or sports information directors). And one out of five athletics directors is a woman, the highest female representation since the mid-1970s.

Are we there yet? Some would point to this progress and say we've arrived, that the trip is complete. But progress is not completion. Movement toward equity is not full equity. How will we know when we have gotten there? Indeed, where is *there*?

"There" includes items that are not part of Title IX but are vital to accomplishing its spirit. Indices of arrival might include the following:

- Title IX requirements are seen as the "normal" paradigm rather than things to be circumvented or feared.
- The institutional role of athletics relates to the mission of the college or university in demonstrable ways.
- The value of the athletic experience is determined not by the fan base but by the experience of the individual athlete.
- College presidents have higher salaries than athletics directors or coaches.
- Coaching compensation relates to the job being done, not to the sex of the athletes being coached, the sex of the coach, or the sport being coached.
- Supporters of athletics teams focus on program-wide loyalty rather than a particular sport.
- Negative pressures on life-balance issues have been eliminated.
- Self-delusional notions that big-time football programs contribute financially to an institution are understood to be false and thus no longer motivate bad administrative decisions.
- Women coaches of men's teams are accepted and supported for their coaching skills, without regard to their sex.
- Women athletics directors are not an endangered species.
- Decisions about hiring and firing coaches and administrative staff are made by school leaders rather than fans and alumni.

In short, equity rather than excuses will be the norm once we have completed our journey.

ROADBLOCKS

As we've noted, much progress, particularly in participation, has been made. Yet three huge issues stand as barricades against arrival: compensation, time, and respect. Overcoming these remaining obstacles hinges on a fourth element: will. The obstacles yet to be traversed can be negotiated only if individual and institutional will exists to traverse them. They cannot be effectively traversed by lawsuits, protests, or legislative enforcement. They are systemic and, in effect, beyond the reach of Title IX, and they have not yet been addressed mostly because of the extreme difficulty involved in surmounting them. Yet they bar the attainment of the spirit and full flower of the law. If they are not dealt with, equity in athletics programs will never become a reality.

When one feels chained to a computer trying to find the best words in the best order to complete a writing task, cleaning out files and closets becomes an appealing alternative. As we prepared to write this article, we succumbed for a while to the appeal of crowded files and closets and came across a long-forgotten article we wrote for the January–February 1991 issue of *Academe* titled, "Back to the Future: Reform with a Woman's Voice." The part of that old article that describes the need for systemic change remains relevant:

> Now a word about reality: there will be no reform of real consequence while the governing principles on individual campuses as well as within the [National Collegiate Athletic Association] define profit on a dollar basis. That means that as long as big-time football and big-time men's basketball continue to be pampered as potential profit makers, there will be no effective reform in inter-collegiate athletics until or unless such programs collapse under the weight of their abuses. There will be more rules and regulations, but no significant reform. Having said such a painful thing, let us hope for a change in principles and consider why now, more than in the past, women's voices have a significant role to play in the call for reform.

Unfortunately, in the almost two decades since our previous *Academe* article, no resolution of these issues has been found. Indeed, the issues of compensation, time, and respect, arguably mired in the profit-dollar pothole, remain truly systemic and vexing.

Compensation

Waiting for an influx of unencumbered money to solve unequal compensation between men and women in college athletics, or other equity-based funding issues, is a wait with no end. In light of today's shrinking endowments and less-wealthy alums, athletics programs will probably not see hefty checks soon from benefactors or institutional sponsors. In fact, institutions are starting to compete with their own athletics departments for support, which does not augur well for institutional budgetary support of athletics. Some evidence suggests that benefactors often favor athletics programs over institutions, because athletics programs give them something tangible in return for their checks, such as better seats at games or travel with teams. If benefactors with limited money give only to athletics programs, academic programs will suffer.

Recently announced new stadium projects and ambitious goals for athletics endowment funds make us wonder about the degree of mental health on some campuses. When institutions that continue to have Title IX and equity problems pursue such efforts, they demonstrate a lack of will for equity beyond the minimum required to avoid administrative complaints and lawsuits. The disconnect on such campuses between athletics and institutional mission may be so great that the old, tired notion that athletics is more important than the institution itself still flourishes.

Yet some schools faced with diminishing resources are finding creative ways to tighten budgets for their more expensive teams. Perhaps putting the entire football team in a hotel the night before a home game is not vital, they say. Maybe taking a bus instead of flying to a competition wouldn't be too bad, they think. Spring trips to warm climates may be a luxury no longer affordable, they conclude. To those outside athletics departments, these budget-conserving techniques seem obvious. These same methods have always been available, if not generally used, to fund greater equity in coaching compensation and athletics programs. Perhaps current financial pressures will lead to their implementation. In any event, institutions are now examining budgets they previously held to be inviolate. It takes will. We hope the presence of will and the changing budgetary terrain combine to bring about constructive change.

Time

Changing the 24-7 time demand on coaches, both men and women, also requires will. Women are often affected more strongly than men by the extraordinary time demands of an athletics career. Solutions to the life-balance issue cannot be found without thoroughly evaluating the role of athletics on campus.

Respect

Two to three percent of men's teams are coached by women. Many of these women coaches suffer from lack of respect, derision, and distrust by the institution, fans, and alums. The issue of respect and its impact on equity extends to the often unspoken yet access-blocking belief that women cannot serve as effective directors of athletics at institutions that field high-profile football teams.

Even subtle and perhaps subconscious semantic choices— such as team names preceded by "Lady"—reflect disrespect, which decreases will. Similarly, referring to men's teams as "X University's basketball team" and to women's teams as "X University's women's basketball team" suggests a second-class status. Along the same lines, talking about "qualified" female coaches while omitting the modifier "qualified" when speaking of male coaches effectively tells the listener that most men are qualified and most women are not. Disrespect is subtle, but it has a deep impact on hiring, firing, funding, supporting, and caring. It also reflects an absence of will to arrive at equity.

So are we there yet? No. Have we made great progress toward arriving? Yes. How much longer until we get there? It depends on the strength of will found in the offices of college presidents and directors of athletics.

There is no road rough enough nor hill steep enough to end the road trip to equity . . . if there is the will to get there.

NOTE

1. This article draws on *Women in Sport: A Longitudinal, National Study on the Status of Women in Sport,* now in its thirty-first year. The authors of this article direct the study. For the first two decades of its life, the study was funded by the City University of New York Brooklyn College. Now it is graciously funded by the Project on Women and Social Change at Smith College. The study solicits data from all National Collegiate Athletic Association member institutions that have a women's athletics program (currently more than 1,100 schools). Over the years, the annual return rate among institutions surveyed has been between 70 and 80 percent. The data are independent of any organizational database. To download a copy of the current study, go to www.acostacarpenter.org.

33

Her Life Depends On It II

Sport, Physical Activity, and the Health and Well-Being of American Girls and Women

Women's Sports Foundation

EXECUTIVE SUMMARY

In 2004, the Women's Sports Foundation published the first edition of *Her Life Depends On It* (Sabo et al.). At that time, it was clear that evidence-based research confirmed that regular physical activity and sport provides the critical foundation, in no small part, that allows girls and women to lead healthy, strong, and fulfilled lives. Now, five years later, *Her Life Depends On It II,* provides an updated, and even more comprehensive, review of the existing research on the links between sports and physical activity and the health and well-being of American girls and women. This expanded review of existing research and health information is co-authored by a team of experts from several related disciplines, including epidemiology, exercise physiology, kinesiology, psychology, and sociology. Some key contributions of this new report include the following:

- Research affirms, even more definitively than five years ago, that engagement in moderate and consistent levels of physical activity and sport for girls and women is essential to good health and well-being.

Source: Women's Sports Foundation, *Her Life Depends On It II* (December 2009).

- Although more research needs to be done, early studies examining the connections between physical activity and academic achievement show there is a positive relationship between the two in girls and women.
- Females from lower economic backgrounds and females of color engage less in physical activity, have less access to sport and physical fitness programs, and suffer negative health consequences as a result.
- Emerging research in prevention and training practices show that gender-conscious approaches to physical training and conditioning for female athletes help to reduce the likelihood of anterior cruciate ligament (ACL) injuries and concussions.

This report could not issue at a more opportune and urgent time. Government leaders, policymakers, and health planners are struggling to reform the health care delivery system, to contain costs, and to initiate preventive strategies. Physical activity is increasingly recognized as a viable strategy for elevating the nation's health. In 1996, on the eve of the Olympic Games in Atlanta, the Surgeon General of the United States released a report on physical activity and health that was described by then United States Secretary of Health and Human Services, Donna Shalala, as representing a "passport to good health for all Americans" (p. 3). The Centers for Disease Control and Prevention followed suit that same year, creating a unit designed to promote health through physical activity (Buchner & Schmidt, 2009). In 2004, the World Health Organization (WHO) put forward the Global Strategy on Diet, Physical Activity and Health, the goal of which was to promote and protect the health of the world's citizens by developing enabling environments for sustainable actions at individual, community, national and global levels. Taken together, these efforts were designed to reduce disease and death rates related to unhealthy diet and physical inactivity. Finally, in July of 2009, a national conference was held in Washington, D.C., to establish the groundwork for America's first National Physical Activity Plan.

Her Life Depends On It II documents the important role physical activity can play in helping to prevent the daunting array of health risks for girls and women such as obesity, coronary heart disease, cancer, osteoporosis, Alzheimer's Disease and related dementias, illicit drug use, tobacco-related disease, sexual risk and teen pregnancy, and eating disorders. In addition to documenting the contributions of sport and physical activity to girls' and women's health and well-being, this version of *Her Life Depends On It* provides an overview of emerging research on several health risks that are associated with overtraining and athletic participation, as well as new studies that point to effective strategies designed to prevent injuries from happening.

Within the United States, the Institute of Medicine defined public health as the collective actions undertaken by a society "to assure the conditions for people to be healthy" (Committee for Assuring the Health of the Public in the 21st Century, 2002). The research compiled in our updated report strongly suggests that sport and physical activity provide conditions that help to ensure girls' health and well-being. Some findings identified in this report relate to:

- **Breast Cancer Risk:** Based on the findings from 23 studies examining the effect of moderate and vigorous physical activity during adolescence on cancer risk, those who had the highest physical activity during adolescence and young adulthood were 20% less likely to get breast cancer later in life (Lagerros et al., 2004).
- **Osteoporosis:** A study following pre-pubertal 10-year-old girls for 20 months found that an exercise program (engaged in three times a week for 12 minutes per session) led to an increase in bone mass. This result was not found for the girls who did not participate in the exercise program (MacKelvie et al., 2001; MacKelvie et al., 2002; MacKelvie et al., 2003; MacKelvie et al., 2004).
- **Smoking:** Female athletes who participated on one or two school or community sports teams were significantly less likely to smoke regularly than female non-athletes. Girls on three or more teams were even less likely to smoke regularly (Melnick et al., 2001).
- **Illicit Drug Use:** Two nationwide studies found that female school or community athletes were significantly less likely to use marijuana, cocaine, opiates, tranquilizers, prescription drugs, or "club drugs" like ecstasy or GHB (Ford, 2008; Miller et al, 2000; Pate et al, 2000; Yusko et al., 2008).
- **Sexual Risk:** Female athletes were less likely to have unprotected sex, sex with multiple partners, or sex under the influence of alcohol/drugs (Lehman & Koerner, 2004; Miller et al., 2002).
- **Depression:** Moderate levels of exercise and/or sports activity helped protect girls and women against depression (McKercher et al., 2009; Sanders et al., 2000).
- **Suicide:** Female high school/college athletes were less likely to consider, plan, or attempt suicide (Brown & Blanton, 2002; Brown et al., 2007; Sabo et al, 2005; Taliaferro et al., 2008a.).
- **Educational Gains:** According to Troutman and Dufur (2007), females who participated in high school sports were more likely to complete college than those who did not participate in sports.

The health benefits realized from the participation of girls and women in sport and physical activity vary by socioeconomic level and racial and ethnic group. Throughout the report, available findings document health risks and vulnerabilities for females of color as well as for girls and women living in urban and rural settings. A special addendum to the report is also available that integrates all of the findings related to these populations.

Despite this ever-expanding body of research, in general girls are still not afforded the degree of encouragement or opportunity extended to boys to participate in sports and fitness activities. Impediments to access remain an ongoing concern, complicated by recent trends that run counter to promoting physical activity, fitness, and sport programs in schools and communities. With schools cutting back on recess, a de-emphasis on physical education nationally, and persistent inequalities in school-sport programs and community-recreation programs, girls and women continue to encounter structural barriers to participation (Cheslock, 2007, 2008; Cooky, 2009; NASPE/AMA, 2006; National Federation of State High School Associations, 2008; National Parent Teacher Association, 2006; Sabo & Veliz, 2008).

While the research base illustrates the importance of physical activity in the lives of girls and women, it is also critical to examine a collection of issues related to performance—overtraining, lack of proper conditioning, poor equipment and unsafe facilities—that impact female athlete experience. In this report, we highlight the emerging areas of research that focus on protecting the health of female athletes and offer insights into the initiatives needed (steps that need to be taken) to ensure their health and safety. For example, a small proportion of female athletes may develop three interrelated conditions—eating disorders, amenorrhea, and osteoporosis—otherwise known as The Female Athlete Triad. Other emerging areas of research focus on female athlete injuries to the head and body, among them tears to the anterior cruciate ligament (ACL) and concussions.

This report's user-friendly format provides a toolbox of information, analysis, and sources for parents interested in the health of their daughters; coaches interested in the well-being of female athletes; media interested in informing readers about strategies to achieve optimal health for females, both young and old, from every sector of society; health consumers; sport leaders and program heads; public health advocates; and public policy makers interested in reducing health care costs while emphasizing prevention and health promotion for female citizens. With increasing specificity and urgency, calls are being sounded across the United States for greater and better opportunities for all Americans to become more physically active. As those calls echo across the land it is imperative that the needs of girls and women be taken into account and met.

REFERENCES

Brown, D. R., & Blanton, C. J. (2002). Physical activity, sports participation, and suicidal behavior among college students. *Medicine & Science in Sports & Exercise 34* (7), 1087–1096.

Brown, D. R., Galuska, D. A., Zhang, J., Eaton, D. K., Fulton, J. E., Lowry, R., & Maynard, L. M. (2007). Physical activity, sport participation, and suicidal behavior: U.S. high school students. *Medicine & Science in Sports & Exercise 39,* 2248–2257.

Buchner, D. M., & Schmid, T. (2009, February). Active living research and public health: Natural partners in a new field. *American Journal of Preventive Medicine 36* (2) (supplement).

Cheslock, J. (2007). *Who's Playing College Sports? Trends in Participation.* East Meadow, NY: Women's Sports Foundation.

Cheslock, J. (2008). *Who's Playing College Sports? Money, Race and Gender.* East Meadow, NY: Women's Sports Foundation.

Cooky, C. (2009). "Girls just aren't interested": The social construction of interest in girls' sport. *Sociological Perspectives 52* (2), 259–284.

De Souza, M. J. & Williams, N. I. (2004). Physiological aspects and clinical sequelae of energy deficiency and hypoestrogenism in exercising women. *Human Reproduction Update 10,* 433–448.

Floriano, V., & Kennedy, C. (2007). Promotion of physical activity in primary care or obesity treatment/prevention in children. *Current Opinion in Pediatrics 19,* 99–103.

Ford, J. A. (2008). Nonmedical prescription drug use among college students: A comparison between athletes and nonathletes. *Journal of American College Health 57* (2), 211–219.

Kirby, D. (2007). Emerging answers: Research findings on programs to reduce teen pregnancy. Washington, DC: National Campaign to Prevent Teen Pregnancy.

Lagerros, Y. T., Hsieh, S. F., et al. (2004). Physical activity in adolescence and young adulthood and breast cancer risk: A quantitative review. *European Journal of Cancer Prevention 13,* 5–12.

Lehman, S. J., & Koerner, S. S. (2004). Adolescent women's sports involvement and sexual behavior/health: A process-level investigation. *Journal of Youth and Adolescence 33* (5), 443–455.

MacKelvie, K., McKay, H., et al. (2001). A school-based exercise intervention augments bone mineral accrual in early pubertal girls. *Journal of Pediatrics 139,* 501–508.

MacKelvie, K., McKay, H., et al. (2002). Bone mineral response to a 7-month randomized controlled, school-based jumping intervention in 121 prepubertal boys: Association with ethnicity and body mass index. *Journal of Bone Mineral Research 17,* 834–844.

MacKelvie, K., Khan, K., et al. (2003). A school-based exercise intervention elicits substantial bone health benefits: A 2-year randomized controlled trial in girls. *Pediatrics 112* (6), 447.

MacKelvie, K., Petit, M., et al. (2004). Bone mass structure are enhanced following a 2-year randomized controlled trial of exercise in prepubertal boys. *Bone 34,* 75–76.

McKercher, C. M., Schmidt, M. D., Sanderson, K. A., Patton, G. C., Dwyer, T., & Venn, A. J. (2009). Physical activity and depression in young adults. *American Journal of Preventive Medicine 36,* 161–164.

Melnick, M. J., Miller, K. E., Sabo, D., Farrell, M. P., & Barnes, G. M. (2001). "Tobacco use among high school athletes and nonathletes: Results of the 1997 Youth Risk Behavior Survey." *Adolescence, 36*: 727–747.

Miller, K. E., Sabo, D., Melnick, J. J., Farrell, M. P., & Barnes, G. M. (2000). *The Women's Sports Foundation Report: Health Risks and the Teen Athlete.* East Meadow, NY: Women's Sports Foundation.

Miller, K. E., Barnes, G. M., Melnick, M. J., Sabo, D., & Farrell, M. P. (2002). Gender and racial/ethnic differences in predicting adolescent sexual risk: Athletic participation vs. exercise. *Journal of Health & Social Behavior 43,* 436–450.

National Association of Anorexia Nervosa and Associated Disorders (2009). General information: Facts about eating disorders. Retrieved July 20, 2009, from http://www.anad.org.

National Association for Sport and Physical Education (NASPE) and American Heart Association (AHA) (2006). *Shape of the nation.* Washington, DC: American Heart Association.

National Federation of State High School Associations (2008). The 2007–2008 High School Athletics Participation Survey. Indianapolis, IN: National Federation of State High School Associations.

National Parent Teacher Association (PTA). (2006). Recess is at risk: New campaign comes to the rescue. Chicago, IL: Author.

National Physical Activity Plan Conference. (2009). Washington, DC, July 1–2, 2009.

Ogden, C. L. (2009). Disparities in obesity prevalence in the United States: Black women at risk. *American Journal of Clinical Nutrition 89,* 101–102.

Pate, R. R., Trost, S. G., Levin, S., & Dowda, M. (2000). Sports participation and health-related behaviors among U.S. youth. *Archives of Pediatric and Adolescent Medicine, 154,* 904–911.

Sabo, D., Miller, K. E., Melnick, M. J., & Heywood, L. (2004). *Her Life Depends On It:*

Sport, Physical Activity, and the Health and Well-Being of American Girls. East Meadow, NY: Women's Sports Foundation.

Sabo, D., Miller, K. E., Melnick, M. J., Farrell, M. P., & Barnes, G. M. (2005). High school athletic participation and adolescent suicide: A nationwide study. *International Review for the Sociology of Sport 40,* 5–23.

Sabo, D., & Veliz, P. (2008). *Go Out and Play: Youth Sports in America.* East Meadow, NY: Women's Sports Foundation.

Sanders, C. E., Field, T. M., Diego, M., & Kaplan, M. (2000). Moderate involvement in sports is related to lower depression levels in adolescents. *Adolescence 35* (140), 793–797.

Staurowsky, E. J., Morris, H., Paule, A., & Reese, J. (2007, October). Travelers on the Title IX compliance highway: How are Ohio's colleges and universities faring? *Women in Sport and Physical Activity Journal.*

Staurowsky, E. J. (in press). Gender equity in two-year athletic departments: Part I. In Hagedorn, L., & Horton, D. (eds.). *New Directions for Community Colleges.* New York, NY: Jossey Bass.

Taliaferro, L. A., Rienzo, B. A., Miller, M. D., Pigg, R. M., Jr., & Dodd, V. J. (2008a). High school youth and suicide risk: Exploring protection afforded through physical activity and sport participation. *Journal of School Health 78,* 545–553.

Theberge, N. (2008). 'Just a normal bad part of what I do': Elite athletes' accounts of the relationship between sport participation and health. *Sociology of Sport Journal, 25* (2), 206–222.

Troutman, K.P., & Dufur, M. J. (2007). From high school jocks to college grads: Assessing the long-term effects of high school sport participation on females' educational attainment. *Youth and Society, 38* (4), 443–462.

United States Department of Health and Human Services (USDHHS). (1996). *Physical activity and health: A report of the Surgeon General.* Atlanta, GA: CDC, 1996. Retrieved July 21, 2009, from http://cdc.gov/nccdphp/sgr/contents.htm.

World Health Organization (2004). *Global strategy on diet, physical activity, and health.* Geneva, SW: Author.

Yusko, D. A., Buckman, J. F., White, H. R., & Pandina, R. J. (2008). Alcohol, tobacco, illicit drugs, and performance enhancers: A comparison of use by college student athletes and nonathletes. *Journal of American College Health 57* (3), 281–289.

34

The Meaning of Success

The Athletic Experience and the Development of Male Identity

Michael A. Messner

> Vince Lombardi supposedly said, "Winning isn't everything; it's the only thing," and I couldn't agree more. There's nothing like being number one.
>
> —Joe Montana

> The big-name athletes will get considerable financial and social remuneration for their athletic efforts. But what of the others, the 99% who fail? Most will fall short of their dreams of a lucrative professional contract. The great majority of athletes, then, will likely suffer disappointment, underemployment, anxiety, or perhaps even serious mental disorders.
>
> —Donald Harris and D. Stanley Eitzen

What is the relationship between participation in organized sports and a young male's developing sense of himself as a success or failure? And what is the consequent impact on his self-image and his ability to engage in intimate relationships with others? Through the late 1960s, it was almost universally accepted that "sports builds character" and that "a winner in sports will be a winner in life." Consequently, some liberal feminists argued that since participation in organized competitive sports has served as a major source of socialization for males' successful participation in the public world, girls and young women should have equal access to sports. Lever, for instance, concluded that if women were ever going to be able to develop the proper competitive values and orientations toward work and success, it was incumbent on them to participate in sports.[1]

In the 1970s and 1980s, these uncritical orientations toward sports have been questioned, and the "sports builds character" formula has been found wanting. Sabo points out that the vast majority of research does *not* support the contention that success in sports translates into "work success" or "happiness" in one's personal life.[2] In fact, a great deal of evidence suggests that the contrary is true. Recent critical analyses of success and failure in sports have usually started from assumptions similar to those of Sennett and Cobb and of Rubin:[3] the disjuncture between the *ideology* of success (the Lombardian Ethic) and the socially structured *reality* that most do not "succeed" brings about widespread feelings of failure, lowered self-images, and problems with interpersonal relationships.[4] The most common argument seems to be that the highly competitive world of sports is an exaggerated reflection of advanced industrial capitalism. Within any hierarchy, one can actually work very hard and achieve a lot, yet still be defined (and perceive oneself) as less than successful. Very few people ever reach the mythical "top," but those who do are made ultravisible through the media.[5] It is tempting to view this system as a "structure of failure" because, given the definition of *success,* the system is virtually rigged to bring about the failure of the vast majority of participants. Furthermore, given the dominant values, the participants are apt to blame themselves for their "failure." Schafer argues that the result of this discontinuity between sports values/ideology and reality is a "widespread conditional self-worth" for young athletes.[6] And as Edwards has pointed out, this problem can be even more acute for black athletes, who are disproportionately channeled into sports, yet have no "social safety net" to fall back on after "failure" in sports.

Both the traditional "sports builds character" and the more recent "sports breeds failures" formulas have a common pitfall: Each employs socialization theory in an often simplistic and mechanistic way. Boys are viewed largely as "blank slates" onto which the sports experience imprints values, appropriate "sex-role scripts," and orientations toward self and the world. What is usually not taken into account is the fact that boys (and girls) come to the sports experience with an *already gendered* identity that colors their early motivations and perceptions of the meaning of games and sports. As Gilligan points out, observations of young children's game-playing show that girls bring to the activity a more pragmatic and flexible orientation toward the rules—they are more prone to make exceptions and innovations in the middle of the game in order to make the game more "fair" and maintain relationships with others.[7] Boys tend to have a more firm, even inflexible orientation to the rules of a game—they are less willing to change or alter rules in the middle of the game; to them, the rules are what protects any "fairness." This observation has profound implications for sociological research on sports and gender: The question should not be *simply* "how does sports participation affect boys [or girls]?" but should add "what is it about a developing sense of male identity that *attracts* males to sports in the first place? And how does this socially constructed male identity develop and change as it interacts with the structure and values of the sports world?" In addition to being a social-psychological question, this is also a *historical* question: Since men have not at all times and places related to sports the way they do at present, it is important to explore just what kinds of men exist today. What are their needs, problems, and dreams? How do these men relate to the society they live in? And how do organized sports fit into this picture?

THE "PROBLEM OF MASCULINITY" AND ORGANIZED SPORTS

In the first two decades of this century, men feared that the closing of the frontier, along with changes in the workplace, the family, and the schools, was having a "feminizing" influence on society.[8] One result of the anxiety men felt was the creation of the Boy Scouts of America as a separate sphere of social life where "true manliness" could be instilled in boys *by men.*[9] The rapid rise of organized sports in roughly the same era can be attributed largely to the same phenomenon. As socioeconomic and familial changes continue to erode the traditional bases of male identity and privilege, sports became an increasingly important cultural expression of traditional male values—organized sports became a "primary masculinity-validating experience."[10]

In the post–World War II era, the bureaucratization and rationalization of work, along with the decline of the family wage and women's gradual movement into the labor force, have further undermined the "breadwinner role" as a basis for male identity, thus resulting in a "problem of masculinity" and a "defensive insecurity" among men.[11] As Mills put it, the ethic of success in postwar America "has become less widespread as fact, more confused as image, often dubious as motive, and soured as a way of life. [Yet] there are still compulsions to struggle, to 'amount to something.'"[12]

How have men expressed this need to "amount to something" within a social context that seems to deny them the opportunities to do so? Again, organized sports play an important role. Both on a personal-existential level for athletes and on a symbolic-ideological level for spectators and fans, sports have become one of the "last bastions" of traditional male ideas of success, of male power and superiority over—and separation from—the perceived "feminization" of society. It is likely that the rise of football as "America's number-one game" is largely the result of the comforting clarity it provides between the polarities of traditional male power, strength, and violence and the contemporary fears of social feminization.

But these historical explanations for the increased importance of sports, despite their validity, beg some important questions: Why do men fear the (real or imagined) "feminization" of their world? Why do men appear to need a separate male sphere of life? Why do organized sports appear to be such an attractive means of expressing these needs? Are males simply "socialized" to dominate women and to compete with other men for status, or are they seeking (perhaps unconsciously) something more fundamental? Just what is it that men really *want*? To begin to answer these questions it is necessary to listen to athletes' voices and examine their lives with a social-psychological perspective.

Daniel Levinson's concept of the "individual life structure" is a useful place to begin to construct a gestalt of the life of the athlete.[13] Levinson demonstrates that as males develop and interact with their world, they continue to change throughout their lives. A common theme during developmental periods is the process of individuation, the struggle to separate, to "decide where he stops and where the world begins." "In successive periods of development, as this process goes on, the person forms a clearer boundary between self and world.... Greater individuation allows him to be more separate from the world, to be more independent and self-generating. But it also gives him the confidence and understanding to have more intense attachments in the world and to feel more fully a part of it."[14]

This dynamic of separation and attachment provides a valuable social-psychological framework for examining the experiences and problems faced by the athlete as he gropes for and redefines success throughout his life course. In what follows, Levinson's framework is utilized to analyze the lives of 30 former athletes interviewed between 1983 and 1984. Their *interactions* with sports are examined in terms of their initial boyhood attraction to sports; how notions of success in sports connect with a developing sense of male identity; and how self-images, relationships to work and other people, change and develop after the sports career ends.

BOYHOOD: THE PROMISE OF SPORTS

Given how very few athletes actually "make it" through sports, how can the intensity with which millions of boys and young men throw themselves into athletics be explained? Are they simply pushed, socialized, or even *duped* into putting so much emphasis on athletic success? It is important here to examine just what it is that young males hope to get out of the athletic experience. And in terms of *identity*, it is crucial to examine the ways in which the structure and experience of sports activity meet the developmental needs of young males. The story of Willy Rios sheds light on what these needs are. Rios was born in Mexico and moved to the United States at a fairly young age. He never knew his father, and his mother died when he was only 9 years old. Suddenly he felt rootless, and at this time he threw himself into sports, but his initial motivations do not appear to be based upon a need to compete and win. "Actually, what I think sports did for me is it brought me into kind of an instant family. By being on a Little League team, or even just playing with all kinds of different kids in the neighborhood, it brought what I really wanted, which was some kind of closeness."

Similar statements from other men suggest that a fundamental motivational factor behind many young males' sports strivings is a need for connection, "closeness" with others. But why do so many boys see *sports* as an attractive means of establishing connection with others? Chodorow argues that the process of developing a gender identity yields insecurity and ambivalence in males.[15] Males develop "rigid ego boundaries" that ensure separation from others, yet they retain a basic human need for closeness and intimacy with others. The young male, who both seeks and fears attachment with others, thus finds the rulebound structure of games and sports to be a psychologically "safe" place in which he can get (nonintimate) connection with others within a context that maintains clear boundaries, distance, and separation from others. At least for the boy who has some early successes in sports, some of these ambivalent needs can be met, for a time. But there is a catch: For Willy Rios, it was only after he learned that he would get attention (a certain kind of connection) from other people for being a good athlete—indeed, that this attention was *contingent on* his *being good*—that narrow definitions of success, based on performance and winning, became important to him. It was years before he realized that no matter how well he performed, how successful he became, he would not get the closeness that he craved through sports. "It got to be a product in high school. Before, it was just fun, and having acceptance, you know. Yet I had to work for my acceptance in high school that way, just being a jock. So it wasn't fun any more. But it was my self-identity, being a good ballplayer. I was realizing that whatever you excel in, you put out in front of you. Bring it out. Show it. And that's what I did. That was my protection.... It was rotten in high school, really."

This conscious striving for successful achievement becomes the primary means through which the young athlete seeks connections with other people. But the irony of the situation, for so many boys and young men like Willy Rios, is that the athletes are seeking to get something from their success in sports that sports cannot deliver—and the *pressure* that they end up putting on themselves to achieve that success ends up stripping them of the ability to receive the one major thing that sports really *does* have to offer: fun.

ADOLESCENCE: YOU'RE ONLY AS GOOD AS YOUR LAST GAME

Adolescence is probably the period of greatest insecurity in the life course, the time when the young male becomes most vulnerable to peer expectation, pressures, and judgments. None of the men interviewed for this study, regardless of their social class or ethnicity, seemed fully able to "turn a deaf ear to the crowd" during their athletic careers. The crowd, which may include immediate family, friends, peers, teammates, as well as the more anonymous fans and media, appears to be a crucially important part of the process of establishing and maintaining the self-images of young athletes. By the time they were in high school, most of the men interviewed for this study had found sports to be a primary means through which to establish a sense of manhood in the world. Especially if they were good athletes, the expectations of the crowd became very powerful and were internalized (and often *magnified*) within the young man's own expectations. As one man stated, by the time he was in high school, "it was *expected* of me to do well in all of my contests—I mean by my coach and my peers, and my family. So I in turn expected to do well, and if I didn't do well, then I'd be very disappointed."

When so much is tied to your performance, the dictum that "you are only as good as your last game" is a powerful judgment. It means that the young man must continually prove, achieve, and then *re*prove, and *re*achieve his status. As a result, many young athletes learn to seek and *need* the appreciation of the crowd to feel that they are worthy human beings. But the internalized values of masculinity along with the insecure nature of the sports world mean that the young man does *not* need the crowd to feel *bad* about himself. In fact, if one is insecure enough, even "success" and the compliments and attention of other people can come to feel hollow and meaningless. For instance, 48-year-old Russ Ellis in his youth shared the basic sense of insecurity common to all young males, and in his case it was probably compounded by his status as a poor black male and an insecure family life. Athletics emerged early in his life as the primary arena in which he and his male peers competed to establish a sense of self in the world. For Ellis, his small physical stature made it difficult to compete successfully in most sports, thus feeding his insecurity—he just never felt as though he belonged with "the big boys." Eventually, though, he became a top middle-distance runner. In high school, however: "Something began to happen there that later plagued me quite a bit. I started doing very well and winning lots of races and by the time the year was over, it was no longer a question for me of *placing,* but *winning.* That attitude really destroyed me ultimately. I would get into the blocks with worries that I wouldn't do well—the regular stomach problems—so I'd often run much less well than my abilities—that is, say, I'd take second or third."

Interestingly, his nervousness, fears, and anxieties did not seem to be visible to "the crowd": "I know in high school, certainly, they saw me as confident and ready to run. No one assumed I could be beaten, which fascinated me, because I had never been good at understanding how I was taken in other people's minds—maybe because I spent so much time inventing myself in their regard in my own mind. I was projecting my fear fantasies on them and taking them for reality."

In 1956 Ellis surprised everyone by taking second place in a world-class field of quarter-milers. But the fact that they ran the fastest time in the world, 46.5, seemed only to "up the ante," to increase the pressures on Ellis, then in college at UCLA.

> Up to that point I had been a nice zippy kid who did good, got into the *Daily Bruin* a lot, and was well-known on campus. But now an event would come up and the papers would say, "Ellis to face so-and-so." So rather than my being in the race, I *was* the race, as far as the press was concerned. And that put a lot of pressure on me that I never learned to handle. What I did was to internalize it, and then I'd sit there and fret and lose sleep, and focus more on not winning than on how I was doing. And in general, I didn't do badly—like one year in the NCAA's I took fourth—you know, in the *national finals.* But I was focused on winning. You know, later on, people would say, "Oh wow, you took fourth in the NCAA?—you were *that good?*" Whereas I thought of these things as *failures,* you know?

Finally, Ellis's years of training, hopes, and fears came to a head at the 1956 Olympic trials, where he failed to qualify, finishing fifth. A rival whom he used to defeat routinely won the event in the Melbourne Olympics as Ellis watched on television. "That killed me. Destroyed me.... I had the experience many times after that of digging down and finding that there was infinitely more down there than I ever got—I mean, I know that more than I know anything else. Sometimes I would really feel like an eagle, running. Sometimes in practice at UCLA running was just exactly like flying—and if I could have carried that attitude into events, I would have done much better. But instead, I'd worry. Yeah, I'd worry myself sick."

As suggested earlier, young males like Russ Ellis are "set up" for disappointment, or worse, by the disjuncture between the narrow Lombardian definition of success in the sports world and the reality that very few ever actually reach the top. The athlete's sense of identity established through sports is therefore insecure and problematic, *not simply* because of the high probability of "failure," but also because *success* in the sports world involves the development of a personality that *amplifies* many of the most ambivalent and destructive traits of traditional masculinity. Within the hierarchical world of sports, which in many ways mirrors the capitalist economy, one learns that if he is to survive and avoid being pushed off the ever-narrowing pyramid of success, he must develop certain kinds of relationships—to himself, to his body, to other people, and to the sport itself. In short, the successful athlete must develop a highly goal-oriented personality that encourages him to view his body as a tool, a machine, or even a weapon utilized to defeat an objectified opponent. He is likely to have difficulty establishing intimate and lasting friendships with other males because of low self-disclosure, homophobia, and cut-throat competition. And he is likely to view his public image as a "success" as far more basic and fundamental than any of his interpersonal relationships.

For most of the men interviewed, the quest for success was not the grim task it was for Russ Ellis. Most men did seem to get, at least for a time, a sense of identity (and even some happiness) out of their athletic accomplishments. The attention of the crowd, for many, affirmed their existence as males and was thus a clear motivating force. Gary Affonso, now 42 years old and a high school coach, explained that when he was in high school, he had an "intense desire to practice and compete." "I used to practice the high jump by myself for hours at a time—only got up to 5'3"—scissor! [*Laughs.*] But I think part of it was, the track itself was in view of some of the classrooms, and so as I think back now, maybe I did it for the attention, to be seen. In my freshman year, I chipped my two front teeth in a football game, and after that I always had a gold tooth, and I was always self-conscious about that. Plus I had my glasses, you know. I felt a little conspicuous." This simultaneous shyness, self-consciousness, and conspicuousness *along with* the strongly felt need for attention and external validation (attachment) so often characterize athletes' descriptions of themselves in boyhood and adolescence. The crowd, in this context, can act as a distant, and thus nonthreatening, source of attention and validation of self for the insecure male. Russ Ellis's story typifies that what sports seem to *promise* the young male—affirmation of self and connection with others—is likely to be *undermined* by the youth's actual experience in the sports world. The athletic experience also "sets men up" for another serious problem: the end of a career at a very young age.

DISENGAGEMENT TRAUMA: A CRISIS OF MALE IDENTITY

For some, the end of the athletic career approaches gradually like the unwanted houseguest whose eventual arrival is at least *known* and can be planned for, thus limiting the inevitable inconvenience. For others, the athletic career ends with the shocking suddenness of a violent thunderclap that rudely awakens one from a pleasant dream. But whether it comes gradually or suddenly, the end of the playing career represents the termination of what has often become the *central aspect* of a young male's individual life structure, thus initiating change and transition in the life course.

Previous research on the disengagement crises faced by many retiring athletes has focused on the health, occupational, and financial problems frequently faced by retiring professionals.[16] These problems are especially severe for retiring black athletes, who often have inadequate educational backgrounds and few opportunities within the sports world for media or coaching jobs.[17] But even for those retiring athletes who avoid the pitfalls of financial and occupational crises, substance abuse, obesity, and ill health, the end of the playing career usually involves a crisis of identity. This identity crisis is probably most acute for retiring *professional* athletes, whose careers are coming to an end right at an age when most men's careers are beginning to take off. As retired professional football player Marvin Upshaw stated, "You find yourself just scrambled. You don't know which way to go. Your light, as far as you're concerned, has been turned out. You miss the roar of the crowd. Once you've heard it, you can't get away from it. There's an empty feeling—you feel everything you wanted is gone. All of a sudden you wake up and you find yourself 29, 35 years old, you know, and the one thing that has been the major part of your life is gone. It's gone."

High school and college athletes also face serious and often painful adjustment periods when their career ends. Twenty-six-year-old Dave Joki had been a good high school basketball player, and had played a lot of ball in college. When interviewed, he was right in the middle of a confusing crisis of identity, closely related to his recent disengagement from viewing himself as an athlete.

> These past few months I've been trying a lot of different things, thinking about different careers, things to do. There's been quite a bit of stumbling—and I think that part of my tenuousness about committing myself to any one thing is I'm not sure I'm gonna get strokes if I go that way. *[Embarrassed, nervous laugh.]* It's scary for me and I stay away from searching for those reasons.... I guess you could say that I'm stumbling in my relationships too—stumbling in all parts of life. *[Laughs.]* I feel like I'm doing a lot but now knowing what I want.

Surely there is nothing unusual about a man in his mid-20s "stumbling" around and looking for direction in his work and his relationships. That is common for men of his age. But for the former athlete, this stumbling is often more confusing and problematic than for the other men precisely because he has lost the one activity through which he had built his sense of identity, however tenuous it may have been. The "strokes" he received from being a good athlete were his major psychological foundation. The interaction between self and other through which the athlete attempts to solidify his identity is akin to what Cooley called "the looking-glass self." If the athletic activity and the crowd can be viewed as the *mirror* into which the athlete gazes and, in Russ Ellis's words, "invents himself," we can begin to appreciate how devastating it can be when that looking-glass is suddenly and permanently *shattered,* leaving the young man alone, isolated, and disconnected. And since young men often feel comfortable exploring close friendships and intimate relationships only *after* they have established their separate work-related (or sports-related) positional identity, relationships with other people are likely to become more problematic than ever during disengagement.

WORK, LOVE, AND MALE IDENTITY AFTER DISENGAGEMENT

Eventually, the former athlete must face reality: At a relatively young age, he has to start over. In the words of retired major-league baseball player Ray Fosse, "Now I gotta get on with the rest of it." How is "the rest of it" likely to take shape for the athlete after his career as a player is over? How do men who are "out of the limelight" for a few years come to define themselves as men? How do they define and redefine success? How do the values and attitudes they learned through sports affect their lives? How do their relationships with friends and family change over time?

Many retired athletes retain a powerful drive to reestablish the important relationship with the crowd that served as the primary basis for their identity for so long. Many men throw themselves wholeheartedly into a new vocation—or a confusing *series* of vocations—in a sometimes pathetic attempt to recapture the "high" of athletic competition as well as the status of the successful athlete in the community. For instance, 35-year-old Jackie Ridgle is experiencing what Daniel Levinson calls a "surge of masculine strivings" common to men in their mid-30s.[18] Once a professional basketball player, Ridgle seems motivated now by a powerful drive to be seen once again as "somebody" in the eyes of the public. When interviewed, he had recently been hired as an assistant college basketball coach, which made him feel like he again had a chance to "be somebody."

> When I say "successful," that means somebody that the public looks up to just as a basketball player. Yet you don't have to be playing basketball. You can be anybody: You can be a senator or a mayor, or any number of things. That's what I call successful. Success is recognition. Sure, I'm always proud of myself. But there's that little goal there that until people respect you, then—[*Snaps fingers.*] Anybody can say, "Oh, I know I'm the greatest thing in the world," but *people* run the world, and when *they* say you're successful, then you *know* you're successful.

Indeed men, especially men in early adulthood, usually define themselves primarily in terms of their position in the public world of work. Feminist literature often criticizes this establishment of male identity in terms of work-success as an expression of male privilege and ego satisfaction that comes at the expense of women and children. There is a great deal of truth to the feminist critique: A man's socially defined need to establish himself as "somebody" in the (mostly) male world of work is often accompanied by his frequent physical absence from home and his emotional distance from his family. Thus, while the man is "out there" establishing his "name" in public, the woman is usually home caring for the day-to-day and moment-to-moment needs of her family (regardless of whether or not she also has a job in the paid labor force). Tragically, only in midlife, when the children have already "left the nest" and the woman is often ready to go out into the public world, do some men discover the importance of connection and intimacy.

Yet the interviews indicate that there is not always such a clean and clear "before-after" polarity in the lives of men between work-success and care-intimacy. The "breadwinner ethic" as a male role *has* most definitely contributed to the perpetuation of male privilege and the subordination and economic dependence of women as mothers and housekeepers. But given the reality of the labor market, where women still make only 62 cents to the male dollar, many men feel very responsible for providing the majority of the income and financial security for their families. For instance, 36-year-old Ray Fosse, whose father left his family when he was quite young, has a very strong sense of commitment and responsibility as a provider of income and stability in his own family.

> I'm working an awful lot these days, and trying not to take time away from my family. A lot of times I'm putting the family to sleep, and working late hours and going to bed and getting up early and so forth. I've tried to tell my family this a lot of times: The work that I'm doing now is gonna make it easier in a few years. That's the reason I'm working now, to get that financial security, and I feel like it's coming very soon ... but, uh, you know, you go a long day and you come home, and it's just not the quality time you'd like to have. And I think when that financial security comes in, then I'm gonna be able to forget about everything.

Jackie Ridgle's words mirror Fosse's. His two jobs and striving to be successful in the public world mean that he has little time to spend with his wife and three children. "I plan to someday. Very seldom do you have enough time to spend with your kids, especially nowadays, so I don't get hung up on that. The wife does sometimes, but as long as I keep a roof over their heads and let 'em know who's who, well, one day they'll respect me. But I can't just get bogged down and take any old job, you know, a filling station job or something. Ah, hell they'll get more respect, my kids for me, right now, than they would if I was somewhere just a regular worker."

Especially for men who have been highly successful athletes (and never have had to learn to "lose gracefully"), the move from sports to work-career as a means of establishing connection and identity in the world is a "natural" transition. Breadwinning becomes a man's socially learned means of seeking attachment, both with his family and, more abstractly, with "society." What is salient (and sometimes tragic) is that the care that a woman gives her family usually puts her into direct daily contact with her family's physical, psychological, and emotional needs. A man's care is usually expressed more abstractly, often in his absence, as his work removes him from day-to-day, moment-to-moment contact with his family.

A man may want, even *crave,* more direct connection with his family, but that connection, and the *time* it takes to establish and maintain it, may cause him to lose the competitive edge he needs to win in the world of work—and that is the arena in which he feels he will ultimately be judged in terms of his success or failure as a man. But it is not simply a matter of *time* spent away from family which is at issue here. As Dizard's research shows clearly, the more "success oriented" a man is, the more "instrumental" his personality will tend to be, thus increasing the psychological and emotional distance between himself and his family.[19]

CHANGING MEANINGS OF SUCCESS IN MIDLIFE

The intense, sometimes obsessive, early adulthood period of striving for work and career success that we see in the lives of Jackie Ridgle and Ray Fosse often begins to change in midlife, when many men experience what Levinson calls "detribalization." Here, the man "becomes more critical of the tribe, the particular groups, institutions, and traditions that have the greatest significance for him, the social matrix to which he is most attached. He is less dependent upon tribal rewards, more questioning of tribal values. . . . The result of this shift is normally not a marked disengagement from the external world but a greater integration of attachment and separateness."[20]

Detribalization—putting less emphasis on how one is defined by others and becoming more self-motivated and self-generating—is often accompanied by a growing sense of *flawed* or *qualified* success. A man's early adulthood dream of success begins to tarnish, appearing more and more as an illusion. Or, the success that a man *has* achieved begins to appear hollow and meaningless, possibly because it has not delivered the closeness he truly craves. The fading, or the loss, of the dream involves a process of mourning, but, as Levinson points out, it can also be a very liberating process in opening the man up for new experiences, new kinds of relationships, and new dreams.

For instance, Russ Ellis states that a few years ago he experienced a midlife crisis when he came to the realization that "I was never going to be on the cover of *Time.*" His wife had a T-shirt made for him with the message *Dare to Be Average* emblazoned on it.

> And it doesn't really *mean* dare to be average—it means dare to take the pressure off yourself, you know? Dare to be a normal person. It gets a funny reaction from people. I think it hits at that place where somehow we all think that we're going to wind up on the cover of *Time* or something, you know? Do you have that? That some day, somewhere, you're gonna be *great,* and everyone will know, everyone will recognize it? Now, I'd rather be great because I'm *good*—and maybe that'll turn

into something that's acknowledged, but not at the headline level. I'm not racing so much; I'm concerned that my feet are planted on the ground and that I'm good.

[It sounds like you're running now, as opposed to racing?]

I guess—but running and racing have the same goals. *[Laughs, pauses, then speaks more thoughtfully.]* But maybe you're right—that's a wonderful analogy. Pacing myself. Running is more intelligent—more familiarity with your abilities, your patterns of workouts, who you're running against, the nature of the track, your position, alertness. You have more of an internal clock.

Russ Ellis's midlife detribalization—his transition from a "racer" to a runner"—has left him more comfortable with himself, with his abilities and limitations. He has also experienced an expansion of his ability to experience intimacy with a woman. He had never been comfortable with the "typical jock attitude" toward sex and women,

but I generally maintained a performance attitude about sex for a long time, which was not as enjoyable as it became after I learned to be more like what I thought a woman was like. In other words, when I let myself experience my own body, in a delicious and receptive way rather than in a power, overwhelming way. That was wonderful! *[Laughs.]* To experience my body as someone desired and given to. That's one of the better things. I think I only achieved that very profound intimacy that's found between people, really quite extraordinary, quite recently. *[Long pause.]* It's quite something, quite something. And I feel more fully inducted into the human race by knowing about that.

TOWARD A REDEFINITION OF SUCCESS AND MASCULINITY

"A man in America is a failed boy," wrote John Updike in 1960. Indeed, Updike's ex-athlete Rabbit Angstrom's struggles to achieve meaning and identity in midlife reflect a common theme in modern literature. Social scientific research has suggested that the contemporary sense of failure and inadequacy felt by many American males is largely the result of unrealistic and unachievable social definitions of masculinity and success.[21] This research has suggested that there is more to it than that. Contemporary males often feel empty, alienated, isolated, and as failures because the socially learned means through which they seek validation and identity (achievement in the public worlds of sports and work) do not deliver what is actually craved and needed: intimate connection and unity with other human beings. In fact, the lure of sports becomes a sort of trap. For boys who experience early success in sports, the resulting attention they receive becomes a convenient and attractive means of experiencing attachment with other people within a social context that allows the young male to maintain his "firm ego boundaries" and thus his separation from others. But it appears that, more often than not, athletic participation serves only to exacerbate the already problematic, insecure, and ambivalent nature of males' self-images, and thus their ability to establish and maintain close and intimate relationships with other people. Some men, as they reach midlife, eventually achieve a level of individuation—often through a midlife crisis—that leads to a redefinition of success and an expansion of their ability to experience attachment and intimacy.

Men's personal definitions of success often change in midlife, but this research, as well as that done by Farrell and Rosenberg,[22] suggests that only a *portion* of males experience a midlife crisis that results in the man's transcending his instrumental personality in favor of a more affective generativity. The midlife discovery that the achievement game is an unfulfilling rat race can as easily lead to cynical detachment and greater alienation as it can to detribalization and expanded relational capacities. In other words, there is no assurance that Jackie Ridgle, as he ages, will transform himself from a "racer" to a "runner," as Russ Ellis has. Even if he does change in this way, it is likely that he will have missed participating in the formative years of his children's lives.

Thus the fundamental questions facing future examinations of men's lives should focus on building and understanding of just what the keys are to such a shift at midlife. How are individual men's changes, crises, and relationships affected, shaped, and sometimes contradicted by the social, cultural, and political contexts in which they find themselves? And what *social* changes might make it more likely that boys and men might have more balanced personalities and needs at an *early* age?

An analysis of men's lives that simply describes personal changes while taking social structure as a given cannot adequately *ask* these questions. But an analysis that not only describes changes in male identity throughout the life course but also critically examines the socially structured and defined meaning of "masculinity" can and must ask these questions.

If many of the problems faced by all men (not just athletes) today are to be dealt with, class, ethnic, and sexual preference divisions must be confronted. This would necessarily involve the development of a more cooperative and nurturant ethic among men, as well as a more egalitarian and democratically organized economic system. And since the sports world is an important cultural process that serves, partly to socialize boys and young men to hierarchical, competitive, and aggressive values, the sporting arena is an important context in which to begin to confront the need for a humanization of men.

Yet, if the analysis presented here is correct, the developing psychology of young boys is predisposed to be attracted to the present structure and values of the sports world, so any attempt *simply* to infuse cooperative and egalitarian values into sports is likely to be an exercise in futility. The need for equality between men and women, in the public realm as well as in the home, is a fundamental prerequisite for the humanization of men, sports, and society. One of the most important changes that men could make would be to become more equally involved in parenting. The development of early bonding between fathers and infants (in addition to that between mothers and infants), along with nonsexist child rearing in the family, schools, and sports would have far-reaching effects on society: Boys and men could grow up more psychologically secure, more able to develop balance between separation and attachment, more able at an earlier age to appreciate intimate relationships with other men without destructive and crippling competition and homophobia. A young male with a more secure and balanced personality might also be able to *enjoy* athletic activities for what they really have to offer: the opportunity to engage in healthy exercise, to push oneself toward excellence, and to bond with others in a challenging and fun activity.

NOTES

1. J. Lever, "Sex Differences in the Games Children Play," *Social Problems* 23 (1976).
2. D. Sabo, "Sport Patriarchy and Male Identity: New Questions about Men and Sport," *Arena Review* 9, no. 2, 1985.
3. R. Sennett and J. Cobb, *The Hidden Injuries of Class* (New York: Random House, 1973); and L. B. Rubin, *Worlds of Pain: Life in the Working Class Family* (New York: Basic Books, 1976).
4. D. W. Ball, "Failure in Sport," *American Sociological Review* 41 (1976); J.J. Coakley, *Sports in Society* (St. Louis: Mosby, 1978); D. S. Harris and D. S. Eitzen, "The Consequences of Failure in Sport," *Urban Life* 7 (July 1978): 2; G. B. Leonard, "Winning Isn't Everything: It's Nothing," in *Jock: Sports and Male Identity*, ed. D. Sabo and R. Runfola (Englewood Cliffs, NJ: Prentice Hall, 1980); W. E. Schafer, "Sport and Male Sex Role Socialization," *Sport Sociology Bulletin* 4 (Fall 1975); R. C. Townsend, "The Competitive Male as Loser," in Sabo and Runfola, eds., *Jock;* and T. Tutko and W. Bruns, *Winning Is Everything and Other American Myths* (New York: Macmillan, 1976).
5. In contrast with the importance put on success by millions of boys, the number who "make it" is incredibly small. There are approximately 600 players in major-league baseball, with an average career span of 7 years. Approximately 6–7% of all high school football players ever play in college. Roughly 8% of all draft-eligible college football and basketball athletes are drafted by the pros, and only 2% ever sign a professional contract. The average career for NFL athletes is now 4 years, and for the NBA it is only 3.4 years. Thus the odds of getting anywhere *near* the top are very thin—and if one is talented and lucky enough to get there, his stay will be brief. See H. Edwards, "The Collegiate Athletic Arms Race: Origins and Implications of the 'Rule 48' Controversy," *Journal of Sport and Social Issues* 8, no. 1 (Winter–Spring 1984); Harris and Eitzen, "Consequences of Failure"; and P. Hill and B. Lowe, "The Inevitable Metathesis of the Retiring Athlete," *International Review of Sport Sociology* 9, nos. 3–4 (1978).
6. Schafer, "Sport and Male Sex Role," p. *50.*
7. C. Gilligan, *In a Different Voice: Psychological Theory and Women's Development* (Cambridge: Harvard University Press, 1982); J. Piaget, *The Moral Judgement of the Child* (New York: Free Press, 1965); and Lever, "Games Children Play."
8. P. G. Filene, *Him/Her/Self: Sex Roles in Modern America* (New York: Harcourt Brace Jovanovich, 1975).
9. J. Hantover, "The Boy Scouts and the Validation of Masculinity," *Journal of Social Issues* 34 (1978): 1.
10. J. L. Dubbert, *A Man's Place: Masculinity in Transition* (Englewood Cliffs, NJ: Prentice Hall, 1979).
11. A. Tolson, *The Limits of Masculinity* (New York: Harper and Row, 1977).
12. C. W. Mills, *White Collar* (London: Oxford University Press, 1951).
13. D. J. Levinson, *The Seasons of a Man's Life* (New York: Ballantine, 1978).
14. Ibid., p. 195.
15. N. Chodorow, *The Reproduction of Mothering* (Berkeley: University of California Press, 1978).

16. Hill and Lowe, "Metathesis of Retiring Athlete," pp. 3–4; and B. D. McPherson, "Former Professional Athletes' Adjustment to Retirement," *Physician and Sports Medicine* (August 1978).

17. Edwards, "Collegiate Athletic Arms Race."

18. Levinson, *Seasons of a Man's Life.*

19. J. E. Dizard, "The Price of Success," in *Social Change and the Family,* ed. J. E. Dizard (Chicago: Community and Family Study Center, University of Chicago, 1968).

20. Levinson, *Seasons of a Man's Life,* p. 242.

21. J. H. Pleck, *The Myth of Masculinity* (Cambridge: MIT Press, 1982); Sennett and Cobb, *The Hidden Injuries of Class;* Rubin, *Worlds of Pain;* and Tolson, *Limits of Masculinity.*

22. M. P. Farrell and S. D. Rosenberg, *Men at Midlife* (Boston: Auburn House, 1981).

* FOR FURTHER STUDY *

Acosta, R. Vivian, and Linda Jean Carpenter. Annual report. "Women in Intercollegiate Sport." Department of Physical Education and Exercise Science, Brooklyn College.

Anderson, Deborah, John J. Cheslock, and Ronald G. Ehrenberg. 2006. "Gender Equity in Intercollegiate Athletics: Determinants of Title IX Compliance." *Journal of Higher Education* 77: 225–250.

Burstyn, Varda. 1999. *The Rites of Men: Manhood, Politics, and the Culture of Sport.* Toronto: University of Toronto Press.

Chronicle of Higher Education. 2002. "Gender Equity in College Sports: 6 Views." (December 6): B7–B10.

Coakley, Jay. 2007. *Sports in Society: Issues and Controversies.* 9th ed. New York: McGraw-Hill.

Conniff, Ruth. 1998. "The Joy of Women's Sports." *Nation* (August 10–17): 26–30.

Eitzen, D. Stanley. 2009. *Fair and Foul: Beyond the Myths and Paradoxes of Sport.* 4th ed. Lanham, MD: Rowman and Littlefield.

Eitzen, D. Stanley, and George H. Sage. 2009. *Sociology of North American Sport.* 8th ed. Boulder, CO: Paradigm.

Hargreaves, Jennifer. 2000. *Heroines of Sport: The Politics of Difference and Identity.* London: Routledge.

Higgs, Catriona T., Karen H. Weiller, and Scott B. Martin. 2003. "Gender Bias in the 1996 Olympic Games: A Comparative Analysis." *Journal of Sport and Social Issues* 27 (February): 52–64.

Hogan, Jackie. 2003. "Staging a Nation: Gendered and Ethnicized Discourses of National Identity in Olympic Opening Ceremonies." *Journal of Sport and Social Issues* 27 (May): 100–123.

Huffman, Suzanne C., A. Tuggle, and Dana Scott Rosengard. 2004. "How Campus Media Cover Sports: The Gender-Equity Issue, One Generation Later." *Mass Communication and Society* 7: 475–489.

Juffer, Jane. 2002. "Who's the Man? Sammy Sosa, Latinos, and Televisual Redefinitions of the 'American' Pastime." *Journal of Sport and Social Issues* 26 (November): 337–359.

Lapchick, Richard E. Annual Report: *Racial and Gender Report Card.* Institute for Diversity and Ethics in Sport, University of Central Florida–Orlando.

McDonagh, Eileen, and Laura Pappano. 2008. *Playing with the Boys: Why Separate Is Not Equal in Sports.* New York: Oxford University Press.

Messner, Michael A. 2002. *Taking the Field: Women, Men, and Sports.* Minneapolis: University of Minnesota Press.

Nylund, David. 2003. "Taking a Slice at Sexism: The Controversy over the Exclusionary Membership Practices of the Augusta National Golf Club." *Journal of Sport and Social Issues* 27 (May): 195–202.

O'Reilly, Jean, and Susan K. Cahn eds. 2007. *Women and Sports in the United States: A Documentary Reader.* Boston: Northeastern University Press.

Suggs, Welch. 2005. *A Place on the Team: The Triumph and Tragedy of Title IX.* Princeton, NJ: Princeton University Press.

Tucker, Lori W., and Janet B. Parks. 2001. "Effects of Gender and Sport Type on Intercollegiate Athletes' Perceptions of the Legitimacy of Aggressive Behaviors in Sport." *Sociology of Sport Journal* 18 (4): 403–413.

Wachs, Faye Linda. 2002. "Leveling the Playing Field: Negotiating Gendered Rules in Coed Softball." *Journal of Sport and Social Issues* 26 (August): 300–316.
Weistart, John. 1998. "Title IX and Intercollegiate Sports: Equal Opportunity?" *Brookings Review* 16 (Fall): 39–43.
Zimbalist, Andrew. 2000. "Backlash against Title IX: An End Run around Female Athletes." *Chronicle of Higher Education* (March 3): B9–B10.

PART TWELVE

Structured Inequality: Sport and Sexuality

Previous sections on structured inequality examined categories of people designated as minorities in society because of their race/ethnicity or gender. The members of these social categories suffer from powerlessness, negative stereotypes, and discrimination. This unit looks at another type of minority group. Unlike the other three minorities, which are disadvantaged because of economic circumstances or ascribed characteristics, the distinguishing feature of the minority examined in this section—homosexuality—is the object of discrimination because it is defined by the majority as different and, therefore, deviant. It is important to underscore a crucial point: *Homosexuality is not inherently deviant, but it is defined and labeled as deviant.*[1] Put another way, "Variance from the societal norm of heterosexuality is not a social problem; *the societal response to it is.*"[2]

An estimated 14 million adults in the United States identify themselves as gay or lesbian. Among these are former elite athletes: Glenn Burke (major-league baseball), David Kopay (professional football), Greg Louganis and Tom Waddell (Olympians), and Martina Navratilova (tennis). Athletes who publicly acknowledge their homosexuality, however, are rare because of the extent of homophobia among athletes, coaches, fans, and the sports media. "The extent of homophobia in the sports world is staggering: manifestations range from eight-year-old boys who put each other down with taunts of 'queer,' 'faggot,' or 'sissy' to high-school locker-room boasting (and, often, lying) about sexual conquests of females, and to college athletes bonding together with a little Saturday night "queer-bashing." To be suspected of being gay, and to be unable to prove one's heterosexual status in the sports world, is clearly not acceptable—indeed, it can be downright dangerous."[3]

Women in sport, more than men, endure intense scrutiny about their sexual identities.[4] This is the subject of selection 35, by Pat Griffin, as she discusses (1) the political functions of homophobia in a sexist and heterosexist culture, (2) the manifestations of homophobia in women's sport, (3) the beliefs that support homophobia in women's sport, and (4) strategies for confronting homophobia in women's sport.

The second selection, by journalist Anthony Cotton, describes the dilemmas that gay athletes face. The final selection, 37, is an overview of the issues related to providing equal opportunities for transgender student-athletes.

NOTES

1. D. Stanley Eitzen, Maxine Baca Zinn, and Kelly Eitzen Smith, *Social Problems,* 11th ed. (Boston: Allyn and Bacon, 2007), p. 288.

2. Ibid., p. 296.

3. Michael A. Messner. "AIDS, Homophobia, and Sports." In Michael A. Messner and Donald F. Sabo, *Sex, Violence, and Power in Sports: Rethinking Masculinity* (Freedom, CA: Crossing Press, 1994), p. 121.

4. See Debra E. Blum, "College Sports' L-Word," *Chronicle of Higher Education* (March 9, 1994): A35–A36.

35

Changing the Game

Homophobia, Sexism, and Lesbians in Sport

Pat Griffin

Throughout the history of Western culture, restrictions have been placed on women's sport participation. These restrictions are enforced through sanctions that evolved to match each successive social climate. Women caught merely observing the male athletes competing in the early Greek Olympic Games were put to death. When Baron DeCoubertin revived the Olympic tradition in 1896, women were invited as spectators but barred from participation. Even in the present-day Olympic Games, women may compete in only one-third of the events.

Although the death penalty for female spectators was too extreme for the late 19th and early 20th centuries, an increasingly influential medical establishment warned white upper-class women about the debilitating physiological effects of vigorous athleticism, particularly on the reproductive system. Women were cautioned about other "masculinizing effects" as well, such as deeper voices, facial hair, and overdeveloped arms and legs. The intent of these warnings was to temper and control women's sport participation and to keep women focused on their "natural" and "patriotic" roles as wives and mothers (Lenskyj, 1986).

During the 1920s and 1930s, as the predicted dire physical consequences proved untrue, strong social taboos restricting female athleticism evolved. Instead of warnings about facial hair and displaced uteruses, women in sport were intimidated by fears of

Source: Reprinted by permission from P. Griffin, "Changing the Game: Homophobia, Sexism, and Lesbians in Sport" *Quest* 44, no. 2 (1992): 251–265.

losing social approval. Close female friendships, accepted and even idealized in the 19th century, became suspect when male sexologists like Freud "discovered" female sexuality sexuality in the early 20th century (Faderman, 1981, 1991; Katz, 1976). In the 1930s, as psychology and psychiatry became respected subfields in medicine, these doctors warned of a new menace. An entire typology was created to diagnose the "mannish lesbian," whose depraved sexual appetite and preference for masculine dress and activity were identified as symptoms of psychological disturbance (Newton, 1989). Social commentators in the popular press warned parents about the dangers of allowing impressionable daughters to spend time in all-female environments (Faderman, 1991; Smith-Rosenberg, 1989).

As a result, women's colleges and sports teams were assumed to be places where mannish lesbians lurked. Women in sport and physical education especially fit the profile of women to watch out for: they were in groups without men, they were not engaged in activities thought to enhance their abilities to be good wives and mothers, and they were being physically active in sport, a male activity. Because lesbians were assumed to be masculine creatures who rejected their female identity and roles as wives and mothers, athletic women became highly suspect.

The image of the sick, masculine lesbian sexual predator and her association with athleticism persists in the late 20th century. The power of this image to control and intimidate women is as strong today as it was 60 years ago. What accounts for the staying power of a stereotype that is so extreme it should be laughable except that so many people believe it to be accurate? Whose interests are served by stigmatizing lesbians and accusing women in sport of being lesbians? Why does sport participation by women in the late 20th century continue to be so threatening to the social order? How have women in sport responded to associations with lesbians? How effective have these responses been in defusing concern about lesbians in sport?

The purpose of this chapter is to discuss the issue of lesbians in sport from a feminist perspective that analyzes the function of socially constructed gender roles and sexual identities in maintaining male dominance in North American society. I share the perspective taken by other sport feminists that lesbian and feminist sport participation is a threat to male domination (Bennett, Whitaker, Smith, and Sablove, 1987; Birrell *and* Richter, 1987; Hall, 1987; Lenskyj, 1986; Messner *and* Sabo, 1990). In a sexist and heterosexist society (in which heterosexuality is reified as the only normal, natural, and acceptable sexual orientation), women who defy the accepted feminine role or reject a heterosexual identity threaten to upset the imbalance of power enjoyed by white heterosexual men in a patriarchal society (Bryson, 1987). The creation of the mannish lesbian as a pathological condition by early 20th-century male medical doctors provided an effective means to control all women and neutralize challenges to the sexist status quo.

To understand the social stigma associated with lesbian participation in sport, the function of homophobia in maintaining the sexist and heterosexist status quo must be examined (Lenskyj, 1991). Greendorfer (1991) challenged the traditional definition of homophobia as an irrational fear and intolerance of lesbians and gay men. In questioning how irrational homophobia really is, Greendorfer highlighted the systematic and pervasive cultural nature of homophobia. Fear and hatred of lesbians and gay men is more than individual prejudice (Kitzinger, 1987). Homophobia is a powerful political weapon of sexism (Pharr, 1988). The lesbian label is used to define the boundaries of acceptable female behavior in a patriarchal culture: When a woman is called a lesbian, she knows she is out of bounds. Because lesbian identity carries the extreme negative social stigma created by early 20th-century sexologists, most women are loathe to be associated with it. Because women's sport has been labeled a lesbian activity, women in sport are particularly sensitive and vulnerable to the use of the lesbian label to intimidate.

HOW IS HOMOPHOBIA MANIFESTED IN WOMEN'S SPORT?

Manifestations of homophobia in women's sport can be divided into six categories: (a) silence, (b) denial, (c) apology, (d) promotion of a heterosexy image, (e) attacks on lesbians, and (f) preference for male coaches. An exploration of these manifestations illuminates the pervasive nature of prejudice against lesbians in sport and the power of the lesbian stigma to control and marginalize women's sport.

Silence

Silence is the most consistent and enduring manifestation of homophobia in women's sport. From Billie Jean King's revelation of a lesbian relationship in 1981 to the publicity surrounding Penn State women's basketball coach Rene Portland's no-lesbian policy (Lederman, 1991; Longman, 1991), the professional and college sports establishment responds with silence to eruptions of public attention to lesbians in sport. Reporters who attempt to discuss lesbians in sport with sport organizations, athletic directors, coaches, and athletes are typically rebuffed (Lipsyte, 1991), and women in sport wait, hoping the scrutiny will disappear as quickly as possible. Women live in fear that whatever meager gains we have made in sport are always one lesbian scandal away from being wiped out.

Even without the provocation of public scrutiny or threat of scandal, silent avoidance is the strategy of choice. Organizers of coaches' or athletic administrators' conferences rarely schedule programs on homophobia in sport, and when they do, it is always a controversial decision made with fear and concern about the consequences of public dialogue (Krebs, 1984; Lenskyj, 1990). Lesbians in sport are treated like nasty secrets that must be kept locked tightly in the closet. Lesbians, of course, are expected to maintain deep cover at all times. Not surprisingly, most lesbians in sport choose to remain hidden rather than face potential public condemnation. Friends of lesbians protect this secret from outsiders, and the unspoken pact of silence is maintained and passed on to each new generation of women in sport.

Silence has provided some protection. Keeping the closet door locked is an understandable strategy when women in sport are trying to gain social approval in a sexist society and there is no sense that change is possible. Maintaining silence is a survival strategy in a society hostile to women in general and lesbians in particular. How effectively silence enhances sport opportunities for women or defuses homophobia, however, is open to serious question.

Denial

If forced to break silence, many coaches, athletic directors, and athletes resort to denial. High school athletes and their parents often ask college coaches if there are lesbians in their programs. In response, many coaches deny that there are lesbians in sport, at least among athletes or coaches at *their* schools (Fields, 1983). These denials only serve to intensify curiosity and determination to find out who and where these mysterious women are. The closet, it turns out, is made of glass: People know lesbians are in sport despite these denials.

In some cases, parents and athletes who suspect that a respected and loved coach is a lesbian either deny or overlook her sexual identity because they cannot make sense of the apparent contradiction: a lesbian who is competent, loved, and respected. In other instances, a respected lesbian coach is seen as an exception because she does not fit the unflattering lesbian stereotype most people accept as accurate. The end result in any case is to deny the presence of lesbians in sport.

Apology

The third manifestation of homophobia in sport is apology (Felshin, 1974). In an attempt to compensate for an unsavory reputation, women in sport try to promote a feminine image and focus public attention on those who meet white heterosexual standards of beauty. Women in sport have a tradition of assuring ourselves and others that sport participation is consistent with traditional notions of femininity and that women are not masculinized by sport experiences (Gornick, 1971; Hicks, 1979; Locke and Jensen, 1970). To this end, athletes are encouraged, or required in some cases, to engage in the protective camouflage of feminine drag. Professional athletes and college teams are told to wear dresses or attend seminars to learn how to apply makeup, style hair, and select clothes ("Image Lady," 1987). Athletes are encouraged to be seen with boyfriends and reminded to act like ladies when away from the gym (DePaul University's 1984 women's basketball brochure).

The Women's Sports Foundation (WSF) annual dinner, attended by many well-known professional and amateur female athletes, is preceded by an opportunity for the athletes to get free hairstyling and makeup applications before they sit down to eat with the male corporate sponsors, whose money supports many WSF programs. The men attending the dinner are not offered similar help with their appearance. The message is that female athletes in their natural state are not acceptable or attractive and therefore must be fixed and "femmed up" to compensate for their athleticism.

Femininity, however, is a code word for heterosexuality. The underlying fear is not that a female athlete or coach will appear too plain or out of style; the real fear is that she will look like a dyke or, even worse, is one. This intense blend of homophobic and sexist standards of feminine attractiveness remind women in sport that to be acceptable, we must monitor our behavior and appearance at all times.

Silence, denial, and apology are defensive reactions that reflect the power of the lesbian label to intimidate women. These responses ensure that women's sport will be held hostage to the *L* word. As long as questions about lesbians in sport are met with silence, denial, and apology, women can be sent scurrying back to our places on the margins of sport, grateful for the modicum of public approval we have achieved and fearful of losing it.

NEW MANIFESTATIONS OF HOMOPHOBIA IN WOMEN'S SPORT

In the past 10 years, three more responses have developed in reaction to the persistence of the association of sport with lesbians. These manifestations have developed at the same time that women's sport has become more visible, potentially marketable, and increasingly under the control of men and men's sport organizations. Representing an intensified effort to purge the lesbian image, these new strategies reflect a new low in mean-spirited intimidation.

Promotion of a Heterosexy Image

Where presenting a feminine image previously sufficed, corporate sponsors, professional women's sport organizations, some women's college teams, and individual athletes have moved beyond presenting a feminine image to adopting a more explicit display of heterosex appeal. The Ladies Professional Golf Association's 1989 promotional material featured photographs of its pro golfers posing pin-up style in swimsuits (Diaz, 1989). College sport promotional literature has employed double entendres and sexual innuendo to sell women's teams. The women's basketball promotional brochure from Northwestern State University of Louisiana included a photograph of the women's team dressed in Playboy bunny outfits. The copy crowed "These girls can play, boy!" and invited basketball fans to watch games in the "Pleasure Palace" (Solomon, 1991). Popular magazines have featured young, professional female athletes, like Monica Seles or Steffi Graf, in cleavage-revealing heterosexual glamour drag (Kiersh, 1990).

In a more muted attempt to project a heterosexual image, stories about married female athletes and coaches routinely include husbands and children in ways rarely seen when male coaches and athletes are profiled. A recent nationally televised basketball game between the women's teams from the University of Texas and the University of Tennessee featured a half-time profile of the coaches as wives and mothers. The popular press also brings us testimonials from female athletes who have had children claiming that their athletic performance has improved since becoming mothers. All of this to reassure the public, and perhaps ourselves as women in sport, that we are normal despite our athletic interests.

Attacks on Lesbians in Sport

Women in sport endure intense scrutiny of our collective and individual femininity and sexual identities. Innuendo, concern, and prurient curiosity about the sexual identity of female coaches and athletes come from coaches, athletic directors, sports reporters, parents of female athletes, teammates, fans, and the general public (South, Glynn, Rodack, and Capettini, 1990). This manifestation of homophobia is familiar to most people associated with women's sport. Over the last 10 to 12 years, however, concern about lesbians in sport has taken a nasty turn.

Though lesbians in sport have always felt pressure to stay closeted, coaches and athletic directors now openly prohibit lesbian coaches and athletes (Brownworth, 1991; Figel, 1986; Longman, 1991). In a style reminiscent of 1950s McCarthyism, some coaches proclaim their antilesbian policies as an introduction to their programs. Athletes thought to be lesbian are dropped from teams, find themselves benched, or are suddenly ostracized by coaches and teammates (Brownworth, 1991). Coaches impose informal quotas on the number of lesbians, or at least on the number of athletes they think look like lesbians, on their teams (Brownworth, 1991). At some schools, a new coach's heterosexual credentials are scrutinized as carefully as her professional qualifications (Fields, 1983). Coaches thought to be lesbians are fired or intimidated into resigning. These dismissals are not the result of any unethical behavior on the part of the women accused but happen simply because of assumptions made about their sexual identity.

Collegiate and high school female athletes endure lesbian-baiting (name-calling, taunting, and other forms of harassment) from male athletes, heterosexual teammates, opposing teams, spectators, classmates, and sometimes their own coaches (Brownworth, 1991; Fields, 1983; Spander, 1991; Thomas, 1990). Female coaches thought to be lesbians endure harassing phone calls and antilesbian graffiti slipped under their office doors. During a recent National Collegiate Athletic Association (NCAA) women's basketball championship, it was rumored that a group of male coaches went to the local lesbian bar to spy on lesbian coaches who might be there. Another rumor circulated about a list categorizing Division I women's basketball coaches by their sexual identity so that parents of prospective athletes could use this information to avoid schools where lesbians coach. Whether or not these rumors are true doesn't matter: The rumor itself is intimidating enough to remind women in sport that we are being watched and that if we step out of line, we will be punished.

Negative recruiting is perhaps the most self-serving of all the attacks on lesbians in sport. Negative recruiting occurs when college coaches or athletic department personnel reassure prospective athletes and their parents not only that there are no lesbians in this program but also that there *are* lesbians in a rival school's program (Fields, 1983). By playing on parents' and athletes' fear and ignorance, these coaches imply that young women will be safe in their programs but not at a rival school where bull dykes stalk the locker room in search of fresh young conquests.

Fears about lesbian stereotypes are fueled by a high-profile Christian presence at many national championships and coaches' conferences. The Fellowship of Christian Athletes, which regularly sponsors meal functions for coaches at these events, distributed a free antihomosexual booklet to coaches and athletes. Entitled *Emotional Dependency: A Threat to Close Friendships,* this booklet plays into all of the stereotypes of lesbians (Rentzel, 1987). A drawing of a sad young woman and an older woman on the cover hints at the dangers of close female friendships. Unencumbered by any reasonable factual knowledge about homosexuality, the booklet identifies the symptoms of emotional dependency and how this "leads" to homosexual relationships. Finally, the path out of this "counterfeit" intimacy through prayer and discipline is described. The booklet is published by Exodus, a fundamentalist Christian organization devoted to the "redemption" of homosexuals from their "disorder."

By allowing the active participation of antigay organizations in coaches' meetings and championship events, sport governing bodies like the NCAA and the Women's Basketball Coaches' Association are taking an active role in the perpetuation of discrimination against lesbians in sport and the stigmatization of all friendships among women in sport. In this intimidating climate, all women in sport must deal with the double burden of maintaining high-profile heterosexual images and living in terror of being called lesbians.

Preference for Male Coaches

Many parents, athletes, and athletic administrators prefer that men coach women's teams. This preference reflects a lethal mix of sexism and homophobia. Some people believe, based on gender and lesbian stereotypes, that men are better coaches than women. Although a recent NCAA survey of female athletes (NCAA, 1991) indicated that 61 percent of the respondents did not have a gender preference for their coaches, respondents were concerned about the images they thought male and female coaches had among their friends and family: 65 percent believed that female coaches were looked upon favorably by family and friends whereas 84 percent believed that male coaches were looked on favorably by family and friends.

Recent studies have documented the increase in the number of men coaching women's teams (Acosta *and* Carpenter, 1988). At least part of this increase can be attributed to homophobia. Thorngren (1991), in a study of female coaches, asked respondents how homophobia affected them. These coaches identified hiring and job retention as problems. They cited examples where men were hired to coach women's teams specifically to change a tarnished or negative (read *lesbian)* team image. Thorngren described this as a "cloaking" phenomenon, in which a team's lesbian image is hidden or countered by the presence of a male coach. Consistent with this perception, anecdotal reports from other female head coaches reveal that some believe it essential to hire a male assistant coach to lend a heterosexual persona to a women's team. The coaches in Thorngren's study also reported that women (married and single) leave coaching because of the pressure and stress of constantly having to deal with lesbian labels and stereotypes. Looking at the increase in the number of men coaching women's teams over the last 10 years, it is clear how male coaches have benefitted from sexism and homophobia in women's sport.

SUSPICION, COLLUSION, AND BETRAYAL AMONG WOMEN IN SPORT

The few research studies addressing homophobia or lesbians in sport, as well as informal anecdotal information, have revealed that many women have internalized sexist and homophobic values and beliefs (Blinde, 1990; Griffin, 1987; Guthrie, 1982; Morgan, 1990; Thorngren, 1990, 1991; Woods, 1990). Blinde interviewed women athletes about the pressures and stress they experienced. Many talked about the lesbian image women's sport has and the shame they felt about being female athletes because of that image. Their discomfort with the topic was illustrated by their inability to even say the word *lesbian.* Instead, they made indirect references to it as a problem. Athletes talked in ways that clearly indicated they had bought into the negative images of lesbians, even as they denied that there were lesbians on their teams. These athletes also subscribed to the importance of projecting a feminine image and were discomforted by female athletes who didn't look or act feminine.

Quotes selected to accompany the NCAA survey and the Blinde study illustrate the degree to which many female athletes and coaches accept both the negative stigma attached to lesbian identity and the desirability of projecting a traditionally feminine image:

> The negative image of women in intercollegiate sport scares me. I've met too many lesbians in my college career. I don't want to have that image. (NCAA, 1991)

> Well, if you come and look at our team, I mean, if you saw Jane Doe, she's very pretty. If she walks down the street, everybody screams, you know, screams other things at her. But because she's on the field, it's dykes on spikes. If that isn't a stereotype, then who knows what is. (Blinde, p. 12)

> Homosexual females in this profession [coaching] definitely provide models and guidance in its worst for female athletes. I'd rather see a straight male coach females than a gay women. Homosexual coaches are killing us. (NCAA, 1991)

> I don't fit the stereotype. I mean the stereotype based around women that are very masculine and strong and athletic. I wouldn't say I'm pretty in pink, but I am feminine and I appear very feminine and I act that way. (Blinde, p. 12)

These attempts to distance oneself from the lesbian image and to embrace traditional standards of femininity set up a division among women in sport that can devastate friendships among teammates, poison coach-athlete relationships, and taint feelings about one's identity as an athlete and a woman. Some women restrict close friendships with other women to avoid the possibility that someone might think they are lesbians. Other women consciously cultivate high-profile heterosexual images by talking about their relationships with men and being seen with men as often as possible. As long as our energy is devoted to trying to fit into models of athleticism, gender, and sexuality that support a sexist and heterosexist culture, women in sport can be controlled by anyone who chooses to use our fears and insecurities against us.

UNDERLYING BELIEFS THAT KEEP WOMEN IN SPORT FROM CHALLENGING HOMOPHOBIA

The ability to understand the staying power of the lesbian stigma in sport is limited by several interconnected beliefs. An examination of these beliefs can reveal how past responses in dealing with lesbians in sport have reinforced the power of the lesbian label to intimidate and control.

A Woman's Sexual Identity Is Personal

This belief is perhaps the biggest obstacle to understanding women's oppression in a patriarchal culture (Kitzinger, 1987). As long as a women's sexual identity is seen as solely a private issue, how the lesbian label is used to intimidate all women and to weaken women's challenges to male-dominated institutions will never be understood. The lesbian label is a political weapon that can be used against any woman who steps out of line. Any woman who defies traditional gender roles is called a lesbian. Any woman who chooses a male-identified career is called a lesbian. Any woman who chooses not to have a sexual relationship with a man is called a lesbian. Any woman who speaks out against sexism is called a lesbian. As long as women are afraid to be called lesbians, this label is an effective tool to control all women and limit women's challenges to sexism. Although lesbians are the targets of attack in women's sport, all women in sport are victimized by the use of the lesbian label to intimidate and control.

When a woman's lesbian identity is assumed to be a private matter, homophobia and heterosexism are dismissed. The implication is that these matters are not appropriate topics for professional discussion. As a result, the fear, prejudice, and outright discrimination that thrive in silence are never addressed. A double standard operates, however, for lesbians and heterosexual women in sport. Although open acknowledgment of lesbians in sport is perceived as an inappropriate flaunting of personal life (what you do in the privacy of your home is none of my business), heterosexual women are encouraged to talk about their relationships with men, their children, and their roles as mothers.

Magazine articles about such heterosexual athletes as Chris Evert Mill, Florence Griffiths Joyner, Jackie Joyner Kersey, Joan Benoit, Nancy Lopez, and Mary Decker Slaney have often focused on their weddings, their husbands, or their children. Heterosexual professional athletes are routinely seen celebrating victories by hugging or kissing their husbands, but when Martina Navratilova went into the stands to hug *her* partner after winning the 1990 Wimbledon Championship, she was called a bad role model by former champion Margaret Court. Although heterosexual athletes and coaches are encouraged to display their personal lives to counteract the lesbian image in sport, lesbians are intimidated into invisibility for the same reason.

Claiming to Be Feminist Is Tantamount to Claiming to Be Lesbian

Claiming to be feminist is far too political for many women in sport. To successfully address the sexism and heterosexism in sport, however, women must begin to understand the necessity of seeing homophobia as a political issue and claim feminism as the unifying force needed to bring about change in a patriarchal culture. Part of the reluctance to embrace the feminist label is that feminists have been called lesbians in the same way that female athletes have and for the same reason: to intimidate women and prevent them from challenging the sexist status quo. Women in sport are already intimidated by the lesbian label. For many women, living with the athlete, lesbian, and feminist labels is stigma overload.

By accepting the negative stereotypes associated with these labels, women in sport collude in our own oppression. Rather than seeking social approval as a marginal part of sport in a sexist and heterosexist society, we need to be working for social change and control over our sport destinies. The image of an unrepentant lesbian feminist athlete is a patriarchal nightmare. She is a woman who has discovered her physical and political strength and who refuses to be intimidated by labels. Unfortunately, this image scares women in sport as much as it does those who benefit from the maintenance of the sexist and heterosexist status quo.

The Problem Is Lesbians in Sport Who Call Attention to Themselves

People who believe this assume that as long as lesbians are invisible, our presence will be tolerated and women's sport will progress. The issue for these people is not that there are lesbians in sport but how visible we are. Buying into silence this way has never worked. Other than Martina Navratilova, lesbians in sport are already deeply closeted (Bull, 1991; Muscatine, 1991). This careful camouflage of lesbians has not made women's sport less suspect or less vulnerable to intimidation. Despite efforts to keep the focus on the pretty ones or the ones with husbands and children, women in sport still carry the lesbian stigma into every gym and onto every playing field.

Women in sport must begin to understand that it wouldn't matter if there were no lesbians in sport. The lesbian label would still be used to intimidate and control women's athletics. The energy expended in making lesbians invisible and projecting a happy heterosexual image keeps women in sport fighting among ourselves rather than confronting the heterosexism and sexism that our responses unintentionally serve.

Lesbians Are Bad Role Models and Sexual Predators

This belief buys into all the unsavory lesbian stereotypes left over from the late 19th-century medical doctors who made homosexuality pathological and the early

20th-century sexologists who made female friendships morbid. In reality, there are already numerous closeted lesbians in sport who are highly admired role models. It is the perversity of prejudice that merely knowing about the sexual identity of these admired women instantly turns them into unfit role models.

The sexual-predator stereotype is a particularly pernicious slander on lesbians in sport (South et al., 1990). There is no evidence that lesbians are sexual predators. In fact, statistics on sexual harassment, rape, sexual abuse, and other forms of violence and intimidation show that these offenses are overwhelmingly heterosexual male assaults against women and girls. If we need to be concerned about sexual offenses among coaches or athletes, a better case could be made that it is heterosexual men who should be watched carefully. Blinde (1989) reported that many female athletes, like their male counterparts, are subjected to academic, physical, social, and emotional exploitation by their coaches. When men coach women in a heterosexist and sexist culture, there is the additional potential for sexual and gender-based exploitation when the unequal gender dynamics in the larger society are played out in the coach-athlete relationship.

It is difficult to imagine anyone in women's sport, regardless of sexual identity, condoning coercive sexual relationships of any kind. Even consensual sexual relationships between coaches and athletes involve inherent power differences that make such relationships questionable and can have a negative impact on the athlete as well as on the rest of the team. This kind of behavior should be addressed regardless of the gender or sexual identity of the coaches and athletes involved instead of assuming that lesbian athletes or coaches present a greater problem than others.

Being Called Lesbian or Being Associated with Lesbians Is the Worst Thing That Can Happen in Women's Sport

As long as women in sport buy into the power of the lesbian label to intimidate us, we will never control our sport experience. Blaming lesbians for women's sports' bad image and failure to gain more popularity divides women and keeps us fighting among ourselves. In this way, we collude in maintaining our marginal status by keeping alive the power of the lesbian label to intimidate women into silence, betrayal, and denial. This keeps our energies directed inward rather that outward at the sexism that homophobia serves. Blaming lesbians keeps all women in their place, scurrying to present an image that is acceptable in a sexist and heterosexist society. This keeps our attention diverted from asking other questions: Why are strong female athletes and coaches so threatening to a patriarchal society? Whose interests are served by trivializing and stigmatizing women in sport?

Women in sport need to redefine the problem. Instead of naming and blaming lesbians in sport as the problem, we need to focus our attention on sexism, heterosexism, and homophobia. As part of this renaming process, we need to take the sting out of the lesbian label. Women in sport must stop jumping to the back of the closet and slamming the door every time someone calls us dykes. We need to challenge the use of the lesbian label to intimidate all women in sport.

Women's Sport Can Progress without Dealing with Homophobia

If progress is measured by the extent to which we, as women in sport, control our sporting destinies, take pride in our athletic identities, and tolerate diversity among ourselves, then we are no better off now than we ever have been. We have responded to questions about lesbians in sport with silence, denial, and apology. When these responses fail to divert attention away from the lesbian issue, we have promoted a heterosexy image, attacked lesbians, and hired male coaches. All of these responses call on women to accommodate, assimilate, and collude with the values of a sexist and heterosexist society. All require compromise and deception. The bargain struck is that in return for our silence and our complicity, we are allowed a small piece of the action in a sports world that has been defined by men to serve male-identified values.

We have never considered any alternatives to this cycle of silence, denial, and apology to the outside world while policing the ranks inside. We have never looked inside ourselves to understand our fear and confront it. We have never tried to analyze the political meaning of our fear. We have never stood up to the accusations and threats that keep us in our place.

What do we have to pass on to the next generation of young girls who love to run and throw and catch? What is the value of nicer uniforms, a few extra tournaments, and occasional pictures in the back of the sports section if we can't pass on a sport experience with less silence and fear?

STRATEGIES FOR CONFRONTING HOMOPHOBIA IN WOMEN'S SPORT

What, then, are the alternatives to silence, apology, denial, promoting a heterosexy image, attacking lesbians, and hiring male coaches? How can women in sport begin confronting homophobia rather than perpetuating it? If our goal is to defuse the lesbian label and to strip it of its power to intimidate women in sport, then we must break the silence, not to condemn lesbians but to condemn those who use the lesbian label to intimidate. Our failure to speak out against homophobia signals our consent to the fear, ignorance, and discrimination that flourish in that silence. If our goal is to create a vision of sport in which all women have an opportunity to proudly claim their athletic identity and control their athletic experience, then we must begin to build that future now

Institutional Policy

Sport-governing organizations and school athletic departments need to enact explicit nondiscrimination and anti-harassment policies that include sexual orientation as a protected category. This is a first step in establishing an organizational climate in which discrimination against lesbians (or gay men) is not tolerated. Most sport governing organizations have not instituted such policies and, when asked by reporters if they are planning to, avoid taking a stand (Brownworth, 1991; Longman, 1991). In addition to nondiscrimination policies, professional standards of conduct for coaches must be developed that outline behavioral expectations regardless of gender or sexual orientation. Sexual harassment policies and the procedures for filing such complaints must be made clear to coaches, athletes, and administrators. As with standards of professional conduct, these policies should apply to everyone.

Education

Everyone associated with physical education and athletics must learn more about homophobia, sexism, and heterosexism. Conferences for coaches, teachers, and administrators should include educational programs focused on understanding homophobia and developing strategies for addressing homophobia in sport.

Athletic departments must sponsor educational programs for athletes that focus not only on homophobia but on other issues of social diversity as well. Because prejudice and fear affect the quality of athletes' sport experience and their relationships with teammates and coaches, educational programs focused on these issues are appropriate for athletic department sponsorship and should be an integral part of the college athletic experience.

Visibility

One of the most effective tools in counteracting homophobia is increased lesbian and gay visibility. Stereotypes and the fear and hatred they perpetuate will lose their power as more lesbian and gay people in sport disclose their identities. Although some people will never accept diversity of sexual identity in sport or in the general population, research indicates that, for most people, contact with "out" lesbian and gay people who embrace their sexual identities reduces prejudice (Herek, 1985).

The athletic world desperately needs more lesbian and gay coaches and athletes to step out of the closet. So far only a handful of athletes or coaches, most notably Martina Navratilova, have had the courage to publicly affirm their lesbian or gay identity (Brown, 1991; Brownworth, 1991; Bull, 1991; Burke, 1991; Muscatine, 1991). The generally accepting, if not warm, reaction of tennis fans to Navratilova's courage and honesty should be encouraging to the many closeted lesbian and gay people in sport. Unfortunately, the fear that keeps most lesbian and gay sports people in the closet is not ungrounded: Coming out as a lesbian or gay athlete or coach is a risk in a heterosexist and sexist society (Brown, 1991; Brownworth, 1991; Burton-Nelson, 1991; Hicks, 1979; Muscatine, 1991). The paradox is that more lesbian and gay people need to risk coming out if homosexuality is to be demystified in North American society.

Another aspect of visibility is the willingness of heterosexual athletes and coaches, as allies of lesbian and gay people, to speak out against homophobia and heterosexism. In the same way that it is important for white people to speak out against racism and for men to speak out against sexism, it is important for heterosexual people to object to antigay harassment, discrimination, and prejudice. It isn't enough to provide silent, private support for lesbian friends. To remain silent signals consent. Speaking out against homophobia is a challenge for heterosexual women in sport that requires them to understand how homophobia is used against them as well as against lesbians. Speaking out against homophobia also requires that heterosexual women confront their own discomfort with being associated with lesbians or being called lesbian, because that is what will happen when they speak out: The lesbian label will be used to try and intimidate them back into silence.

Solidarity

Heterosexual and lesbian women must understand that the only way to overcome homophobia, heterosexism, and sexism in sport is to work in coalition with each other. As long as fear and blame prevent women in sport from finding common ground, we will always be controlled by people whose interests are served by our division. Our energy will be focused on social approval rather than on social change, and on keeping what little we have rather than on getting what we deserve.

Pressure Tactics

Unfortunately, meaningful social change never happens with tension and resistance. Every civil and human rights struggle in the United States has required the mobilization of political pressure exerted on people with power to force them to confront injustice. Addressing sexism, heterosexism, and homophobia in women's sport will be no different. Taking a stand will mean being prepared to use the media, collect petitions, lobby officials, picket, write letters, file official complaints, and take advantage of other pressure tactics.

CONCLUSION

Eliminating the insidious trio of sexism, heterosexism, and homophobia in women's sport will take a sustained commitment to social justice that will challenge much of what has been accepted as natural about gender and sexuality. Addressing sexism, heterosexism, and homophobia in women's sport requires that past conceptions of gender and sexuality be recognized as social constructions that confer privilege and normalcy on particular social groups: men and heterosexuals. Other social groups (women, lesbians, and gay men) are defined as inferior or deviant and are denied access to the social resources and status conferred on heterosexual men.

Sport in the late 20th century is, perhaps, the last arena in which men can hope to differentiate themselves from women. In sport, men learn to value a traditional heterosexual masculinity that embraces male domination and denigrates women's values (Messner and Sabo, 1990). If sport is to maintain its meaning as a masculine ritual in a patriarchal society, women must be made to feel like trespassers. Women's sport participation must be trivialized and controlled (Bennett et al., 1987). The lesbian label, with its unsavory stigma, is an effective tool to achieve these goals.

If women in sport in the 21st century are to have a sport experience free of intimidation, fear, shame, and betrayal, then, as citizens of the 20th century, we must begin to reevaluate our beliefs, prejudices, and practices. We must begin to challenge the sexist, heterosexist, and homophobic status quo as it lives in our heads, on our teams, and in our schools. A generation of young girls—our daughters, nieces, younger sisters, and students—is depending on us.

REFERENCES

Acosta, V., and L. Carpenter. 1988. "Status of Women in Athletics: Causes and Changes." *Journal of Health, Physical Education, Recreation, and Dance* 56, no. 6: 35–37.

Bennett, R., G. Whitaker, N. Smith, and A. Sablove. 1987. "Changing the Rules of the Game: Reflections Toward a Feminist Analysis of Sport." *Women's Studies International Forum* 10, no. 4: 369–380.

Birrell, S., and D. Richter. 1987. "Is a Diamond Forever? Feminist Transformations of Sport." *Women's Studies International Forum* 10, no. 4: 395–410.

Blinde, E. 1989. "Unequal Exchange and Exploitation in College Sport: The Case of the Female Athlete." *Arena Review* 13, no. 2: 110–123.

———. 1990. "Pressure and Stress in Women's College Sports: Views from Athletes." Paper presented at the annual convention of the American Alliance for Health, Physical Education, Recreation and Dance, March, New Orleans.

Brown, K. 1991. "Homophobia in Women's Sports." *Deneuve* 1, no. 2: 4–6, 29.

Brownworth, V. 1991. "Bigotry on the Home Team: Lesbians Face Harsh Penalties in the Sports World." *Advocate* (June 4): 34–39.

Bryson, L. 1987. "Sport and the Maintenance of Male Hegemony." *Women's Studies International Forum* 10, no. 4: 349–360.

Bull, C. 1991. "The Magic of Martina." *Advocate* (December): 38–40.

Burke, G. 1991. "Dodgers Wanted Me to Get Married." *USA Today,* September 18), 10C.

Burton-Nelson, M. 1991. *Are We Winning Yet?* New York: Random House.

Diaz, J. 1989. "Find the Golf Here?" *Sports Illustrated* (February 13): 58–64.

Faderman, L. 1981. *Surpassing the Love of Men: Romantic Friendship and Love Between Women from the Renaissance to the Present.* New York: Morrow.

———. 1991. *Odd Girls and Twilight Lovers: A History of Lesbian Life in Twentieth-Century America.* New York: Columbia University Press.

Felshin, J. 1974. "The Triple Option ... for Women in Sport." *Quest* 21: 36–40.

Fields, C. 1983. "Allegations of Lesbianism Being Used to Intimidate, Female Academics Say." *Chronicle of Higher Education* (October 26): 1, 18–19.

Figel, B. 1986. "Lesbians in the World of Athletics." *Chicago Sun-Times,* June 16, 119.

Gornick, V. 1971."Ladies of the Links." *Look* (May 18): 69–76.

Greendorfer, S. 1991. "Analyzing Homophobia: Its Weapons and Impacts." Paper presented at the annual convention of the American Alliance for Health, Physical Education, Recreation, and Dance, April, San Francisco.

Griffin, P. 1987. "Lesbians, Homophobia, and Women's Sport: An Exploratory Analysis." Paper presented at the annual meeting of the American Psychological Association, August, New York.

Guthrie, S. 1982. "Homophobia: Its Impact on Women in Sport and Physical Education." Unpublished master's thesis, California State University, Long Beach.

Hall, A., ed. 1987. "The Gendering of Sport, Leisure, and Physical Education" [special issue]. *Women's Studies International Forum* 10, no. 4.

Herek, G. 1985. "Beyond 'Homophobia': A Social Psychological Perspective on Attitudes Toward Lesbians and Gay Men." Pp. 1–22 in J. DeCecco, ed., *Bashers, Baiters, and Bigots: Homophobia in American Society.* New York: Harrington Park.

Hicks, B. 1979. "Lesbian Athletes." *Christopher Street* (October–November): 42–50.

"Image Lady." 1987. *Golf Illustrated* (July): 9.

Katz, J. 1976. *Gay American History.* New York: Avon.

Kiersh, E. 1990. "Graf's Dash." *Vogue* (April): 348–353, 420.

Kitzinger, C. 1987. *The Social Construction of Lesbiansim.* Newbury Park, CA: Sage.

Krebs, P. 1984. "At the Starting Blocks: Women Athletes' New Agenda." *Off Our Backs* 14, no. 1: 1–3.

Lederman, D. 1991. "Penn State's Coach's Comments About Lesbian Athletes May Be Used to Test University's New Policy on Bias." *Chronicle of Higher Education* (June 5): A27–28.

Lenskyj, H. 1986. *Out of Bounds: Women, Sport, and Sexuality.* Toronto: Women's Press.

———. 1990. "Combatting Homophobia in Sports." *Off Our Backs* 20, no. 6: 2–3.

———. 1991. "Combatting Homophobia in Sport and Physical Education." *Sociology of Sport Journal* 8, no. 1: 61–69.

Lipsyte, R. 1991. "Gay Bias Moves Off the Sidelines." *New York Times,* May 24, B1.

Locke, L., and M. Jensen. 1970. "Heterosexuality of Women in Physical Education." *Pod* (Fall): 30–34.

Longman, J. 1991. "Lions Women's Basketball Coach Is Used to Fighting and Winning." *Philadelphia Inquirer,* March 10, 1G, 6G.

Messner, M., and D. Sabo, eds. 1990. *Sport, Men, and the Gender Order: Critical Feminist Perspectives.* Champaign, IL: Human Kinetics.

Morgan, E. 1990. *Lesbianism and Feminism in Women's Athletics: Intersection, Bridge, or Gap?* Unpublished manuscript, Brown University Providence.

Muscatine, A. 1991. "To Tell the Truth, Navratilova Takes Consequences." *Women's Sports Pages* (November–December): 8–9. (Available from Women's SportsPages, P.O. Box 151534, Chevy Chase, MD 20825.)

National Collegiate Athletic Association. 1991. *NCAA Study on Women's Intercollegiate Athletics: Perceived Barriers of Women in Intercollegiate Athletic Careers.* Overland Park, KS: National Collegiate Athletic Association.

Newton, E. 1989. "The Mannish Lesbian: Radclyffe Hall and the New Woman." Pp. 281–293 in M. Duberman, M. Vicinus, and G. Chauncey, eds., *Hidden from History: Reclaiming the Gay and Lesbian Past.* New York: New American Library.

Pharr, S. 1988. *Homophobia: A Weapon of Sexism.* Inverness, CA: Chardon.

Rentzel, L. 1987. *Emotional Dependency: A Threat to Close Friendships.* San Rafael, CA: Exodus International.

Smith-Rosenberg, C. 1989. "Discourses of Sexuality and Subjectivity: The New Woman, 1870–1936." Pp. 264–280 in M. Duberman, M. Vicinus, and G. Chauncey, eds., *Hidden from History: Reclaiming the Gay and Lesbian Past.* New York: New American Library.

Solomon, A. 1991. "Passing Game." *Village Voice* (March 20): 92.

South, J., M. Glynn, J. Rodack, and R. Capettini. 1990. "Explosive Gay Scandal Rocks Women's Tennis." *National Enquirer* (July 31): 20–21.

Spander, D. 1991. "It's a Question of Acceptability." *Sacramento Bee,* September 1, D1, D14–15.

Thomas, R. 1990. "Two Women at Brooklyn College File Rights Complaint." *New York Times,* December 12, 22.

Thorngren, C. 1990. "Pressure and Stress in Women's College Sport: Views from Coaches." Paper presented at the annual convention of the American Alliance for Health, Physical Education, Recreation, and Dance, April, New Orleans.

———. 1991. "Homophobia and Women Coaches: Controls and Constraints." Paper presented at the annual convention of the American Alliance for Health, Physical Education, Recreation, and Dance, April, San Francisco.

Woods, S. 1990. "The Contextual Realities of Being a Lesbian Physical Education Teacher: Living in Two Worlds." *Dissertation Abstracts International* 51, no. 3: 788.

36

Gay Athletes' Dilemma

Anthony Cotton

This is the sports guy's favorite time, the season when grown men find themselves as giddy as children on Christmas Eve, waiting to unwrap all the goodies that await inside their widescreen televisions.

There are the Broncos, chasing the most coveted of prizes, the Super Bowl's Lombardi Trophy. There are college football bowl games, capped Wednesday by a Rose Bowl contest that features the season's final two undefeated teams, Southern California and Texas. And though the local franchises may not be title-worthy yet, the National Hockey League is back and the National Basketball Association is taking flight.

Throughout it all, men will root and cheer and agonize and despair, never once considering the psychology of so fiercely celebrating the physical prowess of other men. But as they paint their faces, don their Rod Smith jerseys and plop down onto the couch for the next month or so, former Major League baseball player Billy Bean has a question that might cause them to drop their clickers: What would happen if one of those athletic gods—a Bronco, a Miami Heat player, a USC Trojan—announced he was gay?

"If somebody famous came out, all those sports fans who love him, who run around wearing his T-shirts and jerseys, it would be something where they'd have to start asking questions about themselves," Bean said.

Which is one reason why Bean, one of only three male team-sport athletes to acknowledge being gay—and only after his playing days ended—says male sports are society's last bastion for denial. In a world where talk-show hosts and actors and

Source: Anthony Cotton, "Gay Athletes' Dilemma," *Denver Post,* January 2, 2006. Used by permission.

actresses can come out—with the public still tuning in or forking over nine bucks for their movies—or gay politicians can openly run and win elections, there has never been a gay active male athlete who has announced his sexual orientation.

Of course, Ellen DeGeneres or Nathan Lane never had to share a locker room with 50 of their entertainment peers.

"It would be very tough for someone in that situation," Broncos running back Mike Anderson said. "You're talking men, testosterone, egos.... I just think guys would find it harder to accept—if a guy came out in the locker room and said he was gay, I don't think (his teammates) would accept it."

And yet, coming out is nothing new in women's athletics, the most recent example being basketball star Sheryl Swoopes. During the past 18 months, Swoopes won her third gold medal for the U.S. Olympic team and her third most valuable player award from the Women's National Basketball Association.

In October, Swoopes announced that she was gay, saying life in the closet was "miserable."

Bean called Swoopes' announcement "heroic," in part because it was something he could never do during an eight-year career in Major League baseball.

"I was exhausted from lying about my life every single day," said Bean, who played for Detroit, Los Angeles and San Diego and is now a real estate agent in the Miami area. "I've learned that even if I had trusted just one person, it could have made the whole difference, but I just felt like I was on an island. I was a baseball player, but I knew I had this thing looming in the background, and it just seemed impossible to put the two together and make it work."

After some early struggles, tennis star Martina Navratilova has managed to do so after coming out almost 25 years ago. Professional golfer Rosie Jones has had an even easier time after announcing she was gay in March 2004. As a basketball player, Swoopes may be closer to the athletic sensibilities of the heartland, but even the buzz from her revelation seemed to pass quickly.

"That's because a WNBA player is still sort of on the periphery, compared to an NBA player," Bean said. "If it would have been Tracy McGrady (of the Houston Rockets), now we're talking."

FORCED TO KEEP A SECRET

Statistics suggest that as many as 400 professional male team athletes in the U.S. may be gay. But only three ex-athletes have come out.

According to the Urban Institute, anywhere from 2 percent to 10 percent of the United States population is gay. Applying that percentage to the four major men's professional sports, that means there could be as many as 400 gay athletes.

Yet through all the years of major pro sports, only three athletes—Bean, baseball player Glenn Burke and Esera Tuaolo, a National Football League defensive lineman for nine years in the 1990s—have acknowledged being gay, and each only after the conclusion of their playing careers.

As much as he would like an active male athlete to come out, Bean admits that such a move "would be a little daring."

"There are obviously closeted athletes who have learned to keep that secret in tow because they don't want it to affect their ability to play and make a wonderful living," Bean said. "It takes a long time to get to the top of the sports world, whether it's football or basketball or baseball. By the time someone wades their way through the minor leagues, the colleges, competing against other players, whatever that process of elimination is, you get so hardened by watching friends get peeled away, cut or released, injuries that ruin careers—by the time you get there, you're so damn grateful, however much you might want to come out, it's just another obstacle that makes your day a lot more complicated than it probably needs to be.

"People just make a conscious choice that until they see proof that it's not going to affect their job or the way people look at them or the fans' opinion of them, they're just going to hold on to that secret. It's unfortunate that that's where we are still, but I just think it's going to take more time."

A TABOO SUBJECT

Active athletes don't like discussing the possibility that some teammates may be gay. One player has said he wouldn't stand for a gay teammate.

If you want to see grown men, some of the most accomplished performers in athletics, squirm, just raise the topic of an active male athlete coming out.

"Hold up—do you know something I don't?" Anderson asks.

"No comment," Denver Nuggets center Marcus Camby said. "It's hard to think about. I just don't see it happening too soon."

"The last time I talked about this, I got into trouble," Broncos safety Nick Ferguson said.

"Man, I can't even go there," said PGA Tour golfer and ABC television analyst Paul Azinger. "This is like the taboo subject. It's like talking about race or something. If you talk about it, you're just going to get slaughtered."

Trying to find an example to point out the sensitivity level of some of his peers, Azinger recalls when LPGA star Nancy Lopez married Ray Knight. Although Knight had been an accomplished baseball player and manager, even winning a World Series, when he left his sport and spent the bulk of his time in the golf world travelling with his wife and managing his family, "everybody was just calling him 'Mr. Lopez,'" Azinger said.

As a member of the New York Jets a few years ago, Ferguson was sucked in by the media vortex after Jeremy Shockey of the New York Giants said he "wouldn't stand for" playing with a homosexual.

Ferguson takes a dissenting view.

"I have nothing against someone who wants to live their life in that particular way," Ferguson said. "I don't see why a gay athlete couldn't come out, as long as he handled his business on the field. (But) I don't know what it would be like for him outside of the game. You can have camaraderie inside the locker room, but outside of it, you probably wouldn't see too many people around him because they'd be afraid of getting labeled."

Nuggets general manager Kiki Vandeweghe argues that there's only one label that should matter.

"It's not like 30 years ago, it just isn't," he said. "It just wouldn't factor into what the guy does on the court. If he can play basketball, he can play basketball; that's the end of the story."

Though Bean finds Vandeweghe's sentiment encouraging, he doesn't believe it holds up, even in today's relatively more enlightened age.

"There's a perfect world, and then there's the real world," Bean said. "He's saying the right thing, but he's not the guy who's going to have to go out there in Madison Square Garden and stand at the free throw line with the game on the line and see someone hold up a big sign calling him a faggot."

DIFFERENCES BETWEEN SEXES

A golfer says she eventually made the adjustment after coming out. But it could be harder for men to do so because of sports' macho world.

Swoopes may be in that situation next summer. She is playing overseas for now, and her agent did not return repeated requests to contact her for this story. Swoopes recently signed an endorsement deal with Olivia, a travel company with a predominantly gay and lesbian clientele. Jones is another of the company's spokeswomen, her deal part of the reason she came out last year.

Today, Jones says her sexuality has become "a sidelight" to her play—"People say, 'Oh, yeah, she's gay.'" Though she says there have been no repercussions since coming out, with both gays and heterosexuals expressing thanks and admiration for her choice, Jones admits there was an element of discomfort initially.

"You're coming out to millions of people—it's not like it's just in your workplace, where there may be 30 or 100 people—it's to everybody," she said. "I felt like I was walking around naked for a couple of weeks; I don't know who wouldn't feel uncomfortable walking around naked playing golf in front of thousands of people.

"It was like I had stripped and shed layers off of me, and I felt vulnerable, but I wasn't a wreck emotionally. I played great golf, I was happy, and as time went by, I started playing better, I've had a lot more confidence. I'm just so glad I did it and I don't have to hide that part of my life anymore."

However, Jones feels the cultural chasm between men and women announcing their sexual orientations is miles and miles apart, a gulf that begins at a very early age.

"(Male) friends say to each other all the time, 'Oh, you're so gay,' or 'You're such a wuss' when they're playing sports," Jones said. "When that happens, you're not going to be accepted in that sport. You probably wouldn't survive."

Jean Hodges of Boulder is a regional director for Parents, Families and Friends of Lesbians and Gays. One of her current projects is a study of homophobia in sports, with early indications showing that schoolyard games of touch football or basketball play a strong role in how males begin to perceive their sexuality and the role that plays in interacting with others.

"Boys become afraid. There's such strong motivation for 'men to be men,'" Hodges said. "There's a deep-seated need not to be thought of as effeminate, with the fear factor of being regarded as such pretty great. And as you get older, it gets that much harder because there's so much peer pressure. It would take a huge amount of confidence for a young man to come out."

Bean couldn't do so. But he's hopeful that someone will step forward in time.

"I believe we can make this thing coexist," he said. "If an athlete is strong enough to handle all the scrutiny of being the first one, it's going to dissolve and dissipate as more people do it. But that first one, it's going to be news, and any athlete will tell you it's hard to concentrate and eliminate those variables and distractions when you have people asking you questions 24 hours a day about things that are going on off the field.

"Whoever does come forward will have to think long and hard about that, but they're going to be a hero for some people. But I hope when that happens, their play doesn't drop off. I hope it gets better, because that's what people are going to be looking for."

37

On the Team

Equal Opportunity for Transgender Student Athletes

Pat Griffin and Helen J. Carroll

OVERVIEW

This section of the report provides an overview of issues related to providing equal opportunities for transgender student athletes by addressing the following questions:

- What does transgender mean?
- Why must we address transgender issues in athletics? Why focus on high school and college athletics?
- Should the participation of transgender student athletes raise concerns about competitive equity?
- What are the benefits of adopting fair and inclusive policies?
- What are harmful effects of failing to adopt fair and inclusive policies?

WHAT DOES TRANSGENDER MEAN?

"Transgender" describes an individual whose gender identity (one's internal psychological identification as a boy/man or girl/woman) does not match the person's sex

---

Source: Pat Griffin and Helen J. Carroll, "On the Team: Equal Opportunity for Transgender Student Athletes," National Center for Lesbian Rights and Women's Sports Foundation, 2010, pp. 9–19.

at birth. For example, a male-to-female (MTF) transgender person is someone who was born with a male body, but who identifies as a girl or a woman. A female-to-male (FTM) transgender person is someone who was born with a female body, but who identifies as a boy or a man.[1]

Some transgender people choose to share the fact that they are transgender with others. Other transgender people prefer to keep the fact that they are transgender private.

It is important that other people recognize and respect the transgender person's identification as a man or a woman. In order to feel comfortable and to express their gender identity to other people, transgender people may take a variety of steps: changing their names and self-referencing pronouns to better match their gender identity; choosing clothes, hairstyles, or other aspects of self-presentation that reflect their gender identity; and generally living, and presenting themselves to others, consistently with their gender identity. Some, but not all, transgender people take hormones or undergo surgical procedures to change their bodies to better reflect their gender identity.

Some people are confused by the difference between transgender people and people who have intersex conditions. The key feature of being transgender is having a psychological identification as a man or a woman that differs from the person's sex at birth. Apart from having a gender identity that is different than their bodies, transgender people are not born with physical characteristics that distinguish them from others. In contrast, people with intersex conditions (which may also be called "Differences of Sex Development"), are born with physically mixed or atypical bodies with respect to sexual characteristics such as chromosomes, internal reproductive organs and genitalia, and external genitalia.[2] An estimated one in 2,000 people are born with an anatomy or chromosome pattern that doesn't seem to fit typical definitions of male or female. The conditions that cause these variations are sometimes grouped under the terms "intersex" or "DSD" (Differences of Sex Development).[3]

Most people with intersex conditions clearly identify as male or female and do not have any confusion or ambiguity about their gender identities. In fact, most intersex conditions are not visible, and many intersex people are unaware of having an intersex condition unless it is discovered during medical procedures. Though there may be some similar issues related to sports participation between transgender and intersex individuals, there are also significant differences. This report will focus on the participation of transgender people in sports.

WHY MUST WE ADDRESS TRANSGENDER ISSUES IN SCHOOL ATHLETIC PROGRAMS?

Educators must address transgender issues in athletics for several reasons. First and foremost, core values of equal opportunity and inclusion demand that educational leaders adopt thoughtful and effective policies that enable all students to participate fully in school athletic programs. Over the course of many years, schools have learned and continue to appreciate the value and necessity of accommodating the sport participation interests of students of color, girls and women, students with disabilities, and lesbian, gay, and bisexual students. These are all issues of basic fairness and equity that demand the expansion of our thinking about equal opportunity in sports. The right of transgender students to participate in sports calls for similar considerations of fairness and equal access.

Additionally, as more states, localities, and schools add gender identity and expression to their nondiscrimination policies, and as more courts hold that sex discrimination laws protect transgender people, transgender students and their parents are increasingly empowered to insist that athletic programs accommodate transgender students To avoid decision-making that perpetuates discrimination, school leaders must be proactive in adopting policies that are consistent with school non-discrimination policies and state and federal laws prohibiting discrimination based on gender identity or expression.

Though the number of transgender students is small, research indicates that their number is growing.[4] As the number of people who come out as transgender as teenagers and children increases, so too do the numbers of parents who support their transgender children and advocate for their rights to safety and fair treatment in schools. In response to these demands, K-12 school and college leaders must be prepared to accommodate the educational needs and protect the rights of trans-identified students.

To respond to these realities, sport governing organizations and individual schools are well advised to proactively adopt policies that provide equal opportunities for transgender students to participate on school sports teams. Moreover, in the spirit of encouraging sports participation for all, it is the right thing to do.

In order to design effective policies, educators must understand that gender is a core part of everyone's identity and that gender is more complex than our society generally acknowledges. Learning about the experience of transgender people can help us to see more clearly how gender affects all of our lives, and to put that knowledge into practice in order to better serve all students.

Addressing the needs of transgender students is an important emerging equal opportunity issue that must be taken seriously by school leaders. Because a more complex understanding of gender may be new and challenging for some people, there is a danger that misinformation and stereotypes will guide policy decisions rather than accurate and up-to-date information. Athletic leaders who are charged with policy development need guidance to avoid inscribing misconceptions and misinformation in policies that, ultimately, create more problems than they solve.

WHY FOCUS ON HIGH SCHOOL AND COLLEGE ATHLETICS?

Providing equal opportunities in all aspects of school programming is a core value in education. As an integral part of educational institutions, high school and college athletic programs are responsible and accountable for reflecting the goals and values of the educational institutions of which they are a part. It follows that school athletic programs must reflect the value of equal opportunity in all policies and practices.

Athletic programs affiliated with educational institutions have a responsibility, beyond those of adult amateur or professional sports programs, to look beyond the value of competition to promote broader educational goals of participation, inclusion, and equal opportunity. Because high schools and colleges must be committed to those broader educational goals, they should not unthinkingly adopt policies developed for adult Olympic and professional athletes. Recognizing the need to address the participation of transgender athletes, a few leading international and professional sport governing organizations have developed policies based on overly stringent, invasive, and rigid medical requirements. These policies are not workable or advisable for high school and college athletes for a number of reasons.

For example, in 2004 the International Olympic Committee (IOC) developed a policy addressing the eligibility of transgender athletes to compete in IOC sanctioned events.[5] While the IOC deserves credit for its pioneering effort to address the inclusion of transgender athletes, medical experts have identified serious flaws in the IOC policy, especially its requirement of genital reconstructive surgery, which lacks a well-founded medical or policy basis. Most transgender people—even as adults—do not have genital reconstructive surgery.[6] In addition, whether a transgender person has genital reconstructive surgery has no bearing on their athletic ability. The IOC policy also fails to provide sufficient protections for the privacy and dignity of transgender athletes. Because of these serious flaws, high schools and colleges should not adopt or look to the IOC policy as a model.[7]

There are additional reasons for high schools and colleges to create their own policies rather than adopt policies developed for adults. High school- and college-aged student athletes have developmental needs that differ from those of adults. For example, a core purpose of high school and college is to teach students how to participate and be good citizens in an increasingly diverse society and how to interact respectfully with others. In addition, high school and college athletic programs impose limits on how many years a student athlete can compete that do not exist in adult sporting competitions, where athletes can compete as long as their performances are viable or, in the case of most amateur sports, as long as they wish to.

It is also advisable that high school athletic programs adopt a different policy for including transgender student athletes than college athletic programs. Specifically, this report recommends that high schools permit transgender athletes to play on teams consistent with the student's gender identity, without regard to whether the student has undertaken any medical treatment. In contrast, the report recommends a more nuanced policy for collegiate athletics that is based, in part, upon whether a student athlete is undergoing hormone therapy.

The need for distinct high school and collegiate policies is based on several considerations. First, in high school settings, students are guaranteed the availability of a high school education and a corresponding opportunity to participate equally in all high school programs and activities. At the high school level, the focus should be on full participation in athletics for all students, within the limits of school resources to provide participation opportunities.

Second, intercollegiate sports are governed differently than high school sports. Intercollegiate athletics are regulated nationally by governing bodies that sponsor national competitions and oversee such functions as the random testing of student athletes for the use of banned substances thought to enhance athletic performance. Because testosterone is a banned substance under the current rules for intercollegiate competition, the inclusion of transgender student athletes in college sports must be consistent with those rules.

Third, high school student athletes are still growing and developing physically, cognitively, and emotionally. Because high school-aged students are still growing and maturing, they present a broader range of physical characteristics than collegiate student athletes do, and these differences should be taken into account in developing a policy for high school students.

Finally, high school-aged and younger transgender students are subject to different medical protocols than adults because of their age and physical and psychological development.[8] The World Professional Association for Transgender Health (WPATH) has established guiding medical protocols for transitioning—the process by which a transgender person lives consistently with their gender identity—which may include treatments to have the person's physical presentation more closely align with their identity. Those protocols vary based on the age and psychological readiness of the young person.[9] For children and youth, transition typically consists entirely of permitting the child to dress, live, and function socially consistently with the child's gender identity. For youth who are approaching puberty, hormone blockers may be prescribed to delay puberty in order to prevent the youth from going through the traumatic experience of acquiring secondary sex characteristics that conflict with his or her core gender identity. For older youth, cross-gender hormones or even some sex-reassignment surgeries may be prescribed.

All of these factors point to the need to develop policies for the inclusion of transgender student athletes in high school and college programs that take the relevant differences between the two settings into account. In the high school and college policies recommended below, we have attempted to take account of these differences.

SHOULD THE PARTICIPATION OF TRANSGENDER STUDENT ATHLETES ON SCHOOL TEAMS RAISE CONCERNS ABOUT COMPETITIVE EQUITY?

Concern about creating an "unfair competitive advantage" on sex-separated teams is one of the most often cited reasons for resistance to the participation of transgender student athletes. This concern is cited most often in discussions about transgender women or girls competing on a women's or girls' team. Some advocates for gender equality in high school and college sports are concerned that allowing transgender girls or women—that is, male-to-female transgender athletes who were born male, but who identify as female—to compete on women's teams will take away opportunities for other girls and women, or that transgender girls or women will have a competitive advantage over other non-transgender competitors.

These concerns are based on three assumptions: one, that transgender girls and women are not "real" girls or women and therefore not deserving of an equal competitive opportunity; two, that being born with a male body automatically gives a transgender girl or woman an unfair advantage when competing against non-transgender girls and women; and three, that boys or men might be tempted to pretend to be transgender in order to compete in competition with girls or women.

These assumptions are not well founded. First, the decision to transition from one gender to the other—to align one's external gender presentation with one's internal sense of gender identity—is a deeply significant and difficult choice that is made only after careful consideration and for the most compelling of reasons. Gender identity is a core aspect of a person's identity, and it is just as deep seated, authentic, and real for a transgender person as for others. Male-to-female transgender women fully identify and live their lives as women, and female-to-male transgender men fully identify and live their lives as men. For many transgender people, gender transition is a psychological and social necessity. It is essential that educators in and out of athletics understand this.

Second, while some people fear that transgender women will have an unfair advantage over nontransgender women, it is important to place that fear in context. When examined carefully, the realities underlying this issue are more complex than they may seem at first blush. The basis of this concern is that transgender girls or women who have gone through male puberty may have an unfair advantage due to the growth in long bones, muscle mass, and strength that is triggered by testosterone. However, a growing number of transgender youth are undergoing medically guided hormonal treatment prior to puberty, thus effectively neutralizing this concern. Increasingly, doctors who specialize in treating transgender people are prescribing hormone blockers to protect children who clearly identify as the other gender from the trauma of undergoing puberty in the wrong gender and acquiring unwanted secondary sex characteristics. When the youth is old enough to make an informed decision, he or she can make the choice of whether to begin crossgender hormones. Transgender girls who transition in this way do not go through a male puberty, and therefore their participation in athletics as girls does not raise the same equity concerns that might otherwise be present.

In addition, even transgender girls who do not access hormone blockers or cross-gender hormones display a great deal of physical variation, just as there is a great deal of natural variation in physical size and ability among non-transgender girls and boys. Many people may have a stereotype that all transgender girls and women are unusually tall and have large bones and muscles. But that is not true. A male-to-female transgender girl may be small and slight, even if she is not on hormone blockers or taking estrogen. It is important not to over generalize. The assumption that all malebodied people are taller, stronger, and more highly skilled in a sport than all female-bodied people is not accurate.[10] This assumption is especially inaccurate when applied to youth who are still developing physically and who therefore display a significantly broader range of variation in size, strength, and skill than older youth and adults.[11]

It is also important to know that any athletic advantages a transgender girl or woman arguably may have as a result of her prior testosterone levels dissipate after about one year of estrogen therapy. According to medical experts on this issue, the assumption that a transgender girl or woman competing on a women's team would have a competitive advantage outside the range of performance and competitive advantage or disadvantage that already exists among female athletes is not supported by evidence.[12] As one survey of the existing research concludes, "the data available does not appear to suggest that transitioned athletes would compete at an advantage or disadvantage as compared with physically born men and women."[13]

Finally, fears that boys or men will pretend to be female to compete on a girls' or women's team are unwarranted given that in the entire 40 year history of "sex verification" procedures in international sport competitions, no instances of such "fraud" have been revealed.[14] Instead, rather than identifying men who are trying to fraudulently compete as women, "sex verification" tests have been misused to humiliate and unfairly exclude women with intersex conditions.[15] The apparent failure of such tests to serve their stated purpose of deterring fraud—and the terrible damage they have caused to individual women athletes—should be taken into account when developing policies for the inclusion of transgender athletes.

Rather than repeating the mistakes of the past, educators in high school and collegiate athletics programs must develop thoughtful and informed policies that provide opportunities for all students, including transgender students, to participate in sports. These policies must be based on sound medical science, which shows that male-to-female transgender athletes do not have any automatic advantage over other women and girls. These policies must also be based on the educational values of sport and the reasons why sport is included as a vital component of the educational environment: promoting the physical and psychological well-being of all students, and teaching students the values of equality, participation, inclusion, teamwork, discipline, and respect for diversity.

WHAT ARE THE BENEFITS OF ADOPTING INCLUSIVE POLICIES AND PRACTICES REGARDING TRANSGENDER STUDENT ATHLETES?

All stakeholders in high school and collegiate athletics will benefit from adopting fair and inclusive policies enabling transgender student athletes to participate on school sports teams. School-based sports, even at the most competitive levels, remain an integral part of the process of education and development of young people, especially emerging leaders in our society. Adopting fair and inclusive participation policies will allow school and athletic leaders to fulfill their commitment to create an environment in which all students can thrive, develop their full potential, and learn how to interact with persons from diverse groups.

Many schools and athletic departments identify diversity as a strength and have included sexual orientation and gender identity/expression in their non-discrimination policies. Athletic departments and personnel are responsible for creating and maintaining an inclusive and nondiscriminatory climate in the areas they oversee. Adopting inclusive participation policies provides school athletic leaders with a concrete opportunity to fulfill that mandate and demonstrate their commitment to fair play and inclusion.

Moreover, when all participants in athletics are committed to fair play, inclusion, and respect, student athletes are free to focus on performing their best in athletic competition and in the classroom. This climate promotes the well-being and achievement potential of all student athletes. Every student athlete and coach will benefit from meeting the challenge of overcoming fear and prejudice about social groups of which they are not members. This respect for difference will be invaluable to all student athletes as they graduate and enter an increasingly diverse workforce in which knowing how to work effectively across differences is a professional and personal asset.

WHAT ARE HARMFUL POTENTIAL CONSEQUENCES OF FAILURE TO ADOPT TRANSGENDER-INCLUSIVE POLICIES AND PRACTICES?

When schools fail to adopt inclusive participation policies, they are not living up to the educational ideals of equality and inclusion, and may reinforce the image of athletics as a privileged activity not accountable to broad institutional and societal ideals of inclusion and respect for difference. Moreover, this failure puts schools, athletic conferences, and sport governing organizations at risk of costly discrimination lawsuits and negative media attention.

Failing to adopt transgender-inclusive participation policies is hurtful to and discriminates against transgender students because they may be denied the opportunity to participate in school sports. School sports programs are integral parts of a well-rounded education experience. The benefits of school sports participation include many positive effects on physical, social, and emotional wellbeing. All students, including those who are transgender, deserve access to these benefits.[16]

Failure to adopt inclusive participation policies also hurt non-transgender students by conveying a message that the values of non-discrimination and inclusion are less important than values based on competition and winning. Schools must model and educate about non-discrimination values in all aspects of school programming, not only for students, but for parents and community members as well.

Last but not least, failure to adopt policies that ensure equal opportunities for transgender student athletes may also result in costly and divisive litigation. A growing number of states and localities are adopting specific legal protections for transgender students. In addition, state and federal courts are increasingly applying sex discrimination laws to prohibit discrimination against transgender people.

Several studies show that schools are often hostile places for transgender students and other students who do not conform to stereotypical gender expectations.[17] These students are frequently subjected to peer harassment and bullying which stigmatizes and isolates them. This mistreatment can lead to feelings of hopelessness, depression, and low self-esteem. When a school or athletic organization denies transgender students the ability to participate in sports because of their gender identity or expression, that condones, reinforces and affirms their social status as outsiders or misfits who deserve the hostility they experience from peers.

Finally, the absence of transgender-inclusive policies and practices reinforces stereotypes and fears about gender diversity. When transgender students are stigmatized and excluded, even nontransgender students may experience pressure to conform to gender-role stereotypes as a way to avoid being bullied or harassed themselves.

NOTES

1. Gender Spectrum, "A Word About Words," available online at http://www.genderspectrum.org/images/stories/Resources/Family/A_Word_About_Words.pdf.

2. Intersex Society of North America, "What's the difference between being transgender or transsexual and having an intersex condition?" Available online at http://www.isna.org/faq/transgender.

3. Advocates for Informed Choice, General Brochure, available online at http://aiclegal.files.wordpress.com/2010/02/aic-brochure.pdf.

4. See, e.g., Emily A. Greytak, Joseph G. Kosciw, and Elizabeth M. Diaz, Gay Lesbian Straight Education Network, *Harsh Realities: The Experiences of Transgender Youth in Our Nation's Schools* (2009). Available online at http://www.glsen.org/binary-data/GLSEN_ATTACHMENTS/file/000/001/1375-1.pdf. Despite this evidence of growing numbers, the decision to provide equal opportunity should not be based on the number of transgender students who want to play sports. Even the smallest minority of students deserves the opportunity to participate in all school-sponsored programs.

5. International Olympic Committee, *Statement of the Stockholm Consensus on Sex Reassignment in Sport* (2003), http://www.olympic.org/Documents/Reports/EN/en_report_905.pdf.

6. Lisa Mottet, National Gay and Lesbian Task Force Policy Institute and National Center for Transgender Equality, "Preliminary Findings of the National Transgender Discrimination Survey" (2010).

7. Alice Dreger, "Sex Typing for Sport," Hastings Center Report (March–April 2010).

8. Stephanie Brill and Rachel Pepper, *The Transgender Child: A Handbook for Families and Professionals* (San Francisco: Cleis Press, 2008).

9. World Professional Association for Transgender Health, *The Harry Benjamin International Gender Dysphoria Association's Standards Of Care For Gender Identity Disorders, Sixth Version* (2001). Available online at http://www.wpath.org/documents2/socv6.pdf.

10. In addition, what counts as a competitive advantage may shift dramatically depending on the sport. What is an advantage in one context may be a disadvantage in another. For example, factors such as height, weight, reaction time, and proportion of fast twitch muscle fibers all affect competitive advantage depending on the sport. A female volleyball player may be very tall, and yet few people would consider that to be an unfair competitive advantage in her sport. Similarly, a male swimmer may have a naturally high hemoglobin count enabling him to take in more oxygen, but he is not barred from swimming for that reason. Sarah Teetzel, "On Transgendered Athletes, Fairness and Doping: An International Challenge," *Sport in Society: Cultures, Commerce, Media, Politics,* Volume 9, Issue 2 (2006) Pages 227–251.

11. Assuming that boys have an automatic advantage over girls is particularly false with respect to prepubescent children, where gender plays virtually no role in determining relative athletic ability. For that reason, we strongly recommend that school and recreational sports adopt the policy recommended by the Transgender Law and Policy Institute and endorsed by Gender Spectrum. Transgender Law and Policy Institute, *Guidelines for Creating Policies for Transgender Children in Recreational Sports* (2009).

12. Brenda Wagman, Promising Practices: Working with Transitioning/Transitioned Athletes in Sport Project, AthletesCAN, Canadian Association for the Advancement of Women in Sport, and the Canadian Centre for Ethics in Sport, *Including Transitioning and Transitioned Athletes in Sport: Issues, Facts and Perspectives* (2009). Available online at http://www.caaws.ca/e/resources/pdfs/Wagman_discussion_paper_THE_FINAL.pdf.

13. Michaela C. Devries, "Do Transitioned Athletes Compete at an Advantage or Disadvantage as compared with Physically Born Men and Women: A review of the Scientific Literature" (May 18, 2008). Including Transitioning and Transitioned Athletes, supra note 13. Available online at http://www.caaws.ca/e/resources/pdfs/Wagman_ discussion_paper_THE_FINAL.pdf.

14. Erin Buzuvis, "Caster Semenya and the Myth of the Level Playing Field." *Social Science Research Network* (2009). Available online at http://papers.ssrn.com/sol3/papers.cfm?abstract_id=1521674.

15. Joe Leigh Simpson et al, "Gender Verification in the Olympics," *JAMA* (2000); 284: 1568–1569; see also Sex Typing for Sport, supra note 8.

16. Kirk Mango, "The Benefits of Competitive Athletic Sports Participation in Today's Sports Climate," *Chicago Now* (February 16, 2010). Available online at http://www.chicagonow.com/blogs/athletes-sports-experience/2010/02/ the-benefits-of-competitive-athletic-sports-participation-in-todays-sports-climate.html.

17. Harsh Realities, *supra* note 3.

❋ FOR FURTHER STUDY ❋

Amaechi, John. 2007. *Man in the Middle.* New York: Hyperion.

Broad, K. L. 2001. "The Gendered Unapologetic: Queer Resistance in Women's Sport." *Sociology of Sport Journal* 18 (2): 181–204.

Coakley, Jay. 2007. *Sports in Society: Issues and Controversies.* 9th ed. New York: McGraw-Hill.

Eitzen, D. Stanley, and George H. Sage. 2009. *Sociology of North American Sport.* 8th ed. Boulder, CO: Paradigm.

Fusco, Caroline. 2000. "Lesbians and Locker Rooms." Pp. 91–94 in Peter Donnelly, ed., *Taking Sport Seriously: Social Issues in Canadian Sport,* Toronto: Thompson Education.

Jacobson, Jennifer. 2002. "The Loneliest Athletes." *Chronicle of Higher Education* (November 1): A36–A38.

Lipsyte, Robert. 2000. "An Icon Recast: Support for Gay Athlete," April 30. Available at http://nytimes.com/library/sports/other/043000oth-lipsyte.html.

Lynch, Eamon. 2003. "Having a Gay Old Time." *Sports Illustrated* (June 16): G8–G12.

Nixon, Howard L. II. 2008. *Sport in a Changing World.* Boulder, CO: Paradigm.

Price, Michael, and Andrew Parker. 2003. "Sport, Sexuality, and the Gender Order: Amateur Rugby Union, Gay Men, and Social Exclusion." *Sociology of Sport Journal* 20 (2): 108–126.

Tomlinson, Dylan B. 1998. "Fear and Loathing." *Denver Post,* April 28, 10D.

PART THIRTEEN

Expanding the Horizons: Sport and Globalization

Globalization, according to Joseph Maguire, refers to transnational economics and technological exchange, communication networks, and migratory patterns resulting in interconnected world patterns.[1] Globalization, then, involves, among other things, markets, production, finance, the movement of people, and cultural homogenization. There has been a global economy for 500 years. In the sport realm the cultural imperialism employed by the British colonists of the nineteenth and twentieth centuries brought their sport (soccer, rugby, cricket) to their colonies (e.g., India). The Olympic movement spread around the globe during the twentieth century, and this, too, has been interpreted by some observers as a reflection of the colonial dominance of the West,[2] but in the last twenty-five years or so, it has accelerated rapidly.

While globalization is not new, the pace has quickened rapidly with the transportation and communications revolutions of the late twentieth century. Maguire states: "These globalization processes ... appear to be leading to a form of time-space compression. That is, people are experiencing spatial and temporal dimensions differently. There is a speeding up of time and a "shrinking" of space. Modern technologies enable people, images, ideas and money to criss-cross the globe with great rapidity."[3]

The three selections in this section provide information on the global dimensions of sport in today's world. The first, by anthropologist Alan M. Klein, describes the extent of globalization in Major League Baseball. His question: Will Major League Baseball see players and fans abroad as a twentieth-century-colonialist or as a twenty-first-century-decentered global enterprise?

The second selection (39), by journalist David Macarey, relates the sordid history of the Nike Corporation in its production of sports-related products in lowwagecountries. The final selection in this section is from sports sociologist George H. Sage's book, *Globalizing Sport.* This excerpt focuses on the new media and global sports.

NOTES

1. Joseph Maguire, "Sport and Globalization," in *Handbook of Sports Studies,* Jay Coakley and Eric Dunning (eds.), (London: Sage, 2000), p. 356. For more on the defining characteristics of globalization, see Jeremy Breecher, Tim Costello, and Brendan Smith, *Globalization from Below: The Power of Solidarity* (Cambridge, MA: South End Press, 2000), pp. 1–4; and Robert K. Schaeffer, *Understanding Globalization: The Social Consequences of Political, Economic, and Environmental Change,* 2nd ed. (Lanham, MD: Rowman and Littlefield, 2003), pp. 1–18.

2. H. Eichberg, "Olympic Sport: Neocolonialism and Alternatives," *International Review for the Sociology of Sport* 19: 97–105.

3. Maguire, op. cit., p. 356.

38

Growing the Game

The Globalization of Major League Baseball

Alan M. Klein

Major League Baseball's efforts at globalization are not only provident for the future of the sport but also critical to its current prosperity. The ability of the game to rely upon its domestic base for fans and players has receded to the point where globalizing is imperative. This may be hard to square with the figures on attendance, which reached an all-time high in 2005, and with vigorous television ratings, but from a structural and long-term perspective the current boom is misleading. Major League Baseball must seek players and fans abroad, and indeed it is already doing so. The question is whether it will do so as a twentieth-century colonialist or as a twenty-first-century decentered global enterprise. The former strategy represents familiar ground but is doomed to slow growth and persistent resentment; the latter will at first feel uncomfortable but will aid the worldwide health of the sport.

In an effort to study this question systematically, I selected three of the game's organizations: two teams, the Los Angeles Dodgers and the Kansas City Royals, as well as the Commissioner's Office. All three are structurally representative of key dimensions of the industry, yet each is unique, and each approaches globalization in fundamentally different ways from the others. My attempt to chronicle their efforts spanned seven years (1999–2005) and covered eight countries. The core of this study looks at the political, economic, and structural arrangements of contemporary baseball on a global scale.

Source: Alan M. Klein, *Growing the Game: The Globalization of Major League Baseball* (New Haven, CT: Yale University Press, 2006), 1–9.

THE SPHERE OF BASEBALL

The Commissioner's Office is much like any other multinational corporation: large, complex, guarded, and autocratic. Fortunately, one division within the office deals with international dimensions of the sport: Major League Baseball International (MLBI). At the time of my research, it was presided over by Paul Archey, with Jim Small as the vice president for international marketing and the head of the Japan office.

MLBI is responsible for generating foreign revenue for the major league franchise owners. To that end MLBI sells broadcast rights, secures corporate sponsorships, licenses products, and stages events abroad. Expanding the business opportunities of the game is critical, but within the larger framework of the industry, it is equally important to develop the game itself abroad. Major League Baseball has to deepen its roots where it already exists and engender interest where it is absent or exists only weakly: it must, in the business-inflected jargon of the organization, "grow the game." Hence MLBI is concerned with generating profits as well as with increasing the institutional popularity of the sport internationally. This requires a coherent view of the baseball world outside of the United States.

Jim Small provided me with that social mapping in my first interview. According to him, all countries are divided into three strata according to their baseball sophistication and the potential economic rewards they offer. Tier one countries are those in which "baseball is mature, it's well known. Also, there is some sort of economic activity and the ability for us to market against that love of baseball."[1] In places like the Dominican Republic, Japan, or Mexico, baseball is deeply entrenched, and the number of players signed to professional contracts is significant and consistent.

Tier two includes countries where the game is somewhat less developed. There may be leagues, but they are amateur or semiprofessional, and much less competitive than in the first tier. Nor do these countries produce numbers of major league players comparable to those coming from the first tier. Italy, Australia, and the Netherlands are examples. With a certain kind of inducement (and no one really knows just what that might be), any of these countries might move up. Currently Australia is experiencing something of a baseball renaissance. After almost a decade of decline, the sport seems poised to make significant headway. A new league is planned, and players are being signed in impressive numbers. The 2005 Minnesota Twins, for instance, had sixteen Australians under contract at various levels in their organization.

Tier three comprises those countries in which the sport has a tentative footing, where the game either has only recently been introduced or has not yet taken root in the local sporting tradition. South Africa, England, and Germany are all long-term baseball projects. Players signing contracts with major league organizations are relatively rare in tier three, and the sport itself has yet to establish itself outside of scattered pockets. Because it is a long-term prospect, tier three is not on the radar screen of many major league organizations, but MLBI has worked diligently to grow the game there. Thus far the results have been mixed, but for baseball to become a real global sport, it will have to find a way to become entrenched in Europe and Africa. Jim Small cautions, however, that "tiers are more art than science. We look at a combination of good economies, where we can sell products, and baseball acumen. It's not like we sat down and actually assigned numbers to these."[2] These are all judgment calls, but the classifications can be useful.

In countries where the game is firmly established, the primary interest of Major League Baseball International is economic: "Ultimately, we're charged with returning money to the owners."[3] The largest share of MLBI revenues is derived from the sale of broadcast rights in foreign markets. Japan is the wealthiest such market ever, at $275 million, but deals have been signed in the past few years in Venezuela, the Dominican Republic, Australia, and the United Kingdom. Foreign corporate sponsors have also begun to seek out Major League Baseball with greater frequency. The tier one areas of Asia and Latin America lead the way, as might be expected, because the game is so entrenched there. Corporate sponsorships include everything from promotions to All-Star Game balloting to product lines. Licensing sales have also grown in direct proportion to the numbers of foreign players in major league organizations. The fourth leg of MLBI's revenue program comprises the events that it stages each year. They include preseason exhibition games, such as the weekend series in Valencia, Venezuela, in 2001 between the Houston Astros and the Cleveland Indians; regular-season games such as the 2004 opener between the New York Yankees and the Tampa Bay Devil Rays in Tokyo; and the biennial postseason visit of a major league all-star team to cities throughout Japan to play against stars of the Nippon Professional Baseball league.

In tier two and three countries the emphasis for MLBI is upon deepening the local involvement with the sport via a range of grassroots programs. The most fundamental program in the organization's arsenal is Pitch, Hit, and Run, a curriculum-based program administered through schools for children ages eight to twelve. Started in Australia in 1994, the program grew slowly. By 2002 more than three million children around the world had been introduced to it. Subsequent programs seek to build the base of young players until they are old enough to try out for their respective national teams.

Since these grassroots efforts are designed to change young people's minds as much as to develop the game, MLBI augments its hands-on programs with a range of televised programming. Getting youngsters to watch major league games is a major goal, along with promoting the creation of new sports heroes. Baseball Max, a weekly program filled with clips from games and interviews with stars, is produced by MLBI and disseminated around the world. By exposing young people in a lower-tier country to the game and to its colorful stars, MLBI hopes to make fans and players where few could be found before.

But while Major League Baseball International concentrates on being the game's ambassador to the world, ultimately it is the teams themselves that must be responsible for finding and grooming foreign talent. The Los Angeles Dodgers are an obvious choice for studying globalization in baseball because they pioneered it, and, while no longer alone, they continue to be among the most active in that arena. All major league teams are involved in the international hunt for talent, but big market teams like the Dodgers, the Atlanta Braves, and the New York Mets are exponentially the most involved. The cost of doing business overseas has risen considerably over the past decade. Consider that when Dominican superstars like pitcher Pedro Martinez signed with the Dodgers in 1988, almost no Latin American players signed for more than $10,000. Now a highly coveted prospect will easily get between $500,000 and $1,500,000; the record is Joel Guzmán's signing with the Dodgers for $2.25 million in 2001. It is precisely the wealth of big-market teams, combined with the rapid improvement of foreign talent, that has fueled these changes.

In certain foreign leagues owners who are concerned about losing their best players to the major leagues themselves further drive up the cost of signing their stars. A major league team seeking to sign a Japanese player, for example, must wait for ten years after his initial signing. When the player is finally posted as available to outsiders, interested teams must submit secret bids, the highest of which earns the team the right to negotiate with the player. Ichiro Suzuki cost the Seattle Mariners $13.125 million for the sealed bid, then $14 million for his contract.

The Dodgers may be representative of big-market teams, but they are also distinct in one key way: they are the pioneers in international baseball. While baseball entered the global arena in an institutional and business sense later than the National Basketball Association and the National Football League, in certain respects baseball has had a very long incubation period. The roots of its present-day efforts can be seen in the actions of Brooklyn Dodgers General Manager Branch Rickey more than sixty years ago. It was Rickey who, in 1945, flouted the barrier that had kept African Americans out of "organized baseball"—the major leagues as well as the recognized minor leagues—since late in the nineteenth century. In that monumental act, the first step toward globalization may be seen. On a social level, the Dodgers are to be credited with thinking outside of the box, showing a willingness to find players wherever they may be. This predisposed them to hurdle over national boundaries as quickly as they did racial ones.

Jackie Robinson entered a Dodger organization that was being configured to enable his ascent, and the handprint of Rickey was everywhere evident. Robinson possessed the right combination of personality traits, background, and baseball skill to make Rickey look like a genius, but Rickey planned Robinson's trajectory through three countries (Canada, Cuba, and the United States) to facilitate a smooth transition. Racial integration was a local response that had global repercussions unknown to Rickey and Robinson, but not to Dodger owner Walter O'Malley. Under O'Malley's stewardship (beginning in 1951), a foundation for a global perspective was laid. He built ties with Japan and the Caribbean and created an awareness of global possibilities when no one remotely considered such things. Schooled in proto-globalization, O'Malley's son Peter furthered these efforts when he took over at the helm. His progressive agenda included two signings with international impact: those of Fernando Valenzuela, from Mexico, and Hideo Nomo, from Japan.

While the Dodgers organization is a clear-cut choice for a study of big-market baseball's globalization, at first glance the Kansas City Royals seem anything but an obvious choice for the small-market representative. The Royals came to my attention after I read an article on their general manager, Allard Baird, who had made a grueling fact-finding trip to South Africa. He had hoped that South African baseball would be developed enough that a player might be signed with a good chance of making the majors. When Baird and his associate, Luis Silverio, began traveling about the country and holding tryouts, however, they quickly abandoned any notion of signing a prospect and launched into teaching baseball fundamentals instead. How many general managers would hold clinics for young people whom they know won't "matter" to their standings in the short term? I had to meet Baird, and promptly decided that he and the Royals were embracing a small-market mindset that had them globetrotting in advance of the big boys. Even in baseball-rich countries like the Dominican Republic, Kansas City has to adopt a different posture to sign players: they "shop without a credit card," as Baird puts it. The result is somewhat riskier, but affordable, signings. As a case study the Royals were perfect . . . plus, they always returned my phone calls.

How large- and small-market teams operate in global baseball is one of the core features of this study. I liken the small-market teams to the Portuguese sailors of the sixteenth and seventeenth centuries, who sailed fearlessly to corners of the world and wound up establishing a toehold in the business of colonialism. They did this not because they were intrepid explorers but rather because they couldn't compete directly against the big-market traders like Italy and France. Large-market teams have the option of going where talent is more costly, and when they err in judgment—which can cost millions of dollars—they have the luxury of trying again. Not so for the Milwaukees, the Tampa Bays, or the Kansas Cities of the baseball world. This is why small-market teams shop in Europe, while the behemoths head for Japan.

BASEBALL GLOBALIZATION?

When people think of globalization and baseball, they typically conjure up cosmopolitan team rosters. The pitching staff of the 2005 New York Mets had players from Japan, the Dominican Republic, South Korea, Puerto Rico, and Venezuela, as well as from the United States. More than 29 percent of all major leaguers on opening day rosters in 2005 were foreign born. While most fans know that the Dominican Republic produces a lot of major leaguers (ninety-one of them as the season started), they may not realize that players are increasingly coming from Taiwan, Curacao, South Korea, Australia, and Panama. The face of baseball today looks more like the United Colors of Benetton—Ichiro, Pedro, and the Rocket (Ichiro Suzuki, Pedro Martínez, and Roger Clemens)—than at any time in its past.

But baseball's globalization has many faces that we don't typically see. The face of Ho-Seong Koh, a South Korean manufacturer of sports caps, for example, Koh specializes in producing caps for U.S. teams. Just minutes after a team has won a championship, Koh may receive an order. He has succeeded because he can overnight a shipment anywhere in the United States. His factories in Vietnam, Cambodia, and Bangladesh make two sets of hats ahead of time, awaiting only that last-minute phone order. The phenomenon of Koreans producing for American markets, in factories throughout Asia, and doing so at high speed, is typical of globalization.[4]

Dominicans have become synonymous with baseball excellence. Consider that Dominicans, either native or first generation, have won the American League's Most Valuable Player award each year between 2002 and 2005 (Miguel Tejada, Alex Rodríguez twice, and Vladimir Guerrero), as well as the National League's MVP in 2004 (Albert Pujols). Dominicans' rise to dominance has been nothing short of spectacular, and while their heroics make the front page of most sports sections in newspapers around the United States, in their home country Guerrero's selection was treated as a national story. Guerrero collected his trophy in a ceremony at the Presidential Palace. "It's a celebration all over the country and in the streets," declared Jason Payano, the Dominican sports minister.[5] Dominican accomplishment in baseball has its flip side as well. Young Dominicans—many impoverished—desperately seek to gain a toehold in the sport, giving rise to a host of problems that require action from MLB and the Dominican government. MLB's Commissioner's Office has made serious efforts, for instance, to regulate the way in which young players are signed and groomed to come to the United States—a less conspicuous, but equally important, component of globalizing the sport.

Globalization is found as well in the sudden appearance of an entire Japanese team in a newly formed professional league in California and Arizona. The Golden Baseball League has welcomed this Japanese cohort, the Samurai Bears, not shying away from any of the cultural or logistical issues posed by having such a foreign presence in their midst. When the Japanese players walk into the wrong bathroom or have to navigate an American menu or play their entire schedule on the road because they have no "home" field, the potential awkwardness is handled by all parties with aplomb and the requisite sense of humor.[6] Back in Japan, the megalithic corporation Dentsu signed a $275 million contract with MLB for the broadcast rights to games in Japan. The pact confirms the growing economic partnership between Japanese and North American baseball, as well as the parity of play that is increasingly coming within reach. One sees globalization also in the labyrinthine planning for a baseball World Cup, as the demands and concerns of the nations involved reflect their insistence on a level playing field. The politics of conceiving and producing such an event has been a major learning experience for MLB. In fact, Major League Baseball has had to learn the lessons of globalization on its feet, and to its credit, has come a long way in a short time.

Baseball is globalized even in countries that don't play the game. Máribel Alezondo is Costa Rican. As a citizen of a soccer-playing country, she might be expected to be ignorant of the game of baseball, but in one respect she knows quite a bit. She is one of the workers in the Rawlings sporting goods factory in Turrialba, where eleven hours a day she hand-stitches baseballs used by Major League Baseball. She earns about thirty cents per ball (MLB game balls cost $22.50 each, and regular Rawlings balls retail for $15.00 at stores). Well, she used to anyway; Máribel quit on her doctor's advice, because the work was deforming her fingers and arms. She misses the work nevertheless, and while she may be resentful about the conditions she endured, she grows incredulous upon finding out what happens to the baseballs she labored over: "It's an injustice that we kill ourselves to make these balls perfect, and with one home run they're gone."[7]

Globalization is also about building the game where it barely exists. In South Africa, where until recently hardly anyone knew what the sport was, hundreds of thousands of schoolchildren have been exposed to the game through Major League Baseball International's grassroots programs. Both MLBI and the Royals donated equipment to more than fifteen hundred schools in Black, White, and Colored (the country's three official racial categories) communities. In an unanticipated development, the government has acknowledged the race-free associations of baseball in postapartheid South Africa, proclaiming baseball as part of the "new South Africa." In a country where everything was identified by race, the government is eager to identify cultural elements that reflect new nonracial policies. Suddenly South African baseball is a part of the hoped-for future of the country. The Royals, unprompted, decided to help the game grow as well, teaching young players and holding coaching clinics. The effort has begun to pay off. Since 1999, seven South Africans have signed contracts with major league clubs, and three are still playing (fittingly, two in the Royals organization).

NOTES

1. Jim Small, interview by the author, January 12, 2000.
2. Ibid.
3. Ibid.
4. Ken Belson, "Getting Champions' Caps to the Game Before the Final Whistle," *New York Times,* May 28, 2003.
5. Bob Hohler, "Guerrero Wins by Country Mile," *Boston Globe,* November 17, 2004.
6. Charlie Nobles, "Baseball Players from Over There Get a Shot Over Here," *New York Times,* May 18, 2005.
7. Tim Weiner, "Baseballs Being Made in a Sweatshop," www.sportsbusinessnews.com (The Daily Dose), January 26, 2004 (originally published as "Low-Wage Costa Ricans Make Baseballs for Millionaires," *New York Times,* January 25, 2004).

39

Nike's Crimes

David Macaray

When you're called to testify before Congress, and you've already decided to avoid responsibility or culpability, the standard routine is to resort to amnesia. You know nothing and you remember nothing. Again and again, you lean into the microphone and intone somberly, "Not to my recollection, Senator."

But when you're a manufacturer of sports apparel, like Nike, Inc., who hasn't produced an athletic shoe in the United States since 1984, and has long been accused by labor and humanitarian organizations of exploiting the workers of Third World countries, you can't defend yourself by pretending not to remember.

Instead, you're forced to use that other reliable excuse: ignorance. You build a wall between yourself and the guilty parties. You blame your subcontractors for the shameful policies—i.e., poverty wages, child labor, quasi-slave labor, sweatshop conditions, physical and sexual abuse of workers. Were any Nike management personnel aware of these abuses? "Not to my knowledge, Senator."

On April 9, the University of Wisconsin became the first college to cancel its product licensing agreement with Nike in response to the company's treatment of factory workers in Honduras. The Hondurans claim that when Nike suddenly shut down two manufacturing plants in Choloma and San Pedro Sula, in January of 2009, the employees were denied severance pay totaling more than $2.5 million.

Predictably, Nike professed ignorance of the whole thing, claiming this was a matter between the Honduran workers and Nike's subcontractors. To its credit, the

Source: David Macaray, "Nike's Crimes," *CounterPunch* (April 21, 2010). http://www.counterpunch.org/macaray04212010.html.

University of Wisconsin (which, in 2009, earned $48,000 in Nike royalties) wasn't buying it. Not this time. The university had simply lost patience with the company's tired, old, pass-the-buck tactics.

By now most people are familiar with Nike's glitzy corporate history. They burst upon the scene, then left the country. When Nike shuttered its last shoe factory in the U.S., more than a quarter-century ago, it was estimated that 65,000 American shoe workers had lost their jobs. Worse, of course, was the domino effect it had on the economy.

When you relocate your entire manufacturing base to the Third World, you not only cause your *own* employees to lose their jobs, but you start the dime rolling; you induce your competitors (Reebok, Adidas, Puma, etc.) to move their facilities as well, as they seek to compete with the near slave-wages you're now paying your new employees.

By the time the smoke settles, you have what we have today: $100 shoes being assembled by Vietnamese children making 20-cents an hour ... *literally*.

How predatory is Nike? It has actually moved out of places like South Korea and Taiwan because workers in those countries demanded higher than poverty-level wages, and relocated to places like Thailand, Vietnam, Pakistan and Indonesia. Presumably, when the Vietnamese demand a living wage, Nike will court Sudan and the Congo.

Even if you take the position that Nike is, ostensibly, no worse than any other shoe manufacturer when it comes to trolling for poverty wages, you have to admit that its Chairman of the Board, Phil Knight, is a supreme hypocrite.

Vehemently anti-labor union, Knight nonetheless tries to come off as this above-the-fray enlightened philanthropist/humanitarian. He does charity work; he gives money to colleges. But in truth, Knight is as hard-bitten a businessman as any sweatshop foreman. The only difference is image.

And image is everything to Nike. The company spends an estimated $280 million a year on celebrity endorsements, including those of superstars Michael Jordan and Tiger Woods. It's no exaggeration to say that Knight, the "humanitarian," could feed and clothe all the children of an African city for less than he's paying Jordan *for one year*.

If we argue that it's a bogus comparison, that it's not his job to be anyone's keeper—much less a bunch of African kids—that's fine. But let's also acknowledge that Knight is a money-grubbing shoemaker who made his fortune off the backs of quasi-slave laborers. On Wisconsin!

40

New Media and Global Sports

George H. Sage

The mass communications forms that began with wireless technology have evolved from radio and television broadcasting to computer technology and the Internet. Comparative studies scholar David Leonard asserts that *new media,* the term now used for the latest forms of mass communications, is a "catch-all phrase that includes everything from the Internet and e-commerce, to the blogosphere, video games, virtual reality, and other examples in which media technologies are defined by increased accessibility, fluidity, and interactivity" (2009, 2).

THE INTERNET

The current cutting edge in communications is the Internet (or the Web). Its explosive development in the last decade of the twentieth century was a quantum leap beyond previous forms of communication because it makes possible the inexpensive transmission of messages and images throughout the world in seconds. The Internet had its origins in U.S. Defense Department research done in the late 1960s, but by the mid-1990s it was almost entirely funded by private communications conglomerates, some of them originally founded as Internet firms and others originally founded as print or broadcast corporations.

Source: George H. Sage, *Globalizing Sport: How Organizations, Corporations, Media, and Politics Are Changing Sports.* Boulder, CO: Paradigm Publishers, 2010, pp. 168–175.

According to Internet World Stats, the number of people who use the Internet was nearly 1.5 billion worldwide as of March 2009. Table 40-1 shows the top seven countries in terms of Internet users; some of the numbers are rounded. Although these figures are impressive, it is necessary to keep in mind that only between 15 and 22 percent of the world's population uses the Internet.

The potential of the Internet as a source of sports information of all kinds has created a fundamental change in the delivery of media sports. Some media analysts predict that some time in the next twenty-five years, the Internet will surpass all other forms of mass communication as a source of sports information and entertainment. Currently millions of websites supply sports information to consumers. In September 2009, a Google search using the keywords "sports AND websites" produced a list of 110 million websites. In the short history of the Internet, sports websites regularly are among the leaders in terms of traffic and commercial activity. Table 40-2 lists the top five U.S. sports websites in November 2008.

Because of the popularity of many sporting events, full-motion video of sports events became inevitable. However, to protect their television-rights contracts, most sports organizations have placed limitations on websites' coverage. As the technology was developed to make the Internet respect geographical borders, sports organizations began offering its television-rights holders the option to show video of sports events on their websites. In 2007 Turner Broadcasting System, for MLB.com, produced live online coverage of first-round MLB playoff games and the National League Championship series. Even bigger, several broadcasters, including NBC, BBC, and European Broadcasting Union, posted on the Internet thousands of hours of free live-video coverage of the 2008 Beijing Summer Olympics. In addition, broadcasters worldwide streamed on the Web 2,200 hours of free online Beijing Olympic action that grew exponentially with highlights and replays. ESPN360.com, ESPN's signature 24/7 broadband sports network, is an online website for live sports programming that streams 3,500 hours of live sports coverage from a broad selection of global sports events each year.

Table 40-1 Top Seven World Internet Users

Country	Users (millions)
China	298
United States	220
Japan	94
India	81
Brazil	67
Germany	55
United Kingdom	44

Source: Internet World Stats 2009.

Table 40-2 Top Five U.S. Sports Websites in November 2008

Rank	Website	Unique Visitors (millions)	Percentage Change versus November 2007
1	Yahoo! Sports	22.788	2
2	ESPN	22.198	12
3	NFL Internet Network	14.072	0
4	FOX Sports on MSN	13.766	–10
5	CBS Sports	12.939	–7
	All U.S. sports websites	78.499	5

Source: Google.

VIDEO GAMES

Video games are a form of communication that grew out of the integration of television and computer technologies. The video game industry has had a rapid and sustained global growth and is now a $10 billion industry that rivals the motion picture industry as producing the most profitable entertainment medium in the world.

A sports game, *Tennis for Two* (1958), was one of the first video games. Over the past fifty years, a video game has been developed for virtually every sport played in the world. Like the auto industry, the sports video game industry brings out a new version of its products annually to prime the pump for profits. The processing power of the new generation of video game equipment—Microsoft's Xbox 360, Sony Computer's PlayStation 3, and Nintendo's Wii—has brought the real world into play.

Wii Sports's unique wireless, motion-sensitive remote allows players to make the physical body movements involved in playing a sport. Originally bundled with sports from tennis to bowling, the 2009 version, *Wii Sports Resort,* enables players to engage in over a dozen activities and is expected to generate $400 million in revenue.

As with other forms of entertainment, especially television, questions have arisen about the effects of video game playing on users' habits, behaviors, and social development. For example, how does playing sports video games affect the play habits of children and youth? Do the games influence attitudes and behaviors in terms of sportsmanship, violence, and morality? Does prolonged sports video game playing affect physical fitness, weight management, and social interaction with peers? At this time there has been little research into these questions, and many others, but undoubtedly this will be a rich area for psychological and sociological scholarship in the coming years (Crawford and Gosling 2009; Wolf 2007).

TWITTER, FACEBOOK, MYSPACE, AND YOUTUBE

Sport organizations throughout the world are employing direct communications with customers—mostly fans—through social-media tools such as Twitter, Facebook, MySpace, and YouTube. These popular communications technologies have helped professional sports teams to quickly and inexpensively respond to customers and tailor services for fans. It is the younger fans who flock to Twitter and make it a useful social-media tool.

Twitter is a social-networking application that has taken "immediacy" to new heights; it is rapidly becoming a staple in businesses customer service, and that includes sport organizations (see Box 40-1). In the spring of 2009, during a Stanley Cup play-off game between the Philadelphia Flyers and Pittsburgh Penguins, television sets suddenly went blank. Many cable subscribers Twittered to find out why. One subscriber said, "I did a search on Twitter as soon as the game went off the air. The mystery was resolved in minutes. Before Twitter, it would have been a nightmare trying to find out on the phone what happened" (Swartz 2009, 1B). In the summer of 2009, MLB used Twitter to its maximum advantage leading up to—and during—its 2009 First-Year Player Draft. MLB.com launched the first online "social community" integration of the draft by integrating Twitter into its expanding live interactive media experience, the Draft Caster, and its searchable draft database, the Draft Tracker (Winston 2009).

Other social-media tools, such as Facebook, YouTube, and MySpace, are fostering sports fans service through online communities to exchange comments, ideas, and questions (see Box 40-2). Through their respective services they can offer massive bulletin boards for consumers to weigh in on major issues about athletes and teams.

ONLINE SPORT GAMBLING

Gambling is an economic activity with a history that dates back to antiquity. Betting on sports events was popular with the ancient Greeks five hundred years before the birth of Christ, and it was very popular in all of their Pan-Hellenic Games—one of which was the Olympic Games. Gambling reached some incredible extremes at the Roman chariot races, with rampant corruption and fixed events. Histories of sport over the past two hundred years are replete with accounts of gambling. It is often claimed that wherever you find sport you find gambling. Internet online wagering is the fastest-growing new form of gambling and has become a major force in the global gambling industry. According to *60 Minutes* host Steve Kroft, online gambling is currently an $18 billion industry and growing each year.

Internet gambling is illegal and unregulated in many countries of the world, but bans are almost impossible to enforce since the Internet sites and computers that randomly deal the cards and keep track of the bets are located offshore, beyond the jurisdiction of law-enforcement agencies. Moreover, with the enormous increase of interest in spectator sports over the past thirty years, there has been a corresponding explosion in sports gambling, with online venues being the most convenient. As media analyst Michael Real has observed, "Offshore online sites can be readily accessed by casual betters, children, gambling addicts, and even athletes" (2006, 189).

Box 40-1 Twitter and Global Social Networking in Sports

Hey there! NBA is using Twitter
Hey there! FIFA World Cup is using Twitter
Hey there! Japanese MLB (mlbjapan.com) is using Twitter
Hey there! SportsFanLive is using Twitter
Hey there! Sports Illustrated is using Twitter
Hey there! Professional athletes are using Twitter

Not only are leagues, teams, sporting events, and athletes using Twitter; since its creation in 2006, Twitter has gained global popularity.

Twitter is a free social-networking service that enables users to send and read messages known as "tweets." Tweets are text-based posts sent to the author's subscribers, who are known as "followers." Senders can restrict tweet delivery to those in their circle of friends, or they can allow open access, and they can send and receive tweets via the Twitter website, Short Message Service (SMS), or external applications.

The 140-character limit on message length was initially set for compatibility with SMS messaging and has brought to the web the kind of shorthand notation and slang commonly used in SMS messages. The 140-character limit has also spurred the usage of URL shortening services such as tinyurl, bit.ly, and trim, and content-hosting services, such as Twitpic and NotePub, to accommodate multimedia content and text longer than 140 characters.

It is sometimes described as the "SMS of the Internet" since the use of Twitter's application programming interface for sending and receiving short text messages by other applications often eclipses the direct use of Twitter.

Twitter emphasized their news and information network strategy in November 2009 by changing the question it asks users for status updates from "What are you doing?" to "What's happening?" Although estimates of the number of daily users vary because the company does not release the number of active accounts. A February 2009 Compete.com blog entry ranked Twitter as the third-most-used social network based on their count of 6 million unique monthly visitors and 5 million monthly visits. Twitter had a monthly growth of 1,382 percent, Zimbio of 240 percent, followed by Facebook with an increase of 228 percent. However, only 40 percent of Twitter's users are retained.

Still, in March 2009 Twitter was ranked as the fastest-growing site in the member communities category. By early 2010 Twitter was ranked as one of the fifty most popular websites worldwide.

The Twitter homepage (www.twitter.com) declares that in countries all around the world, people follow the sources most relevant to them and access information via Twitter as it happens—from breaking world news to updates from friends. Join the conversation.

Box 40-2 Facebook and Global Sports Applications

Facebook is a global social-networking website launched In 2004. Users select friends and post messages and personal profiles to notify their friends about themselves. More than 350 million active users are reported for Facebook, about 70 percent of whom are outside the United States. A 2009 study ranked Facebook as the most used social network worldwide by active users.

Over 300,000 applications have been developed for the Facebook platform, with hundreds of new ones being created every month. Many of these allow users to join networks organized by city, workplace, school, and special interests, like sports (even specific sports), to connect and interact with other people with similar interests.

SportsFanLive.com is a premier content and global social-networking site for sports fans. In effect it is its own Facebook. The customizable interface provides easy access to sports information throughout the world. The home page content has a plethora of sports stories about games, athletes, leagues, and so forth. Users can customize the site to highlight the teams and players they are devoted to, and they regularly receive copious amounts of updated news aggregated from over 4,000 sources.

In addition, users of SportsFanLive.com can send articles to like-minded friends on the site through the My FanFeed feature. With an application called FanFinder, which has a ZIP code- and map-based function, they can search for a specific place to watch a game or alert buddies about the sports bar where they are cheering on their team. SportsFanLive users are not just limited to being spectators. Their opinions can be expressed, allowing them to contribute to the daily sports conversation.

To experience this new wave of sports on the Web, log on to www.sportsfanlive.com.

A study by the Annenberg Foundation reported that more than 27 percent of young Americans ages fourteen to twenty-two bet on sports events at least once per month. Even more troubling, sports gambling is rampant and prospering on university campuses throughout the world, and the majority of bookies are students. One writer referred to this phenomenon as "the dirty little secret on university campuses"; another referred to it as a "silent addiction" for many university students. Studies of sports betting by American college students have reported that between 35 and 50 percent of male college students and between 10 and 20 percent of female students have bet on sports events.

There are far too many sports-betting websites to list, and they are being constructed and dismantled weekly, so I will list a few to illustrate their global spread. The European online sports-betting industry is made up of operators that are established, licensed, and regulated in the European Union, some of which are grouped under the

European Gaming and Betting Association, the leading industry body representing online gaming and betting operators in Europe. Eurobet claims to be Europe's leading bookmaker; it offers sports betting, easy withdraw methods, and online casinos, poker, bingo, and games. The European Sports Security Association (ESSA) was established in 2005 by the leading online sports book operators in Europe to monitor irregular betting patterns or potential insider betting from within each sport. ESSA has signed a memorandum of understanding with FIFA and several European sports leagues and has established close relations with the IOC.

In the United Kingdom, BetUK.com advertises itself as the leading online sports-betting bookmaker. But more than that, BetUK.com offers an array of online sports-betting lines for betting on UK events, as well as provides subscribers with a range of sports betting, the latest bets, tips, strategies, and the latest online sports-betting markets from all sports.

Sports Fantasy Leagues

Sports fantasy league "play" is a form of sport gambling, even though at its most local level it is played by a group of friends for very small stakes. At the upper extremes online sport fantasy leagues are huge businesses in which players pay up to several hundred dollars to play by selecting a team of professional athletes from a "draft" and then working the team through the season. Large sums of money can be attained by winning a sports fantasy league championship. A survey by the Fantasy Sports Trade Association (FSTA) indicates that some 30 million individuals actively participate in fantasy sport in the United States alone, spending $800 million yearly on products related to fantasy sports (FSTA 2009). According to its website, in 2008 the National Fantasy Football Championship paid out over $850,000 in prizes—bringing the total payout since 2004 to over $5 million. In the United Kingdom the Fantasy Football Premier League enables players to manage their own teams of players from that league.

Sport fantasy players have an enormous variety of online information sources to help them make good choices in selecting players for their fantasy teams. As Real notes, "The quantity and depth of information available on the Web enables a fantasy league player to be the well-informed general manager of a complex, seemingly realist virtual team" (2006, 178).

REFERENCES

Crawford, Garry, and Victoria K Gosling. 2009. More than a game: Sports-themed video games and player narratives. *Sociology of Sport Journal* 26: 50–66.

Fantasy Sports Trade Association (FSTA). 2009. Welcome to the official site of the FSTA. FSTA. www.fsta.org.

Internet World Stats. 2009. Internet usage statistics: The Internet big picture. www.internetworldstats.com/stats.htm.

Leonard, David. 2009. New media and global sporting cultures: Moving beyond the clichés and binaries. *Sociology of Sport Journal* 26: 1–16.

Real, Michael. 2006. Sports online: The newest player in mediasport. In *Handbook of sports and media,* ed. Arthur A. Raney and Jennings Bryant, 171–184. Mahwah, NJ: Lawrence Erlbaum Associates.

Swartz, Jon. 2009. Businesses get cheap help from a little birdie. *USA Today,* June 26, 1C–2C.

Winston, Lisa. 2009. Fans can share draft takes on Twitter. MLB.com, June 7. http://m1b.mlb.com/news/article.jsp?ymd200906078=content_ id-5197482&vkey-draft2009&fext.jsp.

Wolf, Mark. 2007. *The video game explosion: A history from PONG to PlayStation and beyond.* Westport, CT: Greenwood.

* FOR FURTHER STUDY *

Bairner, A. 2001. *Sport, Nationalism, and Globalization: European and North American Perspectives.* Albany: State University of New York Press.

Barney, Robert K., Stephen R. Wenn, and Scott G. Martyn. 2002. *Selling the Five Rings: The International Olympic Committee and the Rise of Olympic Commercialism.* Salt Lake City: University of Utah Press.

Coakley, Jay. 2007. *Sports in Society: Issues and Controversies.* 9th ed. New York: McGraw-Hill.

Cole, C. L. 2002. "The Place of Golf in U.S. Imperialism." *Journal of Sport and Social Issues* 26 (November): 331–336.

Eitzen, D. Stanley. 2009. *Fair and Foul: Beyond the Myths and Paradoxes of Sport.* Lanham, MD: Rowman and Littlefield.

Eitzen, D. Stanley, and George H. Sage. 2009. *Sociology of North American Sport.* 8th ed. Boulder, CO: Paradigm.

Foer, Franklin. 2004. *How Soccer Explains the World: An Unlikely Theory of Globalization.* New York: Harper Perennial.

Harvey, Jean, Alan Law, and Michael Cantelon. 2001. "North American Professional Team Sport Franchises Ownership Patterns and Global Entertainment Conglomerates." *Sociology of Sport Journal* 18 (4): 435–457.

Harvey, Jean, and Maurice Saint-Germain. 2001. "Sporting Goods Trade, International Division of Labor, and the Unequal Hierarchy of Nations." *Sociology of Sport Journal* 18 (2): 231–246.

Klein, Alan M. 2006. *Growing the Game: The Globalization of Major League Baseball.* New Haven, CT: Yale University Press.

Lafeber, W. 2000. *Michael Jordan and the New Global Capitalism.* New York: W. W. Norton.

Magee, Jonathan, and John Sugden. 2002. "'The World at Their Feet': Professional Football and International Labor Migration." *Journal of Sport and Social Issues* 26 (November): 421–437.

Magnusson, Gudmundur K. 2001. "The Internationalization of Sports: The Case of Iceland." *International Review for the Sociology of Sport* 36 (March): 59–70.

Maguire, Joseph. 1999. *Global Sport: Identities, Societies, Civilizations.* Cambridge, UK: Polity.

Maguire, Joseph. 2000. "Sport and Globalization." Pp. 356–367 in Jay Coakley and Eric Dunning, eds., *Handbook of Sports Studies.* London: Sage.

Nixon, Howard L. II. 2008. *Sport in a Changing World.* Boulder, CO: Paradigm.

Scherer, Jay. 2001. "Globalization and the Construction of Local Particularities: A Case Study of the Winnipeg Jets." *Sociology of Sport Journal* 18 (2): 205–230.

Wong, Lloyd L., and Ricardo Trumper. 2002. "Global Celebrity Athletes and Nationalism." *Journal of Sport and Social Issues* 26 (May): 168–194.

Zirin, Dave. 2005. *What's My Name, Fool? Sports and Resistance in the United States.* Chicago: Haymarket.

Zirin, Dave. 2008. *A People's History of Sports in the United States: 250 Years of Politics, Protest, People, and Play.* New York: The New Press.

About the Editor

D. Stanley Eitzen is Professor Emeritus of Sociology at Colorado State University, where he taught for twenty-one years, the last as John N. Stern Distinguished Professor. Prior to that he taught at the University of Kansas, where he earned his Ph.D. He was editor of *The Social Science Journal* from 1978 to 1984. He began his career as a high school teacher and athletic coach. Although he is well known for his scholarship on homelessness, poverty, social inequality, power, family, and criminology, he is best known for his contributions to the sociology of sport. He has taught a course on sport and society since 1972. He is the author or coauthor of twenty-four books (including three on sport), as well as numerous scholarly articles and chapters in scholarly books. He is a former president of the North American Society for the Sociology of Sport and the recipient of that organization's Distinguished Service Award. Among his other awards, he was selected to be a Sports Ethics Fellow by the Institute for International Sport. He is coauthor with George H. Sage of *Sociology of North American Sport,* 9th edition (Paradigm Publishers, forthcoming).